The Left,
The Right,
& The State

The Left,
The Right,
& The State

Llewellyn H. Rockwell, Jr.

Ludwig von Mises Institute
Auburn, Alabama

Tu ne cede malis,
sed contra audentior ito.

Do not give in to evil,
but proceed ever more boldly against it.

—Ludwig von Mises's childhood motto,
taken from Virgil

CONTENTS

Part II: The Left

Part III: The Right

Part IV: The Market

INTRODUCTION

In American political culture, and world political culture too, the divide concerns in what way the state's power should be expanded. The left has a laundry list and the right does too. Both represent a grave threat to the only political position that is truly beneficial to the world and its inhabitants: liberty.

What is the state? It is the group within society that claims for itself the exclusive right to rule everyone under a special set of laws that permit it to do to others what everyone else is rightly prohibited from doing, namely aggressing against person and property.

Why would any society permit such a gang to enjoy an unchallenged legal privilege? Here is where ideology comes into play. The reality of the state is that it is a looting and killing machine. So why do so many people cheer for its expansion? Indeed, why do we tolerate its existence at all?

The very idea of the state is so implausible on its face that the state must wear an ideological garb as means of compelling popular support. Ancient states had one or two: they would protect you from enemies and/or they were ordained by the gods.

To greater and lesser extents, all modern states still employ these rationales, but the democratic state in the developed world is more complex. It uses a huge range of ideological rationales—parsed out between left and right—that reflect social and cultural priorities of niche groups, even when many of these rationales are contradictory.

The left wants the state to distribute wealth, to bring about equality, to rein in businesses, to give workers a boost, to provide for the poor, to protect the environment. I address many of these rationales in this book, with an eye toward particular topics in the news.

The right, on the other hand, wants the state to punish evildoers, to boost the family, to subsidize upright ways of living, to create security against foreign enemies, to make the culture cohere, and to go to war to give ourselves a sense of national identity. I also address these rationales.

So how are these competing interests resolved? They logroll and call it democracy. The left and right agree to let each other have their way, provided nothing is done to injure the interests of one or the other. The trick is to keep the balance. Who is in power is really about which way the log is rolling. And there you have the modern state in a nutshell.

Although it has ancestors in such regimes as Lincoln's and Wilson's, the genesis of the modern state is in the interwar period, when the idea of the *laissez-faire* society fell into disrepute—the result of the mistaken view that the free market brought us economic depression. So we had the New Deal, which was a democratic hybrid of socialism and fascism. The old liberals were nearly extinct.

The US then fought a war against the totalitarian state, allied to a totalitarian state, and the winner was leviathan itself. Our leviathan doesn't always have a chief executive who struts around in a military costume, but he enjoys powers that Caesars of old would have envied. The total state today is more soothing and slick than it was in its interwar infancy, but it is no less opposed to the ideals advanced in these pages.

How much further would the state have advanced had Mises and Rothbard and many others not dedicated their lives to freedom? We must become the intellectual dissidents of our time, rejecting the demands for statism that come from the left and right. And we must advance a positive program of liberty, which is radical, fresh, and true as it ever was.

Part I: The State

"There will always be those who claim to have special rights over the rest of society, and the state is the most organized attempt to get away with it."

1.

TIMES CHANGE, PRINCIPLES DON'T*

A libertarian must never tire of saying "I told you so." Nor is there a dearth of opportunities to do so. Before 9-11, for example, it was the libertarians who said that 1990s sanctions against Iraq and broader intervention in the Middle East would inspire terrorism. The libertarians also warned that FAA regulations weren't really making the airlines secure. The libertarians further saw that hundreds of billions spent on "defense" and "intelligence" weren't really providing either.

Thus was 9-11, a big I-told-you-so moment for libertarians. The hijackers, seething in anger at US policy in the Gulf region and the Middle East, exploited an FAA-regulated system with plenty of loopholes for bad guys, to crash into a major financial center, and the US government, despite all its spending and promises, was powerless to stop it.

And yet, in this upside-down world, the big message after 9-11 was not that the government and its ways had failed us. Quite the opposite. We were told that the government would save us. It was libertarianism that failed.

Remember? Hillary Clinton, always exploiting the political moment, said of the efforts to cope on that awful day, "we saw government in action. . . . It was the elected officials who were

---

*September 11, 2003

3

leading and comforting." That's an odd way to describe running for their lives, prior to seizing power from their bureaucratic bunkers.

VP Dick Cheney said: "one of the things that's changed so much since September 11th is the extent to which people do trust the government, big shift, and value it, and have higher expectations for what we can do." The triumph of hope over experience!

George Will wrote that "Sept. 11 forcefully reminded Americans that their nation-state . . . is the source of their security. . . . Events since Sept. 11 have underscored the limits of libertarianism." He is speaking here of the same nation-state that stood by and did nothing as 19 guys with box cutters took down the twin towers.

Francis Fukuyama joined in to proclaim the "fall of the libertarians": 9-11 "was a reminder to Americans of why government exists, and why it has to tax citizens and spend money to promote collective interests. It was only the government, and not the market or individuals, that could be depended on to send firemen into buildings, or to fight terrorists, or to screen passengers at airports."

Albert Hunt of the *Wall Street Journal* typified this genre of commentary. "It's time to declare a moratorium on government-bashing," he wrote.

> For a quarter-century, the dominant public culture has suggested government is more a problem than a solution. . . . But, as during previous catastrophes, America turns to government in crisis. . . . For the foreseeable future, the federal government is going to invest or spend more, regulate more and exercise more control over our lives. . . . We will hear much less about the glories of privatization in areas like airport security. . . . Top Bush administration officials will have to dramatically alter their views on regulation. . . . Moreover, more muscular authority must be given to the new Office of Homeland Security. . . . Tougher security measures at home are unavoidable. . . . But there is no real debate over expansion in

general. Sept. 11 has underscored the centrality of government in our lives.

So it went, across the political spectrum. The idea was that the events of that day had somehow refuted all our slogans about cutting government, privatization, personal liberty, markets, and peace. Clearly, they said, it was excessive liberty that had led to this disaster. It was cuts in government, and too little foreign belligerence, that brought it on, while the public sector, from the New York firemen to the military bosses who exacted vengeance abroad, saved us.

Many soft libertarians believed it too, with the DC brand quickly signing up for the wars that followed while issuing weakly worded cautions against going too far in curtailing liberties. David Boaz even tried to put this spin on the largest explosion of government power in half a century:

> The increased support for the federal government makes sense. Finally, the government is focused on its main purpose: the protection of the lives and property of Americans. People who had lost confidence in the government's attempts to run the trains or the post office or to provide everything under the sun can only be pleased to see it concentrating on protecting individual rights.

Or, perhaps they didn't really believe it, but they felt enough heat that they decided to make their ultimate loyalties to the central state known by denouncing the "extreme" versions of libertarianism. They assured everyone that libertarianism is not against government as such, just bad and abusive government.

The rest of us were told to hush up with our petty concerns about foreign entanglements, airport privatization, and what have you. We were told, above all, to stop our broad complaints about government in all its manifestations. September 11 was said to have smashed Rothbardianism, a word that continues to rattle anyone on the public payroll who is in the know.

Why didn't we shut up? Because the libertarian critique of government is not contingent on or tied to time and place, one that can be abandoned when the moment seems to call for government action. The libertarian critique of government is foundational. It says that in all times and places, the coercive power of the state violates rights, and this compulsive rights-violator cannot and should not be trusted to guard our security.

Moreover, because government operates outside the ownership and trade matrixes of society, it lacks both the incentive and the means to carry out an efficient provision of any good or service. Finally, the libertarian critique warns against any grant of sovereign power to anyone, for once granted, it cannot be contained and it will be abused.

Now, these claims might strike many people as absolutist and extreme. So let's say that we alter each sentence with the proviso: "In nonemergency circumstances." Thus: Freedom is great in nonemergency circumstances; property rights work best in nonemergency circumstances; the free market provides for society in most nonemergency circumstances; the government is wasteful and dangerous, unless there is an emergency.

What kind of incentive structure does such a proviso establish for the governing elites? Given that no government is liberal by nature (as Mises says), the emergency proviso gives government a plan of action on how best to take away freedom and accumulate power. It was clear immediately following the 9-11 attacks that this is precisely how DC saw the tragedy. The political establishment and the permanent government saw tragedy as the main chance to intimidate the public into surrendering its rights, property, and liberty in exchange for the promise of security—a security which sophisticated observers knew would not and could not be provided.

And yet in those dark days, our voices were in the minority, especially when warning of the dangers of war. The vengeful state had been unleashed and it was looking for blood wherever it could find it. Wars commenced in Afghanistan and Iraq, leading to unconscionable levels of destruction of life and property. Both countries are now in political chaos, poised between a foreign-imposed martial law and a religious fundamentalist takeover. The sympathy the US had garnered from Europe, Asia, and Latin America after 9-11 quickly turned to hatred against our political elites, and it has yet to go away.

The US government didn't stop with wars. It violated the civil liberties of Americans, and established enormous new bureaucracies. It trampled on the rights of states and localities. It turned flying into a massive police operation. It began a series of protectionist campaigns.

The Bush administration busted the budget and saddled the country with the largest deficit in history. Congress and the presidency engaged in a transparent logrolling whereby the warmongers gave the welfare statists what they want, in exchange for which the welfare statists gave the warmongers what they want. The rest of us watched freedom melt. We did what we could, in our writings and public advocacy, but the government tide was too high to hold back.

Two years later, the themes in the press say nothing about the successes of government. All the headlines are about failure. The American people expect more, not less terrorism. We feel less, not more, secure. Incredibly, Bin Laden, whom the Bush administration blames for 9-11, is still on the loose. The US has more enemies than ever. Let there be no illusions: the people the US "liberated" in Iraq and Afghanistan despise us and want us out. The US can't even provide water and power for the people in Iraq.

Government was given the run of things after 9-11, and what did we get? Wars, bureaucracy, debt, death, despotism, insecurity, and lots of confusing color-coded warnings from our DC masters that seem only designed to keep us ever more dependent. Yes, government has behaved exactly as libertarianism predicted it would behave. It has abused the trust of the American people. And yet, at some level, government has benefited in the end. We have lost, they have gained.

But that moment is coming to an end, or already has. Many people have written off the miserable failure of the proposed tax increase in Alabama as a localized phenomenon, whereas in fact it points the way to a national trend. Bush is not likely to get his new suspensions of civil liberties passed. The neocons are fearful that they no longer hold enough political capital to start more wars. The public is fed up with the mess in Iraq. The much-vaunted advent of the American global empire is under fire. The propaganda no longer seems to be working.

In the real life that most of us live, the private sector is thriving. Technology gets better everyday, thanks to private enterprise. The markets are giving us the security we demand, whether through private communities, private weapons, better alarm systems, and private security guards, or through better systems of information distribution and verification—again, thanks to private enterprise. Homeschooling is still on the rise. Contrary to Hillary Clinton, it is still our friends, family, and clergy who provide us comfort, not our political leaders, whom we trust less and less.

Americans are coming to their senses, and the libertarian theory of society and government is pointing the way. The times change, but the enduring principles that help us to interpret and understand the world do not. It remains true now, as then, as in the future, *saecula saeculorum*, that government provides neither an effective nor a moral means for solving any human problem.

Just as Fukuyama was wrong about the "end of history," he is wrong that 9-11 means the "fall of libertarianism." Perhaps we will look back, with the right lessons in mind, and see that day as the last hurrah of the nation-state and the beginning of a renewed love of liberty and the peace, prosperity, and security it brings.

2.

FREEDOM IS NOT "PUBLIC POLICY"*

Among the greatest failures of the free-market intellectual movement has been allowing its ideas to be categorized as a "public policy" option. The formulation implies a concession that it is up to the state—its managers and kept intellectuals—to decide how, when, and where freedom is to be permitted. It further implies that the purpose of freedom, private ownership, and market incentives is the superior management of society, that is, to allow the current regime to operate more efficiently.

This kind of thinking has been around a while. Murray Rothbard had noted back in the 1950s that economists, even those favoring markets, had become "efficiency experts for the state." There is a small step from that unfortunate stance to providing a free-market rhetorical cover for the state to do what it wants to do anyway, which is surely the ultimate compromise.

Such was at the heart of the Reagan Revolution, when tax cuts were first proposed as a tool to bring in more revenue. Who said that the purpose of freedom was to ensure more lavish funding for the state? And what if the funding didn't materialize? Does that mean that the tax cuts failed? Twenty years later, of course, we see that the strategy was a disaster because it turned out that there is a far surer way to collect more revenue: to collect more revenue.

There are many examples of this awful concession operating today. In policy circles, people use the word privatization to mean not the bowing out of government from a particular aspect of social and economic life, but merely the contracting out of statist priorities to politically connected private enterprise.

---

*June 2002

School vouchers and Social Security "privatization" are the most notorious examples at the national level. At the state and local levels, any government contract awarded to a grafting business interest is deemed "privatization." A Washington think tank recently proposed that the CIA could become more efficient by contracting out to Washington think tanks.

What's at stake is the very conception of the role of freedom in political, economic, and social life. Do we regard freedom as a useful device within the existing structure, or as an alternative to the current political system? This is not a matter of bickering libertarian sects. The very future of the idea of free markets is at stake.

Few opportunities for reform come along. When they do, libertarians ought to be out front not only demanding the full loaf, but also warning against the dangers of a poisoned crumb. The worst mistake our side can make is to sell our ideas as a better means for achieving the state's ends. Yet this approach—advertising market economics as the best political option among a variety of plans—has become the dominant one on our side of the fence.

For starters, this approach typically leads to unfortunate results in the real world, like the California energy "deregulation" fiasco. Such partial reforms can even bring about a worse system than pre-reform, along with a diminished moral authority for free enterprise.

Another case against partial reform was noted by Ludwig von Mises:

> There is an inherent tendency in all governmental power to recognize no restraints on its operation and to extend the sphere of its dominance as much as possible. To control everything, to leave no room for anything to happen of its own accord without the interference of the authorities—this is the goal for which every ruler secretly strives.

The only way out of this problem is for us to strive to eliminate the state's involvement in the life of society and economy.

The tragic case of Poland has been in the news. After the collapse of communism, there was a burst of enthusiasm for the idea of the market economy. The *New York Times* reports that the shipyard in Szczecin was renationalized after workers threatened violence when banks stopped backing a losing business and the paychecks stopped arriving.

This is Poland's first renationalization after the collapse of socialism, undertaken in response to what would be a routine business failure in a market economy. Worse, the country is in the grip of a leftist government. If the *New York Times* is right, disillusionment with capitalism is widespread. Will all-out socialism return? The fear may be exaggerated, but in politics, it is always a mistake to believe that the worst can't happen.

After 1989, Poland underwent a series of economic reforms. Factories were privatized. Most of the 100,000 municipal firms were transferred to private hands. The currency was stabilized. Prices were freed. The government encouraged every manner of enterprise. The result was magnificent: foreign investment and a decade of respectable economic growth.

And yet, as with other East European countries, the privatization was far from complete. Communications were only partially privatized. The health sector was cleaned up but left mostly in government hands. Labor unions managed to retain huge legal privileges, and there was no active market for the control of corporations. Taxes are way too high (30 percent). One quarter of the labor force is still employed in the state sector, though until recently, the trend was heading downward.

Sadly, Poland did not set its sights high enough. The political class looked to the United States and other West European countries as the model, and thus retained or newly instituted a huge range of regulatory impediments to free enterprise, including antitrust law, health and safety regulations, environmental regulations, and labor controls. It's true that they are no more severe than those in the United States or Europe, but Poland can scarcely afford such nonsense after the impoverishment of communism.

Many large factories were never touched by privatization—for fear that they would simply be shut down if they had to compete in a free market. Faced with such a prospect, the only answer is to permit them to go under, for it is absurd to burn money by subsidizing enterprises that are economically unviable. Decisive in the case of shipping, the government made no ironclad commitment to allow factories to fail if they could no longer compete. The reason was fear of the unions.

Interventions to save failing enterprises are bad on their own terms. They don't actually help businesses. They only postpone the day when an enterprise must either become a complete state entity, like the Tennessee Valley Authority, or go belly up.

In Poland, the root of the problem was in the very word "privatization." It implies that everyone and everything will pretty much remain as before, except that ownership will be in private as versus public hands.

The same confusion predominates in the United States. We hear that if we "privatize" the schools with vouchers and other gimmicks, they will be cheaper to run and test scores will go up. We are told that if we "privatize" Social Security, it will produce higher returns for seniors. Here, the establishment libertarian policy people are saying: socialism is possible after all, so long as it is run by private enterprise!

In truth, if the education sector were ever completely in private hands, nothing like the current system would continue to exist. Most administrators would be without jobs in the school system. The schools themselves might become retail centers. Education would be radically decentralized and mixed with private enterprise. Schools would come and go. Teacher salaries would probably plummet. No one would have a right to an education guaranteed by the state. The state could ask for and expect no content or results from education at any level.

A huge range of alternatives would exist, but rare among them would be the current system of megaschools that operate as holding tanks for thousands. Of course we cannot know in advance what this sector would look like, what shapes it might take in the future, but that is precisely the point. The voucher proposal, and all the contracting-out schemes, wouldn't even give the free market a chance to show its stuff. They would only add another layer of public spending and public guarantees to an already socialist system.

The same is true for Social Security. Those who say they want privatization are pushing a system no different in kind from the present one. Your money would still be stolen by the state. Pensions would still be guaranteed by the state. You might even end up paying more, one premium for current retirees and another to fund your own "private" one. The only difference is that a portion of the money will be permitted to be held by private companies, making them in part dependent on public subsidies.

A hundred years ago, a person who proposed such a system would have been considered a socialist. Today, he is a "libertarian public policy expert." If what you desire is true free-market reform, don't call it privatization. We need to stop the present racket. Under real market reforms, no one would be looted and no one would be guaranteed anything. The slogan should be: stop the theft.

In Poland, large factories shouldn't have been "privatized." The state should have just walked away from them, selling the assets to the highest bidder, or turning them over to the workers and managers, and permitting the new owners to do with them whatever they want. In the United States, public schools and Social Security shouldn't be privatized; they should be abandoned and full freedom permitted to take their place. In other words, market institutions shouldn't be used as a tool of "public policy;" they should be the *de facto* reality in a society of freedom.

One objection to my thesis is that partial measures at least take us in the right direction. It's true that even a partially free system is better than a fully socialist one. And yet, partial victories are unstable. They easily fall back into full statism. With US schools and pensions, these privatization schemes could actually make the present system less free by insisting on new spending to cover new expenses to provide vouchers and private accounts.

In a decade of market-oriented reform, capitalism has been seen as a mechanism that might make it possible for failed sectors to continue to do what they have always done. In truth, free-market reforms are far more fundamental.

Free markets are not just about generating profits and productivity. They aren't just about spurring innovation and competition. To make a transition from statism to the market economy means a complete revolution in economic and political life, from a system where the state and its interests rule to a system where the power of the state plays no role. Freedom is not a public-policy option. It is the end of public policy itself. It is time for us to take that next step and call for precisely that.

3.

Legalize Drunk Driving*

[This column was written before the news came out November 2, 2000, that George W. Bush was arrested on a DUI charge 24 years ago. He was stopped in Maine for driving too slowly and briefly veering onto the shoulder of the road.]

Clinton has signed a bill passed by Congress that orders the states to adopt new, more onerous drunk-driving standards or face a loss of highway funds. That's right: the old highway extortion trick. Sure enough, states are already working to pass new, tighter laws against Driving Under the Influence, responding as expected to the feds' ransom note.

---

*November 3, 2000

Now the feds declare that a blood-alcohol level of 0.08 percent and above is criminal and must be severely punished. The National Restaurant Association is exactly right that this is absurdly low. The overwhelming majority of accidents related to drunk driving involve repeat offenders with blood-alcohol levels twice that high. If a standard of 0.1 doesn't deter them, then a lower one won't either.

But there's a more fundamental point. What precisely is being criminalized? Not bad driving. Not destruction of property. Not the taking of human life or reckless endangerment. The crime is having the wrong substance in your blood. Yet it is possible, in fact, to have this substance in your blood, even while driving, and not commit anything like what has been traditionally called a crime.

What have we done by permitting government to criminalize the content of our blood instead of actions themselves? We have given it power to make the application of the law arbitrary, capricious, and contingent on the judgment of cops and cop technicians. Indeed, without the government's "Breathalyzer," there is no way to tell for sure if we are breaking the law.

Sure, we can do informal calculations in our head, based on our weight and the amount of alcohol we have had over some period of time. But at best these will be estimates. We have to wait for the government to administer a test to tell us whether or not we are criminals. That's not the way law is supposed to work. Indeed, this is a form of tyranny.

Now, the immediate response goes this way: drunk driving has to be illegal because the probability of causing an accident rises dramatically when you drink. The answer is just as simple: government in a free society should not deal in probabilities. The law should deal in actions and actions alone, and only insofar as they damage person or property. Probabilities are something for insurance companies to assess on a competitive and voluntary basis.

This is why the campaign against "racial profiling" has intuitive plausibility to many people: surely a person shouldn't be hounded solely because some demographic groups have higher crime rates than others. Government should be preventing and punishing crimes themselves, not probabilities and propensities. Neither, then, should we have driver profiling, which assumes that just because a person has quaffed a few he is automatically a danger.

In fact, driver profiling is worse than racial profiling, because the latter only implies that the police are more watchful, not that they criminalize race itself. Despite the propaganda, what's being criminalized in the case of drunk driving is not the probability that a person driving will get into an accident but the fact of the blood-alcohol content itself. A drunk driver is humiliated and destroyed even when he hasn't done any harm.

Of course, enforcement is a serious problem. A sizeable number of people leaving a bar or a restaurant would probably qualify as DUI. But there is no way for the police to know unless they are tipped off by a swerving car or reckless driving in general. But the question becomes: why not ticket the swerving or recklessness and leave the alcohol out of it? Why indeed.

To underscore the fact that it is some level of drinking that is being criminalized, government sets up these outrageous, civil-liberties-violating barricades that stop people to check their blood—even when they have done nothing at all. This is a gross attack on liberty that implies that the government has and should have total control over us, extending even to the testing of intimate biological facts. But somehow we put up with it because we have conceded the first assumption that government ought to punish us for the content of our blood and not just our actions.

There are many factors that cause a person to drive poorly. You may have sore muscles after a weight-lifting session and have slow reactions. You could be sleepy. You could be in a bad mood, or angry after a fight with your spouse. Should the government be allowed to administer anger tests, tiredness tests, or soreness tests? That is the very next step, and don't be surprised when Congress starts to examine this question.

Already, there's a move on to prohibit cell phone use while driving. Such an absurdity follows from the idea that government should make judgments about what we are allegedly likely to do.

What's more, some people drive more safely after a few drinks, precisely because they know their reaction time has been slowed and they must pay more attention to safety. We all know drunks who have an amazing ability to drive perfectly after being liquored up. They should be liberated from the force of the law, and only punished if they actually do something wrong.

We need to put a stop to this whole trend now. Drunk driving should be legalized. And please don't write me to say: "I am offended by your insensitivity because my mother was killed by a drunk driver." Any person responsible for killing someone else is guilty of manslaughter or murder and should be punished accordingly. But it is perverse to punish a murderer not because of his crime but because of some biological consideration, e.g., he has red hair.

Bank robbers may tend to wear masks, but the crime they commit has nothing to do with the mask. In the same way, drunk drivers cause accidents but so do sober drivers, and many drunk drivers cause no accidents at all. The law should focus on violations of person and property, not scientific oddities like blood content.

There's a final point against Clinton's drunk-driving bill. It is a violation of states rights. Not only is there no warrant in the Constitution for the federal government to legislate blood-alcohol content, the Tenth Amendment should prevent it from doing so. The question of drunk driving should first be returned to the states, and then each state should liberate drunk drivers from the force of the law.

4.
SOCIETY NEEDS NO MANAGERS*

It has been decades since legislatures have struck out daringly in some new and uncharted territory of social and economic management. For the most part, in the United States, Europe, Russia, China, and Latin America, legislatures are constantly at work reforming the systems they created in the past rather than embarking on totally new ventures.

And what are they working to reform? Sectors of governance that are not operating as they should due to dislocations, expense, perceived violations of fairness or some other consideration. We need only think of the financial mess of Medicare and Medicaid, the wholesale crookery of Social Security, the looming dangers of the Alternative Minimum Tax, the unending mess of crisis management, among a thousand other problems in every area of society over which government presumes some responsibility.

The same is true in Western Europe, where there is widespread knowledge that the welfare rolls are too large, that unions exercise too much power, that regulations on enterprise have crippled growth in country after country. Interest groups continue to stop progress toward liberty, but progress is being made on the level of ideology. More large steps toward socialism are not being contemplated, and for this we can be thankful.

ABOLISH PUBLIC POLICY

The main debate in our time thus concerns the direction and pace of reform toward market economics. This is all to the good,

*December 2005

and yet I would like to highlight what strikes me as a great confusion. The reformers here and abroad are widely under the impression that the liberty they seek for their societies can be imposed in much the way that socialist systems of old were imposed. The idea is that if Congress, the president, and the courts would just get hip to the program, they could fix what's wrong with the country in a jiffy. Thus we need only elect liberty-minded politicians, support a president trained in the merit of market incentives, and confirm judges who know all about the Chicago School of economics.

It cannot be, and I predict that if we continue to go down the path, we will replace one bad form of central planning with another. Genuine liberty is not just another form of government management. It means the absence of government management. It is this theme that I would like to pursue further.

I can present my own perspective on this up front: all reform in all areas of politics, economics, and society should be in one direction: toward more freedom for individuals and less power for government. I will go further to say that individuals ought to enjoy as much freedom as possible and government as little power as possible.

Yes, that position qualifies me as a libertarian. But I fear that this word does not have the explanatory power that it might have once had. There is in Washington a tendency to see libertarianism as a flavor of public-policy soda, or just another grab bag of policy proposals, ones that emphasize free enterprise and personal liberties as opposed to bureaucratic regimentation.

This perspective is seriously flawed, and it has dangerous consequences. Imagine if Moses had sought the advice of Washington policy experts when seeking some means of freeing the Jewish people from Egyptian captivity.

They might have told him that marching up to the Pharaoh and telling him to "let my people go" is highly imprudent and pointless. The media won't like it and it is asking for too much too fast. What the Israelites need is a higher legal standing in the courts, more market incentives, more choices made possible through vouchers and subsidies, and a greater say in the structure of regulations imposed by the Pharaoh. Besides, Mr. Moses, to cut and run is unpatriotic.

Instead Moses took a principled position and demanded immediate freedom from all political control—a complete separation between government and the lives of the Israelites. This is my kind of libertarian. Libertarianism is more correctly seen not as a political agenda detailing a better method of governance. It is instead the modern embodiment of a radical view that stands apart from and above all existing political ideologies.

Libertarianism doesn't propose any plan for reorganizing government; it calls for the plan to be abandoned. It doesn't propose that market incentives be employed in the formulation of public policy; it rather hopes for a society in which there is no public policy as that term in usually understood.

TRUE LIBERALISM

If this idea sounds radical and even crazy today, it would not have sounded so to eighteenth-century thinkers. The hallmark of Thomas Jefferson's theory of politics—drawn from John Locke and the English liberal tradition, which in turn derived it from a Continental theory of politics that dates to the late Middle Ages at the birth of modernity itself—is that freedom is a natural right. It precedes politics and it precedes the state. The natural right to freedom need not be granted or earned or conferred. It need only be recognized as fact. It is something that exists in the absence of a systematic effort to take it away. The role of government is neither to grant rights nor to offer them some kind of permission to exist, but to restrain from violating them.

The liberal tradition of the eighteenth century and following observed that it was government that has engaged in the most systematic efforts to rob people of their natural rights—the right to life, liberty, and property—and this is why the state must exist only with the permission of the people and be strictly limited to performing only essential tasks. To this agenda was this movement wholly and completely committed.

The idea of the American Revolution was not to fight for certain rights to be given or imposed on the people. It was not for a positive form of liberty to be imposed on society. It was purely negative in its ideological outlook. It sought to end the oppression, to clip the chains, to throw off the yoke, to set people free. It sought an end to governance by the state and a beginning to governance by people in their private associations.

For a demonstration of how this operated in practice, we need not look any further than the Articles of Confederation, which had no provisions for a substantive central government at all. This is usually considered its failing. We should give the revolutionaries more credit than that. The Articles were the embodiment of a radical theory that asserted that society does not need any kind of social management. Society is held together not by a state but by the cooperative daily actions of its members.

The nation needed no Caesar, nor president, nor single will to bring about the blessings of liberty. Those blessings flow from liberty itself, which, as American essayist Pierre Joseph Proudhon wrote, is the mother, not the daughter of order. This principle was illustrated well during the whole of the Colonial Era and in the years before the Constitution.

But we need not look back that far to see how liberty is a self-organizing principle. In millions of privately owned subdivisions around the country, communities have managed to create order out of a property-rights-based liberty, and the residents would have it no other way. In their private lives and as members of private communities, it may appear that they have seceded from government. The movement to gated communities has been condemned across the political spectrum but evidently consumers disagree. The market has provided a form of security that the government has failed to provide.

Another example of the capacity of people to organize them-selves through trade and exchange is shown in modern techno-logical innovations. The web is largely self-organizing, and some communities of commerce such as eBay have become larger and more expansive than entire countries once were. Firms such as Microsoft or Sun Microsystems are themselves communities of self-organizing individuals, operating under rules and enforcements that are largely private.

The innovations available to us in our times are so astonish-ing that our times have been called revolutionary, and truly they are. But in what sense has government contributed to it? I recall a few years ago that the Post Office suggested that it pro-vide people email addresses, but that was a one-day wonder, since the idea was forgotten amidst all the derisive laughter that greeted the idea.

Modern life has become so imbued with these smaller spheres of authority—spheres of authority born of liberty—that it resembles many aspects of the Colonial period with sectors and complexities. All the great institutions of our epoch—from huge and innovative technology firms to retailers such as Wal-Mart to massive international charitable organizations—are organized on the basis of voluntarism and exchange. They were not created by the state and they are not managed in their daily operations by the state.

IN PRAISE OF ORDERED ANARCHY

This imparts a lesson and a model to follow. Why not permit this successful model of liberty and order to characterize the whole of society? Why not expand what works and eliminate what doesn't? All that needs to happen is for government to remove itself from the picture.

I don't need to tell you that this is not a widely held view. Almost anyone living and working in Washington, DC, or in any major capital of state in the world, believes that there is some sense in which government holds society together, makes it run, inspires greatness, makes society fair and peaceful, and brings liberty and prosperity by enacting a set of policies.

This is a view that bypasses the liberal revolution altogether. It borrows from the ancient world of Pharaohs and Caesars in which a person's rights were defined and dictated by the state, which was seen as the organic expression of the community will as embodied in its leadership class. No clean lines of separation delimited individuals from society, state, and religion. All were seen as part of the organic unity of the civil order.

It was this view that came to be rejected with the Christian view that the state is not the master of the individual soul, which has infinite worth, and had no claim over the conscience. One thousand years later we began to see how this principle was expanded. The state is not the master over property or life either. Five hundred years later we saw the birth of economic science and the discovery of the principles of exchange and the miraculous observation that economic laws work independently of government.

Once the ideological culture began to absorb the lesson of just how unnecessary the state is for the functioning of society—a lesson that clearly needs to be relearned in every generation—the liberal revolution could not be held back. Despots fell, free trade reigned, and society grew ever more rich, peaceful, and free.

It is only natural that people who work for and in government imagine that without their efforts, only calamity would result. But this attitude is ubiquitous today in politics. Nearly all sides of the political debate are seeking to use government to impose their view of how society should work.

GOVERNMENT CANNOT BE RESTRAINED

I have gotten this question: what constitutional amendment would you favor to enact the Misesian agenda. Would you want one that forbids taxes from being raised above a certain amount, or enacts free trade, or guarantees the freedom of contract? My answer is that if I were to wish for amendments, they would look very much like the Bill of Rights. Major swaths of that document are ignored now. Why should we believe that a new amendment is going to perform any better?

The problem with amendments is that they presume a government large enough and powerful enough to enforce them, and a government that is interested more in the common good than its own good. After all, a tendency we've seen over 200 years is for the whole of the Constitution to be rendered by the courts as a mandate for government to intervene, not a restriction on its ability to intervene. Why do we believe that our pet amendment would be treated any differently?

What we need is not more things for government to do, but fewer and fewer until the point where genuine liberty can thrive. Speaking of the Constitution, the grounds on which it was approved were not that it would create the conditions of liberty, but it was rather that it would restrain government in its unrelenting tendency to take away the people's liberties. Its benefit was purely negative: it would restrain the state. The positive good it would do would consist entirely in letting society thrive and grow and develop on its own.

In short, the Constitution did not impose American liberty, contrary to what children are taught today. Instead, it permitted the liberty that already existed to continue to exist and even be more secure against despotic encroachments. Somehow this point has been lost on the current generation, and, as a result, we are learning all the wrong lessons from our founding and other history.

If we come to believe that the Constitution gave us liberty, we become very confused by the role of the United States in the history of the world. Too many people see the United States as the possessor of the political equivalent of the Midas touch. It can go into any country with its troops and bring American prosperity to them.

What is rarely considered an option these days is the old Jeffersonian vision of not imposing liberty but simply permitting liberty to occur and develop from within society itself.

As for foreign countries, the record that the United States has in so-called "nation-building" is abysmal. Time after time, the United States enters a country with its troops, handpicks its leaders, sets up its own intrusive agencies, props up structures that people regard as tyrannous, and then we find ourselves in shock and awe when the people complain about it.

By the way, I'm old enough to remember a time when Republicans didn't call critics of nation-building traitors. They called them patriots. If memory serves, that was about 10 years ago.

As dreadful as this may sound, it does seem that the US government and American political culture are masking their fears of liberty in the name of imposing it. For truly, most political sectors in the United States have a deep fear of the consequences of just leaving things alone—*laissez faire*, in the old French phrase.

The left tells us that under genuine liberty, children, the aged, and the poor would suffer abuse, neglect, discrimination, and deprivation. The right tells us that people would wallow in the abyss of immorality while foreign foes would overtake us. Economists say that financial collapse would be inevitable, environmentalists warn of a new age of insufferable fire and ice, while public policy experts of all sorts conjure up visions of market failures of every size and shape.

We continue to speak about freedom in our rhetoric. Every president and legislator praises the idea and swears fealty to the idea in public statements. But how many today believe this essential postulate of the old liberal revolution, that society can manage itself without central design and direction? Very few. Instead people believe in bureaucracy, central banking, war and sanctions, regulations and dictates, limitations and mandates, crisis management, and any and every means of financing all of this through taxes and debt and the printing press.

THE MYTH OF IRAQ'S FREEDOM

We flatter ourselves into believing that our central planning mechanisms are imposing not socialism but freedom itself, with

Iraq as the most obvious example and the *reductio ad absurdum*, all in one. Here we have a country that the United States invaded to overthrow its government and replace it with martial law administered by tanks on the street and bombers in the air, a controlled economy complete with gasoline price controls, and handpicked political leaders, and what do we call it? We call it freedom.

And yet some 15 years ago, when Saddam invaded Kuwait, threw out its leaders, occupied the country and attempted to impose a new government, the US president called it an aggression that would not stand. He took us to war to send a message that the sovereignty of states must be considered inviolate. It seems that everyone got the message except the United States.

Iraq is hardly the only country. US troops are strewn throughout the world with the mission to bring about the conditions of freedom. Ads for military contractors emphasize the same theme, juxtaposing hymns to liberty with pictures of tanks, bomber's eye views of cities, and soldiers with gas masks on. Then we wonder why so many people in the world bar the door when they hear that the US government is going to bring the blessings of democratic freedom to their doorsteps.

We have developed some strange sense that freedom is a condition that can be imposed by government, one of the many policy options we can pursue as experts in public policy. But it is not real freedom of the sort described above, the kind Jefferson claimed was to be possessed by all people everywhere whose rights are not violated. Rather it is freedom that conforms to a particular model that can be imposed from the top down, whether by the US government domestically or by US troops internationally.

FREEDOM CANNOT BE IMPOSED

It is not only in war that we have come to believe this myth of imposed freedom. The left imagines that by restricting the freedom of association in labor markets, it is protecting the freedom of the marginalized to obtain jobs. But that supposed freedom is purchased at other peoples' expense. The employer no longer has the right to hire and fire. As a result, the freedom of contract becomes one-sided. The employee is free to contract with the employer and quit whenever it seems right, but the employer is not free to contract on his terms and to fire whenever he sees fit.

The same is true for a huge range of activities essential to our civil lives. In education, it is said that the state must impose schooling on all children, else the parents and communities will neglect it. Only the state can make sure that no child is left behind. The only question is the means: will we use the union and bureaucracies favored by the left, or the market incentives and vouchers favored by the right. I don't want to get into a debate about which means is better, but only to draw attention to the reality that these are both forms of planning that compromise the freedom of families to manage their own affairs.

The catastrophic error of the left has been to underestimate the power of free markets to generate prosperity for the masses of people. But just as dangerous is the error of the right that markets constitute a system of social management, as if Washington has a series of levers, one of which is labeled "market-based." If one side wants to build bigger, better bureaucracies, the other side would rather tax and spend on contracting out government services or putting private enterprise on the payroll as a way of harnessing the market's power for the common good.

The first view denies the power of freedom itself but the second view is just as dangerous because it sees freedom purely in instrumental terms, as if it were something to be marshaled on behalf of the political establishment's view of what constitutes the national interest.

The formulation implies a concession that it is up to the state—its managers and kept intellectuals—to decide how, when, and where freedom is to be permitted. It further implies that the purpose of freedom, private ownership, and market incentives is the superior management of society, that is, to allow the current regime to operate more efficiently.

Murray Rothbard had noted back in the 1950s that economists, even those favoring markets, had become "efficiency experts for the state." They would explain how our central planners can employ market incentives to make Washington's plans work better. This view is now common among all people who adhere to the Chicago School of economics. They imagine that judges possess the wisdom and power to rearrange rights in a way that perfectly accords with their view of economic efficiency.

This view also appears in other right-wing proposals for Social Security private accounts, school vouchers, pollution trading permits, and other forms of market-based half measures. They don't cut the chains or throw away the yoke. They forge the steel with different materials and readjust the yoke to make it more comfortable.

There are many examples of this awful concession operating today. In policy circles, people use the word privatization to mean not the bowing out of government from a particular aspect of social and economic life, but merely the contracting out of statist priorities to politically connected private enterprise.

Indeed, the contracted-out state has become one of the most dangerous threats we face. A major part of the Iraq war has been undertaken by private groups working on behalf of government agencies. Republicans have warmed to the idea of contracting out major parts of the welfare state by putting formerly independent religious charities on the public payroll.

After the abysmal performance of FEMA after hurricane Katrina, many lawmakers suggested that Wal-Mart play a bigger role in crisis management. The assumption here is that nothing important is happening unless government somehow blesses the effort through a spending program that goes directly to a particular group or interest.

The worst mistake that free-enterprise supporters can make is to sell our ideas as a better means for achieving the state's ends. In many countries around the world, the idea of capitalism stands discredited not because it has been tried and failed but because a false model of capitalism was imposed from above. This is true in large parts of Eastern Europe and Russia, and also in Latin America. Not that socialism is seen as an alternative but there is a search going on in many parts of the world for some mythical third way.

It doesn't take much for the government to completely distort a market: a price control at any level, a subsidy to an economic loser at the expense of an economic winner, a limitation or restriction or special favor. All of these approaches can create huge problems that end up discrediting reform down the line.

GOVERNMENT ALWAYS GROWS

Another case against partial reform or imposed freedom was noted by Ludwig von Mises:

> There is an inherent tendency in all governmental power to recognize no restraints on its operation and to extend the sphere of its dominance as much as possible. To control everything, to leave no room for anything to happen of its own accord without the interference of the authorities—this is the goal for which every ruler secretly strives.

The problem he identified is how to limit the state once it becomes involved at all. Once you permit the state to manage one aspect of a business sector, you create the conditions that eventually lead it to manage the whole of the sector. Because of government's tendency to expand, it is better to never permit it to have any controlling interest in economic and cultural life.

Airports and airlines are a good example. Fearing the inability of the private sector to provide airline security—under the bizarre assumption that airlines and their passengers have less reason than the government to care about whether they die flying—the government long managed how airlines screen passengers and handle hijacking attempts.

The system was riddled with failure. Then the ultimate failure occurred: 9-11. But instead of backing off the system of bureaucratically administered airline security, Congress and the president created another bureaucracy that specialized in confiscating cosmetic scissors, ripping babies out of mothers' arms, and otherwise slowing down airline check-in to a crawl.

The pressures of new regulations have further cartelized the industry and made genuine market competition even more remote. And when the next catastrophe comes? We can look into our future and see what we might have once thought to be unthinkable: the nationalization of airlines.

It's true that even a partially free system is better than a fully socialist one, but these so-called privatization schemes could actually make the present system less free by insisting on new spending to cover new expenses to provide vouchers and private accounts.

ABDICATE, PLEASE

What is the right thing for Washington policy experts and analysts to advocate? The only thing that government does well: nothing at all. The proper role of government is to walk away from society, culture, economy, and the world stage of international politics. Leave it all to manage itself. The result will not be a perfect world. But it will be a world not made worse by the intervention of the state.

Free markets are not just about generating profits, productivity, and efficiency. They aren't just about spurring innovation and competition. They are about the right of individuals to make autonomous choices and contracts, to pursue lives that fulfill their dreams even if these dreams are not approved by their government masters.

So let us not kid ourselves into thinking that we can have it both ways so that freedom and despotism live peacefully together, the former imposed by the latter. To make a transition from statism to freedom means a complete revolution in economic and political life, from one where the state and its interests rule, to a system where the power of the state plays no role.

Freedom is not a public-policy option and it is not a plan. It is the end of politics itself. It is time for us to take that next step and call for precisely that. If we believe what Jefferson believed, and I think we should, it is time to speak less like managers of bureaucracies, and more like Moses.

5.

DECLARATION CONFUSION[*]

Every July, Americans commence the annual national ritual of noticing that the Declaration of Independence is among the "founding" documents that gave birth to the country. And pundits, following innumerable scholars for 150 years, will twist and mangle the text to discern some other meaning from the document besides the obvious one.

In most parts of the world, the Declaration is understood as a bold announcement and explanation, with an underlying rationale of why the British government needed to be thrown off in an act of American secession. That's why the Eastern Europeans throwing off Soviet tyranny used it as their charter and moral mandate. But right here at home, the Declaration has few real friends. Those who invoke it do so by explaining it as something else.

The industry of twisting the Declaration's clear meaning began only a few years after it was written, as the Federalist camp worked to treat it as a mandate for forming a new central government. The Anti-Federalists, especially Patrick Henry, regarded the Constitution as a step away from the ideals articulated by Jefferson.

[*]July 2000

Why? The Declaration threw off a powerful central government; 11 years later, the Constitution formed one. Indeed, Jefferson himself was no great enthusiast for the Constitution. It was written in his absence, and he only acceded to it on the assumption that the states could escape the union if they chose and the Constitution be amended if the new government threatened to become despotic. It turned out that the first large-scale test of his wish (1860) came only after the central government had accumulated enough power to annul the Declaration.

Federalist distortions were nothing compared with the brazen misrepresentations pushed by President Lincoln. In his hands, the Declaration became nothing more than an affirmation of the equality of all men. It was a rhetorical tactic designed to counter the view held by most people in the South that their secession was nothing but a renewal of the original spirit of the Declaration. Just as the American revolutionaries threw off the British yoke, the South would throw off the Northern yoke.

How could Lincoln promote the Declaration while crushing the right to self-government? There is no better way to counter your opponent's best argument than by taking it up yourself on behalf of a contrary cause. Today this is called triangulation, and it worked as well in the nineteenth century as it has in the Clinton years.

Clinton frequently decried the big government programs of the Republicans even as he pushed big government programs himself. He even (shudder) invokes the name of Jefferson.

The distortions have grown worse as the years have progressed. One faction of the radical left interprets the Declaration as a pre-Marxian revolutionary statement. Another faction treats it as a fraud perpetuated by business elites concerned only for profits. The soft left touts the material in the document about equality. American Tories decry the Declaration's invocations of universal abstractions like human rights, while Straussian neoconservatives see it as a mandate for civil rights and global militarism.

Thank goodness we still have the text itself!

We hold these truths to be self-evident, that all men are created equal, that they are endowed by their Creator with certain unalienable Rights, that among these are Life, Liberty, and the pursuit of Happiness. That to secure these rights, Governments are instituted among Men, deriving their just powers from the consent of the governed. That whenever any Form of Government becomes destructive of these ends, it is the Right of the People to alter or to abolish it, and to institute new Government, laying its foundation on such principles and organizing its powers in such form, as to them shall seem most likely to effect their Safety and Happiness.

Thus we see that the invocation of equality serves a specific purpose: it underscores the point that no man has a mandate from God to rule over other men. That is why a king, even if his name is Lincoln or Clinton or Bush, is not a superior moral agent with rights over the people apart from their consent. No man is endowed with rights superior to anyone else; that is the original American credo.

Next we find that government's power is not prior to the people; its powers are only just when the people institute the government and continue to consent to those powers. When government becomes the enemy of rights, it can be tossed out. Rights are permanent, intrinsic features of men (all men); governments are expedients that can come and go according to the people's wish. Rights cannot be altered or abolished; governments can.

When?

When a long train of abuses and usurpations, pursuing invariably the same object evinces a design to reduce them under absolute Despotism, it is their right, it is their duty, to throw off such Government, and to provide new Guards for their future security.

Thus we find that throwing off government is not only an option; it can also be a positive moral duty.

Indeed, Jefferson, the author of the Declaration, thought that governments should be abolished from time to time just for good measure. He wrote to Abigail Adams just before the Constitution was ratified, "The spirit of resistance to government is so valuable on certain occasions that I wish it to be always kept alive." He sympathized with the people, not the government, during Shays's Rebellion and said, "God forbid we should ever be twenty years without such a rebellion."

Reading on in the Declaration, we find an enormous amount of complaints that revolve around economic issues: taxes, tariffs, revenue investigations, and the like. The British are accused of "cutting off our Trade with all parts of the world" and "imposing Taxes on us without our Consent."

This fact has caused the revisionists on the left to claim that this glorified revolt was nothing other than a fit thrown by the propertied classes. There's a kernel of truth here. Economic liberty and property rights in particular are the foundation of all other liberties. If people are not secure in their earnings and enterprises, there can be no liberty at all (a point obliterated by the ACLU). Other debunkers point out that the infringements against economic liberty were minor, especially as compared with today. But that fact only underscores the point that Jefferson was right: we need more, not fewer, revolutions.

But why did Jefferson say we have rights to "life, liberty, and the pursuit of happiness," rather than use the Lockean phrase "life, liberty, and property?"

As Murray N. Rothbard points out in *Conceived in Liberty*, Jefferson was compressing George Mason's sentence from the Virginia Declaration of Rights, which said that among man's natural rights "are the enjoyment of life and liberty, with the means of acquiring and possessing property, and pursuing and obtaining happiness and safety."

There is no "pursuit of happiness" without property rights.

Also in the text, we find an impassioned hatred of the central government's military and police as instruments of tyranny. The British are accused of quartering troops without the people's permission, of making the military power separate from and superior to the civilian power, and of using "large Armies of foreign Mercenaries to complete the works of death, desolation and tyranny." But now that both left and right are in love with the military (for domestic as well as foreign purposes), these attitudes have fallen completely out of favor with the pundit class.

Jefferson biographer Dumas Malone is right that

> Jefferson's words should make tyranny tremble in any age. They have alarmed conservatives' minds in his own land in every generation, and some compatriots of his have regretted that the new Republic was dedicated to such radical doctrines at its birth.

Frank Chodorov was one of the few to write on the Declaration to get it right, so let's let him have the last word, from his 1945 essay, "Thomas Jefferson, Rebel!"

> It is not at all the charter of a new nation. It is a rationalization of rebellion. The indictment of the British crown was but a springboard from which Jefferson launched a political principle: that government, far from being an end in itself, is but an instrument invented by man to aid him in bettering his circumstances, and when that instrument fails to function properly it is high time to kick it out. And, which is most important, he meant ANY government, not only the particular one which at that time engaged his attention.

Any government. Anytime.

6.

ANATOMY OF AN IRAQI STATE*

If you want to understand what is going on in Iraq—why, for example, the United States is confiscating weapons and forbidding people from taking their small arms out of their

---

*May 2003

homes—turn to a timeless essay: Murray Rothbard's "Anatomy of the State." Here we find the definition of the state, an examination of the ideological props for the state, the fallacies behind the usual justifications for the state, a contrast between state means and social means, a model for understanding relations between states in a federal system and an international system, and arguments concerning the impossibility of a limited state.

That's a lot to absorb from one essay. But once you understand it, it is possible to make sense of the grim scene we are witnessing in Iraq, in which an invader state is attempting to create legitimacy for itself at the same time it is attempting to subjugate the population. It is a perfect case study for understanding the process whereby a small band of conquerors—small relative to the conquered population—attempts to become the one institution in society that produces nothing itself but presumes to make and enforce legislation that everyone in society but itself must obey.

Rothbard defines a state as follows:

> The State is that organization in society which attempts to maintain a monopoly of the use of force and violence in a given territorial area; in particular, it is the only organization in society that obtains its revenue not by voluntary contribution or payment for services rendered but by coercion. While other individuals or institutions obtain their income by production of goods and services and by the peaceful and voluntary sale of these goods and services to others, the State obtains its revenue by the use of compulsion; that is, by the use and the threat of the jailhouse and the bayonet. Having used force and violence to obtain its revenue, the State generally goes on to regulate and dictate the other actions of its individual subjects.

The case of a conquering state like the US in Iraq introduces complicating factors. The state in question does not have a revenue problem. It takes from US taxpayers and spends the money in Iraq, the only remaining problem being that people prefer Saddam dinars to US dollars. But the US does have a compliance problem. It is not at all clear to most Iraqis why, precisely, they have an obligation to obey the US occupiers except to the extent that they are forced to do so. Establishing and maintaining a monopoly on the use of force becomes crucial. That means being the largest possessors of firepower and keeping all competitors at bay.

Now, following Rothbard's definition of the state, whether the state is military or civilian does nothing to change its essential nature. The monopoly on force in normal civic affairs can be disguised through civilian institutions such as courts and peaceful-looking bureaus and the like. Then force is used only after a series of steps defined by legislation. In the military state, such as that running Iraq and much of the third world, it takes a cruder form: men in uniforms driving Humvees and wielding large-caliber machine guns. The only question is whether the state's weapons can be concealed, which suggests a degree of legitimacy, or must be out in the open, which suggests instability.

Now to the news that the US military is confiscating citizens' weapons in Iraq. The goal is to secure a monopoly of force and violence. By decree of the occupation government, broadcast through leaflets and loudspeakers, Iraqis will not be allowed to carry any concealed weapons except by permit issued by the US. All AK-47s, etc. must be turned in. Citizens will be allowed to keep small arms for home protection, but they may not take them out of the house. Open-air arms markets—one of the few sectors of thriving business in Iraq—will be shut down. There will be an amnesty period, but after that? Crackdown. No more shooting in the air at night, for example.

As the *New York Times* explains, "The main emphasis is to enable American forces to protect themselves against attacks." Weapons confiscation is "an important part" of the allied forces "efforts to secure the country. . . . The intention is to reduce attacks against allied forces, reduce crime, and stop violent fights among rival Iraqi groups."

Now, you don't have to be John Lott to know the result. The groups that the US is targeting in particular have the least reason to give up their weapons and every reason to keep them.

We can be sure that anyone who does turn in weapons is not a threat to the US military or to anyone else. The criminals, meanwhile, will feel safer in the knowledge that people on the street and in cars are unarmed.

In short, US efforts to enforce gun control can only result in increased crime and ever more problems with armed gangs using ever more desperate tactics. In the end, this whole project will come to naught. The US government has been unable to enforce gun control in Washington, DC. It sure as heck can't do it in Iraq, and to the extent it is successful, it only means more crime and violence.

What's interesting here is the motivation, which isn't really about stopping petty thievery but primarily about the state's control over society. What's true in Iraq is also true in the United States. The most forthright defenders of gun ownership have made it clear that the best case for permitting it is precisely that it protects citizens against government tyranny.

When the US went into Iraq, no one imagined that months later the military would be searching people for weapons and attempting to impose a gun ban more severe than exists in many US states. But the logic of the situation has propelled the US into acting ever more tyrannically in Iraq, ever more brazenly in its coercive methods, and ever more comprehensively in its degree of attempted control over society. It must do this because it has no other source of legitimacy.

But in politics, every action generates a reaction. Iraqis will not comply with this order. They will keep and hide their weapons. And they will work to acquire more, now that the US has said it has no immediate intention of allowing Iraq to govern itself. Every additional step in attempted control will lead to ever more resistance. The US said it was going into Iraq to liberate that country. But it seems that, with these latest efforts, the end result will be an unending mire of a brutal and unstable military dictatorship or a humiliating pullout that will leave the country in chaos.

Put it this way: if you were an Iraqi, would you turn in your weapon?

7.

WHY THE STATE IS DIFFERENT*

A common accusation against libertarianism is that we are unnaturally obsessed with tracing social and economic problems to the state, and, in doing so, we oversimplify the world.

If you let the people who say this keep talking, they will explain to you why the state is not all bad, that some of its actions yield positive results and, in any case, the state should not always be singled out as some sort of grave evil.

It is not inconceivable, they say, that the state is performing actions that weave themselves into the normal operation of society. The state is not always exogenous to the system but is sometime intrinsic to it. To constantly blame the state for our ills is as cranky as those who single out the Bilderbergers for all the world's ills; it is a half-truth gone mad.

Without attempting a wholesale refutation of this position, what this criticism overlooks is the uniqueness of the state as an institution. Let us turn our attention to a news item that under-scores in what respects the state is different from the rest of society. It concerns the new law passed by Congress and signed by the president that criminalizes the sending of commercial spam. From this one case, we can observe a number of traits of the state that demonstrate just how truly outside of society it really is, and therefore why it is right to focus such close attention on it.

There are a number of commercial products on the market designed to crush spam, which can be defined as email you never asked to receive and do not want. It is not at all clear that sending someone such an email is really a coercive invasion of

---

*December 2003

property rights, but it is surely annoying, and so there is a market for methods of stopping it.

As always in commerce, there are those who stand to make a buck by solving problems. Entrepreneurs dream up new methods and capitalists take risks to bring them to market. Each product that is offered is distinctive. Consumers try out a number of different ones. The ones that work better than others—and sell for the right price and are easy to install—displace those that work less well. Profits flow to those who have done the best job.

This is the way the market works, and all is done voluntarily. The power to judge, to make some products succeed and some fail, is in the hands of consumers. Consumers base their judgments on what is good for them personally, so there is a constant feedback mechanism, from the desktop to the capitalists to the entrepreneurs to the traders who buy and sell stocks of companies that bring the products to market at the least-possible cost.

We can only marvel at how all of this is coordinated by the price system, which is the link between our subjective valuations and the real world of technology and resources. To succeed in this market requires creativity, imagination, a keen sense of judgment, a technological sense, and relentless attention to the needs of others. People make money even as society is served.

Now, let us contrast this gorgeous web of trial and error with the ham-handed approach of Congress and the president. Someone had the idea that spam is bad, and thus does the solution present itself: make it illegal, which is to say, threaten spammers with fines and jail and, if they resist enough, death. It is no more or less complicated than that. There is no trial and error process, no imagination required, no permission from consumers to be sought, and no investors to issue a judgment on the merits or demerits of this approach. Congress speaks, the president agrees, and it is done.

What if it doesn't work? Only under the rarest conditions does the state reverse itself or admit error. Its tendency instead is to keep pounding away with its one and only hammer, even if the nail is all the way in or hasn't budged at all.

Hence Lesson One in the uniqueness of the state: the state has one tool, and one tool only, at its disposal: force.

Now, imagine if a private enterprise tried that same approach. Let's say that Acme Anti-Spam puts out a product that would tag spammers, loot their bank accounts, and hold them in captivity for a period of time, and shoot spammers dead should they attempt to evade or escape. What's more, the company doesn't propose to test this approach on the market and seek subscribers, but rather force every last email user to subscribe.

How will Acme Anti-Spam make money at its operation? It won't. It will fund its activities by taking money from your bank account whether you like it or not. They say that they can do this simply because they can, and if you try to stop it, you too will be fined, imprisoned, or shot. The company further claims that it is serving society.

Such a company would be immediately decried as heartless, antisocial, and essentially deranged. At the very least it would be considered uncreative and dangerous, if not outright criminal. Its very existence would be a scandal, and the people who dreamed up such a company and tried to manage it would be seen as psychopaths or just evil. Everyone would see through the motivation: they are using a real problem that exists in society as a means to get money without our permission, and to exercise authority that should belong to no one.

Lesson Two presents itself: the state is the only institution in society that can impose itself on all of society without asking the permission of anyone in particular. You can't opt out.

A seemingly peculiar aspect of the anti-spam law is that the government exempts itself from having to adhere to its own law. Politicians routinely buy up email addresses from commercial companies and send out unsolicited email. They defend this practice on grounds that they are not pushing a commercial service and that doing so is cheaper than sending regular mail, and hence saves taxpayer money. It is not spam, they say, but constituent service. We all laugh at the political class for its hypocrisy in this, and yet the exemption draws attention to:

Lesson Three: the state is exempt from the laws it claims to enforce, and manages this exemption by redefining its criminality as public service.

What is considered theft in the private sector is "taxation" when done by the state. What is kidnapping in the private sector is "selective service" in the public sector. What is counterfeiting when done in the private sector is "monetary policy" when done by the public sector. What is mass murder in the private sector is "foreign policy" in the public sector.

This tendency to break laws and redefine the infraction is a universal feature of the state. When cops zoom by we don't think of them as speeding but merely being on the chase. Killing innocents is dismissed as inevitable civilian casualties. So it should hardly surprise us that the state rarely or even never catches itself in the webs it weaves. Of course it exempts itself from its anti-spam law. The state is above the law.

The problem of spam will be solved one way or another. The criminal penalties will deter some but the real solution will come from the private sector, just as the problem of crime is lessened by the locks, alarm systems, handguns, and private security guards provided by the private sector. The state of course will take credit. Historians will observe the appearance and disappearance of spam coinciding with the before and after of the criminal penalties, while it will be up to those dismissed as wacky revisionists to give the whole truth.

This is the final feature of the state to which I would like to draw attention: it gets to write the history. Unlike the other three issues, this is not an intrinsic feature of the state but rather is a reflection of the culture. This can change so long as people are alert to the problem. And this is the role, the essential role, of libertarian intellectuals: to change the ideological culture in ways that make people aware of the antisocial nature of the state, and how it always stands outside of society, no matter how democratic it may claim to be.

The case of the latest anti-spam law is only one chapter in a very long book that dates back to the beginning of recorded history, and extends as far as our existence on this earth. There will always be those who claim to have special rights over the rest of society, and the state is the most organized attempt to get away with it. To focus on these people as a unique problem is not an obsession, but the working out of intellectual responsibility.

8.
WHICH WAY THE YOUNG?*

A new poll shows 18–29 year olds turning against Bush, with 58 percent believing that the country is on the wrong track. This, however, doesn't translate into support for John Kerry. In fact the margin of difference between support for either major candidate is negligible. What does seem clear is that the wave of student enthusiasm for the GOP that came about after September 11 has subsided.

But since political polls are both tedious and intellectually vacuous, let's move on to the real question we should be asking: are students tending toward socialist thinking or free-market thinking as compared to the past?

It is hard to discern this based on polls alone, because of the enormous confusion concerning the meanings of liberal and conservative, and left and right. Any poll that stays within these conventions is likely to be misleading (even aside from all the other weaknesses of polling).

---

*May 2004

In the conventional view, to be politically leftist means to have faith in government at home but doubts about the same government abroad—at least that's what it means right now. Thus are the bookstores packed with riveting attacks on the Bush administration's foreign policy for attempting to use the state for messianic purposes in Iraq and Afghanistan, along with all the attendant evils that come with such attempts (lies, debt, death, and all the rest).

At the same time, the same political left decries the Bush administration for not having been messianic enough in its use of government power at home, where they believe the state should equalize incomes, provide free goods and services for one and all, and regulate commerce until it comes to a halt, which would supposedly yield great benefits for the environment.

So partisan have been the attacks that Bush gets no "credit" from socialists for having been the biggest spending president since LBJ. At some point in the future, however, the left may inaugurate Bush revisionism and decide (once he is safely out of office) that he wasn't so bad after all since he brought back government power after its decline in the 1990s—just as the political left discovered after the fact how much they owed to World War I for socializing the economy.

As for the political right and its current literature, we are supposed to be ever vigilant against "big government" unless of course it is the really very big government that seeks world empire in the name of spreading freedom and democracy. In this case—and probably only when the GOP is running the empire—we are supposed to believe every claim of the government, spend hundreds of billions without flinching, arrest dissenters, violate civil liberties, and possibly even draft people into military service. Such positions are said to be "right-wing" (unless the draft is being advocated in the name of racial equality, in which case the position is considered "left-wing").

Is it any wonder that students become confused, especially when there is so little serious discussion of principled ideological issues in popular political literature? The essential message of most political books on the shelf is either: (a) the Bush administration and its friends are fabulous and wonderful, or (b) the Bush administration and its friends are liars, crooks, thieves, and murderers. Come to think of it, the same was true about 10 years ago, when all political books fell into the camp of either pro- or anti-Clinton.

There is nothing wrong with beating up the politicians in charge. It serves a good social function. But serious thought requires a more fundamental rethinking of the role of government in the world, whether at home or abroad, and the true meaning of human freedom.

The attacks on the World Trade Center in September of 2001 did prompt such thinking on the part of a generation of students, but not in a way that suits the cause of liberty. There was the crisis effect, which always seems to cause people to embrace power. There was the heralding of public service, which apparently these students accepted without question. Then there was the nationalistic impulse—among the basest emotions to afflict people—that was unleashed by the idea of swarthy foreigners murdering innocents and demolishing urban landscapes.

The government is always looking for something that appears more dangerous than itself, and these criminals seem to fit the bill. Never mind that it was the government that promised but failed to protect us; it was the government that prevented the airlines from protecting themselves; it was the government that so badly botched the rescue operations; it was the government that had stirred up the hate that led to the terrorism. And there was not much the government could have justly done to fix the problem after the fact, since the perpetrators were all dead.

Nonetheless, all these thoughts are stage two, and most students never went beyond stage one. Joshua Foer, writing for the *New York Times*, reminds us of how pro-war this generation of college students became, and remained until last year, when polls showed far higher support for war among students than people over 30. Pro-war rallies were common on campus. Foer speculates why:

> The class of 2004 grew up at a time when it was easy to have faith in the goodness of our government. Vietnam, Watergate and even Iran-contra were not a part of our direct political memory. For my generation, abuse of power meant sexual indiscretions in the Oval Office—not shifting rationales for war. While President Bush's claims about weapons of mass destruction and links between Iraq and Al Qaeda may have revived memories of the Gulf of Tonkin for some of our parents, my generation wasn't inclined toward incredulousness. After all, according to that same poll, 50 percent of those surveyed under 30 said they trusted government to do the right thing; for Americans older than us, that number was 36 percent.

Thus did the lack of skepticism about power (owing to inattention or lack of experience) translate into support for the war. But it turns out that the war has displayed features of all government programs, and taught close observers a thing or two about the unintended consequences of government action, the ever escalating costs of government programs, the inability of government to control events, the inflated egos and lies of public officials, the tendency of the press to play along, and the inevitable result of government programs that they produce the very opposite of their stated purposes.

No seasoned observer of government can be surprised that the war on terror produced more terror and threats of terror, any more than we should be surprised to see the wars on tobacco, poverty, drinking, fat, speeding, illiteracy, and all the rest, fail just as badly. In short, this war has provided an essential civics lesson that the state is not a friend of truth and liberty but rather its enemy. And so support for the war among students has dropped from 65 percent to 49 percent.

But will the lesson penetrate beyond the superficial level of who should be supported for president? Will the current generation of students see through the partisan fog and observe the core ideological battle of our age and every age? This is the crucial question, and so long as people talk about left and right, liberal and conservative, we are likely to miss it.

Foer closes his *New York Times* op-ed with a thoroughly conventional prediction that the new generation will be liberal on social issues and conservative on national security (he might have added economics to reinforce this repetition of rhetorical conventions). Based on correspondence and applications to Mises Institute programs, it seems to me that we are observing a turn toward a politics that evades the media's radar: libertarianism, which combines free-market politics, opposition to the warfare state, and a peaceful world outlook.

This view borrows from the right's critique of the state at home, and from the left's critique of the state abroad, to forge a political perspective that is as realistic as it is radical. To discover it counts as the great moment in the life of any intellectual because it opens vast vistas for creative thinking on economics, history, philosophy, law, sociology, and even literature.

This summer our humble campus at the Mises Institute is filled with students working in all these fields and coming from many different ideological backgrounds but drawn to something more substantive than the political harangues available at the bestseller rack. This is also a generation that has benefited beyond measure from the products of free enterprise and global trade; they are surrounded by the blessings of the "anarchy of production" and witness to the destructionism of government planning.

To believe in liberty, and understand its application in all affairs in life, is to cease to be buffeted by the winds of partisan politics, and instead to do your part in the preservation and further development of civilization itself. If students are drawn to ideals in our time, the libertarian ideal is poised for a renaissance.

9.

ABSORBED BY THE STATE*

If you have read the *Screwtape Letters* by C.S. Lewis, you know that the Devil is an expert in turning good impulses toward evil ends, and in leading people to misapply virtues in ways that serve the cause of evil.

Well, so it is with the state. In every age, it takes the intellectual and political fashions alive in the culture, and turns them toward power for itself, money for itself, authority and affection for itself. The end is always and everywhere the same and as predictable as the tides. However, the means the state uses to achieve this end are forever changing in ways that surprise us.

This tendency takes peculiar turns in the course of Republican administrations, when the rhetoric of freedom, free markets, and limited government is used for the paradoxical purpose of expanding state power.

Let us begin with the most obvious point.

Most people are ready to concede that defense is one function that government should provide. The first act of a Republican administration is to vastly expand military spending, always with the assumption that unless hundreds of billions more is spent, the country will be left undefended. When Republicans are running the show, it seems that there is no limit to how far this racket can be carried. We proceed as if the need to drink means that we should shove the water hose down our throat.

At the height of World War II, before spending plummeted after the war ended, the federal government spent less than $90 billion on defense, which was the same spent as late as 1961.

---

*February 2005

Today it spends five times that amount in current dollars. Might this spending be a convenient way to slather money on military contractors and to otherwise feed the friends of the government?

So it is with homeland security. For decades, people on the political right have complained that money for defense is being spent on far-flung missions overseas and to subsidize the defense budgets of friendly foreign governments. The left has long brought attention to the subsidies given to authoritarian regimes. And so how does the state absorb these energetic movements? With new programs to provide "homeland security"—more power for the state, but with an even better excuse.

The example of how the cultural conservatives are being absorbed is especially egregious. For decades, conservatives complained that government was waging a war on families by taxing marriage, punishing savings, subsidizing antifamily political movements, and promoting contraception, sex education, abortion, and the like. And yet, if you look at the pro-family movement today, it is all about big government: a federal marriage amendment, ridiculous family programs at the federal level, bureaucratic intervention into family life, and manipulation of American families for Republican purposes.

The pro-family movement used to be plausibly pro-liberty, especially given that the family predates government, exists in a state of anarchy, and is foundational for civilization. But leave it to politics to convert a pro-family movement into one that endorses statism of every sort. It may yet support the state forcing us into associations of which it approves while forbidding all others. That way lies corruption of the worst sort.

The same is true of religion. From the 1970s through the 1990s, religious people had the general sense that the government was against them, attempting to tax their churches, forbidding them from making public expressions of their faith, and funding antireligious propaganda. Then the Bush administration gets control, and what happens? The government is funding religious charities, using religion to justify its foreign policy, courting certain religious groups for votes and support, and doing its best to weave the American faith into the fabric of the American state.

Whereas the Religious right once had just complaints against the government, and an agenda to get the state's hand out of their churches, the opposite now seems true. The state has enlisted the Religious right in a cause that will only lead to more government power over society and economy and the world in general. Here again, we see how the state can turn all movements to its own purposes.

In the last 60 years, the energies of free-market intellectuals have been spent on debunking the need for the social welfare state. But these energies are now being used to expand rather than shrink the state. Consider the cry to "privatize" Social Security. It uses the good work of many great thinkers to debunk a bad system, so that it can be recreated with a wholly new system of forced savings that could end up worse than the original.

The anti-Social Security movement that has existed since the 1930s is being re-channeled into a pro-forced savings movement. A further tragedy: all the efforts of the past to debunk Social Security now risk being discredited when this new program turns out to be wildly expensive, terribly coercive, dangerous to the independence of capital markets, and ultimately fruitless for workers who put their hopes in it. But meanwhile, the energies of the anti-Social Security movement will have been spent.

Education is another area. In the 1970s and '80s, a movement grew among conservative intellectuals and the general public against the dumbing down of curricula in public school. As a result of the collectivism at the heart of centrally controlled public schooling, standards were lowered to the extent that everyone was seen as above average. It was this movement that led to demands for the abolition of the Department of Education and to the rise of homeschooling and the flourishing of alternative schools.

But these days, the movement has been diverted and all its energies put not into tearing down public schools but expanding the state. The voucher program favors federal payments to private schools, which will nationalize an industry and end up making it share in the problems of the public schools. The movement for standards has led to "No Child Left Behind" and regimentation of all schools by Washington, DC. The Department of Education has turned its energies to feeding conservative intellectuals and browbeating everyone into a general "back to basics" movement.

Even homeschooling has not escaped corruption, as the nation's leading college for homeschooled kids works to place smart, decent kids in the worst imaginable place: at the heart of the executive branch of government, and even the CIA.

The tragedy just overwhelms you. These kids have studied hard for many years to prepare themselves to achieve greatness, with moms and dads making enormous sacrifices. So, under the belief that greatness equals power, they are being sent to serve in the state apparatus to learn the main practices that government teaches its drones: to lie, deceive, manipulate, and abuse, without feeling any pangs of conscience. This can turn a good person into a lifelong cynic.

The list goes on. The anti-tax movement becomes a tax-reform movement that ends up making government more expensive, the movement against government bureaucracy becomes a movement for contracting out and putting more people on the payroll, the slogan of "America First" is perverted into a call for protectionism, and so on.

How to avoid the trap? How does any political movement that begins by being opposed to the state avoid being absorbed by the state? The most crucial step is to decide what you are for and what you are against from the very outset. It is not enough to be against a particular government program or for a particular institution such as the family. What we need is a comprehensive ideology of liberty to displace the comprehensive ideology of statism—with no compromises.

In the struggle against power, the battle is too important to risk absorption by the enemy. There are no proxies for genuine liberty. Using rhetorical maneuvers to disguise the movement for freedom as something else is dangerous business indeed.

10.
WORKING AROUND LEVIATHAN*

Permit me to draw your attention to what strikes me as the most profound political paradox of our times. The US government is larger, more consolidated, more powerful, and more intrusive than it has ever been in its history—indeed our sweet land of liberty is now host to the most powerful leviathan state that has ever existed.

Never before has a government in human history owned more weapons of mass destruction, looted as much wealth from a country, and assumed unto itself so much power to regulate the minutiae of daily life. By comparison to the behemoth in Washington, with its printing press to crank out money for the world and its annual $2.2 trillion in largess to toss at adoring crowds, even communist states were powerless paupers.

At the same time—and here is the paradox—the United States is overall the wealthiest society in the history of the world. The World Bank lists Luxembourg, Switzerland, and Norway as competitive in this regard, but the statistics don't take into account the challenges to mass wealth that exist in the US relative to small, homogenous states such as its closest competitors. In the United States, more people from more classes and geographic regions have access to more goods and services

---

*April 2005

at prices they can afford, and possess the disposable income and access to credit to put them to use, than at any other time in history. Truly we live in the age of abundance.

What is the relationship between the rise of big government and the rise of American prosperity? It seems that people on the right and left are quick to confuse correlation with causation. They believe that the US is wealthy because the government is big and expansive. This error is probably the most common of all errors in political economy. It is just assumed that buildings are safe because of building codes, that stock markets are not dens of thieves because of the SEC, that the elderly don't starve and die because of Social Security, and so on, all the way to concluding that we should credit big government for American wealth.

CAUSE AND EFFECT

Now, this is where economic logic comes into play. You have to understand something about the way cause and effect operate in human affairs to understand that big government does not bring about prosperity. Government is not productive. It has no wealth of its own. All it acquires it must take from the private sector. You might believe that it is necessary and you might believe it does great good, but we must grant that it does not have the ability to produce wealth in the way the market does.

Lasting prosperity can only come about through a system that allows people to cooperate to their mutual advantage, innovate and invest in an environment of freedom, retain earnings as private property, and save generation to generation without fear of having estates looted through taxation and inflation. Human effort in the framework of a market economy: this is the source of wealth; this is the means by which a rising population is fed, clothed, and housed; this is the method by which even the poorest country can become rich.

Now, does this system as described characterize the United States? Yes and no. This is, after all, the country that jailed

Martha Stewart, the world's most successful female entrepreneur, for the crime of having not disclosed to the inquisitors every last detail about the circumstances surrounding her choice to sell a stock before its bottom dropped out.

Recently enacted laws, such as the Sarbanes-Oxley Act, empower the federal government to oversee the books of every publicly listed company and even manage their methods and operations in every detail. Some have compared this act to FDR's National Industrial Recovery Act.

This is a country with cradle-to-grave security promises, where the government responds to the eventual inability to keep those promises by making new and more expensive promises. This is a country that, when faced with a problem of airport security, created a whole new federal bureaucracy to gum up the works of every airport in the country.

These are incredibly bad policies, enterprise killers in every way. Why, then, does enterprise continue to thrive? The answer is complex. In many ways we continue to live off the capital of previous generations. Some economic sectors benefit greatly from an artificial injection of newly created credit, making prosperity seem more real than it is in sectors such as housing and perhaps stocks. There is a bitter irony at work here too in that the larger the economy, the more there is to tax, and so government grows as an after-effect of economic growth.

PEOPLE RESIST CONTROL

But here I would like to concentrate on what I think is an explanation that is too often overlooked. It requires that we understand something about the extraordinary capacity of the human mind to overcome obstacles put in its path. In all the history of states, in all the history of reflection on social organization and economics, this component is the most underestimated because it is the least predictable and the most difficult to comprehend. Human beings are creative and determined, and, if they have a love of liberty, and cooperate through exchange, they can overcome seemingly impassable obstacles.

It is because of this power of human ingenuity and determination to improve the world around us, despite the bureaucrats, that a vast gulf has come to separate the accumulated power of the nation-state from its effective power in the management and guidance of society and the world economy.

Now, there is a sense in which the state is nowhere as effective as it claims. Economic law limits what the state can do. The state cannot raise wages for everyone. It cannot dampen prices without causing shortages, or increase prices without causing surpluses. It cannot predict the course of markets or human events. It can control surprisingly few forces that work in the world.

In all its central planning, government is forever declaring that major combat operations are over, whether in foreign or domestic policy, only to discover that its real struggles and battles last and last. A good example is in the area of foreign trade. If a good or service is more efficiently produced abroad, the logic of the market will reassign production patterns until they conform. An attempt to protect domestic industry can do nothing to change this reality. Instead, protection only increases prices for consumers, subsidizes inefficient firms, and brings about ever-increasing amounts of wasted time, work, and resources.

I only mention these few examples of the limits of the state as a prelude to my general claim. It's my view that the gulf between accumulated power and effective power is going to grow ever wider in the coming years, to the point where the nation-state itself will grow effectively weaker, more anachronistic, and finally irrelevant to the course of social development.

I would like to explain more in depth what I mean, and provide an account of how the relationship of society to the state has dramatically changed over the last 50 years and will continue to do so in the years ahead. This change has fundamentally altered our view toward public life and our expectations concerning what institutions we depend upon for our security and well-being. We have come to depend on the state less and less in our daily lives, even as the state has accumulated ever more power. Indeed, unless we work directly for the state, and sometimes even if we do, our activities and affairs owe ever more to the private sector.

In saying this, I am to some extent agreeing with what has become a common complaint made by neoconservative writers and left-liberal pundits. They have said for years that the civic culture is no longer coherent and cohesive. They complain that the nation-state has lost its hold on the public imagination. They whine and wail about how we have all retreated into our suburbs and Internet connections and no longer rally around grand national projects that inspire us with a vision of all that government can do.

Or to put it another way, they worry that the government has run out of good excuses for spending money, taxing us, regulating us, drafting our kids, and getting us embroiled in foreign wars. For the neoconservative crowd, 9-11 really was a godsend, just as the Oklahoma bombing was a godsend to the left-liberals of the 1990s. They were equally adept at exploiting these horrible tragedies to the great advantage of the state, and in browbeating the rest of the population into going along with the political priorities of the regime in power. But in retrospect, it is clear that these events only represented a brief parenthesis in the long-run decline of the nation-state in our social consciousness.

THE MYTHOLOGY OF THE NATION-STATE

Before I proceed further, it would be useful to back up just a bit to remember that the nation-state as we know it is a modern invention, and not an essential feature of society. In many ways, it is, as Bastiat said, nothing but an artifice that permits some to live at others' expense. He was speaking of nineteenth-century France, but all that he wrote applies in our time as well.

But states were not always structured as we know them today. From the fall of the Roman Empire to the Late Middle Ages, societies in Europe were governed not by bureaucrats, elected councils, regulations, or any kind of permanent structural apparatus of coercion and compulsion, but by competing cells of authority that were woven together not by ideology but by separate function. The merchant class managed its affairs, the Church had its purview and courts, the international traders developed their code, feudal lords were masters of their domain, free cities managed themselves, the family was largely autonomous, and the state, such as it was, consisted of extended families and lines of rulers who usually dared not transgress their traditional authority.

Every institution was supremely jealous of its power and authority. The emergence of liberty from feudalism occurred not because any institution brought it about, but because they all tended to stay within their realms, cooperating where necessary but also competing for the loyalty of the public. All the institutions we associate with civilization—such as universities, stock markets, charities, global trade, scientific establishments, vocational schools, courts of law—were born or recaptured from the ruins of the ancient world during these supposed dark ages without nation-states.

Voltaire once wrote of how kings would conduct their wars, raising their own money and employing their own soldiers, always acquiring or losing territory and usually up to no good. But for the most part, though they dominate the history books, their activities had little or no impact on the people. It was during this time, historian Ralph Raico reminds us, that the process of accumulating capital began again and the division of labor began to expand—two features that are essential to rising population and prosperity.

The nation-state as we know it—defined by a fixed governing class that enjoys the legal monopoly on the right to use aggressive force against person and property, and holding a status that is higher in authority than any other institution—was a development of the break-up of Christendom, and the resulting centralization and wars of the late sixteenth century and early seventeenth century, as Martin Van Crevald points out. As competitive sources of authority weakened, the state as an entity separate from its ruler came to be strengthened and consolidated, sometimes in opposition to competing authority centers and sometimes in cooperation with them.

The emergence of the modern state immediately gave rise to a countervailing force: the great liberal movement all over Europe and then in the United States. This liberal movement emphasized a single theme in its writings. It is as follows: (1) society contains within itself the capacity for managing itself in all its affairs, especially its economic affairs, and (2) states, to the extent that they do more than merely punish criminals, are a source of despotism and tyranny.

It was this conviction that was accepted as commonplace during the founding period of the United States, and not just by statesmen but also by merchants, farmers, ministers, and intellectuals. The conviction that society requires no central management, and should thereby be left alone by the governing class, had a name: liberalism. It meant to love liberty.

The structure and founding ideology of the United States were intended to protect that idea of liberty, under the belief that if people are free to pursue their dreams, cooperating with each other and also competing, freely associating to their mutual betterment, and governing their own affairs rather than permitting themselves to be governed from on high, the result would be human flourishing as never before known in history.

THE AGE OF LEVIATHAN

Now, it should be obvious that this model was rejected in the twentieth century, the century of government control. It began with a horrible war that brought the Communists to power in Russia and the managerial class to power in the United States. Economist Thomas DiLorenzo has discussed how we came to be saddled with an income tax, a central bank, and direct democracy, all in one year. The interwar years provided an ever so brief respite before the world became uglier with two models of central control having presented themselves as the only viable systems: fascism and communism. We flatter ourselves if we think the New Deal represented a third choice, for it borrowed from the other two and added only the ingredient of democratic expediency.

World War Two cemented into place the planned society in which all attention was directed toward the public sector as liberator and savior of mankind. The words economic development, technology, and security were bound up with one institution only: the nation-state. It was the nation-state that fought and won the war, launched the bomb, reconstructed economies, rescued the aged, educated the youth, stabilized the economy, and planned the exploration of space. The nation-state was the new god: supposedly omniscient, omnipotent, and omni-competent.

The Mises Institute recently brought out an unpublished essay by Murray Rothbard, "Science, Technology, and Government," written in the late 1950s on the subject of technology and the state. In it he departed from the whole of conventional wisdom at the time by arguing that the government was not the appropriate institution to trust with our technological future. Research and development are best done by the private sector, he said. All major innovations in world history have come about this way, he wrote, and it is from within the private sector that we should expect the next revolution. From government we can only expect technology that reinforces political priorities, but no real innovations that are both useful for the mass of the consuming public and economically viable.

These days the paper is not shocking at all. Not so in those times. The paper was not published because there was no one around to publish it. It was an argument that all his colleagues would have rejected outright. In those days, it didn't even seem to have superficial plausibility. Even those who commissioned the piece found themselves squeamish about its contents. When you think about the public consensus that existed for the state in those days, it does indeed strike us as a different world.

In 1955, the federal government was relatively small but exercised enormous effective power. The federal budget was $68 billion, which is about one thirty-sixth as large as today's government. In fact, the whole federal government was smaller than a single department of the government today: the Department of Education, which, ironically is the one that the Republicans keep saying that they will abolish.

But the size of the state by today's standards masked its effective hold on the public mind. The GI bill, it was believed, would educate all soldiers, while the federal government would reconstruct the Europe the Nazis destroyed even while it protected us from the demonized Soviets who had been our allies in the war the day before yesterday.

The Cold War purported to pit US capitalism against Soviet Communism, but the truth was that there was very little enthusiasm for market economics in the United States. It was not taught in the classrooms. Mises himself could not find a paid position as professor of economics. Keynesian thinking—which imagined the government to be an effective manager of the macroeconomy—was seen as the only real alternative to socialism.

The technological advances of the period mostly involved television and commercial flight, advances widely attributed to government wartime spending. Our information came from three approved networks and a handful of wire services. Publishing books was expensive, so self-publishing was out of the question. Intellectual and economic life was dominated by a kind of forced conformity and the culture seized by an unrelenting fear of nuclear holocaust.

The planned economy that had become fashionable in the 1930s continued its hold on public policy in the 1950s, and successfully kept many innovations at bay. Cell phones are a good example. As with most new technology that enters into mass distribution, we all wonder how we got along without them before. The development and expansion of this industry—which was fully born in 1994—have been entirely a result of private-sector initiative. We own our phones, manage our accounts, deploy the phones for email, web surfing, and even for taking and sending pictures.

The prices and plans are market based, and accessible to a vast amount of the buying public. The industry is incredibly competitive. In every mall in America, cell phone dealers have their booths. When I was a kid we dreamed of personal communication devices that we read about in James Bond novels. We imagined that they would be in our cars. But even Ian Fleming couldn't have imagined their portability or the advance of wireless communications. Nor could we have imagined that they would be a mass product, available not just to spies or the rich but to everyone.

It is highly significant that this industry is rooted so deeply in the private sector. It was not too long ago when economists and political scientists believed that communication technology must always fall within the purview of the state. This belief was the basis of the creation of the old Bell system. I can recall as a young adult that the phone strapped to the wall was the only real-time contact we had with the outside world. It was owned by the one phone company, thanks to government monopoly and regulation. Our right to communicate was sustained and controlled by the state.

In 1947, the federal government, which had by then taken ownership of the entire radio spectrum, graciously relented and permitted the first mobile telephone service. It gave up enough of the frequency spectrum to permit some conversations to take place—23 conversations and no more. This position was not fully reversed until 1988 and it wasn't until 1994 that the government allocated enough spectrum to permit today's cell phones to work as they do. How much earlier we might have enjoyed their use we cannot say for sure. But this much we do know: when the federal government allowed just a little bit of light into the room, entrepreneurs took it from there to create a dazzling display.

So too with the mails. There was only one way to deliver a letter or package when I was a young adult; and very few imagined that it could be done any other way. A few exceptions in the law were made and now look what we enjoy: vast choice in package delivery, with the private sector offering far more choices than the public sector ever dreamed of offering. Here again it was that the federal government had finally permitted an exception to the rule against using any provider but the federal government. Thus a slight ray of light allowed into darkness has brightened the whole world.

Not enough can be said about the way the web has completely reshaped the world. While the Internet was frozen and nearly useless after the government put it in place for purposes of military and bureaucratic communication, the private sector transformed this creaking and poorly constructed structure into the institution that would change the whole world.

A PRIVATIZED WORLD

So it is in sector after sector. We have in these examples the story of the modern world, shaped by private enterprise, driven forward by the power of entrepreneurship, improving in a hundred million ways by employing private property toward the common good. It is done largely outside the government's purview. Sometimes it seems as if government works as little more than an absentee mafia lord, showing up to collect a check and then retreating again to his private estate. You don't want to make him angry but neither do you let the prospect of his sudden appearance deter your activities.

Most of our daily lives are conducted as if we are all striving to live in the absence of government—precisely as the critics say. We live increasingly in private communities and use technologies that are provided for us by private enterprise. We depend on the matrix of exchange and enterprise to give us security in our homes and in our financial affairs. We manage our finances with no sense of anticipation that government will care for us in the future. Our churches and schools and workplaces and families have become the units that draw our social attention. Government and the old-fashioned civic religion just can't find a place for themselves in this scenario. But rather than being a bad thing, this strikes me as a wonderful thing, a return to the America that Tocqueville described rather than the regimented national life of the postwar period.

To celebrate this is not really a matter of ideology. If the market had not been working spectacularly well despite attempts by government to hobble it and channel its energies, we would certainly find ourselves much poorer today than we were 50 years ago. And yet here we are, a country with a population that has fully doubled in size in that period and a GDP that has increased by a multiple of 28. This much we can say: by historical standards, this is a miracle, and the market, not the government, is responsible.

In the meantime, the market has outrun the state to such an extent that the whole planning apparatus of the postwar period, always based on a kind of pseudoscience, has become preposterously untenable.

This is especially true given the size and expanse of the global economy. In 1953, the dollar value of world merchandise trade between all countries totaled $84 billion, not a small sum but about one fourth the size of the total US GDP in the same year. Today, the dollar value of world merchandise trade is $7.3 trillion, or nearly two-thirds the size of the total US GDP. This increasing integration of the world economy, which was given a huge boost by the collapse of Soviet satellites and the opening of China and India, has shattered the dreams of anyone who hoped national economic planning had a future.

Let me present the following metaphor of how I imagine the relationship of the productive matrix of human voluntarism to exist alongside the leviathan state. Imagine a vigorous game of football with fast and effective players, cooperating with their teams and competing with the other team. These, we might say, constitute the activities of the market economy: consumers, producers, savers, investors, innovators, workers, and all institutions associated with the voluntary sector of society such as houses of worship, educational institutions, charitable endeavors, families, and artistic and literary associations of every sort. They are the players in this game.

However, right on the 50-yard line sits a huge, old bull elephant, enormously strong but also sclerotic, slow, and completely unsuited to being a player in this game. Everyone knows that this monstrous animal is there, and they wish it were not. But the game proceeds apace, with runners, kickers, and throwers zipping around it. This mastodon is powerful and authoritative, more so than ever, but it can hardly move. It can bat its trunk at players who prove especially annoying, even impale them on its tusks, but it cannot finally stop the game from taking place. And the longer these players confront this strange obstacle, the better they become at working around it, and growing stronger and faster despite it.

I'll block that metaphor before it becomes too implausible, but let me just say this about the future of the elephant state: like a slowly dying large animal, the state will continue to be an annoyance and even deadly under certain conditions, but it will not be an effective player in our daily lives. The reason is this. The state cannot deal with change, and ours is a time of constant and relentless change. It does not navigate the world with attention to outcomes, and ours is a world in which all human endeavors are expected to achieve. Its bureaucratic structures are fine for dealing with repetitive tasks but it cannot face new challenges. It can consume resources but it is incapable of producing them. It is uninventive, unresponsive, unintelligent, uninformed, and unmotivated to succeed.

Ludwig von Mises provided the first full account for why this is so. The government exists outside the matrix of exchange. There are no market prices for the goods and services it endeavors to produce. The revenue it receives is not a reward for social service but rather money extracted from the public by force. It is not spent with an eye to return on investment. As a result there is no means for the government to calculate its own profits and losses. Its inability to calculate with attention to economic rationality is the downfall of governments everywhere. Its decision-making is ultimately economically arbitrary and politically motivated.

This feature of government can doom whole societies, as it did in the Soviet Union where the government presumed ownership over the whole capital stock. Because government control was complete, and there were few legal channels of escape, society and economy withered and died over time. Eventually the situation became so absurd that even the elite in the Soviet Union did not live as well as the middle class in well-developed countries. As much as power can be its own reward for some, this situation was clearly unsustainable.

But government control doesn't always take that path. It always impoverishes relative to what might otherwise have been the case. But when its control is not comprehensive—or to extend that football metaphor, when the elephant doesn't cover the entire field but still leaves room for the game to take place— the miracle that is the marketplace can still do remarkable things. Sometimes it only takes the government lessening control over one area of life to inspire stunning achievements. The government keeps trying to pave the world, but private enterprise keeps growing up through the cracks.

Socialist Islands

If you want a picture of the contrast between what Murray Rothbard called power and market—or the state and the private sector—consider what you see at most major airports in this country. You have two structures working side by side: the public sector as represented by the Transportation Security Administration and the mostly private sector as represented by the airlines.

So you arrive with your luggage, and the TSA is the first to swing into action. And there you have it: the very picture of the bureaucrat: alternatively inattentive and belligerent, completely disregarding of customer well-being, so slow that they seem to exist out of time itself. They laugh amongst themselves as if they experience a real class identity and pay no mind to others. They treat mere citizens as subordinates, and are quick to accuse us of wrongdoing.

Most of all, they don't do their job well. They will apply a strict chemical test to a tube of Crest, but will let a black ball with a fuse in it go right through unnoticed. They will give a thorough search to a young mother, and think nothing of ripping a baby out of her arms, only because she came up randomly on the list of those to get a thorough check.

Private enterprise could never work this way. If you applied a profit and loss test to such state services, bankruptcy would be a foregone conclusion. But once we get past the TSA, we are greeted with smiles and warmth hitherto unknown in the history of airline travel. Airline employees seem very much aware that the travelers have likely gone through Hell in dealing with the TSA. Even these unionized employees do all they can to serve others. Somehow we arrive at our destinations in one piece and not suffering total humiliation, but this is not due to the TSA. It is due to those forces of private enterprise that still exist in the airline industry.

We can think of this airport scene as a kind of microcosm of the whole economy. It is burdened, vexed, harassed, hampered, and hobbled by the state. But through the miracle of human creativity and determined effort, private enterprise has created a grand and glorious world that has surpassed the most far-flung dreams of the old utopians, a world where food once inaccessible to kings is available to the poorest of the poor, where no one need be without clothing or shelter, where even those we call poor would have been seen as enormously blessed only decades ago.

All of this leaves the question of what our political priorities should be. If it were up to me, I would push a button and reduce government to the size it was after the American Revolution under the Articles of Confederation, and then look forward to debating whether we should get rid of the rest.

But because that is not likely to happen soon, my own sense is that if present trends continue, the years ahead will have more in common with the Gilded Age of the late nineteenth century than the country and the world as we knew them from the Second World War to the end of the Cold War.

Unlike the planned and regimented economy of the postwar period, the Gilded Age was a time when technological advance and demographic shifts made the society essentially ungovernable, even given the vast power of the state. Not that this is any reason for the lovers of liberty to let down their guard: the War on Spain and the Great War that followed the post-Civil War peace shattered civilization. The same can happen again to the great civilization being created and renewed in our own time. After all, a demented elephant can do a lot of damage.

We can do our part to encourage the good developments and forestall the bad. What should our priorities be? Two politicians I saw on C-SPAN recently gave speeches to instruct us on the first question we should ask when we go to vote.

The first one said that we should think mainly about the children, that we should elect politicians who put children's interests first. As an extension of that principle, we should ask the state to further the interests of our families and communities, this person said. Now, if all this means anything, it strikes me as highly dangerous. The state does not own the children and we don't really want to live in a society in which the state is permitted to do with our children, family, or communities what it wishes.

Moreover, there is no such thing as the collective interest of children, families, and communities, and to pretend that there is, is potentially despotic. In any case, it solves no political issue, since right and left have different plans for what they believe is best for our children. These days, their plans reach into every area of their lives, from what program they should be using to learn to read to the conditions under which they are permitted to take their first job. I can't but think of Hannah Arendt's warning that politicians who invoke the children are potential totalitarians.

The second politician said that we should think mainly about our security when we go to vote. The Constitution, he said, empowers the federal government to collect taxes to provide for the common defense, so that is what we should do. He proceeded to justify the whole of the American military empire that has generated so much hatred and opposition around the world, and interfered so seriously with our trading relationships. He was the classic case of a person who completely ignores the Founders' warnings against war, standing armies, and militarism.

Neither Welfare nor Warfare

Now, these politicians disagree profoundly on what the political priorities should be and what we should be asking of the state. The first says we should ask for welfare. The second says we should ask for warfare. They agree to disagree, and spend our money on both. Why? Because, well, because it's no skin off their noses. Such is the nature of public government as Hans-Hermann Hoppe describes it: there is no real ownership so of course there is a squandering of resources and ever-higher costs.

The only real restraint against all forms of government is public opinion. A public that says no to the state is the best defense against despotism, and the best cultural and political context in which liberty grows and thrives. Our times have taught us that world economy does not need the state. As the old liberals said, society contains within itself the capacity for self-management. Our experience in our families and communities has taught that the state does very little to our benefit. Our experience in our workplaces has taught us that the state makes productivity more difficult and gives us very little to nothing in return.

I'm often asked what an average person can do to further liberty. I say that the first and most important step is intellectual. We all need to begin to say no to the state on an intellectual level. When we are asked what we would like the government to do for us, we need to be prepared to reply: nothing. We should not ask it to save our children, nor conscript and kill them in the name of security, nor give us anything at all.

We can still be good citizens. We can be good parents, teachers, workers, entrepreneurs, church members, students, and contributors to society in a million different ways. This is far more important to the future of liberty than how we vote. We must regain our confidence in our capacity for self-governance. I believe this is happening already. The empire is shrinking despite its every attempt to expand. Even if the public sector cannot and will not prepare for a future of liberty, we can. Let us look for and work toward the triumph of liberty unencumbered by Leviathan.

11.
WHY POLITICS FAILS*

The logic of the market is predicated on the pervasive and glorious inequality of man. No two people have the same scales of values, talents, or ambitions. It is this radical inequality, and the freedom to choose our own lot in life, that makes possible the division of labor and exchange.

Through money and contracts, markets allow us to settle differences to our mutual advantage. The result—and here is why people call the market miraculous—is a vast, productive system of international cooperation that meets an incomprehensibly huge range of human needs, and finds a special role for everyone to participate in building prosperity.

---

*January 1999

Now, to politics. The system of voting is designed to replicate the market's participatory features. In fact, it is a perverse distortion of the market system. In markets, you get the goods you pay for. If you don't and there's been a violation of contract, you have legal recourse. In voting, people are not actually purchasing anything but the politician's word, which is not only legally worthless; he has every incentive to lie to produce the desired result.

Politics take no account of individuals. You and I are merely tiny specks on the vast blob called "the American people," and what this blob "thinks" is only relevant insofar as it accords with a political agenda advantageous to the state and its friends.

You think you are voting for tax cuts. Instead you get secret tax increases and perpetual increases in spending. You think you are voting for smaller government. Instead you get ever more government intrusion. This is because it is not the voters who are managing the system. It is well-organized interest groups who feed at the trough managed and owned by the state. Thus there is a vast gulf that separates the average voter from the politician's real day-to-day interests.

The spectacle of elections grows more absurd every year. We are asked to cast ballots for people we do not know because they make promises they are under no obligation to keep. What's even worse, the voting gesture is pointless on the margin. The chances that any one vote (meaning your vote) will actually have an impact are so infinitesimally small as to be meaningless.

In markets, entrepreneurial talent means the ability to anticipate and serve the needs of the buying public. In politics, success means the ability to manipulate public opinion so that enough fools (so regarded by politicians) reaffirm the politician's power and glory. It takes special talents to do this—talents not cultivated in good families.

If American politics were characterized solely by voting and the products of voting, the system would be loathsome enough.

And yet the corruption runs deeper. The real power behind Leviathan is wielded by a vast, unelected army of bureaucrats who fancy themselves specialists in the pseudoscience of public policy. In their minds, the only role for the citizenry, treated as a homogenous blob, is to conform or suffer the consequences. Gone are the cooperation, peace, and genuine diversity of markets. Instead, we experience brute force.

Intellectuals specialize in dreaming up grandiose tasks for government that would be doomed to fail even if perfectly implemented. And yet the most obvious criticism of all government schemes is that they must all be mediated by this corrupt system called politics.

How different is this system from the one envisioned by people like Patrick Henry and George Mason? They hoped to erect a wall of separation between society and government to protect the people from being manipulated by cunning political forces. Indeed, the best of the American revolutionaries hoped for a society free of politics, a society free of any visible signs of government. Albert Jay Nock was right to characterize the state, democratic or not, as a parasite on society. Like a plague bacillus, its only successes are from its own point of view.

12.

PRESIDENT WHO?*

In a truly free society, it wouldn't matter who the president was. We wouldn't have to vote or pay attention to debates. We could ignore campaign commercials. There would be no high stakes for ourselves, our families, or the country. Liberty and property would be so secure that we could curse him, love him, or forget about him.

---

*August 1996

This was the system the framers set up, or people believed they were getting, with the US Constitution. The president would never concern himself with the welfare of the American people. The federal government had no say over it. That was left to the people's political communities of choice; here we were to govern ourselves and plan our own future.

The president was mostly a figurehead, a symbol. He had no public wealth at his disposal. He administered no regulatory departments. He could not tax us, send our children into wars, pass out welfare to the rich and poor, appoint judges to take away our rights, keep dossiers on the citizenry, control a central bank, or change the laws willy-nilly according to the wishes of special interests.

His job was to oversee a tiny government with virtually no powers ("few and defined," Madison said) except to arbitrate disputes among the states, which were the primary governmental units. If the president transgressed his power, he would be impeached as a criminal. But impeachment would not be likely, because the threat was so ominous, it reminded him of his place.

He was also temperamentally unlikely to abuse his power because he was to be a man of outstanding character, well respected by the other leading men in society. He could be a wealthy heir, a successful businessmen, a highly educated intellectual, or a successful farmer. Regardless, his powers were to be minimal.

All this astonished Alexis de Tocqueville in 1830. "No citizen," he wrote, "has cared to expose his honor and his life in order to become the President of the United States, because the power of that office is temporary, limited, and subordinate." The president "has but little power, little wealth, and little glory to share among his friends; and his influence in the state is too small for the success or the ruin of a faction to depend upon his elevation to power."

To make sure it stayed this way, the vice president was to be a political adversary. He was there to remind the president that he was eminently replaceable. In this way, the veep's office was powerful, not over the people, but in keeping the central government in check.

The president was not elected by majority vote, but by electors chosen by the states. Most citizens could not vote. Those who could were deemed the most prudential and far-seeing of their fellows. They owned land, headed households, and were highly educated. And they were to think only of the security, stability, and liberty of the country, and the well-being of future generations.

For nonvoters, their liberty was to be secure no matter who won. They would have no access to special rights. Yet their rights to person, property, and self-government were never in doubt. For all practical purposes, they could forget about the president and, for that matter, the rest of the federal government. It might as well not exist.

People did not pay taxes to it. It did not tell people how to conduct their lives. It did not fight foreign wars, regulate their schools, surround their homes with police, bail out their business, provide for their retirement, much less employ them to spy on their neighbors.

Political controversies were centered at the level of the state and local governments. That included taxes, education, crime, welfare, and even immigration. The only exception was the general defense of the nation. The president was responsible for that. But with a small standing army, it was a minor position, absent a congressionally declared war.

There were two types of legislators in Washington: members of the House of Representatives, a huge body of statesmen that was to grow larger with the population, and members of the Senate, who were elected by powerful state legislatures. The Congress's main power consisted of keeping the executive's power in check.

Under the original design, the politics of this country was to be extremely decentralized, but the community to be united in another respect: by an economy that is perfectly free and a system of trade that allows people to voluntarily associate, innovate, save, and work based on mutual benefit. The economy was not to be controlled, hindered, or even influenced by any central commands.

People were allowed to keep what they earned. The money people used to trade with was solid, stable, and backed by specie. Capitalists could start and close businesses at will. Workers were free to take any job they wanted at any wage or any age. Business's only mission was to serve the consumer and make a profit.

There were no labor controls, mandated benefits, payroll taxes, special benefits, or other regulations. For this reason, everyone was to specialize in what he did best, and the peaceful exchanges of voluntary enterprise caused ever-widening waves of prosperity throughout the country.

What shape the economy took—whether agricultural, industrial, or high-tech—was to be of no concern to the federal government. Trade was allowed to take place naturally and freely, and everyone understood that it was better managed by property holders than by public office holders. The federal government couldn't impose internal taxes if it wanted to, much less taxes on income, and trade with foreign nations was to be rivalrous and free. The only tariffs were to be revenue tariffs, and thus necessarily low to maximize trade and therefore revenue.

If by chance this system of liberty began to break down, the states had an option: to separate themselves from the federal government and form a new government. The law of the land was widely understood to make secession possible. In fact, it was part of the guarantee required to make the Constitution possible to begin with.

This system reinforced the fact that the president is not the president of the American people, much less their commander in chief, but merely the president of the United States. He served only with their permission and only as the largely symbolic head of this voluntary unity of prior political communities.

In this society without central management, a vast network of private associations served as the dominant social authority.

The churches, unrestricted by federal intrusion, wielded vast influence over public and private life, as did civic groups and community leaders of all sorts. They created a huge patchwork of associations and a true diversity in which every individual and group found a place.

This combination of political decentralization, economic liberty, free trade, and self-government created, day-by-day, the most prosperous, peaceful, and just society the world has ever known.

In such a system, there would be little at stake in the upcoming November election. No matter which way it went, we would retain our liberty and property, and our families would never be bothered by any central government.

Today, however, the Washington, DC area is the richest in the country because it's host to the biggest government on the planet. It has more employees, resources, and powers at its disposal than any on the face of the earth. It regulates in finer detail than any other government. Its military empire is the largest and most far-flung in history. Just its tax-take dwarfs the total wealth of the old Soviet Union.

The only remedy is to restore the classical liberal society of the framers. We do not need, as the media claim, the "strong leadership" of a bully with a pulpit. The man for the job is someone who can disappear, and help make the rest of the federal government vanish with him.

13.
KNOW YOUR GOVERNMENT*

No totalitarian state has tolerated even a modicum of financial privacy. That follows from the premise that citizens should not be granted any privacy at all. After all, they might

---

*May 1999

use it in opposition to the government's plans, or support themselves apart from the government.

In contrast, freedom and financial privacy go hand in hand. This is a natural extension of the idea of individual ownership. Just as people put curtains on their windows, bank customers would demand complete confidentiality. The government would have no power to tax our incomes, investments, or savings, or indeed to know anything at all about our financial affairs.

This was the American system before the turn of the century (except during Lincoln's dictatorship). People made as much money as they could, and saved or spent it however they wished. But with income and inheritance taxes came the legal obligation to disclose. As Rep. Robert Adams predicted in 1894, the income tax "will bring in its train the spy and the informer. It will necessitate a swarm of officials and inquisitorial powers."

Today, the United States has the most draconian financial disclosure system in the developed world. People who keep their money in offshore banks to avoid taxes are considered traitors. And when a citizen demands a zone of financial autonomy, the government wants to know: "What exactly are you trying to hide?"

The natural answer of a free people is: Everything.

The state has no more right to know about your affairs than your ne'er-do-well cousin (who at least isn't holding a gun to your head).

The oppressive US system of financial spying is justified in the name of collecting revenue, unearthing "money laundering," and fighting drugs. Even worse, the United States has worked for decades to impose this system on countries around the world.

The Clinton administration recently proposed going even further and imposing "Know Your Customer" regulations on banks. This would have required banks to list their customers as potential launderers and evaders for making a series of "suspicious" transactions. Put in or pull out too much cash in the course of a month or two, and you'd be put on a "Most Wanted" list as a "smurfer." The burden of proof would rest with the citizen to demonstrate his innocence.

In the past, these new regulations would have slid by without notice. Anyone who objected would have been listed as an enemy of the state, investigated and audited, and that would have been the end of it. What the Treasury didn't anticipate was how regulatory politics have changed with the Internet. A news site called WorldNetDaily exposed the Treasury's plot, and a bureaucracy that is used to receiving eight or ten comments on its proposed regs received a quarter of a million against them.

In a magnificent defeat for the spying state, the regulation was killed. Under the leadership of Rep. Ron Paul, Congress passed a resolution condemning the power grab, and the Treasury backed off. It was the most significant blow for financial freedom in many decades, and offers a model for how citizen activism—apart from the usual political channels—can accomplish astounding victories over Leviathan.

Ideally, the United States would have a system even more ironclad than Switzerland's. Bankers would agree never to reveal the contents of their customers' bank accounts to anyone, especially not the government. To achieve that ideal, however, we have to take away from government the excuses it uses to pry into private affairs. That means abolishing the income tax, and not replacing it with gimmicky flat or national sales taxes. Taxes on profits, dividends, and interest need to be scrapped as well.

Frank Chodorov was once asked how the government would get along without such taxes. His response: "I am not concerned so much with how the government can get along without income taxes as I am with how we can get along with them."

Chodorov went on to ask a much more fundamental question: What kind of government do we want? If we want a government that engineers society and pretends to provide for all our needs, we will have to put up with the omnipresent surveillance state.

14.

PRIVATE LIFE?*

Clinton wants his private life back. His personal behavior is his business alone, and his family's. It's a moral outrage that a prosecutor wants to turn a private matter into a public one. Ken Starr's power is wholly illegitimate.

Welcome to the early nineteenth century, when people actually did have private lives because the government dared not intrude. Family was autonomous and so too were extended families. Homes were sacred spaces. Businesses were private property. Neighborhoods managed their own affairs without outside intervention.

There were no spooks listening in on phone calls, reading our mail, investigating our politics, monitoring our income and stealing up to half of it for "public policy." There was no army of social workers telling people how to raise their kids. There was no war on tobacco or drugs. These were all private matters.

Heads of households, pastors, and community leaders were the social authorities, not politicians. The president had no agencies to regulate business, tell property owners whom to hire and fire, much less pretend to manage the national and world economy.

There was no "sexual-harassment" law. People who didn't like their jobs didn't sue. Instead, they sought out a new job. Discrimination on any basis whatsoever was not a crime but a

---

*August 1998

sacred right. There were no laws that punished people for their choices and associations so long as they didn't harm anyone.

It was a system called freedom, and it made possible the most prosperous and humane society in human history. We owe our current prosperity to the remnants of the old system.

But Bill Clinton represents something different, an ideology whose primary tenet is that private life shouldn't exist. All behavior is public behavior.

The state has an interest in managing all aspects of it. What choices and freedoms we have are ours because the state grants them. Children don't belong to the family but to society. Businesses are public property. Our thoughts and motivations—even our jokes—are the business of courts and prosecutors.

But now Clinton, in high-flown libertarian rhetoric, attempts to tap into the seething resentment the public has for big government and demands that the Administrative State he heads and loves leave him alone. In his newfound worldview, he alone enjoys the right to conduct his affairs as he sees fit.

He says no one has a right to know what he is doing with his subordinates. His friends cannot be subpoenaed and forced to rat on him to the feds. "Even presidents have private lives," he says. He means only presidents should have private lives.

Can someone please welcome Bill to the late twentieth century? The power and intrusions of the government now frying him are the same power and intrusions the rest of America is forced to endure every day.

Every penny we spend is subject to investigation by the tax police. No business owner can take a step on his own property without consulting federal agencies. Even in our own homes, we are not free to decide what kind of paint to put on the walls or the size of our toilet tanks.

Recall that Bill would not be in this fix were it not for the preposterous advent of sexual-harassment law. On the day of his speech, thousands of cases are roiling through the courts that will result in million-dollar fines against bosses accused of far less. Managers' lives will be ruined by a subordinate's lewd remark or provocative picture displayed on a desk.

This is a law that Bill defends and champions. His own wife, now bitter that her personal space is invaded by government power, is the icon of the feminist movement that has long claimed that the personal is the political.

Bill is inviting all of us to reject the authority that Kenneth Starr is exercising. Bill didn't like the questions Starr was asking and reportedly even refused to answer them. Why should he? Hey, he's thinking, it's a free country.

It might be possible to be more sympathetic to Bill's predicament. Let him repeal the sexual harassment laws in which he is now entangled. Let him strip the CIA, the IRS, the FBI, the ATF, and the NSA of their power to spy on our private lives.

Let Bill light a bonfire on the White House lawn made of the federal code and a hundred years of the Federal Register. Let him grant to every American the broad rights to private life that he demands for himself. Until then, we are entitled to regard his speech as the plea of a tyrant caught in his own web.

15.

DESPOTISM AND THE CENSUS*

"There went out a decree from Caesar Augustus," says St. Luke on why Mary and Joseph found themselves in Bethlehem, "that all the world should be taxed." Joseph had to go to his own city because the tyrannical Roman government was conducting a census. But the information may have been used for more than just taxation. The Roman government's local

---

*March 2000

ruler later decided he wanted to find the Christ child and kill Him.

Did the government make use of census data to find out where the members of the House of David were? We can't know for sure, although a later Roman despot did. But we can know that Joseph made a huge error in obeying the census takers in the first place. They were up to no good. In fact, another group of religious Jews in Judea decided that they would not comply with the Roman government's demand to count and tax them. The group was known as the "Zealots" (yes, that's where the word came from). They saw complying with the census as equivalent to submitting to slavery. Many ended up paying for their principled stand with their lives.

And yet, their resistance arguably made would-be tyrants more cautious. For 10 centuries after Constantine, when feudal Europe was broken up into thousands of tiny principalities and jurisdictions, no central government was in a position to collect data on its citizens. This is one of the many great merits of radically decentralized political systems: There is no central power to control the population through data gathering and population enumeration.

The only exception in Europe in those years was William the Conqueror who, after 1066, attempted to establish in England a centralized and authoritarian society on the Roman model. That meant, in the first instance, a census. The census was compiled in *The Domesday Book* (*Doomsday Book*), so named by an Anglo-Saxon monk because it represented the end of the world for English freedom.

A predecessor to today's tax rolls, it functioned as a hit list for the conquering state to divide property up as it wished. "There was no single hide nor yard of land," read a contemporary account, "nor indeed one ax nor one cow nor one pig was there left out, and not put down on the record." Eventually the attempt to keep track of the population for purposes of taxes led to the Magna Carta, the foundational statement of limits on the state's power.

The Doomsday Book established the precedent for many other attempts at compiling information. But according to Martin Van Creveld (author of *The Rise and Decline of the State*, 1999), the information-gathering techniques of these times were so primitive, and the governments so decentralized, that the data were largely useless. On the Continent, for example, no government was in the position of demanding a comprehensive census. That began to change in the sixteenth century, when the nation-state began to gain a foothold against the countervailing power of the church, free cities and local lords. In France, the first modern philosopher of the state, John Bodin, urged that a census be taken to better control the people.

Also in France, writes Voltaire, Louis XIV tried but failed to develop a comprehensive accounting of "the number of inhabitants in each district—nobles, citizens, farm workers, artisans and workmen—together with livestock of all kinds, land of various degrees of fertility, the whole of the regular and secular clergy, their revenues, those of the towns and those of the communities." It turned out that this was just a utopian fantasy. Even if the Sun King could have devised the form, it would have been impossible to force people to surrender all that information.

The first censuses of the eighteenth century were taken in Iceland and Sweden using depopulation as an excuse. But America after the revolution of 1776 faced no such problem, and the generation that complained of British tax agents knew better than to invest government with the power to collect information on citizens. In the Articles of the Confederation, drafted in the days of full revolutionary liberty, each state had one vote, no matter how many representatives it sent to Congress. There was no demand for a census because the central government, such as it was, had no power to do much at all.

It was with the US Constitution in 1787 that the real troubles began. The document permitted more powers to the federal government than any free person should tolerate (as Patrick Henry argued), and the inclusion of a census was evidence of the problem. The framers added the demand for a census in the interests of fully representing the people in the legislature, they said. They would have two legislative houses, one representing the states and the other the people in the states. For the latter, they would need a head count. Hence, the government would count heads every 10 years.

Why else was a head count needed? Article I, Section 2, included an ominous mention of taxes, recalling not only Caesar Augustus but the whole tyrannical history of using the census to control people:

> Representatives and direct Taxes shall be apportioned among the several States which may be included within this Union, according to their respective Numbers, which shall be determined by adding to the whole Number of free Persons, including those bound to Service for a Term of Years, and excluding Indians not taxed, three-fifths of all other Persons. The actual Enumeration shall be made within three Years after the first Meeting of the Congress of the United States, and within every subsequent Term of ten Years, in such Manner as they shall by Law direct.

The 1790 census seemed innocent enough, but by 1810, matters were already out of control: For the first time, the government started demanding information on occupations. Fortunately for the American people, the records were burned by the British in 1813, leaving hardly a trace for the state to use to expand its power. And yet, the state would not be held back, and the census became ever more intrusive.

The lesson of the history of the US census is this: Any power ceded to a government will be abused, given time. Today, the long-form of the census asks for details of your life that you would never tell a neighbor or a private business. A total of 52 questions appear on it, some outrageously intrusive.

Every census is worse than the last. The 1990 census asked for the year of your birth, but the 2000 census wants to know the day and the month, not to mention the race and relation of every person in the house, along with the number of toilets and much more. And what is this information used for? Mostly for social and economic central planning—an activity the government shouldn't be engaged in at all.

This isn't a biased rendering of the objectives of the census. The Census Bureau itself says, "Information collected in Census 2000 will provide local area data needed for communities to receive federal program funds and for private sector and community planning."

You only have to ask yourself what any eighteenth- or nineteenth-century liberal would have thought of the idea of "private-sector" and community planning undertaken by the central state.

Indeed, very few Americans trust their government enough to allow it to engage in planning. Consider the incompetent Census Bureau itself. The letters it sent out in advance of the forms put an extra digit in front of the addresses, as the head of the bureau admitted in a February 26, 2000 press release, while trying to blame it on someone else. And these are the people we are supposed to trust to gather information on us to plan our lives? No thanks.

The letter from the government says, "Census counts are used to distribute government funds to communities and states for highways, schools, health facilities and many other programs you and your neighbors need." In short, the purpose is no different from that of William the Conqueror's: to redistribute property and exercise power. Clearly, we've come a long way from the head-counting function of the census. Moreover, there are quite a few of us out here who don't believe that we "need" these programs.

What's worse, the point of the original census was not to apportion a fixed number of House members among the states. It was rationally to expand the number of people serving in the House as the population grew. But after the Civil War, the number of House members stopped growing, so there's not much point to the census at all now—or at least no purpose consistent with liberty.

Moreover, if a head count were all that was needed, the job could be done by using data from private companies or the US Postal Service. But the census wants more than that. Why? Forget all the official rationales. The real reason the government wants the information is to control the population. The promises that the data won't be used at your expense is worth the same as all government promises: zippo.

What is a freeman supposed to do when he receives the form in the mail? First, remember that information is the foundational infrastructure of the would-be total state. Without it, the state is at a loss. And then consider whether the costs associated with noncompliance are outweighed by the subjective benefit one receives from joining with all free people in resisting the government's data-collection efforts. Finally, consider the limited purposes for which the Framers sought to use the census, and ask yourself whether the central government of today really can be trusted with knowing what is better kept to yourself.

For many years, voluntary compliance has been falling. In anticipation of this problem, the Census Bureau has been relying on wholly owned sectors of society to propagandize for its campaign. The Sesame Street character named Count von Count is touring public schools to tell the kids to tell their parents to fill out the census, even as more than a million census kits have been sent to public schools around the country. Think of it as the state using children to manipulate their parents into becoming volunteers in the civic planning project.

It is a bullish sign for liberty that the government only achieved 65 percent mail-in compliance in 1990. And given the decline in respect for government that characterizes the Clinton era, you can bet it will be even lower today. If you do choose to fill out the census, some commentators have recommended you adhere strictly to the Constitution and admit only how many people live in your household. That such a tactic is considered subversive indicates just how far we've come from eighteenth-century standards of intrusion.

In 1941, Gustav Richter, an aide to Adolf Eichmann, was sent to Romania to gather information about the Jewish population in a census, with the ultimate goal of plotting a mass deportation to the Belzec concentration camp. But Romania cut off all political relations with the Nazis and, as a result, the Jewish population was spared the fate of Jews in Poland and Austria. Just as the Zealots of the first century knew, when a government seeks information on people, it is up to no good.

There went out a decree from Clinton Augustus that all the country should fill out the census. But think of this: If Joseph had known what was in store for him, he might have thought twice about taking that long trek to Bethlehem just because the government told him to do so.

16.
TAKE NOT INSULTS FROM CAMPAIGNS*

We already know political campaigns amount to serial fibathons. We know that there is no way to hold these guys to their promises. We know that once they get in charge of our lives and money, we will have less freedom after they are finished with us than before. We are trapped. We also know that democracy offers no way out of this trap, especially not the first-past-the-post kind of democracy that squeezes out all but two candidates who largely agree that the state they are pleading to manage should be all powerful.

We know all this, and it inclines us to despise the campaign season as a parasitical hoax, an advance auction of stolen goods (as Mencken said), an illusion that apes the style but not the substance of genuine choice (as Rothbard said), a betrayal that bears nothing in common with what the Founders envisioned,

---

*March 2004

and a vast waste of resources in which political contributions serve as protection money and victories signal the sounding buzzer for the start of looting and pillaging.

We know all this. And yet there is one consolation. During the campaign, sometimes the candidates insult each other. Thank goodness for this. For our part, we can insult on blogs or letters to the editor. But we can never get close enough to a candidate to insult him to his face, though surely we should want to.

Indeed, we are desperate for the candidates to insult each other. Only they can get away with it these days. Chances are that if you insult the president in private life today, you will be visited by the FBI or locked up in semi-permanent detention without trial. It's like the later Soviet system, there is only one protection in public life: you have to be too prominent to arrest, in order to get away with thumbing your nose at the powers that be.

Mostly we have to depend on the candidates to do this to each other. The primary season is particularly boring for being barren of insults, with no one wanting to call anyone else a name lest he be passed over for the VP slot or otherwise punished.

So general campaigns are much welcome, with the two tribes battling it out with words.

Yes, they lie during this time too. The Democrats accuse the Republicans of having viciously slashed the budget (uh huh) and the Republicans accuse the Democrats of being tax-and-spend liberals (which is why the federal budget goes up so much less under the Democrats?). It's all nonsense of course, and particularly so when the candidates "stick to the issues" and argue about "substance" rather than just deliver *ad hominem* insults.

Far better is when the candidates forget about so-called substance and issues, and just hurl invective. This is the honest way to campaign: In contrast to campaign "substance" which is mostly always wrong or skewed, the invective is mostly entirely true. Statecraft is necessarily an immoral, dirty business. Any incumbent who has done his job has got closets full of bones and piles of dirt under carpets. If an opposing candidate can't come up with a plausible accusation of massive corruption, graft, failures, payoffs, betrayals, cover-ups, and the like, he just hasn't done his homework.

And yet, of course, the media and the official campaign establishment are always trying to crack down on honesty in campaigns, for fear that too much truth telling by one candidate or another will threaten the system. And so currently, John Kerry is being thrashed for an off-camera remark that he made. He called the Republicans "the most crooked . . . lying group I've ever seen," before adding "it's scary."

Well, it is scary. Granted that Kerry has seen a lot of crooks and liars during his years in public life, so perhaps he is going too far. Or perhaps not. The bigger the government the bigger the crooks and the more brazen the liars who run it; Bush presides over the biggest government in human history; and thus do you know the rest. Look: just the other day, Bush denounced the Democrats for favoring "the old policy of tax and spend"— which is a bit like a shark decrying the practice of flesh eating.

In any case, Kerry's comments were a great moment of truth telling, and amount to the only really interesting thing he has said since he emerged as frontrunner. But rather than being praised for his candor and passion, he is being trounced for, you guessed it, negative campaigning.

Let's see how far you can get reading this phony-baloney piety from some Republican muckety-muck:

> Senator Kerry's statement today in Illinois was unbecoming of a candidate for the presidency of the United States of America, and tonight we call on Senator Kerry to apologize to the American people for this negative attack. . . . On the day that Senator Kerry emerged as his party's presumptive nominee, the president called to congratulate him. That goodwill gesture has been met by attacks and false statements.

You believe this GOP guy? He speaks on behalf of a regime that is running several martial law operations around the world at once, killing and pillaging with impunity, and steering the reconstruction contracts to its long-time friends in the otherwise dying sector of old-time US heavy industry—operations that require payoffs, lies, and bloodshed as a matter of policy—but oh when it comes to campaigns, we must not have "unbecoming" statements.

We know what the Bush administration would do if Kerry were an Iraqi, Afghani, or a Haitian. He would be languishing in Guantanamo right now, in fibbercuffs.

Here's something really great: Kerry refused to back down. His spokesmen said: "The Republicans have launched the most personal, crooked, deceitful attacks over the last four years. He's a Democrat who fights back."

And may Bush return fire. A polite, gentlemanly, "becoming" campaign is not one worth noticing. So long as they are slinging mud, at least we know they are saying some true things, and for once, we get something for all our taxes—a little enjoyment.

17.
LIBERTY YET LIVES*

Not for the first time in world history, US voters on November 2 faced a choice between two varieties of statism, two forms of central planning, two types of duplicity, two approaches to rule by the central state. One won, one lost.

In this, our times are not unlike the 1930s, when during a crisis just about everyone believed that there were only two political options worth pursuing. You were either some variety of communist (a.k.a. socialist, Bolshevik, Trotskyite, etc.) or some

---

*November 2004

variety of fascist (a.k.a. corporatist, national socialist, new dealer, etc.). To reject the idea of government control and centralization, it was believed, was to stand outside the main current of history.

In the presidential election, one central plan wanted to soak the rich, the other wanted to spend now and pay later. One had a plan for national life at home, and the other had a plan for the whole world. One emphasized bread and the other circuses, one wanted unilateral war while one wanted lots of consultations and more troops before doing the same thing, but neither knew or cared anything for the great tradition of thought which gave birth to this nation or built the prosperity of our times.

The missing piece in all of this is the forgotten liberal tradition, which affirms the dignity of all human life, believes in the rights of all, and fights for freedom against the never-ending attempts by government, all government everywhere, to restrict and destroy it.

The liberal tradition believes that individuals and society can work out their own problems in the absence of top-down management. It denies to government any role in managing the nation or the world. It embraces private property, cherishes freedom of association, and sees peace as the mother of civilization.

The great intellectual strain of this liberal tradition spans 500 years and longer, and has survived every onslaught from left and right, and will continue to do so. It is the liberal tradition to which we owe the world's prosperity and well-being, all technological innovations, and improvements in health, housing, nutrition, and information distribution. The liberal tradition will continue to thrive, but with no help from the elites in power.

That this tradition is not represented as a political option is not particularly surprising. As Mises wrote in 1929, "government is essentially the negation of liberty." This is why "[a] liberal government is a *contradictio in adjecto.* Governments must be forced into adopting liberalism by the power of the unanimous opinion of the people; that they could voluntarily become liberal is not to be expected."

But elections such as this one present an opportunity for learning. We learn, for example, who the true friends of liberty are, and how to distinguish them from the partisan hacks who are glad to sell out in exchange for getting and staying close to those in power.

That's a pretty good description of just about everyone in DC who works to have "good relations" with the ruling party. This is a tendency you find on the left, right, and center, and even among supposed libertarians. Intellectual sycophancy toward power is always unseemly, but never more so than when it masquerades as a principled attachment to liberty.

We've also learned something about the nature of liberty's most formidable enemies of today as versus most of the twentieth century. In 1989–1990, the party of liberty was witness to the thrilling fact that socialism around the world had collapsed like a house of cards. The ghastly intellectual tradition that had given rise to the bloody communist experiment suffered a blow from which it is not likely to recover.

How pathetic is the soft leftism of today's mainstream Democrat. For most of the election season, Kerry was the voice of this view. He went from place to place seeking dependents for the state among minorities, the aging, public employees, union workers, and anyone else looking for a favor from government. He dutifully invoked those tired soft-left themes about all the wondrous things government will do at home if we could just soak the rich a bit more.

So, Kerry's domestic program looked ridiculous. It seemed to be yanked out of the 1970s and transplanted into another economic world, one ruled by markets and entrepreneurship. We know these issues hurt him among swing voters because it was precisely on these grounds that the Bush camp ridiculed his entire domestic program. If there is a silver lining to the election, it is in the defeat of this program, once again.

However, it is about time that the friends of liberty realize the main threat to liberty in our time in our country comes not so much from the left but from the militarist and imperialist right, which has shown itself uninterested in fiscal discipline, peace, civil liberties, constitutional restraints on power, decentralist decision-making, privacy, or freedom of association. Pillars of Western law and justice have been broken and tossed aside by this regime, under the guise of national emergency and security against threats real and imagined.

So infatuated with power has the Bush administration become that it has bragged that it would place its stamp on the whole world. There is no place that would be or should be immune from its influence and control. It would remake the world, its spokesmen have promised, in Trotsky-like pledges.

This is quite a leap from the "humble" foreign policy Bush campaigned on in 2000, and a measure of how power and crisis can lead to corruption and even insanity.

Imperialism and war are forms of planning, as much as any domestic variety. They presume knowledge over time and place that is ultimately inaccessible to planners. In order to achieve the plan, they do not depend on consent and exchange, but on taking resources by force and imposing their use against the will of their subjects.

The manner in which resources are used is dictated by the will of bureaucrats and politicians, not markets and consumers. They end not in wealth creation and improved living standards—as with market exchange—but in the usual symptoms of government control: debt, destruction, and even death.

Bush started an unnecessary war that has killed tens of thousands of people, and ground into dust a country and a regime that had never done a thing to the United States and represented no threat whatsoever. We were told that this country had weapons of mass destruction. There were none. We were told that the Midas touch of the US government would bring civilization. Instead, it has led to mind-boggling calamity, as citizens flee, reporters hide, and death, abduction, and chaos are routine in what was once the most liberal Arab state.

The claim that the Bush administration provided this country security has no plausibility to it at all. The attacks of 9-11 came about during Bush's rule, and were a result of policies favored by Bush. The response of the administration was to create bigger bureaucracies, put government totally in charge of airline security, impose draconian laws that violated civil liberties, and hold people in prison indefinitely without charge.

What's more, it does not take a foreign-policy genius to see that invading and smashing countries are not very good ways to go about suppressing terrorism, any more than plunging into snake pits is a good way of avoiding snakebites. Of course the analogy doesn't quite work because the government actually benefits from terrorism to some extent because it permits unscrupulous leaders to alarm the public into forking over more money and power, even as life becomes ever less secure.

As for Kerry, he never wanted to be the antiwar candidate. The Bush camp was right that he waffled, providing a sometimes-plausible critique of the imperial state and yet proposing nothing much different as a replacement. It wasn't until Kerry began to discuss the war that his camp made any progress. He gave a series of speeches that affected ideological opposition to what Bush was doing. They weren't great speeches, and parsing them led to the realization that his plan was not that different from Bush's own. But activists poured their hearts into the campaign nonetheless, in the hopes that perhaps he would come around.

In the end, however, there was no great choice to be made. Voters were being asked to choose between two forms of central planning, one domestic, tired, and uninspiring, and another international and promising to conquer ever more countries until the whole region and world were bent at the knee. One plan required higher taxes and more economic regimentation, and the other required higher debt and more death.

At brief moments during the campaign, the regime trotted out the old rhetoric about how Bush was for freedom and for you, whereas his opponent was for the government. This goes beyond cynical. After all, here is an administration that inflated government spending at a rate that compares only to Lyndon Johnson at his Keynesian worst. Here is an administration that used government more than any other in memory. Those who thought Clinton favored big government can only look back nostalgically at a president who seemed to know the limits of power.

Then there are the so-called cultural issues. They are used by the two parties as get-out-the-vote mechanisms. One group runs to the polls to prevent the other group from making headway on a panoply of hot-button causes. But neither party has any real incentive to enact change in either direction, since the whole purpose is to stir people into donating their money and their time, and pulling the right lever at the next election.

The Bush administration views the results of the 2004 election as a mandate. But friends of liberty should know that conceding a mandate to anyone in power is always dangerous business. One form of central planning has been defeated but another form has raised its ugly head. It too must be fought, and on principled grounds.

But the party of liberty is so much better off today than it was in the 1930s. Our intellectual foundation is far stronger. Ours is an international movement with brilliant writers and activists in most all countries of the world, and in all sectors of society. We live amidst the greatest technological advances since the Industrial Revolution, all made possible through liberal means. The globalization of commerce is thinning out the ranks of the war party.

With allies from all walks of life, from many countries, and with passion for truth, the party of liberty works for and joyfully anticipates liberation from despotism—left, right, or center.

PART II: THE LEFT

"Plundering wealth may lead to more equality,
but it's an equality of poverty."

Section 1: Socialism

18.
The New Communism*

The political and ideological forces that gave rise to Bolshevism at the turn of the century are similarly inspiring the movement that looted and burned last month in Genoa, and, before that in Quebec City, Davos, and Seattle. The experience of both causes shows how violent fanatics can gain a political stronghold, and influence the course of history, provided they choose their issues carefully—and just as carefully conceal their ambitions.

From 1916 through 1918, the Bolsheviks engaged in active protest against the Russian war on Germany. They were the party with one nonnegotiable demand: peace. The Communists were wrong on everything but that one issue, yet it was the most important to the general Russian population. An entire generation of young men was being drafted by the Tsar and sent to be killed, even as the war was crushing the economy and spreading misery and suffering.

The Tsar seemed impervious to the suffering. Meanwhile, Lenin and Trotsky, maniacal Communists with a lust for blood,

---

*August 2001

said the war was a symptom of capitalism, which makes no sense, but they called for an end to an undeniable injustice that no one else talked about. Not until after they gained power did the Communists' demonic intentions become obvious to most Russians. But once the Reds consolidated their power by murdering their adversaries, their bloody rule lasted 74 years.

The international communist movement didn't disappear after 1989; it just took on new guises and causes. The media like to talk about how diverse the protesters were in Genoa (the whites, pinks, and blacks), but these labels apply only to their tactics and taste for blood.

All but a few agree that capitalism, as embodied in the leadership of industrialized nations, needs to be displaced by a revolutionary anticapitalist vanguard, or, if that doesn't work, a heavy-handed regulatory and redistributionist regime that would cripple capitalist production.

In these ambitions, the protesters were homogeneous, save for a few straggling libertarians. However, the propaganda strength of the Genoa protesters was also based in genuine complaints about the present state of things. All over Europe, resentments against the consolidation of the international bureaucracies are coming to a boil.

Intimately bound up with this concern is growing opposition to US military imperialism. The United States has most of the guns and cares least about the effects of their use. Everywhere on the global map where you find US soldiers (in more than 100 countries), you will also find locals who despise them for their bad behavior and arrogance. US military dominance has given rise to other complaints: that the United States exercises undue political influence on governments and international agencies.

In fact, many political trends of our times are best seen as attempts to provide some counterweight to the one-super-power world. Despite assurances, for example, this is precisely what the Russia-China accord was all about.

The protest movement has been emboldened by the Bush administration's resolve to build a nuclear shield—the biggest government boondoggle since the superconducting supercollider, and dangerous in the bargain. In true Marxist fashion, the protesters blame capitalism as the root problem (have they noticed that the military itself is a socialist institution, entirely funded by tax dollars?) and favor some sort of communism as the answer.

And so, inevitably, they lump together good positions the US government takes (against the Kyoto treaty) with the bad positions (global military domination). Just as the US military empire discredits its good economic works, the protesters mix their laudable opposition to militarism with a damnable hatred of liberty and property.

But in general these people are long on complaints and short on answers. The stock demand that international agencies do more to protect "human rights" plays right into the hands of the power elite. Thus Jacques Chirac, the French social democrat, made very sympathetic comments toward the protesters. The final statement of the G-8 included all sorts of pious rambling about the world's poor, comments widely interpreted as concessions to the protesters.

The protesters have no principled objection to international agencies as such. Instead, they want to eliminate whatever good they do—opening world markets to capitalist exchange—and expand the bad that they do, which is imposing US-style regulation on the world.

Indeed, a main demand of the protesters is that the international bureaucrats inside be given more, not less, power over economic life. What may look like violent conflict between the plutocrat and the protester is merely a disagreement between moderate and extreme attempts to subject the world to global economic management.

To understand the extent of the ideological confusion, have a look at the manifesto of the antiglobalist movement. The book *Empire* is written by would-be Lenins Michael Hardt and

Antonio Negri, and it is unabashedly promoted as the new *Communist Manifesto.*

The authors (Negri is in jail in Rome and Hardt is a literature professor at Duke) are economic ignoramuses. They live lives entirely shielded from commercial society. They know nothing of the library of books showing that their Marxoid views are nothing short of lunacy. And yet the book is so much in demand that the publisher (Harvard University Press) can barely keep it in stock. If you are paying tuition for your child to go to college, it's a good bet that he or she will be reading this book in the next six months.

Here's what the book says, as gleaned from an equally insane op-ed in the *New York Times* (June 20, 2001). Apart from its arch tone, and cocksure sense that history is on their side, the authors' complaints amount to the usual leftist prattle about racism, sexism, and multinational corporations. But whereas Marx and Engels were specific about what they demanded (the abolition of the family and private property, for example), Hardt and Negri are more circumspect. They merely ask for a "new system" that would "eliminate inequalities between rich and poor and between the powerful and the powerless" and "expand the possibilities of self-determination."

That last point about self-determination could mean anything (I bet not secession, however). But the point about inequality is unmistakable. Think about what it would require to "eliminate" inequality, that is, to make everyone equal in wealth and power. Look it up: equal means the same, as in arithmetic. It cannot happen. The attempt would require a looter state on a scale that we haven't seen since, well, since the early Soviet Union. As F.A. Hayek said, "a claim for equality of material position can be met only by a government with totalitarian powers."

But Hardt and Negri don't deal with Hayek, Ludwig von Mises, or any serious thinkers in the liberal tradition. Their religion, their lunacy, begins with the premise that Marxism is true, and they ignore or dismiss anything that departs from that premise.

Some may call their followers anarchists, but in fact what these people want is total control. What life would be like under a regime inspired by these people is foreshadowed in the streets of Genoa: looting, burning, destruction, and chaos. The protesters did us a favor in previewing exactly what would happen everywhere on the planet if they prevail.

How can they be beaten back? So long as the academic and welfare classes stay on the public payroll, there will always be those who will protest private property and capitalist economics. But what about their growing popular support, such that 100,000 people showed up to protest in Genoa?

Return to the Bolshevik parallel. What if the Tsar had ended the draft, pulled out the troops, stopped the war, and restored normalcy? He would have strangled the Communist movement by eliminating its whole political basis of support. The Russian people would have been spared seven and a half decades of Hell on earth, and 40 million corpses.

So it is with the new Communists. If we fear them, there is only one path to victory over them: the US military empire. Withdraw the troops. Dismantle the nuclear weapons. Scrap plans to build a provocative shield. Repeal sanctions against Iraq, Cuba, and other nations on the bad guy list. Withdraw from international agencies and mind our own business, while trading with the world.

This is not "caving in" to the demands of the protesters. It is simply doing what is right, and thereby denying them a just pretext for their political activities. To be sure, these actions would not stop the fanatic ideologues behind the antiglobalism movement, and it won't stop would-be central planners in international agencies from conspiring. But it would take away whatever popular basis of support they enjoy.

To do this now is more important than any of the elites presently know or understand. The New Bolsheviks, already entrenched in academia and NGOs, are a growing force in world politics. Civilization is fragile, and if the protesters get their way, we will find out just how fragile.

19.

THE NEW FABIANS*

Before the Russian Revolution, the Communist Party had two wings: Bolshevik and Menshevik. The Bolsheviks believed in the immediate establishment of socialism through violence. The Mensheviks (who also called themselves social democrats) argued for a gradual, nonrevolutionary path to the same goal. Liberty and property were to be abolished by majority vote.

The Bolsheviks won, but after committing unimaginable crimes, they have pretty much disappeared. The Mensheviks, however, are taking over America.

At a recent town meeting in Hyde Park, New York, Bill Clinton was asked about a national sales tax (also called a value-added tax or VAT). Clinton—who is happily imposing income, corporate, energy, inheritance, and other taxes—said he could not include a VAT "right now." There is "only so much change a country can accommodate at the same time."

Our local Menshevism has its roots not in Lenin's Russia, but in the London of 1883, when a group of go-slow socialists founded the Fabian Society. Headed by the appropriately named Herbert Bland, its most famous members were playwright George Bernard Shaw, authors Sidney and Beatrice Webb, and artist William Morris.

The Fabians took their name from Quintus Fabius Maximus, the Roman general who defeated Hannibal in the Second Punic War by refusing to fight large set-piece battles (which the Romans had lost against Hannibal), but only engaging in small actions he knew he could win, no matter how long he had to wait.

Founded the year of Marx's death to promote his ideas through gradualism, the Fabian Society sought to "honeycomb"

---

*April 1993

society, as Fabian Margaret Cole put it, with disguised socialist measures. By glossing over its goals, the Fabian Society hoped to avoid galvanizing the enemies of socialism.

Unlike revolutionary Marxists, the Fabian socialists also knew the workings of British public policy. As the original "policy wonks," they did much research, drew up plans, wrote pamphlets and books, and made legislative proposals, drawing on their allies in universities, churches, and newspapers for help. They also trained speakers, writers, and politicians, and Sidney Webb founded the London School of Economics in 1895 as headquarters for this work.

Although the Fabian Society never had more than 4,000 members, they originated, promoted, and steered through parliament most of British social policy in the last 80 years. The result was a wrecked economy and society, until Margaret Thatcher began to defabianize England.

The Fabians succeeded in their goal of establishing the "provider state," a welfare state that would care not just for the poor, but also for the middle class, from cradle to grave.

Whether it was workmen's compensation, old-age pensions, unemployment benefits, or socialized medicine, the Fabians always stressed "social reform," noted John T. Flynn. They

> saw early the immense value of social reform for accustoming the citizens to looking to the state for the correction of all their ills. They saw that welfare agitation could be made the vehicle for importing socialist ideas into the minds of the common man.

Another Fabian innovation: social reform invariably involved some sort of "insurance." People were induced to accept socialism through the model of the insurance company.

Real insurance companies, relying on a random distribution of accidents, pool money to make the world less uncertain for all of us. Pool everyone's wealth in the state—the Fabian argued —and we could be happy, healthy, and wise.

Aneurin Bevan, the Fabian cabinet minister in the post-war Labour government who imposed the National Health Service, actually argued that it would drastically increase everyone's life span, eventually warding off death indefinitely.

The real Fabian vision of the state had been shown, however, in Sidney and Beatrice Webb's *Soviet Communism: A New Civilization?* published in 1935 (the question mark was removed from the title after the first edition). The book praised Stalin's U.S.S.R. as a virtual Heaven on earth.

As fellow Marxists, if of a different stripe, the Webbs were bound to approve of Stalinism—the end if not the means. "The Fabians were in a sense better Marxists than Marx was himself," said Joseph Schumpeter.

> To concentrate on the problems that are within practical politics, to move in step with the evolution of things social, and to let the ultimate goal take care of itself is really more in accord with Marx's fundamental doctrine than the revolutionary ideology he himself grafted upon it.

Bill Clinton was trained by modern Fabians during his Rhodes scholarship days at Oxford. Carroll Quigley, his mentor at Georgetown, was also a sort of Fabian. Perhaps this is why Clinton calls higher taxes "contributions," government spending "investment," blind obedience to him "patriotism," and private property owners "special interests."

Clearly socialism is what Clinton means by "change." As E.J. Dionne has said, "President Clinton's economic plan is a blueprint for recasting" our society into a "social democracy."

For example, just as trade unions were about to die a merciful death in American economic life, Clinton signed several executive orders to ensure their prospering at the expense of property owners.

In his first budget, Clinton called on us to sacrifice ourselves to the government. The Fabians said the same, advocating, in the words of Beatrice Webb, the "transference" of "the emotion of self-sacrificing service" from God to the state.

Like other social democrats, Clinton lies to the public. He says that taxing the rich will have no effect on middle class wealth. But concentration of private capital at the top of the social hierarchy is good. It makes everyone better off. Plundering that wealth may lead to more equality, but it's an equality of poverty.

Clinton has already shown his disdain for the market economy by berating drug companies for their prices and threatening controls on them (while expanding the welfare programs that drive these prices higher).

As to Hillary's health and medical commission, we will get something more socialist than our present system, but short of the total state. More controls will come later.

The Fabian stained glass window, now installed at Beatrice Webb House in Surrey, England, shows George Bernard Shaw and Sidney Webb reshaping the world on an anvil, with the Fabian coat of arms in the background: a wolf in sheep's clothing. That wolf is now at our door.

20.

THE VIOLENCE OF CENTRAL PLANNING*

For today's generation, Hitler is the most hated man in history, and his regime the archetype of political evil. This view does not extend to his economic policies, however. Far from it. They are embraced by governments all around the world. The Glenview State Bank of Chicago, for example, once praised Hitler's economics in its monthly newsletter. In doing so, the bank discovered the hazards of praising Keynesian policies in the wrong context.

---

*August 2003

The issue of the newsletter (July 2003) is not online, but the content can be discerned via the letter of protest from the Anti-Defamation League (ADL). "Regardless of the economic arguments" the letter said,

> Hitler's economic policies cannot be divorced from his great policies of virulent anti-Semitism, racism and genocide. . . . Analyzing his actions through any other lens severely misses the point.

The same could be said about all forms of central planning. It is wrong to attempt to examine the economic policies of any leviathan state apart from the political violence that characterizes all central planning, whether in Germany, the Soviet Union, or the United States. The controversy highlights the ways in which the connection between violence and central planning is still not understood, not even by the ADL. The tendency of economists to admire Hitler's economic program is a case in point.

In the 1930s, Hitler was widely viewed as just another protectionist central planner who recognized the supposed failure of the free market and the need for nationally guided economic development. Proto-Keynesian socialist economist Joan Robinson wrote that "Hitler found a cure against unemployment before Keynes was finished explaining it."

What were those economic policies? He suspended the gold standard, embarked on huge public works programs like Autobahns, protected industry from foreign competition, expanded credit, instituted jobs programs, bullied the private sector on prices and production decisions, vastly expanded the military, enforced capital controls, instituted family planning, penalized smoking, brought about national health care and unemployment insurance, imposed education standards, and eventually ran huge deficits. The Nazi interventionist program was essential to the regime's rejection of the market economy and its embrace of socialism in one country.

Such programs remain widely praised today, even given their failures. They are features of every "capitalist" democracy.

Keynes himself admired the Nazi economic program, writing in the Foreword to the German edition to the *General Theory*:

> [T]he theory of output as a whole, which is what the following book purports to provide, is much more easily adapted to the conditions of a totalitarian state, than is the theory of production and distribution of a given output produced under the conditions of free competition and a large measure of laissez-faire.

Keynes's comment, which may shock many, did not come out of the blue. Hitler's economists rejected *laissez-faire*, and admired Keynes, even foreshadowing him in many ways. Similarly, the Keynesians admired Hitler (see George Garvy, "Keynes and the Economic Activists of Pre-Hitler Germany," *Journal of Political Economy* 83, no. 2 [April 1975]: 391–405).

Even as late as 1962, in a report written for President Kennedy, Paul Samuelson had implicit praise for Hitler:

> History reminds us that even in the worst days of the great depression there was never a shortage of experts to warn against all curative public actions. . . . Had this counsel prevailed here, as it did in the pre-Hitler Germany, the existence of our form of government could be at stake. No modern government will make that mistake again.

On one level, this is not surprising. Hitler instituted a New Deal for Germany, different from FDR and Mussolini only in the details. And it worked only on paper in the sense that the GDP figures from the era reflect a growth path. Unemployment stayed low because Hitler, though he intervened in labor markets, never attempted to boost wages beyond their market level. But underneath it all, grave distortions were taking place, just as they occur in any nonmarket economy. They may boost GDP in the short run, but they do not work in the long run.

"To write of Hitler without the context of the millions of innocents brutally murdered and the tens of millions who died fighting against him is an insult to all of their memories," wrote the ADL in protest of the analysis published by the Glenview State Bank. Indeed it is.

But being cavalier about the moral implications of economic policies is the stock-in-trade of the profession. When economists call for boosting "aggregate demand," they do not spell out what this really means. It means forcibly overriding the voluntary decisions of consumers and savers, violating their property rights and their freedom of association in order to realize the national government's economic ambitions. Even if such programs worked in some technical economic sense, they should be rejected on grounds that they are incompatible with liberty.

So it is with protectionism. It was the major ambition of Hitler's economic program to expand the borders of Germany to make autarky viable, which meant building huge protectionist barriers to imports. The goal was to make Germany a self-sufficient producer so that it did not have to risk foreign influence and would not have the fate of its economy bound up with the goings-on in other countries. It was a classic case of economically counterproductive xenophobia.

And yet even in the United States today, protectionist policies are making a tragic comeback. A huge range of products from lumber to microchips are being protected from low-priced foreign competition. These policies are being combined with attempts to stimulate supply and demand through large-scale military expenditure, foreign-policy adventurism, welfare, deficits, and the promotion of nationalist fervor. Such policies can create the illusion of growing prosperity, but the reality is that they divert scarce resources away from productive employment.

Perhaps the worst part of these policies is that they are inconceivable without a leviathan state, exactly as Keynes said. A government big enough and powerful enough to manipulate aggregate demand is big and powerful enough to violate people's civil liberties and attack their rights in every other way. Keynesian (or Hitlerian) policies unleash the sword of the state on the whole population. Central planning, even in its most petty variety, and freedom are incompatible.

Ever since 9-11 and the authoritarian, militarist response, the political left has warned that Bush is the new Hitler, while the Right decries this kind of rhetoric as irresponsible hyperbole. The truth is that the left, in making these claims, is more correct that it knows. Hitler, like FDR, left his mark on Germany and the world by smashing the taboos against central planning and making big government a seemingly permanent feature of western economies.

The author of the article for Glenview was being naïve in thinking he could look at the facts as the mainstream sees them and come up with what he thought would be a conventional answer. The Anti-Defamation League is right in this case: central planning should never be praised. We must always consider its historical context and inevitable political results.

21.
NATIONAL TREASURES*

It is election time, which means open season on the well-to-do. We are supposed to favor expropriating them in order to meet social needs to be provided by the government. Candidates who want to cut taxes go on the defensive, assuming that they must assure their audiences that the rich won't benefit from their tax plan to any great extent.

It's all nonsense. The rich are the driving force behind wealth creation, economic innovation, job and income growth, and the improvement of living standards generally. Those responsible for the current prosperity daily undertake activities that never

---

*October 2000

make it into the headlines, but they make social and economic progress a reality for society as a whole as well as for themselves.

Forbes Magazine features profiles of many of these people. What amazing and inspiring stories! Their every decision affects the lives of thousands of people and the fate of billions of dollars. Everyone envies their wealth, but who among us would be willing to undertake the risk or bear the enormous burdens they live with on a daily basis?

The total net worth of the top 400 is $1.2 trillion, and the average net worth is $3 billion. Three-quarters of them are billionaires. The price of admission to the club is a cool $725 million. Nearly 1 in 8 of the members are new this year, having displaced 55 who fell from the list; 263 members are entirely self-made, while only 77 inherited their wealth. (The name Rockefeller doesn't appear until No. 104.) One quarter never graduated from college. One quarter live in California—as far from Washington, DC, as possible on the mainland.

The top five include no one from traditional industries. Three represent software (Bill Gates, Paul Allen, Larry Ellison), with one each from hardware (Gordon Moore) and securities (Warren Buffet). Many names you have never heard of are the secret behind the Internet getting faster, websites more navigable, and computers ever more sophisticated.

Unlike the political class, which enjoys fawning interviews from the press and the cheers of servile supporters, the business class is abused and reviled by popular culture. Whereas the news media love nothing better than reprinting government press releases, the only time business leaders make it into the headlines is when they run afoul of government law. They also suffer bad press because they are mostly white men, the class that has been designated as evil oppressors.

It is commonly believed—even taught in business school—that these people are "taking" from the community. Hence, they have a moral obligation to "give back" in the form of philanthropy and other forms of "community service." The problem here is not charity itself. Rich or poor, capitalist or worker, giving is always a good idea (whether that should be done at the expense of stockholders is a different issue). Indeed, American businessmen are the most generous in the world and are the foundation of the half-trillion dollar nonprofit sector in the United States.

The trouble is the idea that charity should be a *quid pro quo* for making money. In truth, making money in a free market is identical to giving to the community. Economic profits are an indication that one is serving one's fellow man. The richer you become in business, the more you have contributed to the betterment of humanity—even if you are doing so for purely selfish reasons.

Even more than the individuals involved, the real miracle is what these 400 represent. Many of them are competitors with each other. Some of them are surely ruthless and greedy rogues; others, however, are pious family men. Some you would find intolerably arrogant; others you could trust with your life. Some are decidedly secular, and others are profoundly religious.

Regardless, the market economy channels their rare impulses in socially productive ways, forcing them to turn their ambitious personalities toward the goal of serving others, and making them constantly accountable to consumers and investors. Their activities coordinate within a capitalist structure to improve every aspect of our lives, whether in education, entertainment, health care, communication or a million and one other products and services. The market economy works to turn the love of money into the service of the consuming public, which is to say the community at large.

Not that most of the rich understand this. They are largely unconscious of their contribution to society, oddly ignorant of the larger picture, and loath to praise the virtue of capitalism in public. They mostly accept the accusations made against them by the media, by the religious establishment, by intellectuals of the left and the right, and by government. Their profession has few defenders. When the attacks are so intense that they threaten their companies, they find themselves without the intellectual resources to explain their social merit.

This is less a problem in the United States than in Europe. But only America has billionaires such as Ted Turner, who make their living off capitalist successes while using their profits to fund socialist activism. This is corporate suicide. Once the journalist John Stossel asked him whether it would be a better idea to invest a billion than to dump it on a bureaucracy like the United Nations. Turner walked off the set in outrage.

Lacking intellectual interest in market economics, some of them also lack principles in the way they conduct their affairs. For example, look at the pictures and profiles of Number 1 and Number 2, which clarify the real nature of the antitrust attack on Microsoft. Gates of Microsoft has $63 billion. Ellison of Oracle has $58 billion, and has been the leading cheerleader behind the attack on Gates, once even hiring people to dig through Microsoft's garbage to find incriminating evidence. Worse, he's got the government on his side. The bottom line is that Ellison can't stand being Number 2 and is using the government to dislodge the guy on top!

Microsoft itself seemed to be on the verge of launching a principled defense of free enterprise, but then weighed in on behalf of an antitrust investigation of America Online for the success of its Instant Messaging software. This was a cheap assault on a competitor, a tactic no better than those used by Ellison against Gates. There's nothing more tragic than seeing people who make their fortunes from voluntary exchange turning to the levers of coercive power to get their way.

But this kind of behavior is the exception, not the norm. The American business class, and in particular the richest 400, deserve our admiration and respect.

SECTION 2: REGULATION

22.

REGULATORY–INDUSTRIAL COMPLEX*

Socialists want socialism for everyone else, but capitalism for themselves, while capitalists want capitalism for everyone else, but socialism for themselves.

Neither Ted Kennedy nor Jane Fonda practices a vow of poverty, nor are they taking any homeless into their mansions, while too many big companies try to short-circuit the market with government privileges. And one way they do it is through the regulatory agencies that acne Washington, DC.

If I may make a public confession (counting on the charity of *Free Market* readers): I used to work for the US Congress. I've since gone straight, of course, but the experience had its value, much as the future criminologist might benefit from serving with the James Gang.

For one thing, being on Capitol Hill showed me that, unlike the republic of the Founding Fathers' vision, our DC Leviathan exists only to extract money and power from the people for itself and the special interests.

---

*September 1990

Ludwig von Mises called this an inevitable "caste conflict." There can be no natural class conflict in society, Mises showed, since the free market harmonizes all economic interests, but in a system of government-granted privileges, there must be a struggle between those who live off the government and the rest of us. It is a disguised struggle, of course, since truth threatens the loot.

When I worked on Capitol Hill, Jimmy Carter was bleating about the energy crisis and promising to punish big oil with a "windfall profits tax." But I saw that the lobbyists pushing for the tax were from the big oil companies.

And, after a moment's thought, it was easy to realize why. There was no windfall profits tax in Saudi Arabia, but it did fall heavily on Oklahoma. And as intended, the tax aided the big companies that imported oil by punishing their competitors, smaller independent firms.

In the ensuing restructuring of the industry, also brought about by the price and allocation regulations of the Department of Energy, the big firms bought up domestic capacity at fire-sale prices, and then the Reagan administration repealed the tax and the regulations. Meanwhile, the big companies received contracts from the Department of Energy to produce money-losing "alternative fuels."

In every administration, the tools of inflation, borrowing, taxation, and regulation are used to transfer wealth from the people to the government and its cronies.

At times, one or another of these tools becomes politically dangerous, so the government alters the mix. That's why the Reagan administration switched from taxes and inflation to borrowing, and it's why the Bush administration, with the deficit a liability, calls for more taxes, inflation, and regulation.

A tremendous amount is at stake in the re-regulation of the economy advocated by the Bush administration. Just one clause in the Federal Register can mean billions for a favored firm or industry, and disaster for its competitors, which is why lobbyists cluster around the Capitol like flies around a garbage can.

While claiming to need more money for—among other vital projects—a trip to Mars supervised by Dan Quayle, the president is boosting the budget of every regulatory agency in Washington.

Here are just some of those agencies, and the way they function: Founded by Richard Nixon, the Occupational Safety and Health Administration is an antientrepreneur agency. Not only does OSHA target small and medium-size businesses, its regulatory cases are easily handled by Exxon's squad of lawyers, while they can bankrupt a small firm.

Also founded by Nixon, the Consumer Product Safety Commission issues regulations drawn up in open consultation with big business—regulations that often conform exactly to what those firms are already doing. Small businesses, on the other hand, must spend heavily to comply.

Another Nixon creation is the Environmental Protection Agency, whose budget is larded with the influence of politically connected businesses, and whose regulations buttress established industries and discriminate against entrepreneurs, by—for example—legalizing pollution for existing companies, but making new firms spend heavily.

The Department of Housing and Urban Development was founded by Lyndon B. Johnson, but its roots stretch back to the housing policy of the New Deal, whose explicit purpose was to subsidize builders of rental and single-family housing. Since LBJ's Great Society, HUD has subsidized builders of public housing projects, and of subsidized private housing. How can anyone be surprised that fat cats use HUD to line their pockets? That was its purpose.

The Securities and Exchange Commission was established by Franklin D. Roosevelt, with its legislation written by corporate lawyers to cartelize the market for big Wall Street firms. Over the years, the SEC has stopped many new stock issues by smaller companies, who might grow and compete with the industrial and commercial giants aligned with the big Wall

Street firms. And right now, it is lessening competition in the futures and commodities markets.

The Interstate Commerce Commission was created in 1887 to stop "cut-throat" competition among railroads (i.e., competitive pricing) and to enforce high prices. Later amendments extended its power to trucking and other forms of transportation, where it also prevented competition. During the Carter administration, much of the ICC's power was trimmed, but some of this was undone in the Reagan administration.

The Federal Communications Commission was established by Herbert Hoover to prevent private property in radio frequencies, and to place ownership in the hands of the government. The FCC set up the network system, whose licenses went to politically connected businessmen, and delayed technological breakthroughs that might threaten the networks. There was some deregulation during the Reagan administration—although it was the development of cable TV that did the most good, by circumventing the networks.

The Department of Agriculture runs America's farming on behalf of producers, keeping prices high, profits up, imports out, and new products off the shelves. We can't know what food prices would be in the absence of the appropriately initialed DOA, only that food would be much cheaper. Now, for the first time since the farm program was established by Herbert Hoover, as a copy of the Federal Food Administration he ran during World War I, we are seeing widespread criticism of farm welfare.

The Federal Trade Commission—as shown by the fascist-deco statue in front of its headquarters—claims to "tame" the "wild horse of the market" on behalf of the public. Since its founding in 1914, however, it has restrained the market to the benefit of established firms. That's why the chief lobbyists for the FTC were all from big business.

When then-Congressman Steve Symms (R-ID) tried to partially deregulate the Food and Drug Administration in the 1970s to allow more new drugs, he was stopped by the big drug companies and their trade association. Why? Because the FDA exists to protect them.

OSHA, CPSC, EPA, HUD, SEC, ICC, FCC, DOA, FTC, FDA—I could go on and on, through the entire alphabet from Hell. I have only scratched the villainous surface. But according to the average history or economics text, these agencies emerged in response to public demand. There is never a hint of the regulatory-industrial complex. We're told that the public is being served. And it is: on a platter.

23.

THE INCREDIBLE STUFF MACHINE*

So those scurvy bums at Wal-Mart are finally getting what is coming to them! The state of Maryland will force all companies with more then 10,000 employees to spend at least 8 percent of their payroll on health insurance. Lots of companies have that many employees, but only one falls under the 8 percent threshold, which is You-Know-Who.

It is only the latest legislative blow dealt against the company that is finally accomplishing what everyone throughout all of human history dreamed of: plentiful food and goods available to all people in all places at low prices. What's to complain about? This is the mystery that cries out for investigation.

That success breeds destructive attacks is part of business lore. A classic in modern libertarian literature, for example, is the poem "The Incredible Bread Machine" by R.W. Grant. It tells the story of Tom Smith, who invents a great machine to bake bread and package bread so cheaply that it could sell for

---

*January 2006

less than a penny. "The first time yet the world well fed, And all because of Tom Smith's bread."

But then Tom Smith developed a problem: success. His bread was everywhere, and he was rich. But soon the public began to decry the Bread Trust, and regulation smashed his company. The last two stanzas:

> Now bread is baked by government.
>
> And as might be expected,
>
> Everything is well controlled.
>
> The Public well protected.
>
> True, loaves cost a dollar each,
>
> But our leaders do their best!
>
> The selling price is half a cent. . . .
>
> Taxes pay the rest.

The key to the story is antitrust regulations pushed by business competitors and cheered on by an envious public ignorant of economics. It's pretty much the same with Wal-Mart. Companies with whom Wal-Mart competes are only too happy in the short term to see the company get hammered for undercutting them on price. If you have been trying to fob off products for high prices for years—and these are essential to your profit margins—it must be torture to see Wal-Mart doing so well selling at a fraction of the old market price.

Herein lies not only the origin of antitrust but of vast numbers of business regulations. They are advocated by dominant firms that seek to impose harmful costs on smaller competitors (such as when Wal-Mart itself was pushing for a higher minimum wage) or by smaller firms that hope to impose punishing costs on more successful firms. The notion that these regulations are designed to benefit the public is just the ideological junk food that is fed to Congressional committees and the general public.

The way to address this problem is for the state to cease to offer business the chance to unfairly compete in this way. If there were no regulations and no antitrust laws, businesses would not face the near-occasion of sin to use government as a way to clobber its enemies. They would face no choice but to innovate, cut costs, and serve consumers better than the other guy.

Much more troubling and mysterious are public attitudes. Wal-Mart was made successful because people like buying there. They like the prices and convenience. The public could bankrupt the company in a matter of weeks simply by failing to show up to make purchases. People are free to do so. That's the way the market works.

Maybe you hate Wal-Mart. Fine. Don't shop there. What's so hard to understand about that?

Why would the same people who enjoy the fruits of Wal-Mart's entrepreneurship also celebrate laws that harm the company? They believe that they can have their cake and eat it too. There is a lack of economic understanding in operation here. They have failed to understand that one of the reasons Wal-Mart can offer such good deals is that they are running an efficient enterprise.

But does it not come at the expense of the labor force? Of course all workers want raises in all forms, just as all consumers want products and services to be available at the lowest price. These are conflicting demands. At some point in the scale of wages and prices, the tradeoff between the two demands finds a clearing point. What that point is cannot be worked out by a central planner. It has to be discovered by the market.

The moral import of the market is its noncoercive core. The workers who work at Wal-Mart would rather be doing so than any other activity that is open to them. So too for the shoppers. It is the matrix of exchange that has made Wal-Mart a success. Unlike with government, no one has a gun pointed at his head. Everyone is making a noncoerced choice in favor of exchanging as versus not exchanging. Everyone benefits.

Does that seem elementary to you? Then you understand something that most sociologists, literary scholars, news commentators, preachers, and government officials apparently do not understand. You understand that mutually beneficial exchange is the cornerstone of civilization itself.

You probably also understand that this law is not going to be good for Maryland. Fewer Wal-Marts will start up in that state than otherwise would. A legal climate hostile to business will deter future businesses from locating there. Some businesses may leave. Also, a less competitive environment for business will mean higher prices and less consumer choice. And why? So that Wal-Mart's competition can thrive on an inefficient business model. This law, then, rewards waste and punishes efficiency.

Now, there is a further complication in this case. A main complaint against Wal-Mart's wage policies is that its employees were draining too much from the state's Medicaid budget. This is an interesting point. Is it possible that Wal-Mart was, in effect, free riding off the taxpayers? Would it then be better just to roll those costs onto the back of the company itself? There is a superficial logic at work here, but it is the logic that leads to all-out business regimentation.

It is doubtful that in a truly free market business would normally provide any health benefits at all, anymore than they provide you shoes, movie tickets, or scotch delivered to your door. These are things that you buy on your own. Medical benefits tied to employment originated as a scheme to get around government wage controls.

If the Medicaid free ride is a problem, there is a more direct solution. Get rid of this program too. What we need are Wal-Marts in the medical industry, firms that provide great services at low prices. But they won't come about until we rid ourselves of the subsidies attached to public provision.

Meanwhile, the Incredible Stuff Machine will pay and pay for all the glorious things it has brought the world population, and the ignorant among us will clamor for the machine to be destroyed. Then the only big companies will be those created, run, and subsidized by the government.

24.

WAL–MART WARMS TO THE STATE[*]

The CEO of Wal-Mart, H.Lee Scott, Jr., surprised many by calling for an increase in the minimum wage. And what accolades were heaped on him! The company was even cast in a new role, from the exploiter of workers to the responsible advocate of pro-worker policies.

And how selfless, for who has to pay such higher wages but companies like Wal-Mart? And thus do we see a corporation set aside its business interests on behalf of the long-term interests of society.

The whole thing befuddled Wal-Mart haters as much as it disgusted its free-market defenders.

Ted Kennedy wouldn't go so far as to praise the company, but he did say that "If the CEO of Wal-Mart can call for an increase in the minimum wage, the Republicans should follow suit on behalf of the millions of working men and women living in poverty."

Other lefties just wouldn't believe it. The spokesman for Wal-Mart Watch said that Scott's call for a higher wage floor was "disingenuous and laughable."

And yet, let us think this through. Might there be another reason Wal-Mart would advocate a higher minimum wage?

Before looking at the evidence, let's do some *a priori* theorizing based on the history of US corporate regulation. Historians such as Robert Higgs, Butler Shaffer, Dominick Armentano, and Gabriel Kolko have chronicled how the rise of business regulation, including intervention in market wages, was pushed by

---

[*]October 2005

large companies for one main reason: to impose higher costs on smaller competitors.

This is how child labor legislation, mandated pensions, labor union impositions, health and safety regulations, and the entire panoply of business regimentation came about. It was pushed by big businesses that had already absorbed the costs of these practices into their profit margins so as to burden smaller businesses that did not have these practices. Regulation is thus a violent method of competition.

Think of it this way. Let's say you run a retail coffee shop that sells only "fair trade" coffee, which is expensive to acquire, but for which consumers are willing to pay a high price. All is going swimmingly until a competitor shows up and sells unfair coffee that tastes just as good for half the price.

Let's say consumers begin to change their minds about the merit of your "fair trade" coffee and your profits fall. You must make a change to survive. You can compete by offering a wider range of choice. Or you can lobby the local government in the name of "social responsibility" (oh, such high ideals!) to require that all coffee sold in your town be "fair trade."

Who does that benefit? Your company. Who does it hurt? Their company.

Moving from theory to reality, we find that this is precisely what Wal-Mart is up to. The hint comes from the news stories: "Wal-Mart maintains that it pays above the current $5.15 an hour minimum wage to its employees."

Now, most readers might just look at this as a case of leading by example. Would that everyone were as fair as the wonderful Wal-Mart! But a second look suggests another interpretation, namely that it wants to slam its smaller competition, which will be seriously harmed by having to pay more for labor.

The current minimum is $5.15. According to studies, Wal-Mart pays between $8.23 and $9.68 as its national average. That means that the minimum wage could be raised 50 percent and still not impose higher costs on the company.

Wal-Mart itself makes even more elaborate claims on Wal-martfacts.com: "The national average for regular hourly Wal-Mart wages is nearly twice the federal minimum wage, and higher in urban areas." If true, the national minimum could be raised by 100 percent and leave the company unaffected.

So who would it affect if not Wal-Mart? All of its main competitors. And the truth is that there are millions of businesses that compete with it every day. Many local stores have attempted to copy Wal-Mart's price-competitive model, but face lower costs and can actually thrive.

There are many ways to compete with Wal-Mart. Not all shoppers like sprawling stores. Others like better service with more experts on the floor. Others just hate crowds. But a main way to compete is to hire lower-priced labor. This could mean that your employees are from a "lower" rung on the social ladder, but they too need opportunities. The savings can be reflected in other amenities that Wal-Mart does not offer. There can be nonstandardized products otherwise not available. The location might be better. Even prices for goods can be lower.

Even similar stores such as K-Mart can pay lower wages, and that can make the margin of difference. K-Mart pays over a much wider range, as low as $6.75 an hour. A major competitor is mainstream grocery stores, where workers do indeed start at minimum wage. Target too pays starting employees less than Wal-Mart, if members of Target's labor union can be believed.

Now, if Wal-Mart can successfully lobby the government to abolish lower-wage firms, it has taken a huge step toward running out its competition. The effect of requiring other firms to pay wages just as high as theirs is the same as if the company lobbied to force other companies to purchase only in high quantities, to open large stores only, or to stay open 24 hours. By making others do what Wal-Mart does, the company manages to put the squeeze on anyone who would dare vie for its customer base.

Now here is the great irony. The left has long been in a total frenzy about how Wal-Mart saunters into small towns and outcompetes long-established local retailers. They claim that the company's success always comes at a huge social cost.

Now, most of this rhetoric is overblown and ignorant. Wal-Mart would not have made any profits or grown as it has without having convinced the consuming public to purchase from the store. Consumers could put the company out of business tomorrow, just by failing to show up to buy.

The left's claims of unfair practices would be valid if Wal-Mart did indeed work to impose legal disabilities on its competitors—in effect making it illegal to outcompete the company. And yet that is precisely what raising the minimum wage would do: impose a legal disability on those companies engaged in lower-wage competition with Wal-Mart. So the economically ignorant left advocates raising the minimum wage.

Thus has our CEO friend Mr. Scott discovered a viciously devious tactic. He sees a way to drive out the competition by doing precisely what Wal-Mart's biggest critics are advocating! And what will be the result? Wal-Mart's share of the market will go up, and its degree of cartelization over the mass consumer market will increase, not by market means but through government intervention. Then we can expect the left to once again fly into another hysteria about the size and growth of the company—totally oblivious to how they worked to bring it about.

Free-market advocates who have long defended Wal-Mart can only be disgusted at this shift in the company's methods from competing on market grounds to calling for the state to crush its competition. Even more disgusting is how the company can count on the economic ignorance of its critics to help do it.

The minimum wage should not be raised but abolished. If free competition and a nonmonopolized market are what you favor, you too should favor abolishing the minimum wage. In a purely free market, Wal-Mart would discover that there are indeed limits to growth, and that others are willing and able to learn from its successes.

25.

THE TROUBLE WITH LICENSURE*

Not too long ago, the Tennessee Dental Society sued to stop a "danger to patients": professional tooth cleaning. Not that they had anything against professional tooth cleaning; they wanted the professionals to be dentists and their employees, not dental hygienists in independent practice.

One of the hygienists protested that her price was lower, and therefore people would get their teeth cleaned more often. "It also helps that they don't have to fear the drill, although I refer any problems I see to dentists." But she was driven out of business because she wasn't licensed as a dentist. What her customers thought meant nothing.

A few years before, the Oklahoma State Dental Society lobbied for a toughened law against "denturists": dental technicians who make false teeth directly for customers, bypassing the dentist.

At a press conference, the head of the dental society was asked if this wasn't already against the law. Yes, he said, but a patient had to bring a complaint, and none would. It seems the denturists would give dissatisfied customers their money back —and let them keep the teeth in the bargain. A reporter wondered aloud whether a dentist had ever returned an unhappy patient's money, and was told the question was irrelevant.

I like my dentist, and would never go to a less qualified if cheaper professional. But why should it be illegal, in a free market, for me to do so?

For centuries, professionals have sought to cartelize their occupations, that is, to limit competition. The stated reason is protecting consumers, but the real reason is financial.

---

*August 2000

Just recently, a legal secretary was threatened with jail in Florida. She was helping people fill out legal documents, something she had done in a law firm for 20 years. But now she was doing it on her own, for pay. In Florida, as in all other states, the actual crime is practicing unlicensed law, medicine, or dentistry for money, which alone tells us the real nature of the offense.

Medical organizations argue that only licensure enables us to distinguish the qualified from the goof-off. In fact, it is the reverse. Licensure endangers consumers by making them less watchful, since they assume that any state-licensed doctor is competent.

With specialists—where the market process of certification rules—consumers are very watchful. Any doctor may legally do plastic surgery, for example, but customers look for a highly qualified, well-recommended, board-certified surgeon. The same is true in every other specialty, as it would be for all physicians without licensure.

Why should it be illegal for a pediatric nurse to set up an independent practice in Harlem, or a geriatric nurse in West Texas? Yet both would be tossed in jail.

Again, I would never go to anyone but my family doctor. But why, in a free society, should I not be allowed to choose?

Restricting the supply of medical care has a long history. Hippocrates built a thriving medical center on the Greek island of Cos in the fourth century B.C., and taught any student who could pay the tuition. But when the great man died, there was fierce competition for students and patients, and the doctors sought to cartelize the system with the Hippocratic Oath.

The oath pledged devoted care to the sick, but also that "I will hand on" my "learning to my sons, to those of my teachers, and to those pupils duly apprenticed and sworn, and to none others."

In the modern world, England's Royal College of Physicians (RCP)—a state-approved licensing agency—has long been the model medical monopoly, exercising iron control over its members' economic conduct. But this guild-like system wasn't salable in *laissez-faire* America.

In 1765, John Morgan tried to start an intercolonial medical licensing agency in Philadelphia, based on the RCP. He failed, thanks to bitter infighting among the doctors, but did begin the first American medical school, where he established the "regular mode of practice" as the dominant orthodoxy. Those who innovated were to be punished.

After the Revolution, said historian Jeffrey Lionel Berlant, "a license amounted to little more than a honorific title." In Connecticut and Massachusetts, for example, unlicensed practitioners were prohibited only from suing for fees. And in the free-market 1830s, one state after another repealed penalties against unlicensed practice.

By the mid-nineteenth century, there were virtually no government barriers to entry. As economist Reuben A. Kessel noted, "Medical schools were easy to start, easy to get into, and provided, as might be expected in a free market, a varied menu of medical training that covered the complete quality spectrum." Many were "organized as profit-making institutions," and some "were owned by the faculty."

From time to time, doctors attempted to issue tables of approved fees—with price-cutting called unprofessional—but they failed, because price-fixing cannot long survive in a competitive environment.

Organized medicine's lobbying against new doctors and new therapies began to be effective in the middle of the century, however. The official reason was the need to battle "quackery." But as historian Ronald Hamowy has demonstrated in his study of state medical society journals, doctors were actually worried about competition lowering their incomes.

The American Medical Association (AMA) was formed in 1847 to raise doctors' incomes. Nothing wrong with that, if it had sought to do it through the market. Instead, its strategy, designed by Nathan Smith Davis, was the establishment of state licensing boards run by medical societies. He attacked medical school owners and professors who "swell" the number of "successful candidates" for "pecuniary gain," fueled by the "competition of rival institutions." These men advance "their own personal interests in direct collision" with "their regard for the honor and welfare of the profession to which they belong." The answer? "A board of examination, to sit in judgment" to restrict entry and competition, which he did not point out could only have a pecuniary motive.

As philosopher William James told the Massachusetts legislature in 1898: "our orthodox medical brethren" exhibit "the fiercely partisan attitude of a powerful trade union, they demand legislation against the competition of the 'scabs.'" And by 1900, every state had strict medical licensure laws.

The Flexner Report of 1910 further restricted entry into the profession, as legislatures closed non-AMA-approved medical schools. In 1906, there were 163 medical schools; in 1920, 85; in 1930, 76; and in 1944, 69. The relative number of physicians dropped 25 percent, but AMA membership zoomed almost 900 percent.

During the great depression, as Milton Friedman notes, the AMA ordered the remaining medical schools to admit fewer students, and every school followed instructions. If they didn't, they risked losing their AMA accreditation.

Today, with increasing government intervention in medicine —often at the AMA's behest—the organization exercises somewhat less direct policy control. But it still has tremendous influence on hospitals, medical schools, and licensing boards.

It limits the number of medical schools, and admission to them, and makes sure the right to practice is legally restricted. The two are linked: to get a license, one must graduate from an AMA-approved program. And there is a related AMA effort to stop the immigration of foreign physicians. The AMA also limits the number of hospitals certified for internships, and licensure boards will accept only AMA-approved internships.

The licensure boards—who invariably represent medical societies—can revoke licenses for a variety of reasons, including "unprofessional conduct," a term undefined in law. In the past, it has included such practices as price advertising.

Medical licensure is a grant of government privilege. Like all such interventions, it harms consumers and would-be competitors. It is a cartelizing device incompatible with the free market. It ought to be abolished.

26.
ILLUSIONS OF POWER*

Critics accuse libertarians of reveling in government failures. Yes and no. No one is pleased to see the destruction caused by government policies, whether small scale, as when a tighter regulation causes business failures, or large scale, as when wars destroy life for millions.

The kernel of truth to the claim is this: the failure of government illustrates something extremely important about the structure of reality that most people are likely to forget. It comes down to this: statesmen and public officials, no matter how powerful they may be, cannot finally control social outcomes.

If I might offer a summary of a point emphasized in all of Mises's works: the structure of society and world affairs generally is shaped by human actions, stemming from imaginative human minds working out individual subjective valuations, and their interactions with the material world, which is governed by laws that are beyond human control.

What that means is that you and I cannot on our own, even if we have maximum political power, control all of human society, and especially not its economic side.

---

*December 2003

Let's first consider an example from current popular wisdom about the manufacturing base. Many products that were once made in the United States—thinking here of televisions, pianos, firecrackers, plastics, and bicycles—are now made in China. This has caused a great deal of alarm—all unwarranted, so far as sound economics is concerned.

But let's say we have the ambition to change this social outcome. Anyone is free to build a bicycle and attempt to market it to willing buyers. Let's say you rent some property, hire the workers, acquire all the necessary capital, and then put your bike on sale. In order to cover your costs and make a profit, you find that you must price your bikes above the going market price. Maybe you can persuade people that you have a special product that is better than the others. Or maybe yours will sit on the floor. Or maybe you will have to lower your price and you will find that your revenue does not cover your costs, and you have to go out of business.

No matter what you decide, this much is clear: you are not dictating the outcome. You wanted to build bikes, but it is the consuming public that decides whether it is in our interest to do so. There is nothing you have to say about it. You cannot make people fork over the money. I would venture to suggest that you will ultimately come to the conclusion that you should be doing other things besides attempting to keep up with other businesses that have lower labor and capital costs and hence can make a profit through selling goods at much lower prices.

But let's say you decide that you don't want to bow to the realities of the market. Instead you lobby Congress to tax everyone who buys a bike from overseas. The tax is high enough that you can continue to charge exorbitant prices for your bikes. You make a profit. But at what expense? The consumers who buy your bikes have less income left over for other pursuits, whether consumption, saving, or investment. The workers you are employing are being kept from other pursuits as well, and the capital you are consuming is not available for other projects.

Ultimately, you have skewed the entire economic system in a way that benefits you at everyone else's expense. Others have found a way to do what you are doing much more efficiently, but because you lobbied and got your way, society is prevented from benefiting from others' innovations. And how long must this distorted system last? That you managed to tax everyone to benefit you does nothing to change the reality that others can do what you are doing more cheaply and better. Do workers really want to be employed in an industry that is something of an artifice? Do consumers really want to pay high prices just so that you can continue to indulge in your bike-making passion?

Clearly not. At some point, people will catch on to the racket, and find other ways to go about acquiring bikes. Maybe they will exploit loopholes in the law that allow them to import bike parts. An industry of do-it-yourself bike building becomes a threat to your profits. Or perhaps black markets will take over. Or maybe people will turn away from bikes altogether and starting trying out new forms of informal transportation. Skateboards are fitted with handlebars. Gas-powered scooters develop a peddle-only option. The very definition of a bike comes into question. Increasingly, enforcement will have to become ever more onerous.

At some point in this game, we face a choice. We can continue to impose an ever more absurd and preposterous system of regulations and protections just so that you can benefit, or we can bow to reality and let in foreign bikes for consumer purchase. Let's say your tariff lasts a year or even 10 years. What will it accomplish? In that time, vast resources are wasted. Consumers of all sorts are exploited. Capital is consumed in economically wasteful ways. People are pushed around and the police powers of the state grow. It does society no good at all.

My point is that whatever the fate of the so-called manufacturing base, there is nothing in the long run that can be done to turn it in one direction or another. The fate of manufacturing is in the hands of consumers at large, and subject to the laws of economics which no man can repeal. It is the outcome of human choice.

Now, the Bush administration has thought otherwise and imposed a huge range of protections to benefit its supporters and people who the administration hoped would become its supporters. The result has been to skew the world economy, hobble markets, delay inevitable transitions, and impose massive social costs.

What this example shows is that governments are not omnipotent. Many try to be, and no government is liberal by nature. But there are limits. Governments bump up against human valuations time and again. Even in the highly rarified event of a despotic government that rules a population unanimously in support of despotism, government still bumps up against the structure of the world, which resists control.

Let us consider another example. Let us say that government desires a strong dollar. But it still wants to print dollars and ship them around the world. In this case, there is nothing that government can do to insure the dollar's strength against depreciation. Nothing. This is due to the laws of economics. All else equal, the value of a currency in terms of goods falls as its quantity increases. Governments that desire otherwise can only shake their fist in anger.

The same is true domestically. The government wants economic recovery before a recession has fully run its course. It thereby drops interest rates, spends vast amounts of money to gin up demand, and otherwise encourages as much consumption as possible. These tactics can result in some short-term gains but it doesn't work in the long run. These tactics deplete savings and capital and weaken the foundation for solid future growth.

The issue of the price of prescription drugs will be a big one in this coming campaign. The problem is high prices. Popular wisdom has it that this is because of the greed of the medical industry. The truth is that these high prices are partly a result of subsidized demand due to Medicare and Medicaid, insurance regulation, and the restricted supply due to patent laws. In other words, the political class is responsible for the high prices. It's true that the pharmaceutical industry is not complaining. In fact, high prices are precisely what its friends in government want to bring about.

They may regret that the poor have to pay the higher prices, but not enough to do anything substantive about it. Prices would plummet today if patents were repealed, free trade (including re-importation) allowed, and subsidized demand ended by the abolition of Medicare and Medicaid. But no one wants to consider that solution, so Congress creates ever more intrusive programs designed to control prices, keeping the prices high enough to satisfy the industry but low enough to reduce the political clamor.

The problem is that the government can't have it both ways. It cannot reward its friends with high prices and keep consumers happy at the same time. The current system with its large subsidies is only creating massive new liabilities in programs that cannot be funded in perpetuity without massive tax increases that no one is willing to advocate. Absent tax increases, the only answer is inflation, which taxes us in other ways.

One way to think about government is as a rat wandering through a maze with no escape. There is no magic solution to getting around basic economic laws. All lunches must be paid for by someone, prices cannot be both high and low at the same time, and all attempts to coerce generate counter-reactions. In short, there is no alternative universe in which the fantasies of politicians come true.

But try telling that to the political class. The last thing they want to hear is that their power is limited, that their will is not a way. They are prone to believe that membership in the political class comes with the privilege of shaping the world to their liking. If you read the social science literature, you find the same error at work on a nearly universal basis. Very rarely does anyone come along and say: great theory but it has nothing to do with reality. You are just playing intellectual games.

Socialism was really nothing other than an intellectual game. People from the ancient world to the present conjured up some vision of how they would like the world to work and then advocated a series of measures of how to achieve it. Mises and his generation explained that their vision was fundamentally at odds with reality. In the real world, capital must have prices rooted in the exchange of private property in order for it to be employed in its highest-valued capacity. It solves nothing to say that everyone should own capital collectively. This was the equivalent of pointing out that the Emperor was wearing no clothes.

In some ways, what we do as commentators on economic affairs is to follow this model again and again. The other day, a candidate for president suggested that the answer to our economic woes was more regulation. He had it all figured out in his mind. Immediately, free-market economists from all over the world joined forces to point out that his goal of higher economic productivity could not be achieved this way. It was an unwelcome message but one necessary to deliver regardless.

The experience of Iraq has provided myriad examples of the same. The US government wants to pump oil. It wants to start factories, stores, and commerce generally. But it refuses to put private owners in charge. As a result, all its military muscle has amounted to very little at great expense. It is a classic example of how governments fail when they try to fight against forces they cannot control. Factories in Iraq that have gone into operation have done so without support of the occupying government.

And think of the war generally. At the outset, the visionaries in the Bush administration imagined that Iraq was really a very simple problem to solve. It only needed to be decapitated and the magic dust of the US presence would otherwise create an orderly and prosperous society that would be a model for the region.

Then reality hit. Crime was unleashed. Feuding political factions clamored for control. Production stopped. Society flew into chaos. This was not because of the absence of political leadership. It was because of the presence of foreign martial law in a country that was seething in resentment against the United States.

Time and again, we have seen evidence that the Iraq war only accomplished the opposite of its aims. Its purpose was to find weapons, punish terrorism, and bring order to the region. Instead it has fueled terrorism and brought new levels of disorder to the region. Having failed to achieve its stated goals, the administration then redefined the war in terms that reflect whatever was accomplished: namely to toss out and capture Saddam.

In this sense, the war was like any other government program: bringing about the opposite of its stated intentions and doing so at greater expense. Thus do we see the intersection between foreign and domestic policy. Government is famously ham-handed at home and similarly incompetent abroad. No matter how much government claims that it is master of the universe, it constantly confronts forces beyond its control.

In all the talk of the calamity of this war, never forget the broader picture: what an incredible opportunity was squandered after the end of the Cold War. The West had emerged as the universally acknowledged ideological victor in that 40-year struggle. That the Cold War was not actually an ideological struggle so much as a classic standoff between two empires is irrelevant for understanding the implications of this fact: totalitarian communism collapsed while the free economic system of the market remained standing in total triumph. The world was ready for a new period of genuine liberalism, and looking to the United States. On the verge of an amazing period of technological advance, we were perfectly situated to lead the way.

There had never been a time in US history when George Washington's foreign policy made more sense. A beacon of liberty. Trade with all, belligerence toward none. Commercial engagement with everyone, political engagement with as few as possible. The hand of friendship. Good will. This was the prescription for peace and freedom. It was within our grasp. Our children might have grown up in a world without major political violence. A world of peace and plenty. It could have been.

But it was not to be, mainly because George W.'s father decided that he wanted to go down in the history books for doing something big and important. What else but war? The United States was now the world's only superpower and itching for some fight somewhere. It's a bit like a playground filled with wimps and one boy with a black belt in karate who never absorbed the lesson in how and where to use his fighting skills. And then there was this oil-drilling dispute between Iraq and Kuwait, and Bush decided to intervene. Twelve years later, US forces are still there, causing unrelenting havoc for those poor people.

Here at home we are given constant examples of the huge gulf that separates government's perceptions of itself versus the reality. The Bush administration wanted to give the steel industry a boost. The administration established tariffs, which amounts to a tax on all consumers of steel. American manufacturers faced a choice of paying the tax to buy imported steel or paying the higher prices for domestic steel. Those who could do neither had to cut back production and hiring in other areas. Other consumers had to pay higher prices, which diverted income from other pursuits.

As for the steel industry itself, the tariffs did nothing to help it achieve greater efficiency, which is the only way to deal with more efficient competitors. They only ended up subsidizing inefficiency. Even then, it wasn't enough. During the period of tariffs, the industry dramatically consolidated in order to become more efficient in other ways.

Once faced with the prospect of trade wars—the ultimate cost of protectionism—the Bush administration pulled back and repealed the new tariffs, thereby landing the industry in exactly the same predicament it was in before the tariffs were passed. As for commercial society as a whole, it paid dramatically higher steel costs, and faced sporadic shortages, for absolutely no reason.

Faced with failure on every front, the Bush administration did the right thing and repealed the tariffs. Not that it was honest about the failure. Instead it claimed its policy worked so well that it could now repeal it. This is like a physician prescribing poison and then changing his mind. He can't but try to put the best spin on it, I suppose.

But what a beautiful example of the powerlessness of government this is! The Bush administration wanted to save American industry and only ended up vastly raising the costs of doing all forms of business. More cutbacks are inevitable as steel production shifts to other countries and the United States finds its comparative advantage elsewhere.

Much legislative energy is poured into helping some groups gain favorable treatment in the workplace. I'm thinking here of the usual litany of victim groups as identified according to race, ability, sex, national origin, religion, and the like. Have these laws actually helped the group in question? The results are mixed at best. If you send people out into the workforce with a high price attached to their heads—and the prospect of a lawsuit is a very high price indeed—you only make employers less likely to hire them.

I don't doubt that some people have been helped by these laws, but they are not the people most in need of help. Today, the disabled, blacks, women, and religious minorities go in search of jobs with a major problem: employers fear them on the margin, and, on the margin, are less likely to hire them relative to others, provided they can get away with it. It is the least qualified among them who pay the highest price. A good test case is disability: it is a documented fact that unemployment among the truly disabled is higher today than it was when the Americans with Disabilities Act was passed.

Because libertarians know in advance that government policies are destructive, we tend to focus our editorial energy on pointing to its destructive effects. But in our zeal to draw attention to issues others ignore, let us not forget the bigger picture. There are always limits to what the government can do, and the government's destruction is always accompanied by examples of great creativity on the part of the market.

Even as government dominates the headlines, private entrepreneurs are busy every day working to improve products and services that improve our lives. They do it without taxing us or regulating us, or making us suffer through tedious elections or political debates. They make their products and offer them to us in a way that pleases the consuming public the most. We can choose whether we want them or not.

Consider the success of Wal-Mart. If government had set out to create a volume discounter that made a world of material goods and groceries available to the multitude in all countries, it might have tried for a thousand years and not created anything resembling this company. Even the military has relented and now routinely points its employees not to its on-base stores but to Wal-Mart, Office Depot, and others for the best prices.

Foreign development aid is another example. It took decades to get the message across, but today finance ministers in the developing world understand that they have far more to gain through integration into the world economy than from development aid and all the restrictive policies that come with it. Today, as Sudha Shenoy points out, the largest resistance to new trade deals comes from the developing world, not because they don't want trade but because they desire trade without the labor and environmental controls the US demands.

The same is true in the area of communications. In the last century, governments aspired to control them all: the phones, the mails, the media. Today, we see that government, in practice, controls very little of the communications industry, despite every attempt to hobble private enterprise.

In that same vein, a major issue for everyone these days is computer viruses and spam, which threaten to make our chief mode of communication less reliable. Congress passes ineffectual legislation against spam and viruses, while private enterprise has given us dozens of means of winning the battle.

Private enterprise creates; government destroys. That is the great economic lesson of our times and all times.

Of course there is one way in which government never fails. It can loot. It can gain footholds into society's command centers. It can punish enemies. It can even indoctrinate people in its preferred vision of the world through propaganda.

This is the best way to understand the public school system. It doesn't work to educate but it does work to transfer vast sums from the private to the public sector. And here too, we see the power of private enterprise: booster clubs in public schools represent a *de facto* source of privatization, and the clubs and groups connected to them are the only really successful things going on in public school.

We'll hear much in the coming months about all the wonderful reforms politicians are going to bring us. This is the time when politicians vie for our allegiance by telling all about their ideas and vision for the future. As usual, they will parse their words in ways to maximize the numbers of people who are persuaded and minimize the amount of trouble they get into for inadvertently telling people something they don't want to hear.

As an aside, whoever came up with this idea of a mass democracy just wasn't thinking things through very clearly. Nothing runs well by majority vote, to say nothing of the fact that a truly free society shouldn't be "run" at all; it works on its own without would-be masters-and-commanders grasping at the helm.

Let me then offer to you my own top 10 list of political lies you are told, all designed to make you believe that government should have more power than it already has, so that it can create more of the disasters we are accustomed to:

(10) *My new program will generate jobs.*

Truth: Only the market generates jobs on net.

(9) *My education program will reform schools so that they leave no child behind.*

Truth: The public schools do not work for the same reason no government program can work. They exist outside the market economy.

(8) *My program will save industry X.*

Truth: Industry must be part of the market or else it is not really industry at all.

(7) *I won't raise your taxes but I will pass lots of new programs.*

Truth: All programs must be paid for.

(6) *As president, I will pursue a humble foreign policy.*

Truth: Nothing in the office of the president encourages humility.

(5) *This war is humanitarian and winnable.*

Truth: War is nothing but a government program on a massively destructive scale, and just as error-prone.

(4) *My reform will bring market-based competition.*

(Note: Be on the lookout for this lie, which market partisans are likely to believe.)

Truth: There is only one kind of genuine market, and it is rooted in private property and nothing else.

(3) *We will secure the nation.*

Truth: Government cannot provide security better than markets, any more than it can provide food or houses better than the market.

(2) *Government is compassionate.*

Truth: Men who seek power over the lives of others are the coldest, cruelest humans of all.

(1) *You can't love your country and hate your government.*

Truth: A person who loves his country loves liberty first.

One hundred years from now, the great story of the latter part of the twentieth century and the first part of the twenty-first century will be the vast improvements in life wrought by technology. Consider the web, the cell phone, the PDA, the affordable laptop computer, advances in medicine, and the spread of prosperity to all corners of the globe. What has government had to do with this? The answer is: nothing contributory. It has worked only to impede progress, and we can only be thankful that it hasn't succeeded.

Through all of human history, governments have caused frightening levels of bloodshed and horror, but in the end, what has prevailed is not power but the market economy. Even today governments can only play catch-up. This is because of the reasons that Mises outlined. Government cannot control the human mind, so it cannot, in the long run, control the choices people make. It cannot control economic forces, which are a far more powerful and permanent feature of the world than any government anyway.

Governments have a propensity to overreach in so many areas of life that their exercise of power itself leads to their own undoing. The overreach can take many forms: financial, economic, social, and military. In this way, and with enough passion for liberty burning in the hearts of the citizenry, governments can be responsible for their own undoing. It comes about as a result of overestimating the capacity of power and underestimating its limits.

I believe this is happening in our time. It may not be obvious when taking the broad view, but when you look at the status of a huge range of government programs and institutions, what you see is a government that is at once enormously powerful and rich, but also fragile and teetering on the brink of bankruptcy. Events of the last year indicate just how far the government has slipped in its ability to manage the economy, society, culture, and world order. Despite the exalted status of the state today, the vast and sprawling empire called the US government may in fact be less healthy than it ever has been.

A few months back, we had a special speaker come to Auburn, probably the most famous man who has visited us since the Country and Western star Alan Jackson was in town. He was Mikhail Gorbachev, a very interesting figure in the history of nations. He came to power with the reputation of a reformer and instituted many reforms that were designed not to give more liberty to the people, but to stop the unraveling of an empire before it was too late. But it was too late. All his talk of *perestroika* and *glasnost* couldn't fool the people, who had become convinced that the Soviet machine was something of a hoax.

The empire unraveled not because of him, but despite his efforts to save it. When it came time to make the critical decision of whether to try to hold the empire together by more and more force, or not, history had already made the choice for him. The empire dissolved in the blink of an eye. Not too many months later, he was out of a job, not because he was recalled in some formal process, but because the forces of history had run him over.

Democratic governments are not immune from the forces of history that overthrew Soviet tyranny. All governments over-reach and no government is permanent. So let us fear government but not exaggerate its powers. It can cause enormous damage and it must always be fought. But in this struggle, we are on the right side of history. The power of human choice, aided by the logic of economics and the laws that operate without any bureaucrat's permission, are our source of hope for the future.

SECTION 3: THE ENVIRONMENT

27.

GOVERNMENT GARBAGE*

In the loony leftist town where I live, we're ordered to separate our trash into seven neatly packaged piles: newspapers, tin cans (flattened with labels removed), aluminum cans (flattened), glass bottles (with labels removed), plastic soda pop bottles, lawn sweepings, and regular rubbish. And to pay high taxes to have it all taken away.

Because of my aversion to government orders, my distrust of government justifications, and my dislike of ecomania, I have always mixed all my trash together. If recycling made economic sense—and this is an economic question, not a dogma of the mythical earth goddess Gaia—we would be paid to do it.

For the same reason, I love to use plastic fast-food containers and nonreturnable bottles. The whole recycling commotion, like the broader environmental movement, has always seemed to have a large malarkey component. So I have never felt guilty —just the opposite—nor have I yet been arrested by the garbage gendarmes. But I was glad to get some scientific support for my position in the December 1989 issue of *The Atlantic Monthly*.

---

*February 1990

Professor William L. Rathje, an urban archaeologist at the University of Arizona and head of its Garbage Project, has been studying rubbish for almost 20 years, and what he's discovered contradicts almost everything we're told.

When seen in perspective, our garbage problems are no worse than they have always been. The only difference is that today we have safe methods to deal with them, if the environmentalists will let us.

The environmentalists warn of a country covered by garbage because the average American generates 8 pounds a day. In fact, we create less than 3 pounds each, which is a good deal less than people in Mexico City today or Americans 100 years ago. Gone, for example, are the 1,200 pounds of coal ash per year each American home used to generate, and our modern packaged foods mean less rubbish, not more.

But most landfills will be full in 10 years or less, we're told, and that's true. But most landfills are designed to last 10 years. The problem is not that they are filling up, but that we're not allowed to create new ones, thanks to the environmental movement. Texas, for example, handed out 250 landfill permits a year in the mid-1970s, but fewer than 50 in 1988.

The environmentalists claim that disposable diapers and fast-food containers are the worst problems. To me, this has always revealed the anti-family and pro-elite biases common in any left-wing movement. But the left, as usual, has the facts wrong as well.

In two years of digging in seven landfills all across America, in which they sorted and weighed every item in 16,000 pounds of garbage, Rathje discovered that fast-food containers take up less than 1/10th of one percent of the space; less than 1 percent was disposable diapers. All plastics totaled less than 5 percent. The real culprit is paper—especially telephone books and newspapers. And there is little biodegradation. He found 1952 newspapers still fresh and readable.

Rather than biodegrade, most garbage mummifies. And this may be a blessing. If newspapers, for example, degraded rapidly, tons of ink would leach into the groundwater. And we should be glad that plastic doesn't biodegrade. Being inert, it doesn't introduce toxic chemicals into the environment.

We're told we have a moral obligation to recycle, and most of us say we do so, but empirical studies show it isn't so. In surveys, 78 percent of the respondents say they separate their garbage, but only 26 percent said they thought their neighbors separate theirs. To test that, for seven years the Garbage Project examined 9,000 loads of refuse in Tucson, Arizona, from a variety of neighborhoods. The results: most people do what they say their neighbors do: they don't separate. No matter how high or low the income, or how left-liberal the neighborhood, or how much the respondents said they cared about the environment, only 26 percent actually separated their trash.

The only reliable predictor of when people separate and when they don't is exactly the one an economist would predict: the price paid for the trash. When the prices of old newspaper rose, people carefully separated their newspapers. When the price of newspapers fell, people threw them out with the other garbage.

We're all told to save our newspapers for recycling, and the idea seems to make sense. Old newspapers can be made into boxes, wallboard, and insulation, but the market is flooded with newsprint thanks to government programs. In New Jersey, for example, the price of used newspapers has plummeted from $40 a ton to minus $25 a ton. Trash entrepreneurs used to buy old newspaper. Now you have to pay someone to take it away.

If it is economically efficient to recycle—and we can't know that so long as government is involved—trash will have a market price. It is only through a free price system, as Ludwig von Mises demonstrated 70 years ago, that we can know the value of goods and services.

Environmentalists don't seem to understand this. They ask their followers to ignore price signals and cut their consumption of everything from gasoline to paper towels. This one plank in the environmental platform I agree with, since it will make these goods cheaper for the rest of us. I'm happy to have my standard of living raised by voluntary poverty from what Ronald Reagan once called "the tree huggers."

Some left-liberal economists claim prices can't solve the garbage problem because of "external diseconomies." Since greedy capitalists are out to make a fast buck, the theory goes, they produce goods that impose costs external to their businesses, i.e., trash. But all businesses have spillover effects, good and bad, and in a free market, this creates opportunities for other entrepreneurs. The donut industry may help make people fat (an external diseconomy). Should it be forced to sponsor Weight Watchers? Or, more to the point, should the public be taxed for a new federal Department of Corpulent Affairs?

The cave men had garbage problems, and so will our progeny, probably for as long as human civilization exists. But government is no answer. A socialized garbage system works no better than the Bulgarian economy. Only the free market will solve the garbage problem, and that means abolishing not only socialism, but also the somewhat more efficient municipal fascist systems where one politically favored contractor gets the job.

The answer is to privatize and deregulate everything, from trash pickup to landfills. That way, everyone pays an appropriate part of the costs. Some types of trash would be picked up for a fee, others would be picked up free, and still others might command a price. Recycling would be based on economic calculation, not bureaucratic fiat.

The choice is always the same, from Eastern Europe to my town: put consumers in charge through private property and a free price system, or create a fiasco through government. Under the right kind of system, even I might start separating my trash.

28.

Gross Domestic Bunk*

The Commerce Department, which costs $3 billion a year, is touting one of the most brainless economic ideas of our generation. What ought to be called the Anti-Commerce Department announced the concept on Earth Day, which appropriately enough is also Lenin's birthday.

In cahoots with the environmentalists, the bureaucrats have dreamed up a new formula to calculate the Gross Domestic Product, resulting in a Green GDP. The present GDP attempts (and fails) to calculate economic productivity. The new GDP would make a bad figure worse by subtracting the alleged "environmental cost" of productivity.

The Greens have a zero-sum attitude toward economic growth, and so we are supposed to deduct "resource depletion" from the productive employment of capital and time. Such a figure could come in handy on Sunday morning talk shows.

"The economy is growing at 3 percent," an economist might say. "But that drains our resources by 3 percent," responds the environmentalist. "And that comes out to zero," concludes the moderator.

Agriculture might seem like a useful activity, but not if we reduce productivity by supposed soil depletion. How is that to be measured? Not by a mere farmer, whose livelihood depends on preserving the soil, but by an official in Washington, DC.

Did building a new house require the cutting down of some trees? Subtract them from the GDP. Is that juicy steak delicious? Too bad. Steak requires cows, which environmentalists hate. Reduce the GDP by that T-bone too. Enjoy driving? It harms Mother Earth, so take it away as well.

---

*June 1994

In fact, every human activity except dying offends some environmentalist. It's enough to make you glad to be alive. Artificial lighting, eating, driving, logging, plowing, building, heating, cooling, showering, using paper bags, having children, and even breathing are all objectionable to the Greens. Taken to their logical end, in fact, environmentalism requires bringing the economy to a standstill, and then reversing it. As is clear from their own literature, only the subordination of man to plants and animals (except cattle, who should be killed but not eaten) will please them in the long run.

Using the regulatory state, the Greens have been moving us toward their totalitarian goal. All over the country, Americans have been forbidden to use their own land as they see fit. If it's a swamp or bog (i.e., a "wetland") or holds an "endangered" species, such as the recently sanctified Delhi Sand Fly, shut it down. Your name may be on the deed, and you may pay taxes on it, but the government is the real owner, since it decides how the land is to be used, if at all.

Environmental regulations are why it costs so much to get your air conditioner repaired, why wood prices are so high, why your car can't pass emissions inspection even though it's only a few years old, why you are forced to collect old newspapers so the city can recycle them at tremendous expense, and charge you for it. That trees are a crop, like asparagus, that can be grown, used, and grown again, is inadmissible.

There's no science or logic to the bulk of their claims, whether it's global warming, holes in the ozone layer, acid rain, or any of the other Mother Green fairy tales.

But just as the American people are catching on, the Greens are trying to trick us again. They tell us the GDP ought to be reduced—not by the cost of their fanatical controls—but by the costs of capitalism itself. They want us to believe that free markets, not the "Clean Air" Act and other crippling laws, are the problem.

With the Green GDP even the craziest regulation could be made to appear beneficial. The statistical construct is so perverse, in fact, that it will increase as our standard of living declines. The poorer the people, the richer the Earth.

Not that the present GDP is any great shakes. Constant Commerce Department revisions—we call them mistakes in the private sector—are enough to make the figure a laughing stock. George Bush lost the 1992 election in part because the Commerce Department said we were in a recession. After the election, the department said, whoops, we'd been in a recovery.

And floods and earthquakes account for a substantial rise in the GDP, because the figure does not and cannot account for wealth destruction. Los Angeles can be devastated by failing offices and burning homes, but once the repairs begin, the government records a building boom.

Henry Hazlitt tells the story of the boy who breaks a store window, as Keynesians stand around and convince themselves it's a productive act. But the story was intended to illustrate an economic fallacy, not provide the intellectual foundation for a Commerce Department model.

Before the government started trying to calculate productivity, it should have taken time to define it. The Austrian economist Herbert Davenport, in his 1913 book *The Economics of Enterprise*, is helpful. He suggests that: "Economic production is the bringing about of changes appropriate to command a price." A price suggests scarcity, utility, and profit. "Anything that meets this test is economic production," he adds. "And nothing else is."

What if a good or service seems useful, but it doesn't command a price in the market? If nobody wants it, it's not economic production. "Pianos could not be wealth in a society lacking musical tastes," says Davenport, "or books wealth to savages."

Davenport then asks: "Are thieves producers?" No, for the holdup man does not "give us anything for our money." He simply takes it by force. This is not productive behavior.

Davenport's discussion raises another question: what about the grandest larceny of all, $1.6 trillion taken from the private sector by the central government every year? If that property weren't seized, it could be put to private, productive use. Taxation, like theft, is a net loss to society, and should be subtracted from the GDP. Government spending is also a net loss, although it increases the GDP just like an earthquake.

In his book *America's Great Depression*, Murray N. Rothbard suggested an alternative figure: the Private Product Remaining. It subtracts government spending and taxing from overall productivity. Economist Robert Batemarco picked up the idea and prepared an alternative set of statistics that shows declines in living standards where the government wants us to believe we're richer.

Instead of subtracting the supposed costs of economic liberty from the GDP, as the Greens propose, we need to take away the costs of government, including environmental regulations, which interfere with private property and cost hundreds of billions of dollars a year.

As usual, then, the Commerce Department has it backwards. If we are going to attempt national income accounting, it should be an honest undertaking. It certainly should not be more dishonest than the present figure. And by Davenport's and Rothbard's definition, and Batemarco's calculation, our economy is getting less and less productive. Big government and its allies are responsible.

29.
MY VICE: HATING THE ENVIRONMENT*

I am a sinner but unrepentant. You see, I don't practice environmentalism, and I don't believe in it. I don't recycle and I don't conserve—except when it pays to do so. I like clean air—really clean air, like the kind an air conditioner makes. I like the

---

*August 2000

bug-free indoors. I like development, as in buildings, concrete, capitalism, prosperity. I don't like swamps (and that goes for any "wetland," even the ballyhooed "Everglades") or jungles ("rainforests"). I see all animals except dogs and cats as likely disease carriers, unless they're in a zoo.

When PBS runs a special on animal intelligence, I am unmoved. I'm glad for the dolphins that they can squeak. I'm happy for the ape that he can sign for his food. How charming for the bees that they organize themselves so well for work. But that doesn't give them rights over me. Their only real value comes from what they can do for man.

According to modern political and religious doctrine, all these views make me a sinner. The mainline churches long ago became quasi-Manichaean, heralding blessed poverty and swearing never to disturb blessed nature with the stain of human action. And we all know about the vogue of New Age religions. Public-school kids are taught the religion of eco-sentimentalism.

Even the new Catholic Catechism seems mushy on the subject. "Man's dominion over inanimate and other living beings granted by the Creator is not absolute . . . it requires a religious respect for the integrity of creation" (par. 2416). I have no idea what this means. It seems like a sop to the new paganism. Do killer bees and killer bacteria have "integrity" worthy of "religious respect"? To my mind, nature is only valuable if it serves man's needs. If it does not, it must be transformed.

Even in free-market circles, I'm expected to herald the beauty and moral integrity of nature before I discuss property rights and markets. In fact, "free-market environmentalists" insist that we accept the goals of the greens, while only rejecting some of their statist means as the best way to achieve those goals. I don't buy it. The environmentalists are targeting everything I love, and the struggle between them and us is fundamental.

Only the Randians can be counted on to make any sense on this issue. They assert what used to be the Christian position only a few decades ago: namely, that man occupies the highest spot in the great chain of being. The interests of no animal, no species, no living thing, should be permitted to trump the need for human flourishing. But for such outrageous talk, the Randians have been banished by many libertarians on grounds that their strategy is all wrong.

One wise Randian once implored me to closely examine the word "environment." What does it refer to? he asked. Well, you can tick through the list of environmental concerns: air, water, animals, trees, the ozone, etc. But where does it stop? What are the boundaries of what is called the environment? What it really means, he said, is: "anything but man." He was right. A perfect environment would be a world without people. How monstrous to allow the greens to take even one step toward this goal!

Not just Rand, but also St. Augustine believed that the purpose of nature is to serve man:

> Some attempt to extend this command ["Thou Shalt Not Kill"] even to beasts and cattle, as if it forbade us to take life from any creature. But if so, why not extend it also to the plants, and all that is rooted in and nourished by the earth? For though this class of creatures have no sensation, yet they also are said to live, and consequently they can die; and therefore, if violence be done them, can be killed. So, too, the apostle, when speaking of the seeds of such things as these, says, "That which thou sowest is not quickened except it die;" and in the Psalm it is said, "He killed their vines with hail." Must we therefore reckon it a breaking of this commandment, "Thou shalt not kill," to pull a flower? Are we thus insanely to countenance the foolish error of the Manichaeans? Putting aside, then, these ravings, if, when we say, Thou shalt not kill, we do not understand this of the plants, since they have no sensation, nor of the irrational animals that fly, swim, walk, or creep, since they are dissociated from us by their want of reason, and are therefore by the just appointment of the Creator subjected to us to kill or keep alive for our own uses.

How glorious, St. Augustine also wrote, to see human habitations spreading where once unchecked nature reigned. That's my view too. I don't care how many homilies I hear about the glories of nature, from the pulpit or Congress or the media, I'm against it, unless it has been changed by man into something useful or otherwise valuable. Things that grow are for food, clothing, decoration, or lawns. All swamps should be drained, all rain forests turned over to productive agriculture.

Not being a do-it-myselfer, my favorite section of the hardware store features bug killers, weed killers, varmint traps, and poisons of all sorts. These killer potions represent high civilization and capitalism. The bags are decorated with menacing pictures of ants, roaches, tweezer-nosed bugs, and other undesirable things, to remind us that the purpose of these products is to snuff out bug life so it won't menace the only kind of life that has a soul and thus the only kind of life that matters: man.

The only problem with pesticides is that they aren't strong enough. "Fire-ant killer" only causes the little buggers to pick up and move. Why? Some time back, the government banned the best pesticide of all: DDT. As a result, the country is filled with menacing, disease-carrying flying and crawling insects. Whole swaths of formerly wonderful vacation property have been wrecked because we are not permitted to use the only substance that ever really worked to wipe these things out. In the third world, many thousands have died since the abolition of DDT thanks to increased malaria and other bug-borne diseases. All this because we have decided that bugs have a greater right to life than we do. All this because we ignore a key tenet of Western thought: all things not human are "subjected to us to kill or keep alive for our own uses."

Such thoughts can get you arrested these days because environmentalism is our official religion. Consider the Styrofoam question. I refuse to hold a paper cup with hot coffee, not when a perfectly wonderful insulated cup is available. When I demand the coffee shop give me Styrofoam, they shrink back like Dracula before the crucifix. I explain that Styrofoam takes up less than 0.001 percent of landfill space, and that inked paper is actually more poisonous for ground water, so maybe they better not subscribe to the *New York Times*, but it doesn't matter. For them, paper cups are holy and Styrofoam is the devil. Evidence just doesn't matter.

We know where environmentalism actually came from. The left once claimed that the state could make us better off. The bigger the government, the more prosperous we would be. When that turned out not to be true, they changed their tune. Suddenly, they began to condemn prosperity itself, and the place of the oppressed proletariat was taken by oppressed members of the animal, plant, and insect kingdoms. We have adopted poverty as a policy goal, complete with its own civic code of ethics.

From time immemorial until the day before yesterday, Western man has seen nature as the enemy, and rightly so. It is dangerous and deadly. For the sake of our own survival it must be tamed, cut, curbed, controlled. That is the first task of civilization. The first step to civilization's destruction is the failure to understand this, or to call this attitude a sin.

SECTION 4:
FREE TRADE & GLOBALIZATION

30.
BASTIAT WAS RIGHT*

Frédéric Bastiat was a French economist, a passionate and articulate believer in free enterprise, who lived from 1801 to 1850. But his writings speak to us today, and help explain why the recent conflict with China has ended through diplomacy and peace rather than belligerence and war.

The answer can be summed up in one word: commerce. Glorious, peaceful, prosperity-making, peace-preserving commerce. It was the overwhelming fact that the health of our economies are linked that made the Chinese and US governments realize that both sides have more to gain from good relations than hatred and war.

It was Bastiat who observed the trade-off between commerce and war. When goods don't cross borders, armies will. Without trade, there is less to lose from the mass destruction that war implies. Countries that trade have a mutual stake in the preservation of open, friendly relations. This is one reason that free

---

*April 2001

commercial activities promote peace, and why protectionism and trade sanctions generate war tensions.

History shows that war is good for government. In wartime, government gains massive power over society. It is granted a degree of latitude in its use of emergency powers that would not otherwise be permitted. War allows politicians and bureaucrats with a passion for power to use it to the hilt, through taxation, inflation, and regimentation. War destroys things and then permits governments to profit from rebuilding them. It drains the private sector of capital and entrepreneurial energy, and enriches the parasitical institutions of the state. No free society stays free after war begins.

The mystery isn't why war exists but rather why, given the nature of government, it isn't the norm. Bastiat explained that free trade helps quell government's passion for war. It creates powerful lobbying groups on all sides that demand the preservation of peace and the triumph of diplomacy over hostility. International trade networks create intermediating structures of business relations that work as a barrier to bombs and belligerence.

This observation was further elaborated on by Ludwig von Mises, who responded to the Marxist-Leninist theory that capitalism leads to war. Lenin saw war as the internationalization of the intractable conflict between capital and labor. On the contrary, Mises said, the basis of capitalism is trade and mutual cooperation to the benefit of everyone. Capitalism creates networks of commerce—including capital markets and wide circles of labor and entrepreneurial specialization—that become dependent on each other.

The socialists of today understand this, which is why, since the end of the Cold War, so many of them have joined the war party. They too recognize that freedom, trade, and peace go together, so they've decided to oppose all three. Only last year, for example, the website of the World Socialists complained that

> The pledge to restart the talks [with China] came after a barrage of lobbying pressure by US companies alarmed over the

prospect of losing the billions of dollars in trade and investment opportunities.

Indeed, commercial ties are the very basis of international friendship, particularly that which thrives between the United States and China. Each year, China exports $200 billion in goods to the world, and imports $170 billion, for a total dollar value of commercial world traffic in and out of China of nearly half a trillion.

China's top trade partner is Japan but next in line is the United States, which annually imports from China $81 billion in electrical machinery and equipment, apparel, shoes, toys, games, iron and steel, furniture, leather goods, and a million other things, while China imports $13 billion in machinery, fuel, medical equipment, paper product, aircraft, and a million other things.

Our lives—by which I mean the lives of regular people in the United States and in China—are made immeasurably better because of the freedom to trade. Our networks of exchange build private-sector prosperity in both countries. Was the "corporate lobby" influential in preventing the tensions over the US spy plane from degenerating into outright conflict? Very possibly, even likely—a fact that we should celebrate, not condemn.

So entrenched are US-China business ties that the warmongers among us have to think creatively to come up with excuses for protectionism and hostility. Lately they have been fulminating about human rights in trade, the supposed existence of forced and child-based labor, the claim that China is spying on the United States, and the trade deficit. They say that all these things raise good reasons to curb or cut off commercial relations.

The crucial question to ask about all these complaints is: will less trade make matters better or worse? The typical political dissident in China wants more contact with the outside world, more of the economic opportunity that trade brings. Commerce opens up societies and gives the powerless greater opportunities to have control over their destinies. Besides, if it were possible to use embargoes and sanctions to shape up foreign countries, Cuba and North Korea would have become paradises of human rights long ago.

Bastiat had a radical goal. In addition to the protection of private property, he wanted

> the abolition of war, or rather (what amounts to the same thing), the fostering of the spirit of peace in public opinion, which decides the question of war or peace. War is always the greatest of the upheavals that a people can suffer in its industry, the conduct of its business, the investment of its capital, and even its tastes.

In the recent conflict with China, some Americans (even, I'm sorry to say, many American conservatives) tasted blood. But they didn't get their way, *Deo Gratias*. With free trade between the United States and China, the opportunities for our governments to go to war are greatly reduced.

It is because peace and freedom go together, and mutually reinforce each other, that we need ever more trade and commercial relations with all countries everywhere, with no exceptions, ever. May private enterprise continue to save the world from destruction by governments.

31.

DOES WORLD TRADE NEED WORLD GOVERNMENT?*

This much we know: prosperous nations have the fewest barriers to trade, while poor nations have the most. That fact alone does not prove the case for free trade, but adding a bit of logic sews up the case.

---

*September 2003

The wider the pool from which a country can draw labor and capital, the more likely it is that resources will be used efficiently and to the betterment of all. By opening up an economy beyond the borders of the nation-state, the workers and capital resources of a country find the best possible employments toward the goal of serving society as a whole.

The case for free trade has been made for hundreds of years, and yet the fight for the right to buy and sell outside the borders is never ending. The situation is complicated by a major confusion that exists among free-trade advocates. Many believe that world trade, because it is a good thing, ought to be sanctioned, managed, and otherwise regulated by the government or a coalition of governments. This was the intellectual error behind the creation of the World Trade Organization, an international bureaucracy that was supposed to open up trade but has ended up politicizing it and creating international conflict where none need exist.

Consider the crazy, mixed-up politics at work at the trade talks in Cancun, Mexico. The rich nations (meaning, mainly, the United States) swaggered into Cancun with an aggressive, three-pronged agenda: to foist a stricter system of investment rules (including patent and copyright enforcement) on developing nations, to extend US-style environmental and labor regulations to cover poorer nations, and to reduce restrictions on exports to poor nations and foreign investment in them from the industrialized world. What was missing here was the good will to make a change in their own protectionist policies, much less to reduce the production supports for their own inefficient industries.

Trade was certainly on the agenda, but free trade as traditionally understood was nowhere in the mix. From the beginning, the WTO was based on the idea that industrialized nations need to find markets for their products among the sad-sack nations of the world—not that the poor nations might have something to sell that consumers in rich nations might want to buy. That's why "intellectual property rights" (coercive monopolies for particular producers in rich countries) was high on the agenda but real-life free trade in agricultural goods was off the table completely.

Nor are the rich nations a monolith. Because the United States has long been the driving force behind global economic growth, US officials naturally assume that they have the right to exercise hegemonic control over the world economy, an assumption that makes EU finance ministers (embroiled in their own harmonization controversies) very wary indeed. This follows several years of unrelieved protectionist regulation by the US against anyone anywhere who would dare build a better mousetrap than is produced in the land of the free (which just so happens to be host to the largest, best-armed, most well-funded government in the history of the world).

Meanwhile, poor nations arrived in Cancun with a history of bad experiences at world trade conferences. The last time around, finance ministers from rich nations made some perfunctory promises to address the agricultural question, but moved on to preach to poor nations that they had better shape up and start regulating their economies more heavily. In particular, they were told that they need to crack down on alleged copyright and patent abuses in their countries, raise wages so that their workers can't "unfairly" compete with those from industrialized nations, and start enforcing stricter environmental laws. This is a composite agenda cobbled together by the main labor, environmental, and business interests that are so influential in US politics.

Now, the problem here is obvious to anyone who knows basic economics. The comparative advantage that poor nations have in attracting investment and producing their own goods for export is precisely their unregulated labor and environmental regimes. Given that their object is to become more competitive, not less, it would make no sense to legislate higher wages that would only drive out capital and lead to more unemployment. If they stand a chance for development, tighter regulations on production are not the answer. What they need instead is an open marketplace in which to compete using their comparative advantage.

In the past, the anti-WTO protesters have claimed to be standing with the poor nations of the world against capitalist globalization, but the reality is much more complicated. By resisting the trend to "upwardly harmonize" regulations, poor nations of the world have stood firmly with the free-trade tradition. What they were arguing for, in reality, is not less globalization in general but less political globalization in order to make possible more economic globalization. The two forces are at odds with each other.

Having been burned too many times in the past, this time, poor nations arrived at the talks with a set of demands of their own. If the rich countries are going to preach about "free trade," they'd best start living up to it themselves. That rich countries export highly subsidized farm products to the third world, to sell at prices cheaper than these countries can produce, is notable enough. But to then turn around and refuse to accept imports of low-priced goods on grounds that this constitutes "dumping," is adding injury to insult.

At the talks, each side tried to change the subject as much as possible until it became obvious that there was little point in talking. The legal and regulatory reforms that the US demanded were never seriously considered. The idea of cuts in subsidies and tariffs was ruled out completely. Indeed, the Bush administration is moving in the opposite direction, toward the dangerous idea of national sufficiency, even though it is a sure prescription for economic depression. Of course the whole scene was punctuated by hysterical protests from the throngs of activists that the WTO attracts like flies to a picnic.

As for the leftists who railed against globalization, they are right to have an inchoate sense that the WTO is up to no good. Beyond that, there is no agreement. If they are in solidarity with the poor nations of the world, does that mean they favor cutting agricultural subsidies in industrialized nations? That would mean job losses of course, and further hardship for their beloved "family farms." You can't stand with both the poor and oppressed agricultural workers in the United States and the poor and oppressed agricultural workers in the third world; ultimately they are in competition with each other, and should be.

What's more, the left can't simultaneously endorse the full panoply of phony and expensive "rights" in the charter of the International Labor Organization and link arms with the workers of the third world. The bottom line is that if the US labor unions get their way, the workers and peasants in the third world would find themselves without jobs and even more destitute than they already are. The same goes for foreign investment, which, contrary to the left, is a boon for all poor nations.

As for the business lobby, it needs to worry less about forcing foreign governments to enforce their copyrights and think more about how to compete in an increasingly competitive world. It ought to spend at least as much time and energy reducing barriers to imports as it does pushing for the elimination of barriers to exports. In short, they need to stop acting so much like mercantilists and act more like entrepreneurs.

The irony is that the WTO bears much of the blame, though there is plenty to go around. Somehow world trade proceeded apace for the entire history of civilization without this outfit serving as a sounding board for fanatics, protectionists, and would-be global regulators. When so many free traders supported the WTO's creation, were they being naïve or were they being paid off? Regardless, the WTO is no friend of free trade.

Everyone says that the collapse in Cancun could mean the end of multilateral trade negotiations for the duration. For the cause of free trade, there could be a downside to this, especially if it means that the US will treat the issue of world trade with as much political finesse as it managed the Iraq situation.

But the upside is even more obvious. It means a setback in the movement to upwardly harmonize regulations. It means a setback for global government generally. It is all to the good if it means that businesses around the world work on striking up their own deals instead of relying on governments, and the organizations that governments create, to do it for them.

As a side benefit, it is now exposed for all to see, and possibly for the first time in our generation, that industrialized nations represent a great threat to free trade. What is needed is not another round of negotiations. Let every nation, right now, do what is best for all citizens of the world: eliminate every form of intervention that would prevent or otherwise hobble mutually beneficial trade between any two parties anywhere in the world. No bureaucracy can help us toward that goal; it must come from a growing realization of the merit of freedom itself.

32.
BUY BETHLEHEM?*

Some of the most vociferous attacks on free trade in recent years have come from religious lobbies, and are led by people who believe that they have the best interests of the workers in mind. They call on us to buy products labeled fair trade, or to boycott growers who employ low-cost labor, or to refuse products made by international corporations operating in the third world, or to join protesters at any international conferences where it is believed that the conspirators inside are seeking to lower barriers to trade. They do all of these things under the conviction that to limit the right to buy and sell is part of the mission of spreading the social gospel.

Actually, what they are doing is raising the prices of consumer products, harming opportunity for workers to find good

*April 2005

employment, hindering growth of economies in the developing world, and inadvertently serving as foot soldiers for the mercantile interest groups that seek to shield themselves from more efficient but foreign competitors. Their campaigns may be cast in a different light, but the substance of their program is no different from those who say that we should only buy American, which in turn makes no more sense than a campaign to buy only Michigan, or buy only Lansing, or, *reductio ad absurdum*, buy only from me.

The push to restrict people's opportunities to buy and sell based on region is an attempt to bring about what economists call autarky, or economic self-sufficiency. It is the economic system that decries the expansion of the division of labor and urges all production to take place in the smallest possible geographical unit. In practice, the campaign for economic autarky takes place at the level of the nation-state and thereby works as a handmaiden of those who see nationalism and even war as a better program than peace and mutual betterment through trade.

I know of only one setting in which autarky is economically viable. It is the Garden of Eden. Here the ground did not need to be prepared for growing. It produced on its own. Animals did not need to be hunted, slaughtered, and cooked. Economic scarcity did not exist. There was no scarcity of resources, no scarcity of time, and no economic problem to overcome at all. Mortality was unknown. Man and woman lived in perfect contentment in the presence of God. Economic autarky was viable here.

But with sin came death and banishment from this garden. Man and woman would have to work to produce. Pain and suffering entered into the world. Time and resources were scarce. But God did not leave the human population with no means to overcome the new limits on what could be consumed. God made it possible for the human population to use intelligence to exchange. People would divide their labor based on their own unique talents and capacities. This division took place between peoples and regions. Trade became a means to achieve a kind of cooperative unity even though the Garden of Eden was nowhere to be found.

Thus was born the concept of free trade.

The Christian tradition teaches that the sin of the Garden was finally destroyed at the Incarnation, when God became Man and walked among us. The Gospel of Matthew records for us that the first gifts given to him came from the Magi, wise men who traveled from foreign lands. And what did they bring? Gold, frankincense, and myrrh—products from the East. Jesus was thus presented products acquired from international lands, imports to Bethlehem.

One can only imagine the scene had the social gospel autarkists been present. They would have demanded to know whether the workers who mined the gold, made the incense, or produced the myrrh were paid a fair wage. They might have demanded, lacking proof of such, that the Wise Men should have refrained from buying. Certainly Jesus should only be given gifts acquired through fair trade, they might say. They might have demanded that instead of traveling from afar that the Wise Men might have been socially conscious enough to Buy Bethlehem.

In his ministry Jesus recruited from among the merchant class, most famously from among fishermen, whose produced commodity knows no nation or state. There were tent makers who traveled to provide people goods and services that they needed where they needed them. There is not a word in the whole of the Gospels that speaks of some alleged need to keep production local or to establish some arbitrary geographic limits on buying and selling. Such an attitude is completely alien to Biblical times, where the need to overcome poverty through trade was everywhere understood.

Jesus's parables are filled with references to commerce and its ethical obligations. In the story of the Laborers in the Vineyard, we find a vineyard owner who hires based on contract and adheres to that contract even when it means paying people who worked a full day the same as those who worked only a few hours. There was no talk of fair wages here. The lesson we are taught rests on the right of the owner to make contracts, the right of the laborer to accept or refuse work, and the failure of vision of those workers who complain about the terms after the fact.

Again, we can imagine what the social gospel autarkists would say about this situation. They would probably advocate nationalizing the vineyard and unionizing the workers, who would then promptly strike for shorter hours and higher wages and benefits all around.

Moving on to the parable of the talents from Saint Matthew, scripture notes that the master is preparing for another trip to a foreign land. We are told that he is the kind of person who reaps where he has not sown and gathers where he has not planted. In other words, he used the division of labor, the surest path to wealth. He was a trader and entrepreneur who saw his business as extended to all places, not just those of his residence. It is through foreign trade that the man most likely made his money, which was then given to the servants as a test of their prowess as investors. Some passed and others failed.

We as individuals and as a nation can choose to bury our talents or seek out the best and most profitable uses for them. That could mean that our capital should travel just as the master in the parable has traveled. To insist that we use our scarce resources wastefully means to behave as the man who was cast out of the kingdom on grounds that he hadn't even deposited his money with the bankers to earn a market rate of return.

Today, we face relentless demands to establish a system of autarky, to buy local or national rather than divide up the labor, specialize, and trade to our mutual advantage. But this is not the path to prosperity. It is the path to conflict and war. Among the charges that the Declaration of Independence leveled against King George was that he was attempting to cut off colonial trade with all parts of the world but Britain. This the Founders saw as a violation of human rights and a policy of impoverishment.

As F.A. Hayek wrote in the neglected conclusion to his 1944 book *The Road to Serfdom,*

> If international economic relations, instead of being between individuals, become relations between whole nations organized as trading bodies, they will inevitably become the source of friction and envy.

Ludwig von Mises concluded his 1944 book *Omnipotent Government: The Rise of the Total State and Total War* with a similar warning. "The establishment," he said, "of an international body for foreign trade planning will end in hyperprotectionism." These two great free marketeers understood how government uses the period immediately following a war as it does the war itself for state power and special-interest rewards.

When we think of the conflicts of our own time, we can see how they stem from a failure to engage in exchange. Ten years of sanctions against Iraq cut off that country's trade with its most profitable markets. This act of protectionism was a prelude to a ghastly war. In contrast, our relations with China have been of growing amounts of trade, and a potential setting of conflict has turned to one of mutual benefit.

After the fall of Communism and the rise of economic liberalization around the world, it is no longer feasible to deny the reality of economic globalization. Rather than bemoan this, we need to see the benefits for all peoples. It means more goods and services and lower prices. It means more opportunities for improving the standard of living. It means better relationships between all cultures and peoples. In free trade, I believe, we see the hand of the Creator. We are given the means to cooperate to overcome banishment from the Garden. We will also contend with scarcity. But that should never stop us from living out the Gospel command to go forth into all the world.

It is the earth and the fullness thereof, not the nation-state, that is the Lord's. Not just ministers but also merchants and consumers should be free to go forth into all the world.

33.
WHY THEY HATE US*

Journalists pride themselves on their power of observation. It is observation that is the first step toward putting a picture of the world into words and print, bringing to the rest of us an image they have seen but we have not. Journalists are often very good at seeing small pictures, but not big pictures. Actually, in their profession, it is bad form to even attempt to see the big picture until you have reached the highest level of professional achievement.

Thomas Friedman of the *New York Times* has achieved that level and thus acquired the right to pronounce. With three Pulitzer Prizes under his belt (1983, 1988, 2002) and a National Book Award for *The Lexus and the Olive Tree* (2000), his opinion on everything from economics to politics to war is highly regarded. Why? Presumably because he has seen so much, reported on so much, and been so long on his beat, he has mastered his craft. And it's true that his commentary is usually worth reading. He can be unpredictable and even manage to dissent from established opinion, if only on the margin.

But even unimpeachable public intellectuals like Friedman tip their hand from time to time, and reveal that they have no better an understanding of the world than any man on the street who has never taken a class in economics or read deeply in political thought. His column titled "A Theory of Everything," which ran June 1, 2003, is just such a case. For all his observations and reporting, he has missed the most elementary distinction and for that reason ends up falling back on a line of thought so conventional and confused that it could have been written by any college freshman on a term-paper deadline.

---

*June 2003

He begins with the question concerning the entire Muslim world after 9-11: why do they hate us? And after the most recent war, the question has broadened into: why does everybody else hate us? By now everyone knows these questions, but little thought is put into the phrasing of the question, namely, who exactly is "us."

Am I supposed to believe that the average Muslim hates you and me as much as they hate Richard Cheney, George Bush, and Donald Rumsfeld? The fact is that Muslims don't hate you or me. They don't know you or me. But they do know the names of people at the top of the US government, and for good reason: these people have ordered the military occupation of Muslim countries. We did not order this; they did, and the citizens of these countries hate them for it. To conglomerate you and me with Dick, George, and Donald is to engage in a very slippery rhetorical tactic.

But let's leave that profoundly important problem aside, and assume that by "us," Friedman means America in general. There can be no question that world opinion on America has sunk. What is his answer to the question of why they hate America?

Friedman tells the story of the collapse of the Soviet Union and the amazing rise of American power in the 1990s, when the technology revolution led to the undisputable dominance of the United States as an economic and political power. As a "hyper-power," we began to touch their lives in their countries more than their own governments. People around the world began to sense that America was shaping their lives in ways they could not control. The world economy is too intertwined for anyone to consider an official military response, Friedman goes on, so that left it to people who have no real stake in the system to try to beat back the hegemony. Thus terrorism—warfare by private groups as versus states—became the preferred means of fighting.

After the US military crushed the Taliban and then Iraq, more and more people have begun to fear the United States. People who once believed that the United States was a benign power began to believe that it was a dangerous one, especially given the Bush administration's go-it-alone approach. Friedman says that the world's real frustration is that people cannot vote over the uses of American power and thus have no choice over their fate, and this is fueling hatred. He concludes that we need to find "a stable way to manage this situation."

What is Friedman's error? In a phrase, he conflates "power and market" (to borrow a phrase from the title of Murray Rothbard's great book). In missing this point, Friedman shows that he has done too much reporting and not enough thinking. He sees angry people all over the world, from Muslims in a rage over US troops and US movies, to the French bourgeoisie, attacking McDonald's, and draws the most trivial conclusion possible: people always hate the dominant power. He makes no sharp distinction between econo-cultural influence and politico-military imperialism, whereas any serious understanding of the world must begin with this distinction.

What is the difference between econo-cultural influence and politico-military imperialism? It begins with the elementary divide between things that people choose to embrace and those that are foisted upon them. American commerce is not dominant around the world because people are buying products at the point of a gun. Consumers of the world have chosen, of their own free will, to purchase these goods offered by entrepreneurial companies.

It is an act of voluntary cooperation that has made American commerce dominant. Big Macs are not forced on the world; they are purchased by people who choose them over other options. If the French stopped buying Big Macs, the burger chain would pull out in a matter of months.

There is no reason to expect that market saturation would give rise to resentment. Let's understand this by way of analogy. Let's say that Persian rugs become hugely fashionable and inexpensive. They are on the floors of half of American homes. People don't want rugs of other types or designs, just Persian. Now, if a person saw this fact and started to whip up a huge frenzy about the scary power of Iranian rug makers, everyone would think this person was a bit loopy. Far from being a threat, Iranian rug makers have merely made it possible for Americans to acquire the goods they want. If the American hegemony were limited to Starbucks, McDonalds, and Nike, who would care? None of these companies have any power to coerce anyone. There is no reason to resent them, anymore than we resent the Finns for cell phones, the Swiss for watches, or the Russians for vodka. We are free to buy or abstain from buying any of these goods at any time. It is our choices as consumers that give these products prominence in the global economy.

But don't leftist protesters target US companies and even burn them down from time to time? Yes, they do, and I don't doubt that anticapitalism has something to do with it. And yet these companies have come to serve as proxies for the aspect of the American hegemony that the world really hates: the military power, which is to say, the US state. But don't Muslims despise the decadence of American movies and music? Certainly. But would their opposition turn to violence if the United States were not bombing and invading their countries? Highly doubtful.

There is a huge difference between setting up a company and inviting people to buy your product versus bombing people and bribing politicians to do your will. It is the difference between what Franz Oppenheimer called the social and political means. One way is peaceful, the other violent. One asks for people's cooperation and the other demands it. One way is based on hope for voluntary choice and the other presumes that choice is a dangerous thing. Economic globalism and military globalism are not just distinct; they represent opposing forces in the world today.

The great tragedy of the American hegemony is that these two ways of doing things have been intertwined, such that people of the world are no longer able to distinguish between the voluntary choice to watch an American movie and the coercive mandate to turn in your gun. That Thomas Friedman does not draw attention to the difference makes him culpable for grave intellectual error but hardly unique: both the friends and opponents of American commercial globalism have presumed that it goes along with military domination.

Friedman himself has famously written that: "The hidden hand of the market will never work without a hidden fist." For this he is called an apologist of corporate power. But here again, the phrase corporate power is highly misleading. In a market economy, no corporation has power, only profits and influence, which come to it by the voluntary choices of consumers. Only the military exercises power as such, and it does so without seeking the input of others.

Friedman hints at this with his comment that people of the world do not have a vote on the behavior of the American hegemony. But a political vote would be useless. Do we really want to subject the fate of world trade to the political votes of the world population? Who or what would they vote for? What if the vote ended up granting the United States the right to do whatever it wanted? Those who voted against this outcome would be no better off for having slogged to the polling stations.

Nonetheless, he is right that people want some say in world affairs. That requires, in the first instance, a rejection of war and military occupation. The appropriate means to grant people a say over the shape and direction of the world economy and culture is the market. The market is the stable way to manage the situation. But in order for the market to do its work, the military means must be rejected in favor of the peaceful means, which is all about commercial activity and cultural exchange.

As Mises writes:

> The free traders want to make peace durable by the elimination of the root causes of conflict. If everybody is free to live and to work where he wants; if there are no barriers for the mobility of labor, capital, and commodities; and if the administration, the laws, and the courts do not discriminate between citizens and foreigners, the individual citizens are

not interested in the question where the political frontiers are drawn and whether their own country is bigger or smaller. They cannot derive any profit from the conquest of a province. In such an ideal—Jeffersonian—world of democracy and free trade war does not pay.

However, so long as the United States has troops in 100 countries, overthrows regimes at will, slaughters people in its wars, decides which countries may defend themselves and how, and otherwise assumes the right to manage all world politics, the wonderful aspects of the American "hegemony"— namely the superiority of its economic and cultural exports, and their integration with countries and cultures around the world—will live in the shadow of the threat of coercion.

The American commercial sector has brought great blessings to the world. However, the great tragedy of a huge economy operating under a central state is precisely that it can be used to fund that state's imperial impulses. When people of the world are looking for a way to curb the military power, they invariably turn their anger against the vulnerable symbols of capitalism (hence the Twin Towers calamity). It is up to the citizens of the hegemony to make their will known and restrain the state so that the blessings of commerce can thrive.

The journalist's skill as an observer can only take him so far, if he is observing with the wrong theory in mind. As Friedman's column shows, without the distinction between power and market—the very core of the libertarian idea—a theory of everything can easily turn into a theory of nothing.

SECTION 5: CULTURE

34.
CAPITALISM AND CULTURE*

From left and right, capitalism is condemned for all the cultural failings of the modern world—everything from mindless TV to dirty books to slatternly art to trashy movies to debasing music. It's an extension of the left-liberal habit of blaming a system for what are actually the failings of individuals.

Ludwig von Mises identified Victorian art critic John Ruskin as the intellectual source of this ceaseless griping. Ruskin saw civilization, embodied in the arts, as going down the tubes, and he labeled the market economy as the cause. This allowed him to be a socialist without surrendering upper-class affectations or having to prattle about workers and peasants.

Ruskin thus qualifies, said Mises, as "one of the grave-diggers of British freedom, civilization and prosperity."

"A wretched character in his private no less than in his public life," Ruskin eulogized the ancient producer cartels called guilds. "Government and cooperation are in all things the laws of life," wrote Ruskin in *Unto This Last* (1862), "anarchy and competition the laws of death."

---

*October 1995

Nowadays, practically everyone with a college degree is a tacit Ruskinian. Americans may understand the productive power of the market, but many are blind to its virtue as a civilizing agent, to its ability to sustain tradition, create what's beautiful and grand, and preserve what's right and good.

The left (still essentially Marxian) wants us to think of capitalism as modern and industrial. More correctly, capitalism is just a name for the social recognition of private property, trade, and contract enforcement. It was as much a part of ancient Athens as nineteenth-century America. In its total absence, civilization would crumble, and the arts vanish.

In modern times, the confusion usually starts this way. Someone flips on the television to find the usual rotten show and offensive commercials. He concludes that's the market at work: base, vulgar, and insulting to our intelligence.

Once on this track, the anticapitalist mentality runs wild. The decadence of the cash nexus appears everywhere. Strip malls and yellow M's in the sky. Boxing, moshing, tabloids, rap, and low pay for intellectuals. It's all horrible, sniffs this person, and it's all capitalism's fault.

If this theory were correct, the prophets, saints, and ancient philosophers were wasting their breath. They called on people to abandon sin and adopt virtue, when they could have taken the fast track to social salvation by condemning free exchange and private property.

What the great moralists knew, and we've forgotten, is that people and cultures are products of human choice. Good lives can flourish in any social setting, whether the prison camp, the Wild West, or even Washington, DC.

Sin and stupidity will, of course, always be with us. From an economic perspective, our goal should be to make sure sinners pay for their sins, and that minimal resources are used to cater to them. In this process, capitalism is our ally. In addition to making prosperity possible, the whole point of economics and markets is to make sure the minimum amount of resources is used to satisfy any particular demand of any particular group.

The free economy is efficient because it deals with tastes and preferences as a given, it organizes resources in an economically practical way, and it arranges for the consumer to get what he wants at the least possible cost to everyone else.

The junk on television may indeed speak volumes about our culture. People should care about more important things. Thanks to capitalism, however, society isn't wasting excess resources on it. Trash is delivered in the least costly manner, leaving more resources for the pursuit of what really matters.

Entrepreneurs have learned to provide services to even the smallest niche. When I watch television—and I don't very often—the most intelligent network is EWTN. It features 50-part lectures by learned academics on subjects like Scholasticism.

This is a profitable enterprise that would be considered wasteful in a socialist country—not to mention politically incorrect. In a less prosperous society, it couldn't survive. Yet I can't remember anyone crediting capitalism for making St. Thomas Aquinas accessible to the masses.

It used to be said that government had to fund the arts for them to be of good quality. That argument no longer flies. Take a look at the malevolent and stupid creations of the National Endowment for Arts. The government's "sculptures," "architecture," and "music" have littered the country with rubbish.

Economists say that the market "internalizes externalities." This means, in part, that people who are offended by some goods and services can structure their lives to avoid exposure. That's mostly true, especially in the case of sleazy television and movies, pornography, and weird services like telephone sex. Thanks to capitalism—which restricts such services to the people who purchase them—the rest of us don't have to be affected.

A shop selling Satanic trinkets recently opened up in Auburn, Alabama. "Anything for a buck," people sneered, until the store went belly-up for lack of business. It's true that some people will do anything for a buck, but in a market economy, they have to be subservient to the consuming public.

The market delivers plenty of similar good news, though most of it goes unremarked. Let's consider the case of big cities, which the productive public has been clawing its way out of for decades.

The government has done everything in its power to make cities uninhabitable by regular people. Government welfare has fostered a whole class of citizens that is at once indolent and criminal. Public housing and rental subsidies have destroyed settings that were once middle-class. Many cities today are only "cultural" centers if you like freaks and muggers.

Yet, thanks to capitalism, there is hope. Private individuals and developers take buildings that appear beyond repair and revive them. House by house, block by block, whole sections of cities have been gentrified. It's not charity work. Without a system of profit and loss, it wouldn't happen.

Yet you can't satisfy those with an anticapitalist mentality. They invariably complain that gentrification raises property values and "squeezes" out the poor, while forgetting to notice how much better off everyone is when degraded resources are made more valuable.

Beach housing has long been a magnet for cultural complaints against capitalism. High-rise buildings were routinely called evil for destroying the view from a mile away. Yet it is this type of structure that makes beach living possible for the masses in the first place.

Some architects, in revulsion against beach high rises, have worked with investors to buy miles of property on the beach. Then they create communities with quaint houses and shops. The result is magnificent, and entirely private, if affordable only for a few.

These architects think they're repudiating the tackiness of capitalism. They fail to realize that their private, planned communities are as much a part of capitalism as the high rises. Far from making a left-wing ideological point, they are catering to different tastes, marketing a product, and vastly increasing the value of property as a result. High rises and private communities both represent capitalism at work.

What about the materialism of capitalism? This too is a misnomer. Strictly speaking, capitalism is not about material goods; it's about exchangeable goods. Leisure, love, beauty, and art are all exchangeable, and as much a part of economic life as Big Macs and Must-See-TV.

It's said that markets bring about short-term thinking. Quite the contrary. Markets often focus on the extreme long-term, in ways the government never can. Consider the wine industry. It can take decades before a vineyard produces a really great bottle of wine. Even common table wines require that entrepreneurs plan many years in advance. The more forward-looking the capitalist, the more he can be rewarded for setting aside temporary pleasures.

Every good and service has a timetable, and the entrepreneur must plan in the most cost-effective manner. It's bureaucratic man—not the mythical economic man—who is prone to consumption and immediate gratification. And the more the state intervenes in an economy, the more it penalizes long-term thinking and rewards short-term. Inflation is the most obvious example.

But hasn't the capitalist mentality forced everyone in the family to work 60 hours per week, just to keep up with material desires? In fact, it's the government that has brought it about. A conspiracy against sound money and private property is what drove wives and mothers into the workforce in the 1970s and 1980s. A return to unfettered capitalism would allow those who desired it to return home, so that we could restore family and community life, both of which thrive under *laissez-faire*.

As Schumpeter noted, every socialist is an enemy of the bourgeois values of home, family, community, property, honesty, diligence, and hard work. The more socialist our economy becomes, the more vice displaces virtue in public and private life.

As for the culturally uplifting aspects of capitalism, the profit and loss system makes possible—to take just a few examples—

our economy's amazing bounty of recorded classical music, the greatest cabernets in the world, an abundance of culinary treats even kings couldn't imagine two centuries ago, and some good movies. If that doesn't convince, consider that it's under capitalism that the Bible became the all-time best-selling book.

35.
WHO'S THE AMERICAN TALIBAN?*

The political buzz for weeks has centered on whether the Democrats are going to employ the "Taliban Strategy," claiming that the Republican Party's right flank is the "Taliban Wing."

How does the left get away with describing right-wing thought as Talibanish, especially when compared to the left-wing agenda of speech codes, economic regulation, and authoritarian intervention in every aspect of American private life?

Recall that the Taliban consisted of a pack of young people just out of specialized Islamic school where their heads were filled with political ideology stemming from a maniacal rendering of a handful of books they considered holy writ. Once in power, they attempted to impose this rendering on the entire population in the hopes of creating a kingdom of God on earth.

That is also a short description of the career of countless numbers of left-wing reformers in America, where colleges and universities filled their heads with otherworldly socio-political theory that they then attempted to impose on a resisting population.

Eggheaded utopianism is only one similarity between the Taliban and the American left. Who favors:

---

*January 2002

- punishing and even criminalizing speech and thought that contradicts egalitarian ideology on issues of race, sex, disability, and sexuality;

- enacting national restrictions on eating fast food or driving fast cars;

- police enforcement of rules against smoking, drinking, gambling, or otherwise indulging in traditional but socially harmless "vices;"

- punishing people for failing to piously separate their own private garbage, can by can and bottle by bottle, into five types of recyclable material;

- spying on families to discover whether they are spanking their kids and/or failing to expose them to politically correct attitudes and a sufficiently diverse social circle;

- regulating the content of films and music to ensure that they do not send messages to youth that the politicians regard as culturally inappropriate;

- making end-runs around parents by having public schools indoctrinate children in all the recent political priorities of the ruling regime;

- abolishing the freedom of association and mandating adherence to detailed government rules concerning all uses of private property in hiring, firing, consumer service, and housing;

- curtailing property rights in the name of federally protected species and plants, and even claiming omniscience in seeking to alter weather patterns one hundred years in the future;

- restrictions on the right to advertise;

- outlawing mining, drilling, logging, and other forms of commerce considered insufficiently devoted to holy mother earth;

- cracking down on any form of humor that pokes fun at any politically favored group;

- imposing ceilings on the ability of lenders to charge market-determined interest rates and passing other forms of anti-usury laws (as favored by the Taliban);

- special protection for women in the law on grounds that they constitute an inherently weaker sex that would otherwise be exploited by powerful men;

- restrictions on the right to display religious symbols or otherwise reveal religious preferences that are contrary to political priorities;

- regulating the right to reproduce to prevent supposed overpopulation;

- extreme regulations on the ability of individuals and families to acquire weapons of self-defense, on grounds that all people ought to entrust their safety to public employees;

- consolidation of all political power in the center to prevent that emergence of local leaders who might enact policies contrary to the ruling ethos.

Sure, there are people on the right who may go along with such policies, though in doing so they contradict their general principles favoring freedom and limited government. On the left, however, such extreme measures of social, cultural, and economic control are endemic to the ideology itself. We can only imagine the type of controls that would weigh on our national life if the left had its entire way.

For reasons hard to fathom, however, the political left still enjoys the reputation of favoring civil rights, civil liberties, and the rights of individuals. But it has been years, even decades, since that was true in the United States. All the old talk of civil liberties and free speech turn out to have been a ploy to gain power so that the left could impose its own form of controls. Look at what they have imposed on the universities they control!

What's more, the regimes with which the left has variously sympathized over the years—Soviet and Chinese communism—have been the most despotic antifreedom regimes in the history of the world. After all this, the left has lost any right to claim the mantle of freedom, much less to contrast itself with the tyranny of Talibanism.

The problem with the right in America isn't that it is like the Taliban. It is that it is too often willing to abandon libertarian principles and kowtow to the intrinsic Talibanism of the left, which is just another variant of big-government control.

36.
MISES ON THE FAMILY*

The family is an anarchistic institution, G.K. Chesterton wrote. He meant that it requires no act of the state to bring it about. Its existence flows from fixed realities in the nature of man, with its form refined by the development of sexual norms and the advance of civilization.

This observation is consistent with a brilliant discussion of the family in Ludwig von Mises's masterwork *Socialism*, first published in 1922. Why did Mises address family and marriage in an economics book refuting socialism? He understood—unlike many economists today—that the opponents of the free society have a broad agenda that usually begins with an attack on this most crucial bourgeois institution.

"Proposals to transform the relations between the sexes have long gone hand in hand with plans for the socialization of the means of production," Mises observes. "Marriage is to disappear along with private property. . . . Socialism promises not only welfare—wealth for all—but universal happiness in love as well."

Mises noted that August Bebel's *Woman and Socialism*, a paean to free love published in 1892, was the most widely read left-wing tract of its time. This linkage of socialism and promiscuity had a tactical purpose. If you don't buy the never-never

*January 2002

land of magically appearing prosperity, then you can focus on the hope for liberation from sexual responsibility and maturity.

The socialists proposed a world in which there would be no social impediments to unlimited personal pleasure, with the family and monogamy being the first impediments to go. Would this plan work? No chance, said Mises: the socialist program for free love is as impossible as its economic one. They are both contrary to the restraints inherent in the real world.

The family, like the structure of the market economy, is a product not of policy but of voluntary association, made necessary by biological and social realities. Capitalism reinforced marriage and family because it insisted on consent in all social relations.

The family and capitalism thus share a common institutional and ethical foundation. By attempting to abolish them, the socialists would replace a society based on contract with one based on violence. The result would be total societal collapse.

When the democratic socialists Sidney and Beatrice Webb traveled to the Soviet Union, a decade after Mises's book, they reported a different reality. They found women, liberated from the yoke of family and marriage, living happy and fulfilled lives. It was as much a fantasy—actually a bloody lie—as their claim that Soviet society was becoming the most prosperous in history.

No sane intellectual embraces full-blown social economics anymore, but a watered-down version of the socialist agenda for the family is the driving force behind much of US social policy. This agenda goes hand in hand with the hobbling of the market economy in other areas.

It is no accident that the rise of free love in the United States accompanied the rise of the fully developed welfare state. The goals of liberation from work (and saving and investment) and liberation from our sexual natures stem from a similar ideological impulse: to overcome fixed realities in nature. The family has suffered as a result, just as Mises predicted it would.

While the advocates of the family and the proponents of capitalism should be united in a single political agenda of smashing the interventionist state, they typically are not. Family advocates, even conservative ones, often decry finance capitalism as an alienating force, and advocate ill-advised policies like tariffs, union monopolies, and wage floors for married people.

At the same time, free enterprisers show little interest in the genuine concerns of family advocates. And neither seems interested in the radical attack on both freedom and family life that government policies like child labor laws, public schooling, Social Security, high taxes, and socialized medicine represent. In Mises's view, this breech is unnecessary.

> It is no accident that the proposal to treat men and women as radically equal, to regulate sexual intercourse by the state, to put infants into public nursing homes at birth and to ensure that children and parents remain quite unknown to each other should have originated with Plato,

who cared nothing for freedom.

Neither is it an accident that the same proposals these days are pushed by people who have little to no regard for family or economic law.

37.
Why Professors Hate the Market*

The anticapitalism of college professors is legendary even if its genesis and basis are somewhat mysterious. If anything should be clear to those who care about evidence, it's that the market economy is superior to all forms of economic planning. Even minimal amounts of government intervention produce sector-specific stagnation.

Compare Fed-Ex, for example, to the post office, or public schools to private schools, or the unregulated high-tech sector

---

*June 2000

with the highly regulated and unionized steel industry. Many heroic professors today do understand this. But that's not the norm. Why is it that so many professors in so many fields, particularly in elite institutions, and despite all evidence and good sense, still hate the market?

A clue comes from this year's hiring season. It turns out that college graduates, particularly in fields touching on computers and business, are hugely in demand. Colleges are flooded with recruiters vying for the students' attention. They are being courted as never before: wined and dined by executives, offered sign-up bonuses, paid salaries unheard of a decade ago.

But here's the kicker: the large majority are not planning to attend graduate school. Apart from a real vocation to teach and research, why should they, especially in this extremely tight job market? Their skills are marketable in business and that's where the money is.

In one case cited by the *New York Times*, Columbia University once had 70 percent of its graduating class planning to go forward with higher degrees. Now, only 20 percent are planning to do so. That's only one out of five students, at a prestigious school where you might expect that most students would seek higher degrees.

What does this imply about the remaining 20 percent? Among them, there are probably some potentially great scholars, people whose calling it is to live and work in the world of ideas. On the other hand, college officials fear that many of them are going on, not because they are brilliant, but precisely for the opposite reason: that they can't cut it in the marketplace. As the *Times* puts it, "this trend makes many college officials fear that a smaller, and possibly less capable, group will choose to become professors."

It makes sense that grad school will be less attractive to people in boom times. But the *Times* also reveals that the trend is very conspicuous in the reverse as well: it turns out that grad schools are most in demand during times of recession. Bad economic times equals high enrollment. It's no wonder that the intellectual class tends to hate the market: their very fortunes are bound up with creating more recessions, if only to fill seats in the classroom.

Ludwig von Mises once speculated, in his 1956 book *The Anti-Capitalistic Mentality*, that the socialism of the professors was driven in part by government funding of universities, but also by the psychological factor of envy. Intellectuals consider themselves to be society's most valuable assets, and look around to find businessmen, entertainers, and sports stars earning vastly more than they do.

They conclude that the market is fundamentally unfair in the way it distributes resources, and resolve to do what they can to destroy it through teaching and writing. The current sorting trend is bound to increase the likelihood of professors in top schools being filled with envy toward capitalism. And the vast gulf that separates academic and business elites will grow ever wider.

Now, the university faces a problem of an additional kind: not only leftism but also a general dumbing down. If the economic boom continues, and students continue to enter the marketplace rather than grad school, elite universities will no longer be the place where the best and brightest dwell.

This process of dumbing down has actually been going on for some time, and not only because the smartest are entering the business world. Affirmative action and politically correct degrees (women's studies, black studies, Chicano studies, etc.) have dramatically diminished the prestige of graduate schools in general. And with police-state-style thought control and severe restrictions on intellectual life in general, campuses have lost the air of freedom that is necessary for creating a vibrant intellectual life.

The people who are inclined to put up with this are not going to be the fighters and the independent thinkers. Rather, they are the types who appreciate an environment of safe leftism, enjoy conformism to rigid socialist ideologies, and fear and loathe the rough and tumble of the market economy. They are inclined to do what they are told, adopt a conventional PC curriculum that avoids all controversy, and otherwise play it safe.

On the one hand, this kind of stagnation is a benefit to colleges because it permits them to squeeze out the troublemakers. On the other hand, their product will become less and less attractive to smarter people, and the social status of professors will decline. The decline will tend to feed on itself, with inferior teachers teaching inferior students at universities that once had the best reputations.

Thank goodness, the sad situation in elite schools is not representative of all universities. I know a historian who had impeccable credentials but had a hard time finding a position that reflected his qualifications. There was no other reason than that he was the wrong color (white), wrong sex (male), and held the wrong political views (conservative and free market). He ended up at a small college hardly anyone has heard of. On the other hand, he was astonished to find a very competent faculty filled with like-minded colleagues. It was a veritable haven of white male conservatives who had been shut out of name universities!

His story is a common one. Why did he and the thousands like him decide to pursue the academic life despite all the frustrations, low pay, and degrading treatment from the elites of the profession? Because they have a calling to teach and research, and can do no other. That is the original idea of the academic life, while the original idea of the university was a place set aside where others can benefit from their wisdom. In the long run, it is the body of thought taught by these idealists that will shape our world.

If the flight from elite academia ends up leaving only drones in place, who end up teaching only those whom the market rejected, while the brilliant few find alternative means of doing the hard and essential work of advancing knowledge, it will have been all to the good.

SECTION 6: CIVIL RIGHTS

38.

HOW GOVERNMENT PROTECTS POTENTIAL WORKPLACE KILLERS*

On July 8, Doug Williams, a 48-year-old assembly-line worker at the Lockheed Martin plant in Meridian, Mississippi, walked out of a meeting with managers on how to get along with fellow employees—just the sort of meeting encouraged by federal law to assure that everyone appreciates the merit of diversity and that no one is being harassed in the workplace. Minutes later, he returned with shotgun and a rifle. He shot two people in the room and three more on the factory floor. Then, he killed himself.

Co-workers were not surprised. He had long threatened people. He had been to anger counseling. He made it known that he was mad as heck that black employees were getting promotions and he wasn't. Only last month, he put on a KKK hood and paraded around the plant. Told to take it off, he chose instead to leave the factory and stay away for five days.

Perhaps it is too much to speculate that federally mandated affirmative action (practiced with great élan in companies like Lockheed, which specialize in federal contracts) pushed this

---

*July 2003

189

guy over the edge. Even so, some reasonable questions present themselves:

Why would a company continue to employ a person who posed a potential threat to others?

Why wasn't he fired rather than put through seminars on working and playing well with others?

In short, what the heck were his supervisors thinking in continuing to keep him around?

There's a short answer: The Americans with Disabilities Act, a law passed 13 years ago by the first Bush administration that protects disabled people from job discrimination. It may have sounded like a good idea. The idea of turning someone down for a job he or she can otherwise do solely on grounds that he or she is in a wheelchair offends our sense of fairness.

People often feign surprise at how the law has come to be a lawsuit machine while doing virtually nothing to help the disabled. As the economists at the Federal Reserve Bank of San Francisco concluded,

> at the end of the 1990s, despite seven straight years of substantial economic growth, a smaller fraction of working-age individuals with disabilities worked and a larger fraction relied on federal disability income transfers than ever before.

But anyone who looked at the law closely knew what was going on. The definition of disability was so vague that it clearly represented yet another massive encroachment of the government and its courts into the workplace. It made the disabled more expensive and more risky to hire. It made them more difficult to fire, and hence less likely to be hired. If anything, workplace discrimination against them has increased rather than decreased. Employers would rather find sneaky ways to keep them at bay than to risk unending lawsuits.

And then there are the absurdities. You see, the ADA covers people with mental impairments. This includes, according to the EEOC's online guide, "any mental or psychological disorder, such as . . . emotional or mental illness," examples of which include major depression, anxiety disorders, obsessive compulsive disorder, schizophrenia, and "personality disorders."

The ADA covers such disabilities if they "limit one or more major life activities" such as "learning, thinking, concentrating, interacting with others." The disability is covered if it

> significantly restricts the condition, manner, or duration which an individual can perform a life activity, as compared to the average person in the general population.

The more severe the disability, the more bound the employer is to accommodate it. Take, for example, the worker who is consistently hostile to fellow employees and bosses. The more hostile he is, the more the worker enjoys a right not to be fired: "consistently high levels of hostility, social withdrawal, or failure to communicate when necessary," is a sign of disability. If they are "long-term or potentially long-term, as opposed to temporary," it is enough "to justify a finding of ADA disability."

Can the employer ask about the existence of an emotional or psychiatric disability before hiring the person? The EEOC is unequivocal: "No."

What if the employer begins to suspect that the person poses a direct threat? In this case, the employer can inquire, but such inquiries

> must not exceed the scope of the specific medical condition and its effect on the employee's ability, with or without reasonable accommodation, to perform essential job functions or to work without posing a direct threat.

So let's say an employer suspects he has a nutcase working at the factory. Once all the bureaucratic hurdles have been cleared, can the employer fire the guy? Not yet. The employer must first make "reasonable accommodation."

> For example, room dividers, partitions, or other soundproofing or visual barriers between workspaces may accommodate individuals who have disability-related limitations in concentration.

What is reasonable accommodation? The courts are still working on that. They'll get back to you in a few years. Or maybe never.

Does this mean that violent people are protected in civil-rights law? It would seem so. But the EEOC says otherwise: "nothing in the ADA prevents an employer from maintaining a workplace free of violence or threats of violence." An employer can discipline an employee, to be sure, so long as discipline is "job-related for the position in question and consistent with business necessity."

What if a person poses a "direct threat" to others? Can he be fired then, simply as a safety precaution? The EEOC purports to explain that a person who is a direct threat can be fired.

See if you can follow this:

> Under the ADA, an employer may lawfully exclude an individual from employment for safety reasons only if the employer can show that employment of the individual would pose a "direct threat." Employers must apply the "direct threat" standard uniformly and may not use safety concerns to justify exclusion of persons with disabilities when persons without disabilities would not be excluded in similar circumstances.

> The EEOC's ADA regulations explain that "direct threat" means "a significant risk of substantial harm to the health or safety of the individual or others that cannot be eliminated or reduced by reasonable accommodation." A "significant" risk is a high, and not just a slightly increased, risk. The determination that an individual poses a "direct threat" must be based on an individualized assessment of the individual's present ability to safely perform the functions of the job, considering a reasonable medical judgment relying on the most current medical knowledge and/or the best available objective evidence. With respect to the employment of individuals with psychiatric disabilities, the employer must identify the specific behavior that would pose a direct threat. An individual does not pose a "direct threat" simply by virtue of having a history of psychiatric disability or being treated for a psychiatric disability.

Thus do we see that there is a way that a violent person can be tossed out on his ear, provided all similarly behaving nondisabled people have been and would be treated the same way, the threat is significant and high, that the threat is truly job related, and that it cannot be reasonably accommodated using the newest and best available medical knowledge.

In short, if you are preparing to fire someone on grounds that he or she is dangerous, you had better have darn good legal counsel! Chances are you will be sued. Chances are that you will have to settle either with a large cash payment or go to court. You might win in court or you might not. In either case, you will have expended massive resources just to exercise what the free enterprise system should guarantee in the first place: the right to hire and fire.

So, yes, in the end, it might be true that Lockheed could have fired Doug Williams. But who is to say for sure? In retrospect, it is clear that he was a direct threat. By the standard of good sense, it is clear he was a threat before. But that is not enough. The whole bias of the law works against any definitive judgment to prevent violence before it happens. The culture of the workplace, especially in large corporations, is to overlook oddities, even potentially violent oddities, accommodate them in whatever way, or otherwise keep good sense on the shelf in the name of human rights.

We have no way of knowing whether Williams's supervisors wanted to fire the guy but feared doing so on grounds of the ADA. But it would make sense if Lockheed's managers were far more attentive to the particularities of the law than the safety of the workplace. That is precisely what laws such as the ADA have done. In this case, a federal law ostensibly devoted to making sure employers respect the dignity of life has cost five lives. It has surely cost American employers the right to keep their payrolls free of nutcases who would snap and mow down their fellow workers.

There is no way that the federal government can spell out the particularities of every employment situation and regulate them with an eye toward economic and managerial good sense. If the EEOC did fix up its regs to make it easier to fire the likes of Williams, other cases will come along that similarly cry out for reform. There is really only one alternative to the ADA: let the employers manage their workplace, and let employees choose among them.

39.
THE TRIAL OF LOTT*

Following the media campaign against Senator Trent Lott, many people were astonished by the Senator's willingness to jettison all political principle for the sake of saving his status as Majority Leader. Why would a conservative Republican suddenly find himself embracing the full panoply of the left-wing racial agenda and flog himself so mercilessly?

Consider what a Chinese political prisoner under Maoist Communism had to say about the role of self-criticism, denunciation, and confession:

> It doesn't take a prisoner long to lose his self-confidence. Over the years Mao's police have perfected their interrogation method. . . . Their aim is not so much to make you invent non-existent crimes, but to make you accept your ordinary life, as you led it as rotten and sinful and worthy of punishment, since it did not accord with the police's conception of how life should be led. The basis of their success is despair, the prisoner's perception that he is utterly and hopelessly and forever at the mercy of his jailers. He has no defense, since his arrest is absolute and unquestionable proof of his guilt. (*The Black Book of Communism*, p. 510)

Such means are the tried and true method of assuring the supremacy of an ideology. Lott was accused of segregationism

---

*December 2002

and racism for saying something kind about the presidential bid of Senator Strom Thurmond in 1948. Most likely, his comments reflected an affection for the attempt by the South to resist federal encroachments against the liberties and rights of the states after the Second World War. But you would never know that by listening to either Lott or his critics. As under Mao, the accused was already guilty as charged so he had only one right: to repent of his errors. If he appeared insufficiently repentant, the attacks were renewed until the accused was completely destroyed.

Even at the outset, it was clear that no effort would be made to understand the deeper issues involved about the history or political issues. There would be no tolerance for anyone who might say that Thurmond's bid reflected a just political aspiration, that his States' Rights Party might have had a point to make that extended beyond race hatred. The thousand-year struggle for liberty made possible by decentralized political orders was swept away or completely recast in light of racial politics—as if the United States had not been founded as anything but a unified state, and as if this conclusion were never in question.

No, there was one goal at the outset of Lott's trial: extract a confession, an apology, and bring about what the Chinese communists called "rectification": a visible sign that one accepts the reality of one's ideological apostasy, and declares publicly that the regime is right and you are wrong. Anything short of that is regarded as a personal indictment and further evidence that you, as the enemy, must be vanquished.

Even so, perhaps it is worth examining the deeper historical and political issues. It is not true that supporting the Dixiecrats in 1948 necessarily reflected a racial bias against blacks. The real issue was not race; it was the place of freedom and federalism—concepts that are apparently not understood by the national press or by any of Lott's critics right and left—in the post-war period. Both parties were split on the direction they would take after long years of depression and war. The industrial planning of the New Deal was shocking enough, but the wartime planning of the Second World War was as bad as the fascist governments the United States opposed on the battlefront.

The crucial political question concerned the direction the country would take in the future—pushing headlong into the welfare-warfare state or returning to founding principles—just as the country faced this same question in 1989 at the end of the Cold War. In 1948, the key domestic question concerned the uses of federal power for purposes of social planning and redistribution. On the international front, the Marshall Plan had already been passed, shocking many in both parties who had a principled opposition to foreign aid and international management on this scale. And Truman and his advisers were already embroiling the United States in a Cold War against Russia, a government that had been a close US ally only a few years earlier.

Many Democrats had hoped that FDR would be an aberration—a man who betrayed his 1932 election promises (for a balanced budget, for limited government, for lower taxes, for peace) for personal power. A strong faction hoped for a return to the older style Democratic Party that favored free trade, decentralization, peace, and other Jeffersonian policies.

Harry Truman, meanwhile, was untested by any presidential election until 1948. It was unclear until the convention that year which part of the party would be dominant. What the limited-government faction had underestimated was the extent to which the party had come to depend on vote-buying through welfare schemes for its very lifeblood, and many in the libertarian-oriented faction of the Democratic Party saw the foray into civil-rights politics as nothing more than an extension of the same scheme.

A similar split had emerged in the Republican Party, whose Congressional wing had largely resisted the New Deal and the drive to war. One faction hoped to deep-six this "negative" attitude toward consolidation—pushing for the Cold War and for retaining the New Deal—while another faction favored free enterprise, spending cuts, and small government at home and abroad. The issue came to a head in 1952 with the great battle between Dwight Eisenhower and Robert Taft, a battle that was won (through the basest convention trickery) by the nationalist-consolidationist faction.

Triangulation was taking place all around. Truman had hoped to outflank the nationalist and anticommunist faction of the GOP with his Cold War rhetoric, while the militarists within the GOP hoped that an embrace of the welfare-warfare state would win enough votes to break the stranglehold that the Democrats held over the White House. Neither of the dominant branches of either party saw much electoral advantage in calling for radical cuts in government or returning to a foreign policy of peace and free trade. The vote-buying and industrial subsidies of the previous twenty years had reduced the Jeffersonians in both parties to an extent that few but the most pessimistic observers had anticipated.

J. Strom Thurmond's faction of the Democratic Party bolted after it became clear who would dominate the party. It founded an optional party that it hoped could compete, which of course it could not (as most every third party discovers within a system constructed by the dominant two). Today it is said that Thurmond's party pandered to the racist elements in the South, but it is more correct to say that the dominant factions of the major parties were pandering to the always-present desire on the part of pressure groups for special favors from the federal government.

Thurmond's party announced its first principle in the platform of the States Rights Party:

> We believe that the protection of the American people against the onward march of totalitarian government requires a faithful observance of Article X of the American Bill of Rights which provides that: "the powers not delegated to the United States by the Constitution, nor prohibited by it to the states, are reserved to the states respectively, or to the people."

A long train of abuses and usurpations of power by unfaithful leaders who are alien to the Democratic parties of the states here represented has become intolerable to those who believe in the preservation of constitutional government and individual liberty in America.

The Executive Department of the government is promoting the gradual but certain growth of a totalitarian state by domination and control of a political minded Supreme Court. (Citing, e.g., "national domination and control of submerged oil-bearing lands in California.")

By asserting paramount Federal rights in these instances a totalitarian concert has been promulgated which threatens the integrity of the states and the basic rights of their citizens.

We believe that the Constitution of the United States is the greatest charter of human liberty ever conceived by the mind of man. We oppose all efforts to invade or destroy the rights vouchsafed by it to every citizen of this republic. We stand for social and economic justice, which we believe can be vouchsafed to all citizens only by a strict adherence to our Constitution and the avoidance of any invasion or destruction of the constitutional rights of the states and individuals. We oppose the totalitarian, centralized, bureaucratic government and the police state called for by the platforms of the Democratic and Republican conventions.

We stand for the checks and balances provided by the three departments of our Government. We oppose the usurpation of the legislative function by the executive and judicial departments. We unreservedly condemn the effort to establish nation-wide a police state in this republic that would destroy the last vestige of liberty enjoyed by a citizen.

We favor home rule, local self-government, and a minimum interference with individual rights.

The above points, which are more prominent in the platform than anything concerning race, are eminently defensible by any libertarian or conservative. But in the current climate, a taboo exists against expressing any regret for the astonishing centralization of power in American politics since World War II. Question that, and you will have few friends and legions of opportunistic enemies. We are supposed to accept this reality, which stands on its head every hope of the Founding Fathers.

It is nonetheless true that federalism of the sort mentioned in this platform is the essential genius of the American republican system of government—its great contribution to the modern political experience, as Lord Acton noted. In American law, federalism is guaranteed by the enumerated powers in the Constitution, which restrict the federal government to only a few functions while leaving the rest to the states and the people, as the Tenth Amendment says.

In the American lexicon, federalism is the same as the Jeffersonian phrase "states' rights," which means that the states as legal entities have rights over the federal government. "The true theory of our Constitution," wrote Jefferson, "is surely the wisest and best—that the states are independent as to everything within themselves, and united as to everything respecting foreign nations."

As James Madison said, summing up the American structure of government:

> The powers delegated . . . to the federal government are few and defined. Those which are to remain in the state governments are numerous and indefinite.

FDR himself affirmed his dedication to this idea in 1930:

> As a matter of fact and law, the governing rights of the states are all of those which have not been surrendered to the national government by the Constitution or its amendments.

In this way, America was different from Prussia or any other nation-state of the old world that had a unitary state apparatus that exercised sole sovereignty. In American federalism, we saw the embodiment of divided sovereignty, political tolerance, and decentralization—the expression of the liberal conviction that society can manage itself and needs no central plan. As for government, its power should be close to the people and shared only by consent. As Montesquieu wrote:

> this form of government is a convention by which several small states agree to become members of a large one, which they intend to form. . . . As this government is composed of small republics, it enjoys the internal happiness of each.

No, the system of federalism and states' rights does not lead to perfection in every way. But it provides a check on corruption and despotism from the center, and the political tolerance of federalism permits flexibility and competition between legal regimes, which provides a check on petty despotisms. It is this very flexibility that would have best handled the issue of race relations in the period after World War II. It was an enormous error to scrap foundational American principles for the political expediency of the moment, and we've paid a big price in freedom for having done so.

As for segregation, the platform of the States Rights Party did endorse it, but it also endorsed "the constitutional right to choose one's associates" (free association, once a pillar of liberal theory) as well as the right to "accept private employment without governmental interference, and to earn one's living in any lawful way." When was the last time a party platform so unreservedly embraced liberty as a principle of the labor market? These principles have been overthrown by the regime, and now what was once taken for granted as part of the fabric of liberty is neither discussed nor understood.

In 1948, most Southerners, however, understood that the federal government wanted to do more than end legally sponsored segregation at the state level, which was on its way out in any case. They understood that the federal government wanted to take charge of their schools and communities, not only ending legal segregation but also managing their lives by prohibiting voluntary choice in the exercise of private property rights. They worried about the effects of a new social planning attempt, complete with mandatory and subsidized demographic upheavals. This is what they predicted and this is what occurred.

So intense was the campaign for centralization that in 1950, journalist John T. Flynn wrote of the "War on the South," which he described as an attempt to use racial conflict to shore up support for the New Deal planning state. And let's not forget, too, that the South was put through a cruel "Reconstruction" after the Civil War; 83 years earlier, the right of self-government was taken from the South and military governments were installed. All people everywhere resent imperial government intrusion, but Southerners could speak with experience on the question. That memory was still alive in 1948, and the threat that another round was coming was everywhere perceived.

Instead of allowing segregation to fade away, the federal government usurped state functions and created a very ugly backlash in the South, pitting blacks against whites and vice versa. This has resulted in unnecessary racial conflict and the consolidation of federal power. This has not been helpful to American race relations, and it has taken away essential freedoms and property rights from all Americans.

Today we see every manner of socialistic meddling imposed on the states, not just in the South but in all states and against all businesses and communities and schools. The assumption is that DC managers know best how to bring about social cooperation, and that people cannot be trusted in their daily lives to treat each other humanely. Instead, we are told, they need inhumane bureaucracies to tell communities how to run their schools, to tell businesspeople whom to hire and whom not to fire, to tell cities how much public housing to build and how much to distribute by way of welfare dollars.

Would the country have been better off had the Dixiecrats won in 1948? Of course this is conjectural history, and Lott was wrong to imply that we can know the answer with certainty. If Thurmond's party behaved the way the Democrats and Republicans typically behave—betraying election promises in favor of building the welfare-warfare state—the party might not have made any difference at all.

However, we can say that the country would have been far better off by preserving freedom and federalism rather than empowering a managerial, therapeutic state that today intrudes itself into every aspect of public and private life, often in the name of quelling racial conflict but in fact only creating more.

In every state, there is racial conflict, and we should hope and pray and work for an end to it and the laws that inflame it. But it does not compare to the suspicion and anger that dominate race relations in Washington, DC, a place where the racial divide is obvious to anyone with eyes to see. In Washington, the home of the people who claim they know what is best for everyone in the country, crime and poverty are higher, and the races can't manage the everyday civilities that Southerners take for granted.

Lott might have apologized for any misunderstanding his remarks created, owing to the lack of historical understanding of our nation's press corps and punditry class. Moreover, there is no evidence that Lott had any clue about these underlying issues. Like the jailed dissident in Mao's China, he embraced his guilt and pleaded for mercy. But no one should have to apologize for being a defender of freedom and federalism, and an opponent of the Leviathan state, which uses any excuse, including race, to trample on the essential rights of all.

40.

THE ECONOMICS OF
MARTIN LUTHER KING, JR.*

We're supposed to venerate Martin Luther King, Jr., but that's not easy for a believer in economic liberty. Time and again, King called on us to "question the capitalistic economy" and "restructure America."

"You see, my friends," said King, "you begin to ask the question, 'Who owns the oil?' You begin to ask the question, 'Who owns the iron ore?' You begin to ask the question, 'Why is it that people have to pay water bills in a world that is two-thirds water?'"

Privately owned oil and iron ore mean rational use, whereas government-owned resources, as in the USSR, mean chaos and poverty.

Although America's water systems—municipalized or regulated—are not exactly free enterprise in action, we have to pay for water for the same reason we have to pay for anything valuable. Fresh, clean water is scarce, and the price system ensures that it will not be squandered, while encouraging further production.

When government intervenes in the price system, as it does to sell water to agriculture at below-market rates, the results are waste, and shortages elsewhere.

When the Soviets invaded Afghanistan, they didn't collectivize agriculture, but they did collectivize agricultural water distribution. Within months, there was no water at all, as centuries-old private distribution channels silted up.

Only a capitalistic water system—with private property rights in water and freely adjusting prices—can ensure that

---

*February 1991

there is enough water for all who want it, instead of allocation through nonprice political battles with the most powerful pressure groups winning out.

King had no use for the price system, calling it "violence" responsible for blacks paying "higher consumer prices" than whites. "Do you know," he asked, "that a can of beans almost always costs a few cents more in grocery chain stores located in the Negro ghetto than in a store of that same chain located in the upper-middle-class suburbs?"

This led, said King, to black "disillusionment and bitterness." But why, unless—as a recent *New York Times* poll tells us is more and more the case—blacks believe their plight is the result of a white conspiracy?

In a free market, prices are set by consumers when they buy, or don't buy, a particular product. If storeowners set prices too high, even by a few cents, competitors will make a profit by undercutting them.

The ghetto has far too little of the "cutthroat competition" King so often denounced. Non-black businessmen can be greeted with hostility; rampant street crime is a barrier to entry; widespread welfare blunts the desire to work while encouraging a short-term orientation; and government holds sway to a degree found elsewhere in this country only on Indian reservations, which are also poverty stricken.

King, however, believed in government sway, calling capitalism a system "permitting necessities to be taken from the many to give luxuries to the few." The "profit motive" has "encouraged smallhearted men to become cold and conscienceless."

What was his alternative? The loss motive?

The profit motive means that resources are not systematically wasted, as under the political motive, and that innovation, entrepreneurship, and hard work are rewarded. Surely this, rather than the reverse as under socialism, is the moral system.

King claimed that the "good and just society is neither the thesis of capitalism nor the antithesis of communism, but a socially conscious democracy which reconciles the truths of individualism and collectivism."

In fact, the good society, upon whose back big government sits like a succubus, is composed of cooperative endeavors from the corporation to the church, from the family to the university. Bureaucratic intrusion weakens and destroys these endeavors, whether it's justified in the name of "socially conscious democracy" or any other high-sounding but low-acting construct.

King favored a "higher synthesis"—part individualism, part collectivism—as in Sweden. But one of the least-known aspects of the antisocialist revolution has been its effect on Sweden, which has been getting poorer and poorer thanks to decades of redistributionism. Today, the people are demanding lower taxes and less government, much to the consternation of the Swedish establishment. As Ludwig von Mises demonstrated, the mixed economy is inherently unstable. It must tend toward either statism or the free market; there is no economically rational way of reconciling the two.

"When machines and computers, profit motives and property rights are considered more important than people, the giant triplets of racism, materialism, and militarism are incapable of being conquered," said King.

Aside from the fact that "The Giant Triplets" sounds like a companion film to "Attack of the Killer Tomatoes," there are enough false dichotomies in that one sentence for a Congressman. Suffice it to say that it is people who build and use machines and computers, which have much improved people's lives; that property rights are the most important people's right, with their absence leading to economic fiasco; and that there's nothing wrong with people desiring material improvements in their lives.

Naturally King disliked that engine of capitalism, the entrepreneur, whom he called responsible for "thousands of working people displaced from their jobs with reduced incomes as a result of automation while the profits of the employers remain intact." Automation, he said, is "skimming off unskilled labor from the industrial force. The displaced are flowing into proliferating service occupations."

The "individual capitalists of the West" also invest "huge sums of money in Asia, Africa, and South America, only to take the profits out with no concern for the social betterment of the countries."

But King was advancing a left-wing myth. Foreign investment in the third world has put bread on the tables of millions impoverished by socialist governments. That is real "social betterment." And automation, i.e., improved technology, raises standards of living.

Electric clothes washers save homemakers much hard labor, and "cost" the jobs of laundry workers, but so what? Homemakers, and society as a whole, are much better off. And so are the laundry workers, who can get better jobs in a more prosperous society.

If automation were evil, we could ban all motorized transportation between New York and Los Angeles, and "create jobs" for drivers of horse-drawn wagons. Does anyone think we'd be better off?

Nor are service jobs less desirable than industrial, although socialists have always been partial to large industrial entities which seem easier to centrally plan, and to unionize.

"The Negroes pressed into these services need union protection, and the union movement needs their membership to maintain its relative strength in the whole society," said King. Yet unions are organized rip-offs, using their privileges to enrich themselves at the expense of nonunion workers and businessmen. By helping bring about a centralized labor market (through minimum wages and closed shops), unions have deliberately injured unskilled workers, many of them black, by shutting them out of the market.

But King had far more in mind than unionism:

> If a city has a 30 percent Negro population, then it is logical to
> assume that Negroes should have at least 30 percent of the

jobs in any particular company, and jobs in all categories rather than only in menial areas.

To bring this about, he wanted "preferential treatment"—a racial test for hiring and firing, promotion and transfer, and all other personnel decisions. How this squared with his dream of a society based on "the content of a person's character" rather than the "color of their skin," he didn't say.

Whether people were working or not, said King, there should be a government-guaranteed "minimum—and livable—income for every American family" as part of a "radical reconstruction of society itself." Nothing else would cure America's "interrelated flaws of racism, poverty, militarism, and materialism."

What good can come of taking the earnings of some families by force, skimming them in DC, and bestowing the remainder on other families? As we have seen all too clearly, welfare makes the economy less efficient, the recipients less independent, the taxed less productive, and the government bigger.

King also advocated massive federal compensation for blacks because "for two centuries the Negro was enslaved," although "all of America's wealth today could not adequately compensate its Negroes for his centuries of exploitation and humiliation."

He didn't mention that the people who would be getting the money were not the victims and the people paying it were not the perpetrators.

Race-based public policies create social conflict, and King knew it. But his answer was more government: a "federal program of public works, retraining, and jobs for all."

The received wisdom on the right these days is that King would have rejected the excesses of the modern civil rights movement. But that clearly isn't the case. Indeed, David Garrow in his Pulitzer Prize-winning biography says that in private gatherings King endorsed "democratic socialism," while making "it clear to close friends that economically speaking he considered himself what he termed a Marxist."

PART III: THE RIGHT

"The real choice isn't between liberty and security;
it is between our security and the state's."

SECTION 1: FASCISM & THE POLICE STATE

41.
THE REALITY OF RED–STATE FASCISM*

Year's end is the time for big thoughts, so here are mine. The most significant socio-political shift in our time has gone almost completely unnoted, and even unnoticed. It is the dramatic shift of the red-state bourgeoisie from leave-us-alone libertarianism, manifested in the Congressional elections of 1994, to almost totalitarian statist nationalism. Whereas the conservative middle class once cheered the circumscribing of the federal government, it now celebrates power and adores the central state, particularly its military wing.

This huge shift has not been noticed among mainstream punditry, and hence there have been few attempts to explain it—much less have libertarians thought about what it implies. My own take is this: the Republican takeover of the presidency combined with an unrelenting state of war, has supplied all the levers necessary to convert a burgeoning libertarian movement into a statist one.

---

*December 2004

The remaining ideological justification was left to, and accomplished by, Washington's kept think tanks, who have approved the turn at every crucial step. What this implies for libertarians is a crying need to draw a clear separation between what we believe and what conservatives believe. It also requires that we face the reality of the current threat forthrightly by extending more rhetorical tolerance leftward and less right-ward.

Let us start from 1994 and work forward. In a stunningly prescient memo, Murray N. Rothbard described the 1994 revolution against the Democrats as follows:

> a massive and unprecedented public repudiation of President Clinton, his person, his personnel, his ideologies and programs, and all of his works; plus a repudiation of Clinton's Democrat Party; and, most fundamentally, a rejection of the designs, current and proposed, of the Leviathan he heads . . . what is being rejected is big government in general (its taxing, mandating, regulating, gun grabbing, and even its spending) and, in particular, its arrogant ambition to control the entire society from the political center. Voters and taxpayers are no longer persuaded of a supposed rationale for American-style central planning. . . . On the positive side, the public is vigorously and fervently affirming its desire to re-limit and de-centralize government; to increase individual and community liberty; to reduce taxes, mandates, and government intrusion; to return to the cultural and social mores of pre-1960s America, and perhaps much earlier than that.

This memo also cautioned against unrelieved optimism, because, Rothbard said, two errors rear their head in most every revolution. First, the reformers do not move fast enough; instead they often experience a crisis of faith and become overwhelmed by demands that they govern "responsibly" rather than tear down the established order. Second, the reformers leave too much in place that can be used by their successors to rebuild the state they worked so hard to dismantle. This permits gains to be reversed as soon as another party takes control.

Rothbard urged dramatic cuts in spending, taxing, and regulation, and not just in the domestic area but also in the military and in foreign policy. He saw that this was crucial to any small-government program. He also urged a dismantling of the federal judiciary on grounds that it represents a clear and present danger to American liberty. He urged the young radicals who were just elected to reject gimmicks like the balanced-budget amendment and the line-item veto, in favor of genuine change. None of this happened of course. In fact, the Republican leadership and pundit class began to warn against "kamikaze missions" and speak not of bringing liberty, but rather of governing better than others.

Foreshadowing what was to come, Rothbard pointed out:

> Unfortunately, the conservative public is all too often taken in by mere rhetoric and fails to weigh the actual deeds of their political icons. So the danger is that Gingrich will succeed not only in betraying, but in conning the revolutionary public into thinking that they have already won and can shut up shop and go home.

The only way to prevent this, he wrote, was to educate the public, businessmen, students, academics, journalists, and politicians about the true nature of what is going on, and about the vicious nature of the bipartisan ruling elites.

The 1994 revolution failed of course, in part because the anti-government opposition was intimidated into silence by the Oklahoma City bombing of April 1995. The establishment somehow managed to pin the violent act of an ex-military man on the right-wing libertarianism of the American bourgeoisie. It was said by every important public official at that time that to be antigovernment was to give aid and support to militias, secessionists, and other domestic terrorists. It was a classic intimidation campaign but, combined with a GOP leadership that never had any intention to change DC, it worked to shut down the opposition.

In the last years of the 1990s, the GOP-voting middle class refocused its anger away from government and leviathan and toward the person of Bill Clinton. It was said that he represented some kind of unique moral evil despoiling the White House. That ridiculous Monica scandal culminated in a pathetic and pretentious campaign to impeach Clinton. Impeaching presidents is a great idea, but impeaching them for fibbing about personal peccadilloes is probably the least justifiable ground. It's almost as if that entire campaign was designed to discredit the great institution of impeachment.

In any case, this event crystallized the partisanship of the bourgeoisie, driving home the message that the real problem was Clinton and not government; the immorality of the chief executive, not his power; the libertinism of the left-liberals and not their views toward government. The much heralded "leave us alone" coalition had been thoroughly transformed into a pure anti-Clinton movement. The right in this country began to define itself not as pro-freedom, as it had in 1994, but simply as antileftist, as it does today.

There are many good reasons to be antileftist, but let us revisit what Mises said in 1956 concerning the antisocialists of his day. He pointed out that many of these people had a purely negative agenda, to crush the leftists and their bohemian ways and their intellectual pretension. He warned that this is not a program for freedom. It was a program of hatred that can only degenerate into statism.

> The moral corruption, the licentiousness and the intellectual sterility of a class of lewd would-be authors and artists is the ransom mankind must pay lest the creative pioneers be prevented from accomplishing their work. Freedom must be granted to all, even to base people, lest the few who can use it for the benefit of mankind be hindered. The license which the shabby characters of the quartier Latin enjoyed was one of the conditions that made possible the ascendance of a few great writers, painters and sculptors. The first thing a genius needs is to breathe free air.

He goes on to urge that antileftists work to educate themselves about economics, so that they can have a positive agenda to displace their purely negative one. A positive agenda of liberty is the only way we might have been spared the blizzard of government controls that were fastened on this country after Bush used the events of 9-11 to increase central planning, invade Afghanistan and Iraq, and otherwise bring a form of statism to America that makes Clinton look *laissez-faire* by comparison. The Bush administration has not only faced no resistance from the bourgeoisie. It has received cheers. And they are not only cheering Bush's re-election; they have embraced tyrannical control of society as a means toward accomplishing their anti-leftist ends.

After September 11, even those whose ostensible purpose in life is to advocate less government changed their minds. Even after it was clear that 9-11 would be used as the biggest pretense for the expansion of government since the stock market crash of 1929, the Cato Institute said that libertarianism had to change its entire focus:

> Libertarians usually enter public debates to call for restrictions on government activity. In the wake of September 11, we have all been reminded of the real purpose of government: to protect our life, liberty, and property from violence. This would be a good time for the federal government to do its job with vigor and determination.

The vigor and determination of the Bush administration have brought about a profound cultural change, so that the very people who once proclaimed hatred of government now advocate its use against dissidents of all sorts, especially against those who would dare call for curbs in the totalitarian bureaucracy of the military, or suggest that Bush is something less than infallible in his foreign-policy decisions. The lesson here is that it is always a mistake to advocate government action, for there is no way you can fully anticipate how government will be used. Nor can you ever count on a slice of the population to be moral in its advocacy of the uses of the police power.

Editor & Publisher, for example, posted a small note the other day about a column written by Al Neuharth, the founder of

USA Today, in which he mildly suggested that the troops be brought home from Iraq "sooner rather than later." The editor of *E&P* was just blown away by the letters that poured in, filled with venom and hate and calling for Neuharth to be tried and locked away as a traitor. The letters compared him with pro-Hitler journalists, and suggested that he was objectively pro-terrorist, choosing to support the Muslim jihad over the US military. Other letters called for Neuharth to get the death penalty for daring to take issue with the Christian leaders of this great Christian nation.

I'm actually not surprised at this. It has been building for some time. If you follow hate-filled websites such as FreeRepublic.com, you know that the populist right in this country has been advocating nuclear holocaust and mass bloodshed for more than a year now. The militarism and nationalism dwarfs anything I saw at any point during the Cold War. It celebrates the shedding of blood, and exhibits a maniacal love of the state. The new ideology of the red-state bourgeoisie seems to actually believe that the United States is God marching on earth—not just godlike, but really serving as a proxy for God Himself.

Along with this goes a kind of worship of the presidency, and a celebration of all things public sector, including egregious laws like the Patriot Act, egregious bureaucracies like the Department of Homeland Security, and egregious centrally imposed regimentation like the No Child Left Behind Act. It longs for the state to throw its weight behind institutions like the two-parent heterosexual family, the Christian charity, the homogeneous community of native-born patriots.

In 1994, the central state was seen by the bourgeoisie as the main threat to the family; in 2004 it is seen as the main tool for keeping the family together and ensuring its ascendancy. In 1994, the state was seen as the enemy of education; today, the same people view the state as the means of raising standards and purging education of its left-wing influences. In 1994, Christians widely saw that Leviathan was the main enemy of the faith; today, they see Leviathan as the tool by which they will guarantee that their faith will have an impact on the country and the world.

Paul Craig Roberts is right:

> In the ranks of the new conservatives, however, I see and experience much hate. It comes to me in violently worded, ignorant and irrational emails from self-professed conservatives who literally worship George Bush. Even Christians have fallen into idolatry. There appears to be a large number of Americans who are prepared to kill anyone for George Bush.

Again:

> Like Brownshirts, the new conservatives take personally any criticism of their leader and his policies. To be a critic is to be an enemy.

In short, what we have alive in the United States is an updated and Americanized fascism. Why fascist? Because it is not leftist in the sense of egalitarian or redistributionist. It has no real beef with business. It doesn't sympathize with the downtrodden, labor, or the poor. It is for all the core institutions of bourgeois life in America: family, faith, and flag. But it sees the state as the central organizing principle of society, views public institutions as the most essential means by which all these institutions are protected and advanced, and adores the head of state as a godlike figure who knows better than anyone else what the country and world needs, and has a special connection to the Creator that permits him to discern the best means to bring it about.

The American Right today has managed to be solidly anti-leftist while adopting an ideology—even without knowing it or being entirely conscious of the change—that is also frighteningly antiliberty.

This reality turns out to be very difficult for libertarians to understand or accept. For a long time, we've tended to see the primary threat to liberty as coming from the left, from the socialists who sought to control the economy from the center.

But we must also remember that the sweep of history shows that there are two main dangers to liberty, one that comes from the left and the other that comes from the right. Europe and Latin America have long faced the latter threat, but its reality is only now hitting us fully.

What is the most pressing and urgent threat to freedom that we face in our time? It is not from the left. If anything, the left has been solid on civil liberties and has been crucial in drawing attention to the lies and abuses of the Bush administration.

No, today, the clear and present danger to freedom comes from the right side of the ideological spectrum, those people who are pleased to preserve most of free enterprise but favor top-down management of society, culture, family, and school, and seek to use a messianic and belligerent nationalism to impose their vision of politics on the world.

There is no need to advance the view that the enemy of my enemy is my friend. However, it is time to recognize that the left today does represent a counterweight to the right, just as it did in the 1950s when the right began to adopt anticommunist militarism as its credo. In a time when the term patriotism means supporting the nation's wars and statism, a libertarian patriotism has more in common with that advanced by *The Nation* magazine:

> The other company of patriots does not march to military time. It prefers the gentle strains of *America the Beautiful* to the strident cadences of *Hail to the Chief* and *The Stars and Stripes Forever*. This patriotism is rooted in the love of one's own land and people, love too of the best ideals of one's own culture and tradition. This company of patriots finds no glory in puffing their country up by pulling others' down. This patriotism is profoundly municipal, even domestic. Its pleasures are quiet, its services steady and unpretentious. This patriotism too has deep roots and long continuity in our history.

Ten years ago, these were "right wing" sentiments; today the right regards them as treasonous.

What should this teach us? It shows that those who saw the interests of liberty as being well served by the politicized proxies of free enterprise alone, family alone, Christianity alone, law and order alone, were profoundly mistaken. There is no proxy for liberty, no cause that serves as a viable substitute, and no movement by any name whose success can yield freedom in our time other than the movement of freedom itself. We need to embrace liberty and liberty only, and not be fooled by groups or parties or movements that only desire a temporary liberty to advance their pet interests.

As Rothbard said in 1965:

> The doctrine of liberty contains elements corresponding with both contemporary left and right. This means in no sense that we are middle-of-the-roaders, eclectically trying to combine, or step between, both poles; but rather that a consistent view of liberty includes concepts that have also become part of the rhetoric or program of right and of left. Hence a creative approach to liberty must transcend the confines of contemporary political shibboleths.

There has never in my lifetime been a more urgent need for the party of liberty to completely secede from conventional thought and established institutions, especially those associated with all aspects of government, and undertake radical intellectual action on behalf of a third way that rejects the socialism of the left and the fascism of the right.

Indeed, the current times can be seen as a training period for all true friends of liberty. We need to learn to recognize the many different guises in which tyranny appears. Power is protean because it must suppress that impulse toward liberty that exists in the hearts of all people. The impulse is there, tacitly waiting for the consciousness to dawn. When it does, power doesn't stand a chance.

42.

WHICH WAY FOR LIBERTY?*

An interview request from a famed center-left publication allowed me to put together some further thoughts on the rise of red-state fascism in America, and the libertarian response. So here are my notes on the topic, prior to publication.

Our times are much like the 1930s, when it was widely assumed that there are only two viable ideological positions: communism or fascism. Liberalism of the old school was considered to be a failure, and not even worth considering.

Why does libertarianism never entirely disappear, despite every attempt to kill it? In part, because a strain of American ideology from the colonial period to the present supports it. Murray N. Rothbard's 4-volume *Conceived in Liberty* demonstrates that the theory and practice of radical libertarian thinking can even be thought of as the very core of American political values.

Just to cite one case, the preachers and religious leaders who spoke out prior to the American Revolution were knowledgeable of and friendly toward the liberal tradition. They cited Locke as freely as they cited the Bible. Americans of all classes resented the smallest intrusions on liberty and property as tyranny itself. After the revolution, we enjoyed some 10 blissful years of near-anarchy under the Articles of Confederation.

This is our heritage. It is also why every president appeals to libertarian ideals to gain public backing. Clinton did, and Bush does as well. They all invoke Jeffersonian rhetoric. The problem is that the middle class continues to be bamboozled by this rhetoric, even as the power elite continues to conspire for ever more money and power.

---

*December 2004

The interests of all classes, not just the middle class, are for liberty. The heartland bourgeoisie is the most supportive of libertarian economics, but it is also the most easily distracted by nationalist and cultural appeals. These days, they tend to back the Republicans. For this reason, they don't notice that the Republicans are actually worse than the Democrats when it comes to expanding government power and shredding all sorts of liberties, including the economic ones.

RETHINKING THE LEFT, FOR NOW

The extent to which the Bush regime owns the conservative middle class is a wonder to behold. Again, it is probably for cultural and nationalist reasons, and not because the typical American household is for slaughtering foreigners, suppressing free speech, and bankrupting the country.

These days you are far more likely to find libertarian sentiments expressed on the left side of the political spectrum: outrage about what's happened to civil liberties, truth-telling about the war, and even disgust at the spending and regulating machine of the Bush regime.

Some of the strongest resistance to American fascism right now comes from black Americans, who have suffered disproportionately in this war. Polls from a year ago show black support for the war dipping below 20 percent. Today it must be even lower. Defense Department studies have expressed alarm that 41 percent fewer blacks are willing to sign up to be fodder, which is why the Army is behind in its recruiting goals.

Women too provide strong resistance to war fever. As more women are drawn to the expectation of a full-time professional life, women voters are also going to increasingly develop a commercial-class consciousness concerning taxes and regulations. The victim mentality that agitates for privilege in the workplace could give way to a free-market feminism. If this is united to a consistent anti-war view, resistance against the state could increase among women.

Also, libertarians increasingly find themselves in sympathy with a range of interest groups they would otherwise oppose.

Many people find themselves in circumstances, for whatever reasons—whether personal difficulties, life choices, or other factors—that bring about associations that fall outside the Bush-approved bourgeois family arrangements. No libertarian can support federal penalties against such people. Freedom of association is a first principle of civilization, and it is a disgrace to see that principle attacked in the name of family values.

Also, the Bush administration wants to feed tax dollars to private schools, religious charities, and handpicked mutual fund companies. Even if the teachers unions, the Religious Left, and the AARP oppose these plans for different reasons, we can't but cheer them on.

I used to complain about the universities and their indoctrination of students in leftist theory. But these days, one has to be grateful that there are at least some pockets of resistance remaining.

It is no accident that both parties make an appeal to libertarian notions about the dangers of power. Love of liberty is what unites us as Americans. Our most important job right now is to work to show how nationalist warmongering, cultural agit-prop, and government belligerence of all sorts work at cross purposes with libertarian ideals.

Also, the left needs to learn a lesson from the Bush regime: the answer to fascism is not socialism but freedom itself. They need to lose whatever romantic attachments to power they still have.

COOPERATING WITH THE STATE

I've been asked many times about the role of a leading DC libertarian think tank and its unfortunate cooperation with the Bush administration. I've always declined to comment, but this interviewer convinced me that it can't be ignored.

The problem is this: In the hours and days after 9-11, the cause of liberty cried out for defenders to stand up and say, "This crime is not a license for government to grab power."

Instead, and notoriously, this libertarian think tank went the other direction and backed the wholly unwarranted invasion of Afghanistan and otherwise offered only utilitarian cautions about the creation of massive new bureaucracies.

To some extent, I can understand the fear factor. In those days, sedition trials didn't seem out of the question. One wrong word and you risked destroying every relationship with government you had worked to achieve for 25 years. But even then, was it really necessary, two months later, for a think-tank spokesman to say that increased public support for the federal government "makes sense" since it is "concentrating on protecting individual rights"?

This was one of many such pronouncements in which this think tank made it clear that it would not stand in the way of what the Bush administration planned. In the meantime, of course, they have further speeded the revolving door between their offices and the government. This is hardly unusual for DC think tanks, but it is especially injurious given the source.

People look for libertarians to provide a principled alternative. When they do not, the perception is that there are no legitimate reasons to resist the state. What's more, the state knows that if the libertarians are not making trouble, the regime can pretty well do what it pleases.

It is in the state's interest to keep a tame libertarian wing alive and thriving for precisely these times. It is for the same reason the state has always courted the church: it needs moral cover from a credible source.

Logrolling with the state also does intellectual damage and harms recruitment among students. It is as if some libertarians want to live up to the leftist caricature of capitalist intellectuals in league with the state, cheering on war and imperialism, and taking money from Wall Street to back corporate boondoggles such as Social Security privatization.

Libertarians Contra Fascism

It is as important for libertarians to be anti-fascist as it is for them to be antisocialist. But first we need to recognize that fascism is a reality, not just a smear term.

What began as expedience in the Bush administration has turned, over time, into a full-blown program. Militarism, of course, is an old Republican standby, useful, for example, during the Cold War to keep the masses distracted from noticing what was happening to their liberty. What makes it different today is how it is united to an overarching ideology, a distinctly right-wing form of central planning, which takes careful thought to understand.

The ideology of the Bush regime is nationalist and culturally conservative. It is consistently antileftist in the sense that it rejects egalitarianism, cultural toleration, free speech, and overt appeals to socialist envy. It is religious and Christian in rhetoric. It makes an appeal for family, country, patriotism, and traditional American values. It is pro-business. It is anti-intellectual. It backs middle-class welfare to the hilt.

Behind the rhetoric you find the iron fist of the state, forcing conformism and regimentation. Bush-style fascism has created a kind of cult of personality too, in which the public is led to believe through hints and nudges that the president has a direct line to God. More than any president in my living memory, he peppers his speeches with personal pronouns: "I will defend America."

What the Bush regime has taught us is that there is a difference between being antileftist and being pro-liberty. They have demonstrated that the threats to liberty emanate not only from leftist thought but also rightist thought in which the state is used to impose a particular view of the good at home and abroad. I don't think the United States has ever had a left-wing president as convinced as the Bush administration is of the ability of government to work miracles.

The confluence of these ideological factors and their success in appealing to the middle class can only prompt us to look at history to find its predecessors. Where do we find right-wing central planning, right-wing warmongering, right-wing justifications for cracking skulls on a global scale? The twentieth century offers many examples of dictatorial anti-left regimes. It is not a stretch to call these fascist or national socialist.

Just as socialism is different in every country, so too is fascism. We don't see the appeal to racial solidarity of the Nazis at work here. The Italian and Spanish cases of interwar right-wing dictatorship come to mind, but there are differences there too. In the case of Chile or pre-Castro Cuba, you had business working with government to monopolize the economy.

So while the Bush case borrows from all of these, it is its own unique variety of fascism: evangelical Christianity and a global crusade, with anti-leftist but pro-statist policies that show complete contempt for individual liberty at home and abroad.

THE BAD SEED ON THE RIGHT

How did conservative intellectuals and activists go from hating big government in the 1990s to loving it and celebrating it today? There is a bad seed in the ideology of American conservatism that spawns power worship. If you can get a group of people to pledge the government flag and sing the murderous *Battle Hymn of the Republic* in their churches, and to take a position on war that is Mark Twain's *War Prayer* come to life, the rest is just a mop-up operation. The Germans too were a very religious and conservative people.

There is also an American precedent. Reagan played the war card to great effect, and Nixon manipulated the cultural issues to his advantage. FDR, Wilson, and Lincoln demonstrated that presidents can ignore the Bill of Rights in wartime, and historians have faithfully celebrated their legacies. Bush invokes this American tradition and thereby taps into the form of patriotism inherent in conservative ideology. It is as cynical as it is effective.

We will have to wait to see what follows the Bush regime to discover the closest historical analogy. Is he a Nicholas II who will inspire a bloody backlash of left-wing dictatorship? Will his successor be even worse? Or is he a Pinochet who inspires revulsion against militarism and dictatorship of all sorts, so that his rule will be eventually followed by normalcy, liberalism, and peaceful commercialism?

THE ROLE OF THE NEOCONSERVATIVES

I'm actually of the opinion that the "neo" part of conservatism has been overplayed. The problem is really just plain old conservatism. But speaking as a matter of history, the neoconservatives made two unique contributions to conservative ideology. They convinced conservatives and Republicans to make their peace with the domestic welfare and regulatory state. And they convinced the same groups that democracy represents a political ideal that can and should be imposed on the world.

American fascism doesn't need these two additives to exist and thrive, but the inclusion of them helped round out the ideology, and helped it become particularly dangerous for the world.

More and more, I fear that the Bush administration is doing terrible ideological damage, demolishing what remained of the old liberal impulse in the middle class and shoring up support for imperialist practices in the post-Cold War world.

The allure of Bush has corrupted evangelicals, homeschoolers, the pro-family movement, the pro-life movement, the tax-cut lobbies, the gun lobbies—all these groups that hated Washington only the day before yesterday are suddenly the storm troopers of the regime. Every day that goes by, the resistance to power on the right weakens, even as it strengthens only marginally on the left.

FUTURE PROSPECTS

The libertarian tradition stretches from the ancient world through the Middle Ages to our own day. But I do think we are living through a high point in intellectual development and recruitment. The body of theoretical work is vast and the intellectuals are hardened and ready for battle. The web and blogosphere give us the means to compete in the world of ideas as never before.

There is no sure blueprint for success other than for libertarians to do what each individually does best, whether that means teaching students, organizing anti-war rallies, writing large books on technical economic topics, or tirelessly managing a compelling blog.

I'm wary of all formal alliances but I do think libertarians need to be strategically flexible and entrepreneurial in finding intellectual allies, even if it means admitting that far better arguments are being made by *CounterPunch* than by *National Review*.

What desperately needs to be rethought is this tendency of libertarians to avert their eyes from the reality of what's going on at places like *National Review.* Their main dishes consist of calling for ever more war, approving the killing of civilians, backing the surveillance state, and even torture. Libertarians have traditionally provided the side dishes that call for petty deregulatory measures and tax cuts. This really must stop.

The libertarian revolution will come when we least expect it, and it will unfold in a way we cannot fully anticipate. In the mid 1980s, everyone assumed that the Soviet empire would last forever. Five years later, it was gone without a trace. So too, the expectation of eternal world rule by Washington, DC, could evaporate very quickly.

43.

SLOUCHING TOWARD STATISM*

Which is a greater cause of cultural and moral decline: the private sector or the government? Asked another way, which is doing more to promote a return to civilized social norms: the market or the central state? The answer highlights a dividing line between left and right.

Robert Bork's book *Slouching Towards Gomorrah* provokes this query. He chronicles a dizzy array of depressing cultural data that even left-liberals can't ignore. His thesis is that civilization is slipping through our fingers, and he's probably right. However, his suggestions for change require new forms of government intervention, a grave error that dooms his analysis.

Bork has confused the cause with the cure. It's government policy, not the private sector, that has caused social collapse by politicizing culture in the first place. Whether it's fostering welfarism, backing ugly art and music, punishing society's natural elites with income and inheritance taxes, or shortening time horizons through persistent inflation, the government has debased tastes, subsidized moral squalor, and dumbed down social norms.

Before we put government in charge of cultural uplift, consider that prototype of government social and cultural hegemony: the military base. Once seen as model communities of discipline and moral high standards, bases have recently been rocked by revelations of widespread sexual impropriety. This hardly surprises anyone who's spent time in or around the military.

Young people are put in distant places where they face no supervision from family or an organic community. They have

_____

*January 1997

little work to do and an abundance of discretionary income. Their housing, food, medical care, and clothing are provided at no charge by the government. Nobody need plan, for example, to come up with next month's rent.

The grayness and regimentation of the military base mask a deep debasement. Illegal drug use is rampant, on and off the base, and has long involved more than half of the enlisted men (recent declines in reported drug use measure only a rise in dishonesty). Alcoholism is more than double civilian levels. Tattooing is normal, gambling is rampant, and in its discount stores, the US military is the biggest purveyor of pornography in the world.

Go to any military base in the country and look at the kinds of outlying enterprises taxpayers unwittingly support. Once-nice communities have been turned into magnets for nude dancing, prostitution, and every manner of sexual profiteering.

Look at Georgia's Fort Benning. Apart from the military, the area is populated by traditional people with traditional morals. Yet along the main drag, you pass dozens of brightly lit sex parlors, an alarming sight in the Deep South. The military here is a cultural cancer that lives off the taxpayer. It's no surprise that the military is riddled with sexual abuse: in their off-hours, these guys are feeding our tax dollars to naked performers. It reflects the absence of chivalry inherent in all government operations.

Other businesses popular around military bases are pawn shops and the sort of car dealers that cater to people who don't pay their debts. That reflects another dirty secret of the military: live-for-the-moment attitudes and bad credit are typical, as in any welfare culture.

Relieved of the burdens of making themselves productive, exercising economic choices, or managing finances, the troops in these bases tend to collapse into a state-of-nature barbarism, despite the best efforts of a few officers.

Conservatives like Bork, who complain about the culture, should take notice of this, but as avid supporters of the warfare state, they carefully avert their eyes.

Now consider the other side of the question: can the private sector rescue us from a Borkian fate? Left-liberals like to cite Disney to show that free enterprise is also a social menace. They say Disney preys on kids' voracious material appetites, wrecks and trivializes classic literature, and erects enormous monuments to the indulgence of pleasure.

There's no need to defend Disney's more recent animated movies (let alone those released under subsidiary labels). For example, the pagan environmentalism and anti-European propaganda of Pocahontas are unbearable for anyone who knows economics or history. Nobody claimed the private sector produces only what is beautiful and true.

However tacky some of Disney's products are, remember this: the company has no power of its own. It only profits when it succeeds in persuading the buying public to purchase its products. The tastes of the consuming public are the driving force behind every product the company produces, and not the reverse. If people decided not to buy, Disney's market power would instantly collapse.

Moreover, the real triumph of Disney has nothing to do with its movies. This corporation, founded by a hard-core believer in free markets, and a cultural reactionary to boot, has demonstrated new frontiers of private-property creativity. It has erected entire communities of perfect order and freedom organized on the principles of free enterprise.

Disney World is 45 square miles, an area the size of San Francisco. The rides are the least interesting part. Disney World contains upwards of 300 retail stores, plus nature preserves, streams and lakes, nature trails, recreation areas, yacht clubs, resorts, beach clubs, golf courses, office space, and campsites. There are 12,000 rooms available for rent, and total employment is 35,000, most of them young people who behave themselves because they have to.

Infrastructure like roads and bridges are entirely private, as are police services, fire protection, sewage, and trash disposal. Despite having no taxes or mandates, and being entirely free from outside zoning, this massive park is arguably the best "governed" place on earth. There is no crime, no vandalism, and no sexual profiteering. There are no gangs, no slums, no homeless bums, no panhandlers, and no loiterers. Because it is private, every inch is cared for.

If you're looking to restore the old days of charming architecture and safe, clean streets, look to the Disney-created town of Celebration, Florida. Again, it is entirely private. Ten minutes south of the Magic Kingdom, it is a bustling place that will soon be home to 20,000 people. New houses are grabbed up instantly, as are spots in the new private school. There's no cultural rot here. How interesting that it's become the target of left-wing attacks for "artificiality."

The economics literature is always fretting about "public goods" that markets supposedly can't produce, including police protection and infrastructure. Nonsense, said Disney, and proceeded to demonstrate how orderly a micro-society can be when there's no government to push property owners around.

Indeed, Disney World points the way toward solving most of our social and cultural troubles: put more property in private hands. It has even shown us how the immigration problem can be handled. Disney World attracts 30 million visitors per year without disruption.

As economist Fred Foldvary points out, Disney shows that the less government intervenes, the more private enterprise can satisfy human wants; supposed "public goods" are no exception.

The stark contrast between the ordered liberty of Disney World and the deep corruption of the military base is no accident. These two communities demonstrate, in contrasting microcosms, the difference between the market's means of social organization and the government's.

Yet micro-secessionism isn't the only way the market overcomes cultural disintegration. Wal-Mart is hated by the left, but it too has become a source of cultural uplift. As the nation's largest distributor of compact discs, it supervises everything that appears on its shelves. Producers must take out degrading lyrics, electronically mask dirty words, and supply clean cover art. This approach is not for everyone. But Wal-Mart saw a market niche and filled it. Only capitalism allows that.

Our society may be slouching toward Gomorrah, but government is the least likely institution to reverse the trend. The free market not only gives us prosperity, it can also make us better people by requiring and rewarding old-fashioned virtues like thrift, prudence, courage, and stewardship. Government, which has made us so much poorer by its invasions of private property, has also wrecked the culture.

44.
ECONOMIC IGNORANCE*

The essence of the economic order is the price system. Without it, as Ludwig von Mises demonstrated in 1920, society is doomed to mass starvation.

Even the KGB and the Gulag couldn't entirely wipe out the price system, so the USSR managed to stagger along, but only through suffering and bloodshed.

Our own Gosplan, the US Congress, hasn't been as extreme, thanks to the American people and our traditions of liberty. But it's still the biggest collection of economic meddlers and ignoramuses west of Moscow.

When the price system functions freely, it brings supply and demand into rough equality, ensuring that resources are put to their most-valued uses. To the extent that government meddles with prices, it creates waste, hampers entrepreneurship, and makes people poorer. That's true with energy and natural

---

*October 1990

resources; perverting the price system even makes our drug problems worse.

If tomatoes—for whatever reason—become scarcer, their price goes up, which tells consumers to eat less. If more tomatoes come on the market, their price goes down, telling consumers they can eat more. Prices thus constitute a system of resource conservation.

But Congressmen pretend—exactly like Soviet central planners—to know economic values without prices, as we can see in the recent frenzy over oil prices. They denounced "price gouging" while planning tax gouging, including new energy taxes designed to raise the price of gasoline!

The recent hysteria over African elephant tusks was another problem of prices and property rights. If people were allowed to raise elephants and sell their tusks—as even the socialist government of Zimbabwe pointed out—there would be no more and no fewer elephant tusks than there should be. The same principle applies to all other resources. If left in common ownership, there will be misuse. If put in private hands, we will have the right amount: supply will meet demand.

An example of market response in the animal market was the Cayman Turtle Farm in the British West Indies. The green sea turtle was considered endangered, thanks to overharvesting due to common ownership. The farm was able to hatch eggs and bring the hatchlings to maturity at a far higher rate than in nature. Its stock grew to 80,000 green turtles. But the environmentalists hated the Cayman Turtle Farm, since in their view it is morally wrong to profit from wildlife, and they drove the farm out of business. The green turtle is again on the endangered species list.

Left-liberals justify government intervention in the price system because of "public goods" and "externalities."

A public good is supposed to be something we all want, but can't get unless government provides it. Environmentalists claim everyone wants national parks, for example, but the market won't provide them, so the government must. But how can we know, independent of the market, that everyone does want these expensive parks? Or how many parks of what sort?

We could take a survey, but that doesn't tell us the intensity of demand. More important, it's not enough to know that people want, for example, diamonds; we would have to know if they are willing to give up other things to obtain them, and we can only know that by watching their actions in a free market.

If we realize that only the market can give us economic information, the alleged problem of public goods disappears. Absent government prohibitions and subsidies, or competition from "free" parks, the market will ensure that we have exactly the number and type of parks that the American people want, and are willing to pay for.

An externality is a side effect. Your neighbors' attractive new garden is a positive externality; their barking dog is a negative one. One is a blessing, the other an irritant, but you voluntarily purchase neither.

Environmentalists claim, for example, that trash is a negative externality of consuming, so they advocate government suppression of "wasteful" consumption. Yet the free market handles this justly and efficiently through property rights. Privatize everything and the externalities are "internalized;" that is, those who ought to bear the costs do.

Making a product such as drugs illegal hampers this process. Given the incentives, there are no measures severe enough to suppress the trade. Even within the federal prisons, where the criminals are all in cages, there's a lucrative drug market.

Government drug warriors regularly announce the goal of raising the price of illegal street drugs. This is supposed to be a sign that they are winning their unwinnable war on drugs. But what do higher drug prices mean? Higher profits for the drug dealers.

Simple economics teaches that if the price of drugs is driven higher, and the costs of production and consumer demand remain the same, drug producers and distributors can pocket the difference. In economic jargon, the marginal revenue of drug sales already outstrips the marginal cost of production by an artificially huge margin. Profit differentials reach 2,000 percent in some drug markets!

Higher prices also mean that users will steal more money to buy their drugs—more robbings, beatings, killings, and break-ins in cities across America. Last year drug users stole more than $7 billion from innocent Americans. Higher prices will guarantee an increase in that figure.

The high murder rate in the inner cities is also a direct result of drug laws that make the peaceful settlement of disputes impossible. Drug laws have insured the continuance of a market that relies on violence and the threat of violence.

Tougher law enforcement is not a sufficient deterrent. Pushers already face the prospect of imminent death when they step out onto the streets to sell their goods. As long as a ghetto kid can earn $4,000 a week selling drugs, he will continue to take the risk.

That leaves decriminalization, which would subject the drug industry to full market discipline. Drug prices would plummet, profits would crash, and street crime would drop—by 75 percent according to some estimates.

This wouldn't create a utopia, but that is not one of our options. Once the violence stops, we can focus our energies and resources on private treatment for those who want to stop, and private antidrug education for the young.

But we should not spend any public money on treatment or education. Some left-liberal legalizers want to redirect the billions now spent on enforcement into government-run clinics instead. About 80 percent of treated addicts return to drugs within a year, however, showing that the problem is not lack of treatment.

Some people are natural addicts, who will harm themselves with drugs. There's nothing the rest of us can do about it, except prevent them—through decriminalization—from spreading their misery to the rest of society.

It would be nice to have another choice, but the laws of economics do not allow us one.

45.
DRUG WAR DEATH TOLL*

Give it up, drug warriors. You will never stop the production and consumption of marijuana, cocaine, or any other substance that people want to grow and repackage for others who want to buy. The attempt to do so vastly increases the price and thereby benefits some producers at the expense of others, breeds crime and corruption in public agencies, and violates people's civil liberties.

The drug war leads people to believe that the federal government, not the people who can actually do something about drug use, is taking care of the problem. It breeds parental dereliction of duty. Meanwhile, the government's constant message of "Say No to Drugs" has the opposite effect on young people always willing to bite the forbidden fruit that government doesn't want them to touch.

For bureaucratic reasons, the drug warriors are unwilling to make distinctions about the severity of drugs, so that pot and heroin are considered equally bad. This is so absurd that it discredits the entire message. Meanwhile, other forms of drugs such as alcohol and tobacco enjoy legal approval, even as the government has programs to make drugs by prescription as cheap as possible.

The hypocrisy is flagrant and outrageous, and the effects are deeply corrupting of the culture and the political process. The

---

*April 2001

drug warriors first federalized drug control, on grounds that state-level interdiction had too many leaks. Then the federal government, always glad for more power, made it a foreign-policy issue, brow-beating governments all over the world to run roughshod over their citizens in an attempt to stamp out drugs.

Today, Veronica Bowers and her 7-month-old adopted daughter Charity are dead. They were killed by military bullets raining in on a small civilian aircraft flying to bring the Gospel of Jesus Christ to the Indians of Peru. The CIA and the Peruvian military mistook a plane of missionaries for drug dealers. There were no warning shots.

Drug lords, for all their malice, are careful to keep noncombatants out of the line of fire. Governments don't care. We are all in the line of fire so far as they are concerned, so the blood of civilian missionaries is the price we pay for keeping cocaine away from those who will find some way to get it anyway.

It was a mistake, the US government says. Sorry. But where is the accountability? Who is going to fry for this murderous act? The sub commander whose irresponsible behavior led to the death of Japanese high-school students was "punished" with an early retirement so he can continue to live off the tax-payers while doing nothing.

Does anyone believe that those responsible for the death of the missionaries will receive any worse treatment? So far no one has been willing to accept responsibility. Who investigates the investigators? Who prosecutes the prosecutors? Isn't it time the Christian Right begins to rethink the drug war, which has now taken two of their own?

In a drug war, the government treats us all as suspects. Our bank accounts are investigated, we are harassed at the airport, and we are spied on at every turn. Recreational users, who pose no threat to anyone but themselves, are treated as worse than felons and given mandatory sentences that ruin their lives. Meanwhile, murderers can't be kept in prison because prisons are overcrowded with small-time tokers.

After decades of experience, we know the drug war can't work. Anyone who says otherwise is a liar or a fool. We also know that the costs are huge, to our liberty and our tax dollars. The drug lords don't entirely mind; they will continue to earn monopoly profits so long as their competition is kept at bay. It is the rest of us who should protest.

But can we really make drugs legal at the federal level? There is no constitutional basis for doing otherwise. Nothing in that founding document permits government bureaucrats to control what we smoke, inhale, or inject. By letting them attempt to do so, we invite every form of tyranny. And no amount of increased power by the feds will do the job. Consider that one of the worst drug problems exists in federal prisons. Prisons can't keep them out! A free society shouldn't even try.

If we make illicit drugs legal, people warn, they will be available for anyone who wants them. But that is precisely the situation we are in now. Can it get worse?

What happens if people take more drugs after legalization than before?

So be it.

People do lots of things that are bad for them. They eat too many cheeseburgers and they skydive. They watch tacky movies and listen to rap. They wear sloppy clothes and forget to floss their teeth. They get too fat and pick their noses. And they ingest, sniff, and smoke mind-altering drugs. A free society deals with these problems at the level of the family, the church, and community norms, not through the leviathan state.

Ludwig von Mises, in 1949, said:

> The problems involved in direct government interference with consumption are not catallactic problems. They go far beyond the scope of catallactics and concern the fundamental issues of human life and social organization. If it is true that government derives its authority from God and is entrusted by Providence to act as the guardian of the ignorant and stupid populace, then it is certainly its task to regiment every aspect of the subject's conduct. The God-sent ruler knows better

what is good for his wards than they do themselves. It is his duty to guard them against the harm they would inflict upon themselves if left alone.

Self-styled "realistic" people fail to recognize the immense importance of the principles implied. They contend that they do not want to deal with the matter from what, they say, is a philosophic and academic point of view. Their approach is, they argue, exclusively guided by practical considerations. It is a fact, they say, that some people harm themselves and their innocent families by consuming narcotic drugs. Only doctrinaires could be so dogmatic as to object to the government's regulation of the drug traffic. Its beneficent effects cannot be contested.

However, the case is not so simple as that. Opium and morphine are certainly dangerous, habit-forming drugs. But once the principle is admitted that it is the duty of government to protect the individual against his own foolishness, no serious objections can be advanced against further encroachments. A good case could be made out in favor of the prohibition of alcohol and nicotine. And why limit the government's benevolent providence to the protection of the individual's body only? Is not the harm a man can inflict on his mind and soul even more disastrous than any bodily evils? Why not prevent him from reading bad books and seeing bad plays, from looking at bad paintings and statues and from hearing bad music? The mischief done by bad ideologies, surely, is much more pernicious, both for the individual and for the whole society, than that done by narcotic drugs.

These fears are not merely imaginary specters terrifying secluded doctrinaires. It is a fact that no paternal government, whether ancient or modern, ever shrank from regimenting its subjects' minds, beliefs, and opinions. If one abolishes man's freedom to determine his own consumption, one takes all freedoms away. The naive advocates of government interference with consumption delude themselves when they neglect what they disdainfully call the philosophical aspect of the problem. They unwittingly support the case of censorship, inquisition, religious intolerance, and the persecution of dissenters.

46.
PRISON NATION*

Americans, perhaps like all people, have a remarkable capacity for tuning out unpleasantries that do not directly affect them. I'm thinking here of wars on foreign lands, but also the astonishing fact that the United States has become the world's most jail-loving country, with well over 1 in 100 adults living as slaves in prison. Building and managing prisons, and locking people up, has become a major facet of government power in our time, and it is long past time for those who love liberty to start to care.

Before we get to the reasons why, look at the facts as reported by the *New York Times*. The United States leads the world in prisoner production. There are 2.3 million people behind bars. China, with four times as many people, has 1.6 million in prison.

In terms of population, the United States has 751 people in prison for every 100,000, while the closest competitor in this regard is Russia with 627. I'm struck by this figure: 531 in Cuba. The median global rate is 125.

What's amazing is that most of this imprisoning trend is recent, dating really from the 1980s, and most of the change is due to drug laws. From 1925 to 1975, the rate of imprisonment was stable at 110, lower than the international average, which is what you might expect in a country that purports to value freedom. But then it suddenly shot up in the 1980s. There were 30,000 people in jail for drugs in 1980, while today there are half a million.

Other factors include the criminalization of nearly everything these days, even passing bad checks or the pettiest of

---

*April 2008

thefts. And judges are under all sorts of minimum-sentencing requirements.

Before we move to causes, please consider what jail means. The people inside are slaves of the state. They are captured and held and regarded by their captors as nothing other than biological beings that take up space. The delivery of all services to them is contingent on the whims of their masters, who have no stake in the outcome at all.

Now, you might say that this is necessary for some people, but be aware that it is the ultimate assault on human dignity. They are "paying the price" for their actions, but no one is in a position to benefit from the price paid. They aren't working off debts or compensating victims or struggling to overcome anything. They are just "doing time," costing taxpayers almost $25,000 a year per person. That's all these people are to society: a cost, and they are treated as such.

The communities in which they exist in these prisons consist of other unvalued people, and they become socialized into this mentality that is utterly contrary to every notion of civilization. Then there is the relentless threat and reality of violence, the unspeakable noise, the pervasiveness of every moral perversity.

In short, prisons are Hell. It can be no wonder that they rehabilitate no one. As George Barnard Shaw said, "imprisonment is as irrevocable as death."

What's more, everything we know about government applies to this ultimate government program. It is expensive (the states alone spend $44 billion on prisons every year), inefficient, brutal, and irrational. The modern prison system is also a relatively new phenomenon in history, one that is used to enforce political priorities (the drug war) rather than punish real crimes. It is also manipulated by political passions rather than a genuine concern for justice. The results of the drug war are not to reduce consumption but rather the opposite: illegal drugs are now a $100 billion industry in the United States, while the drug war itself cost taxpayers $19 billion, even as the costs of running the justice system are skyrocketing (up 418 percent in 25 years).

People say that crime is down, so this must be working. Well, that depends on what you mean by crime. Drug use and distribution are associated with violence solely because they are illegal. They are crimes because the state says they are crimes, but they do not fit within the usual definition we find in the history of political philosophy, which centers on the violation of person or property.

What's more, the "crime" of drug use and distribution hasn't really been kept down; it has only gone further underground. In a major irony and commentary on the workability of prisons, drug markets are very active there.

Now to causes. Some social scientists give the predictable explanation that all this is due to the lack of a "social safety net" in the United States. In the first place, the United States has had such a net for a hundred years, and yet these people seem not to have noticed. No such net is big enough for some people. Moreover, it is more likely that the very presence of such a net—which creates a moral hazard so that people do not learn to be responsible for their own well-being—contributes to criminal behavior (all else being equal).

There are those on all sides who attribute the increase to racial factors, given that the imprisoned population is disproportionately black and Hispanic, and noting the disparity in crime rates in such places as Minnesota with low levels of minority populations. But this factor too could be illusory, especially with regard to drug use, since it is far more likely that a state system will catch and punish people with less influence and social standing than those whom the state regards as significant.

A more telling point comes to us from political analysts, who observe the politicization of judicial appointments in the United States. Judges run on their "tough on crime" records, or are appointed for them, and so have every incentive to lock people up more than justice truly demands.

One factor that hasn't been mentioned so far in the discussion is the lobbying power of the prison industry itself. The old rule is that if you subsidize something, you get more of it. And so it is with prisons and the prison-industrial complex. I've yet to find any viable figures on how large this industry is, but consider that it includes construction firms, managers of private prisons, wardens, food service providers, counselors, security services, and 100 other kinds of companies to build and manage these miniature societies. What kind of political influence do they have? Speculation here, but it must be substantial.

As for public concern, remember that every law on the books, every regulation, every line in the government codebook, is ultimately enforced by prison. The jail cell is the symbol and ultimate end of statism itself. It would be nice if we thought of the interests of those who are prisoners in society and those who will become so. But even if you are not likely to be among them, consider the loss of privacy, the loss of liberty, the loss of independence, the loss of all that used to be considered truly American in the course of building prison nation.

47.

OUR KIND OF CENTRAL PLANNING[*]

During the 1990s, many of us complained bitterly about rule by the left. We were outraged at how the Clinton administration had so much faith in government's ability to bring about universal fairness and equality. Government, we were told, would make right all relations between groups, equalize access to health care, curb every corporate abuse, and stop all forms of exploitation of man against man, and man against nature.

---

*April 2007

Except that behind every regulation, every bill, and every central plan, no matter how humane it appeared on the outside, an informed person could discern the iron fist of the state, which the Clinton administration freely used against its enemies. Clinton himself was perhaps never as convinced of the cure of power as the worst Clintonites, but it remained and remains his default worldview.

What was wrong with the leftists' worldview in the 1990s and today? Essentially it is this: they see society as unworkable by itself. They believe it has fundamental flaws and deep-rooted conflicts that keep it in some sort of structural imbalance. All these conflicts and disequilibria cry out for government fixes, for leftists are certain that there is no social problem that a good dose of power can't solve.

If the conflicts they want are not there, they make them up. They look at what appears to be a happy suburban subdivision and see pathology. They see an apparently happy marriage and imagine that it is a mask for abuse. They see a thriving church and think the people inside are being manipulated by a cynical and corrupt pastor. Their view of the economic system is the same. They figure that prices don't reflect reality but instead are set by large players. There is a power imbalance at the heart of every exchange. The labor contract is a mere veneer that covers exploitation.

To the brooding leftist, it is inconceivable that people can work out their own problems, that trade can be to people's mutual advantage, that society can be essentially self-managing, or that attempts to use government power to reshape and manage people might backfire. Their faith in government knows few limits; their faith in people is thin or nonexistent. This is why they are a danger to liberty. We knew this in the 1990s, and we know it today.

The remarkable fact about the conflict theory of society held by the left is that it ends up creating more of the very pathology that they believe has been there from the beginning. The surest way to drive a wedge between labor and capital is to regulate the labor markets to the point that people cannot make voluntary trades. Both sides begin to fear each other. It is the same with relations between races, sexes, the able and the physically and mentally challenged, and any other groups you can name. The best path to creating conflict where none need exist is to put a government bureaucracy in charge.

And yet the left is hardly alone in holding this essential assumption about the way the world works. We have lived through six years of a Republican president. The regime is dominated by a different philosophical orientation. And we have thereby been reminded that there are many flavors of tyranny. Bush's spending record is far worse than Clinton's. After promising a humble foreign policy, war and war spending define our era. We're told that every problem with war can be solved through more force; that there is nothing necessarily wrong with imprisoning people without cause and without legal representation; that torture can be a legitimate wartime tactic; that some countries have to be destroyed in order to be made free; and that we can have all the warfare and welfare we desire at virtually no cost, thanks to the miracle of debt-driven economic growth.

Traveling on airplanes reminds us how much freedom we've lost and how we have become accustomed to it. Government bureaucrats presume the right to search us and all our property. We are interrogated at every step. The slightest bit of resistance could lead to arrest. We mill around airports while the loudspeakers demand that we report all suspicious behavior. Sometimes it seems like we are living in a dystopian novel.

Some people say that the real problem with the Bush administration is that it is too far left, and that a genuine right-wing government would be better. I'm disinclined to believe that, for I detect in the Bush administration a particular philosophy of governance that departs from that of the Clinton regime in many ways, except in its unlimited faith in government, that is, force and the threat of force.

I would go so far as to say that the most imminent threat that we face is not from the left but from the conservative right. I would like to defend the idea that rule by the right is as dangerous as rule by the left. Elsewhere, I've referred to members of political groups that support the conservative right as "red-state fascists," and I don't use that phrase merely for rhetorical purposes. There was and is such as thing as fascism as a non-leftist form of social theory that puts unlimited faith in the state to correct the flaws in society.

In the American postwar tradition, the political right has been a mix of genuine libertarian elements together with some very dangerous tendencies. Mises wrote in *Omnipotent Government* that there is a breed of warmonger who sees war not as an evil to be avoided as much as possible, but rather a productive and wonderful event that gives life meaning. To these people—and Mises of course was speaking of Nazis—war and all its destruction is a high achievement, something necessary to bring out the best in man and society, something wonderful and necessary to push history and culture forward.

Reading Mises's claim in peacetime makes it seem implausible. Who could possibly believe such things about war? And yet I think we know now. There have been hundreds of articles in the conservative press in the last six years that have made the precise claims we see above. Even in the religious world, we see the shift taking place, with new emphasis on the God of War over the Prince of Peace.

During the New Deal and before the Cold War, the libertarian tendencies of the American Right prevailed. But after the Cold War began, the mix became unstable, with the militarists and statists gaining an upper hand. It was during this period that we first heard the term "conservative" applied to people who believe in free enterprise and human liberty—a ridiculous moniker if there ever was one. Frank Chodorov was so fed up with it that he once said: "anyone who calls me a conservative gets a punch in the nose." Neither did Hayek or Mises, much less Rothbard, permit that term to be applied to their world-view.

Nonetheless, it stuck, and the bad habits of mind along with it. It would be impossible to say what policy of the current-day right constitutes the biggest danger to liberty. For now, I would like to leave aside the most commonly talked about issues of the Bush administration, such as its ahistorical view of the power of the executive branch and its post 9-11 violations of civil liberties, which are very real indeed. Instead let's look at the grimmest aspect of the state: its enforcement arm.

LOCK 'EM UP

The American Right has long held a casual view toward the police power, viewing it as the thin blue line that stands between freedom and chaos. And while it is true that law itself is critical to freedom, and police can defend rights of life and property, it does not follow that any tax-paid fellow bearing official arms and sporting jackboots is on the side of good. Every government regulation and tax is ultimately backed by the police power, so free-market advocates have every reason to be as suspicious of socialist-style police power as anyone on the left.

Uncritical attitudes toward the police lead, in the end, to the support of the police state. And to those who doubt that, I would invite a look at the US-backed regime in Iraq, which has been enforcing martial law since the invasion, even while most conservatives have been glad to believe that these methods constitute steps toward freedom.

The problem of police power is hitting Americans very close to home. It is the police, much militarized and federalized, that are charged with enforcing the on-again-off-again states of emergency that characterize American civilian life. It is the police that confiscated guns from New Orleans residents during the flood, kept residents away from their homes, refused to let the kids go home in the Alabama tornado last month, and will be the enforcers of the curfews, checkpoints, and speech controls that the politicians want during the next national emergency. If we want to see the way the police power could treat US citizens, look carefully at how the US troops in Iraq are treating the civilians there, or how prisoners in Guantanamo Bay are treated.

A related problem with the conservative view toward law and justice concerns the issue of prisons. The United States now incarcerates 730 people per 100,000, which means that the US leads the world in the number of people it keeps in jails. We have vaulted ahead of Russia in this regard. Building and maintaining jails is a leading expense by government at all levels. We lock up citizens at rates as high as eight times the rest of the industrialized world. Is it because we have more crime? No. You are more likely to be burglarized in London and Sydney than in New York or Los Angeles. Is this precisely because we jail so many people? Apparently not. Crime explains about 12 percent of the prison rise, while changes in sentencing practices, mostly for drug-related offenses, account for 88 percent.

Overall, spending on prisons, police, and other items related to justice is completely out of control. According to the Bureau of Justice Statistics, in the twenty years ending in 2003, prison spending has soared 423 percent, judicial spending is up 321 percent, and police spending shot up 241 percent. When current data become available, I think we will all be in for a shock, with total spending around a quarter of a trillion dollars per year. And what do we get for it? More justice, more safety, better protection? No, we are buying the chains of our own slavery.

We might think of prisons as miniature socialist societies, where government is in full control. For that reason, they are a complete failure for everyone but those who get the contracts to build the jails and those who work in them. Many inmates are there for drug offenses, supposedly being punished for their behavior, but meanwhile drug markets thrive in prison. If that isn't the very definition of failure, I don't know what is. In prison, nothing takes place outside the government's purview. The people therein are wholly and completely controlled by state managers, which means that they have no value. And yet it is a place of monstrous chaos, abuse, and corruption. Is it any wonder that people coming out of prison are no better off than before they went in, and are often worse, and scarred for life?

In the US prison and justice system, there is no emphasis at all on the idea of restitution, which is not only an important part of the idea of justice but, truly, its very essence. What justice is achieved by robbing the victim again to pay for the victimizer's total dehumanization? As Rothbard writes:

> The victim not only loses his money, but pays more money besides for the dubious thrill of catching, convicting, and then supporting the criminal; and the criminal is still enslaved, but not to the good purpose of recompensing his victim.

Free-market advocates have long put up with jails on grounds that the state needs to maintain a monopoly on justice. But where in the world is the justice here? And how many jails are too many? How many prisoners must there be before the government has overreached? We hear virtually nothing about this problem from conservatives. Far from it, we hear only the celebration of the expansion of prison socialism, as if the application of ever more force were capable of solving any social problem.

KILL 'EM ALL

This ideology of power is particularly clear when it comes to war. In the 1970s, there developed a myth on the right that the real problem with Vietnam was not the intervention itself, but the failure to carry it out to a more grim and ruthless end. This seems to be the only lesson that the Bush administration garnered from the experience. So the solution to every problem in Iraq—at least, I can't think of an exception to the rule—has been to apply more force through more troops, more bombs, more tanks, more guns, more curfews, more patrols, more checkpoints, and more controls of all sorts. It's as if the administration were on an intellectual trajectory that it cannot escape.

Why the lack of any critical thinking here? How is it that the war planners and their vast numbers of supporters do not question the underlying assumption that government is capable of achieving all its aims, provided that it is given enough time and firepower? It's as if they are unable to apply the logic behind their support of free enterprise in any other area of politics.

What's more, it is not even clear that American conservatives are temperamentally inclined to support free enterprise. Let us never forget that it was the Nixon administration that finally destroyed the gold standard and gave us price and wage controls, and it was the Reagan administration that set the world record on government spending and debt, before it was broken by the current Republican administration. There is no doubt in my mind that under the right conditions, the Bush administration would institute wage and price controls in the same way that it has pursued an intermittently protectionist program, regulated business, erected new bureaucracies, and failed to seriously cut taxes.

Why is it the case that American conservatives cannot be trusted with the defense of liberty? Here is where we have to penetrate more deeply into the philosophical infrastructure of American conservatism. I wish I could say it is derived from the Republicanism of Madison, or the libertarianism of Jefferson, or the aristocratic old-style liberalism of Edmund Burke, or the rabble-rousing faith in freedom exhibited by that American original Patrick Henry. Sadly, this is not the case. Nor do the conservatives show evidence of having been influenced by the thinkers discussed in Russell Kirk's book *The Conservative Mind*, such as John C. Calhoun, John Randolph of Roanoke, John Adams, much less the eccentric Orestes Brownson.

Conservatives have become addicted to entertainment radio and television as the source of their news, and the underlying philosophy seems not to have any connection to history in any way. But because we are all intellectually indebted to some body of ideas, we have to ask: which one is it that informs modern-day conservatism?

Law-Keeper, Law-Breakers

What we have at work here is a crude form of Hobbesianism, the political philosophy hammered out by the seventeenth-century Englishman Thomas Hobbes. His book *Leviathan* was published in 1651 during the English Civil War in order to justify a tyrannical central government as the price of peace. The natural state of society, he said, was war of all against all. In this world, life is "solitary, poor, nasty, brutish, and short." Conflict was the way of human engagement. Society is rife with it, and it cannot be otherwise.

What is striking here is the context of this book. Conflict was indeed ubiquitous. But what was the conflict about? It was over who would control the state and how that state would operate. This was not a state of nature but a society under Leviathan's control. It was precisely the Leviathan that bred that very conflict that Hobbes was addressing, and he proposed a cure that was essentially identical to the disease.

In fact, the result of the Civil War was the brutal and ghastly dictatorship of Oliver Cromwell, who ruled under democratic slogans. This was a foreshadowing of some of the worst political violence of the twentieth century. It was Nazism, Fascism, and Communism that transformed formerly peaceful societies into violent communities in which life did indeed become "solitary, poor, nasty, brutish, and short." Leviathan didn't fix the problem; it bred it—and fastened it on society as a permanent condition.

What is striking about Hobbes is that he thought not at all about economic problems. The problem of human material well-being was not part of his intellectual apparatus. He could not have imagined what England would become only a century to a century and a half later: a bastion of freedom and rising prosperity for everyone.

He wrote at the tail end of an epoch before the rise of old-style liberalism. At the time that Hobbes was writing, the liberal idea had not yet become part of public consciousness in England. In this respect, England was behind the Continent, where intellectuals in Spain and France had already come to understand the core insights of the liberal idea. But in England, John Locke's *Two Treatises on Government* would not be written for another thirty years, a book that would supply the essential framework of the Declaration of Independence and lead to the formation of the freest and most prosperous society in the history of the world.

Because Hobbes didn't think about economic issues, the essential liberal insight was not part of his thinking. And what is that insight? It is summed up in Frédéric Bastiat's claim that "the great social tendencies are harmonious."

WE CAN GET ALONG

What he means by this is that society contains within itself the capacity to resolve conflicts and create and sustain institutions that further social cooperation. By pursuing their individual self-interest, people can come to mutual agreement and engage in exchange to their mutual benefit. A critical insight here, one that needs to be taught to every generation, relates to the law of association.

The law of association points out that people of radically different abilities, backgrounds, religions, races, and capacities can successfully cooperate to achieve ever-higher levels of social welfare through negotiation and trade. The law of association is what explains the method by which humans were able to move out of caves, away from isolated production, beyond the hunter-gatherer stage, and into what we call civilization. This law makes it possible for people to stop stealing from each other, stop killing each other, and begin to cooperate. It is the basis of society.

Note that the law of association does not suppose that everyone in society is smart, enlightened, talented, or educated. It presumes radical inequality and points to the paradox that the world's smartest, most talented person still has every reason to trade with his polar opposite because scarcity requires that the tasks of production be divided between people. Under the division of labor, everyone plays an essential role. It is the basis of families, communities, firms, and international trade. Another fact that needs to be understood is this: the law of association is a fact of human existence whether or not there is a state. Indeed, the foundation of civilization itself precedes the existence of the state.

What the law of association addresses is the core problem of freedom itself. If all people were equal, if everyone had the same skill level, if there were racial, sexual, and religious homogeneity in society, if people did not have differences of opinion, there would be few if any problems in society to overcome because it would not be a human society. It would be an ant heap, or a series of machine parts that had no volition. The essential problem of social and economic organization, aside from scarcity, is precisely how to deal with the facts of inequality and free will. It is here that freedom excels.

Let us be clear. Bastiat was not saying that there are no such things as criminals. He was saying that society can deal with malevolence through the exchange economy, and in precisely the way we see today: private security companies, private production of locks and guns, private arbitration, and private insurance. The free market can organize protection better than the state. Private enterprise can and does provide the police function better than the state. As Hayek argued, the state is wildly overrated as a mechanism of order-keeping. The state is and has been in history a source of disorder and chaos.

This essential insight of liberalism is what led the founding fathers to take such a radical step as throwing off the rule of Britain. They had to be firmly convinced that chaos would not ensue, that the American people could manage their own affairs without overarching leviathan control. They believed that the source of any conflict in their society was the central state, and that society itself could be self-regulating. In place of control by the king, they put the Articles of Confederation, which was a type of government that more closely approximated anarchy than any system in the modern period. The government was barely in existence, and had essentially no power.

Why did anyone believe it could work? It was the new science of liberty that led to this conviction. The American consensus was precisely that Hobbes was wrong. In the state of nature, life is not nasty and brutish, or, rather if it is, there is nothing that a nasty and brutish state can do to improve it. The only way a society can advance out of barbarism is from within by means of the division of labor.

This logic has been forgotten by the American Right. Instead they have bought into the view that society is fundamentally unstable and rife with a conflict that only the state can solve. That root conflict is between those who adhere to the law and those who are inclined to break it. These they define as good guys and bad guys, but it is not always true, since the law these days is not that written by God on our hearts, but rather the orders handed down by our political masters.

This seemingly important point is completely lost on the Republican mind, since they believe that without the state as lawmaker, all of society and all of the world would collapse into a muddle of chaos and darkness. Society, they believe, is a wreck without Leviathan. This is why they celebrate the police and the military more than merchants and entrepreneurs, and why they think that war deserves more credit than trade for world prosperity.

ONE FAITH PER SOCIETY

The conviction that society, no matter how orderly it appears, is really nothing more than a gloss on deep-rooted conflict, expresses itself in the romantic attachment to the police power and war. But it also affects the right's attitude toward religion. Many people are convinced that, in the end, it is not possible that society can be religiously heterogeneous. In particular, these days, most conservatives believe that the United States cannot abide the presence of Muslims and other religious minorities.

Now, on this question, we can grant that the existence of the universal franchise does create problems with religious heterogeneity. But this is a problem created by the state itself. In conditions of freedom, there is no reason why all religions cannot peacefully coexist.

The current-day view of conservatives that we are in an intractable war against Islam also stems from the conflict-based view of society. In the absence of the state, people find ways to get along, each preserving their own identities. Religious heterogeneity presents no problems that freedom cannot solve.

And yet conservatives today are disinclined to accept this view. They seem to have some intellectual need to identify huge struggles at work in history that give them a sense of meaning and purpose. Whereas the founding generation of old liberals was thrilled by the existence of peace and the slow and meticulous development of bourgeois civilization, the right today is on the lookout for grand morality plays into which they can throw themselves as a means of making some mark in history. And somehow they have come to believe that the state is the right means to fight this battle.

In short, their meta-understanding of politics bypassed the liberal revolution of the eighteenth century and embraced the antiliberal elements of the Enlightenment. Up with Hobbes, down with Locke: that is their implied creed. Liberty is fine but order, order, is much more important, and order comes from the state. They can't even fathom the truth that liberty is the mother, not the daughter, of order. That thought is too complex for the mind that believes that the law alone, legislated or by executive fiat, is what separates barbarism from civilization. Freedom, to them, is not a right but something conferred as a reward for good behavior. The absence of good behavior justifies any level of crackdown.

I once heard a leading Republican intellectual, a respected figure with lots of books on everyone's shelves, express profound regret when the Soviet Union was falling apart. The problem, from this person's perspective, is that this led to disorder, and order—meaning control even by the Soviet state—is the fundamental conservative value. That about sums it up. Even Communism is to be tolerated so long as it keeps away what they dread more than death: people within their rights doing whatever they want.

At the end of the Cold War, many conservatives panicked that there would be no more great causes into which the state could enlist itself. There were about 10 years of books that sought to demonize someone, somewhere, in the hope of creating a new enemy. Maybe it would be China. Maybe it would be the culture war. Maybe it should be drugs. At last, from their point of view, 9-11 presented the opportunity they needed, and thus began the newest unwinnable war in the tradition of LBJ: The War on Terror.

So must government rule every aspect of life until every last terrorist is wiped off the face of the earth? Must we surrender all our liberty and property to this cause, as the regime and its apologists suggest?

This view of society is certainly not sustainable in these times or in the future. Ever more of daily life consists in seceding from the state and its apparatus of edicts and regulations. In the online world, billions of deals are made every day that require virtually no government law to enforce. The technology that is pushing the world forward is not created by the state but by private enterprise. The places we shop and the communities in which we live are being created by private developers. Most businesses prefer to deal with private courts. We depend on insurance companies, not police, to reduce the risks in life. We secure our homes and workplaces through private firms.

What's more, these days we see all around us how liberty generates order and how this order is self-sustaining. We benefit daily, hourly, minute-by-minute, from an order that is not imposed from without but rather generated from within, by that remarkable capacity we have for pursuing self-interest while benefiting the whole. Here is the great mystery and majesty of social order, expressed so well in the act of economic exchange.

Many Republicans by contrast live intellectually in a world long past, a world of warring states and societies made up of fixed classes that fought over ever-dwindling resources, a world unleavened by enterprise and individual initiative. They imagine themselves to be the class of rulers, the aristocrats, the philosopher kings, the high clerics, the landowners, and to keep that power, they gladly fuel the basest of human instincts: nationalism, jingoism, and hate. Keeping them at bay means keeping the world of their imaginations at bay, and that is a very good and important thing for the sake of civilization.

THE ROTHBARD REVIVAL

Having said all of this about the modern-day right, I do want to draw your attention again to the forgotten tradition of the Old Right of the 1930s and '40s. These were times when Garet Garrett was celebrating free enterprise against New Deal planning, John T. Flynn was exposing the warfare state as a tool of socialism, Albert Jay Nock was heralding the capacity of private education to create literacy and artistry, and when politicians on the right were advocating peace and trade. This period came to an end in the 1950s with the emergence of the first neoconservatives attached to *National Review*.

Very few people today know anything about this aspect of American intellectual history. But in a few months, this period of ignorance is going to come to an end. The Mises Institute is publishing a remarkable document. It is Murray Rothbard's unpublished history of the postwar American Right. The name of the book is *The Betrayal of the American Right*. It chronicles both his life and the life and death of a movement. Ultimately his outlook is hopeful, just as mine is hopeful.

The manuscript has circulated privately for 30 years. It will soon see the light of day. He names names. He spares no enemy of freedom. Many people will cheer. Many others will weep. It will be a great day. The Mises Institute is the powerhouse for publishing and educating in the libertarian tradition. The young are listening and we are having a great effect in bringing to life the vision of society that animated the American Revolution and, indeed, gave rise to civilization as we know it.

I've spoken about the problem of those who look at society and see nothing but conflict and no prospect for cooperation. It is a view shared by the left and the right. But truly there is an actual conflict at the root of history—but it is not the one most people understand or see. It is the great struggle between freedom and despotism, between the individual and the state, between the voluntary means and coercion. The party of freedom knows where it stands.

SECTION 2: WAR

48.
FALSE GLORY*

Why does the bourgeoisie support war? Why the state goes to war is not a mystery—at least the general reasons are not mysterious. War is an excuse for the state to spend our money on its friends. It can punish enemies that are not going with the program. It intimidates other states tempted to go their own way. It can pave the way for politically privileged commercial interests. The regime that makes and wins a war gets written up in the history books. The reasons for war are the same now as in the ancient world: power, money, glory.

Why the bourgeoisie back war is another matter. It is self-evidently not in their interest. The government gains power at their expense. It spends their money and runs up debt that is paid out of taxes and inflation. It fosters the creation of permanent enemies abroad who then work to diminish our security at home. It leads to the violation of privacy and civil liberty. War is incompatible with a government that leaves people alone to develop their lives in an atmosphere of freedom.

Nonetheless, war with moral themes—we are the good guys working for God, and they are the bad guys doing the devil's

---

*May 2005

work—tends to attract a massive amount of middle-class support. People believe the lies, and once the lies are exposed, they defend the state's right to have lied in the first place. People who are otherwise outraged by murder find themselves celebrating it on a mass industrial scale. People who harbor no hatred toward foreigners find themselves attaching ghastly monikers to whole classes of foreign peoples. Regular middle-class people, who otherwise struggle to eke out a flourishing life in this vale of tears, feel hatred well up within them and confuse it for honor, bravery, courage, and valor.

Why? Nationalism is one answer. To be at war is to feel at one with something much larger than oneself, to be a part of a grand historical project. They have absorbed the civic religion from childhood—Boston tea, cherry trees, log cabins, Chevrolet—but it mostly has no living presence in their minds until the state pushes the war button, and then all the nationalist emotions well up within them.

American nationalism is usually associated with attachment to a particular set of state managers that you think can somehow lead the country in a particular direction of which you approve. So the nationalism of the Iraq war, for instance, was mostly a Republican Party phenomenon. All Democrats are suspected as being insufficiently loyal, of feeling sympathy for The Enemy, or defending such ideas as civil liberty at a time when the nation needs unity more than ever.

You could tell a Republican nationalist during this last war because the words peace and liberty were always said with a sneer, as if they didn't matter at all. Even the Constitution came in for a pounding from these people. Bush did all he could to consolidate decision-making power unto himself, and even strongly suggested that he was acting on God's orders as Commander in Chief, and his religious constitutionalist supporters went right along with it. They were willing to break as many eggs as necessary to make the war omelet. I've got an archive of a thousand hate mails to prove it.

But nationalism is not the only basis for bourgeois support of war. Longtime war correspondent Chris Hedges, in his great book *War Is a Force that Gives Us Meaning* (First Anchor, 2003), argues that war operates as a kind of canvas on which every member of the middle and working class can paint his or her own picture. Whatever personal frustrations exist in your life, however powerless you feel, war works as a kind of narcotic. It provides a means for people to feel temporarily powerful and important, as if they are part of some big episode in history. War then becomes for people a kind of lurching attempt to taste immortality. War gives their lives meaning.

If you know something about the sociology of religion, you can recognize what he is describing: the sacraments. In Christian theology they are derived from periodic ceremonies in the Jewish tradition that cultivate the favor of God, who grants our lives transcendent importance. We receive sacraments as a means of gaining propitiation for our sins, an eternal blessing on worldly choices, or the very means of eternal life.

War is the devil's sacrament. It promises to bind us not with God but with the nation-state. It grants not life but death. It provides not liberty but slavery. It lives not on truth but on lies, and these lies are themselves said to be worthy of defense. It exalts evil and condemns the good. It is promiscuous in encouraging an orgy of sin, not self-restraint and thought. It is irrational and bloody and vicious and appalling. And it claims to be the highest achievement of man.

It is worse than mass insanity. It is mass wallowing in evil.

And then it is over. People oddly forget what took place. The bloom on the rose of war fades, leaving only the thorns—the awful reality, the dashed hopes, the expense, the lame, the limbless, the widows, the orphans, the death on all sides, and the resulting instability.

The rose wilts, and the thorns grow, but people go on with their lives. War no longer inspires. War news becomes uninteresting. All those arguments with friends and family—what were they about anyway? All that killing and expense and death—let's just avert our eyes from it all. Maybe in a few years, once the war is out of the news forever and the country we smashed recovers some modicum of civilization, we can revisit the event and proclaim it glorious. But for now, let's just say it never happened.

People have long accused the great liberal tradition of a dogmatic attachment to peace. It would appear that this is precisely what is needed to preserve the freedom to find true meaning in our lives.

Do we reject war and all its works? We do reject them.

49.
My Speech at the Antiwar Rally*

I was invited to speak at a peace march and rally in Birmingham, Alabama, sponsored by the Alabama Peace and Justice Coalition, and gladly accepted the offer to speak against the war in Iraq.

Yes, as you might guess, the program was dominated by leftists who rightly oppose the war but want big government to run the economy. I accepted for the same reason I would accept an engagement to speak against taxes even if sponsored by a right-wing group that also favored the war and militarism.

The opportunity to make a difference in favor of freedom should not be passed up, even if one's associates have a mixed-up ideology. After all, most ideologies these days are mixed up, and have been for the better part of a century.

Those who want free markets domestically typically want central planning and socialism when it comes to war and peace, while those who see the merit of diplomacy and minding one's

---

*September 2005

own business in foreign policy can't reconcile themselves to capitalism as the only economic system that lets people alone to live happy, prosperous lives.

Now, one might think that the old liberal view, the view of Jefferson and his school, might be more widely held: namely that the government ought not lord it over anything. But somehow everyone seems to have a stake in big government, whether to rule the world or expropriate the rich. So what can we do but encourage the good parts of what people believe and discourage the bad parts?

In any case, I was glad to speak before this group, and they were gracious to ask. The challenge was to put together a three-minute speech that summed up the libertarian case against the Iraq War—not easy to do.

I was aware that I was a token non-leftist speaking to a largely leftist audience.

Among the slogans of the day was that we should spend less on the war and more on social needs. Libertarians can agree in some way: give everyone back their money and let each individual spend on his or her social needs!

There are two potential failings in such a venue: kowtowing to the audience or, the opposite error, ungraciously rubbing their noses in their inconsistencies. It strikes me that the only way to proceed here is simply to tell what's true as best as one is able, and to heck with rhetorical strategy.

The speech seemed well received. A minister from an African Methodist Episcopal church came up to me and said "you express my views exactly!" I had my doubts, but that's great if true. Similarly, there was a young kid wearing a shirt that said: "War is the symptom; capitalism is the disease." He was cheering very loudly, so who knows? Maybe I made him think.

What follows is my text. If you read it yourself, you will see that I went longer than three minutes. I might have just reduced it all to: "down with the warfare-welfare state, and up with peace and free trade."

War and Morality

By what ethical standard should we judge the state? One tradition, which we might call anti-liberal, asserts that there are special laws of morality that apply to the state alone. Another tradition, the liberal tradition, says that states must abide by the moral standards that apply to everyone in all times and all places.

The first view is the ancient one. It permitted and expected states to pillage and kill. The right and wrong of statecraft was dictated by the sword. The idea of universal moral laws and universal human rights did not find favor among the Caesars and Pharaohs, any more than this idea appealed to later dictators.

Yet the liberal tradition gradually abolished the idea of caste and special legal privilege. It asserted, more generally, that no group possesses a special license to lord it over others.

St. Augustine might have been the first to observe that the moral status of Alexander the Great's conquests was more egregious than the pirate's depredations. The pirate molests the sea, but the emperor molests the world.

The view that states can do wrong is the most powerful theory of politics in the history of the world. It led to the birth of the dream of universal freedom. Slavery, imperialism, colonialism, militarism, and authoritarianism all came to exist under a moral cloud.

At the same time, freedom and individualism unleashed human energies and, in the setting of free economies, created a prosperity beyond any ever known. This made possible the vast expansion of the world's population, and human flourishing as never seen before.

Given this history, and the central role that the American Revolution had in furthering the liberal idea, we must ask the question: what does the US government not understand about the evil of imperialism, the immorality of enslaving a foreign people, the malice of colonialism, and the intolerable brutality of authoritarianism?

In fact, the theory of the modern American regime is a throwback to the ancient view that the United States operates under special rules.

The US government believes it can starve foreign countries such as Iraq by imposing killer sanctions that a high US official said were worth the lives of hundreds of thousands of children.

The US believes that it can use its weapons of mass destruction to threaten any country in the world on the very suspicion that it might be trying to defend itself. The US can then phony up intelligence, overthrow a leader, and install a regime of its choosing. Not to worry: its magical military Midas touch will transform that country into a paragon of democratic freedom—just as soon as all political opposition is silenced or destroyed.

In short, the US government believes that it operates under a different moral standard, not only from the moral standard that regular people apply to their own affairs, but even different from the moral standard that the US applies to other states.

And who pays the price for this moral hypocrisy? The victims of war.

Of all forms of collectivist central planning, war is the most egregious. It is generated by the coercive force of taxation and monetary depreciation. Its means are economic regimentation and the violation of the freedom to associate and trade. Its ends are destruction and killing—crime on a mass scale.

War leaves in its wake orphans, widows, parents without children, sickness, hatred, and spiritual and psychological trauma. It gives power to dictators on all sides. It is based on a lie that mass death can ever accord with justice. It attempts to silence those who tell the truth.

Indeed, war is a kind of totalitarianism. It is a policy without limit. It demands from us all that we have to give: our money, our children, our minds, even our souls. Too often people give it all. Too often, Americans give it all.

George Bush was brazen enough to make the doctrine explicit. If you are not for him, he says, you are for the terrorists.

He said it because the state fears the advocates of peace. It fears the truth, and those who tell the truth. It fears those who dare to judge the state by normal standards of morality.

The state fears you. Why? Because you hold the opinions that you do, and refuse to surrender your mind, your talents, your soul. By joining the resistance, you help thwart their plans. You help establish the basis for peace in the future. You help preserve and develop civilization, for the human family can only thrive in a setting of peace.

So I say to you: Keep making the sacrifice. Believe in peace. Proclaim peace. Stand up to the state. Be a dissident. Tell what is true. And do not fear the emperor-pirates. They, after all, fear you. For you help tilt the balance of history against their barbarism, and in favor of peace and freedom.

50.

ANYTHING FOR A BUCK*

When it comes to Wall Street scandals, the widely held assumption is that accountants, stock traders, investment bankers, CEOs, and CFOs will do anything for a buck. If a broker recommended a stock that sunk in price, the courts and media are ready to assume a financial scam. He was cheating his own clients to line his pockets!

If a stock was sold before bad news was announced, the assumption is that insider information was employed. If an audit report seems to bury the bad news, the assumption is that

---

*November 2002

the CEO and CFO conspired to cook the books to enrich themselves. Hey, money makes the capitalist world go round!

But might these have been mistakes stemming from lack of knowledge of the future? Perhaps all decisions at any point in time seemed to be the best ones but only later turned out to be wrong? Never. To say that is to reveal a crazy pro-business bias and fail to understand that making money (not ethics or customer service or whatever else) is all these people care about. So we are told.

In general, then, when reporting and adjudicating matters that pertain to business, the widely held assumption is that these people will do anything for a buck, whether lie, cheat, or steal. The burden of proof that wrongdoing does not exist falls entirely on the capitalist or stock dealer. Reasonable people are free to see money grubbing as the secret and sole motivation behind every action. Who would be so naïve as to think otherwise?

Ah, but when it comes to foreign policy—even that of a presidential administration sitting on an oil fortune and heading a global crude empire—matters are entirely different. To think that Bush's plans for Iraq are driven by the desire to control Iraq's oil supplies is seen as unseemly, unsavory, base, and contrary to every norm of proper opinion holding. Woe to anyone who would suggest that something other than national interest is the driving force!

Thus does Nicholas Kristof of the *New York Times* tell us that he is against war but even more against a certain line of argument against war. "One can disagree with the calls for war, as I do," he says,

> but liberals discredit themselves when they claim that the only reasons Mr. Bush could be planning an invasion are finishing Daddy's work, helping his oil buddies, or diverting voters from corporate scandals.

Liberals are discrediting themselves by saying what is true? How could this be? Because "If we're to convince Americans of the perils of invasion, it'll be by citing arguments rather than epithets." But this is a false choice. To cite the real reasons for Bush's war, and provide reasons why you think that the administration is lying, is to provide an argument, and that argument is that things are not always as they seem. With government, who is naïve enough to think otherwise?

With all the unrespectable, nonserious claims that the Iraq war is really about spilling blood for oil, the *New York Times* examined the issue of the oil motive at great length in its Sunday edition, and concluded the following: "No serious expert believes the charge made by Mr. Hussein that Washington's one real goal is to seize his oil."

How does one define a "serious expert"? In the case of Iraq, it means a person who does not believe that the war is all about oil. If you conclude that it is, you are de-listed from the ranks of serious experts.

In fact, this is generally true in public life: disagree fundamentally with the state and you are no longer considered a serious expert on anything. People in public life work their entire careers to make sure this does not happen, which is another way of saying that they work to stay within the bounds of opinions set by the ruling regime.

And yet the *New York Times* story goes on to point out that Iraq has five times more proven reserves of oil than the United States and the second largest supply of any country in the world (Saudi Arabia is number one). The story by Serge Schmemann grants that

> 112 billion barrels of proven reserves is also something nobody can overlook. So even if it's not only about oil, or even mainly about oil, Iraq's "ability to generate oil" is always somewhere on the table, even if not in so many words.

We might also say that bank robbers just like being mischievous, though the fact that banks have money is always somewhere on the table. In the same way, a rapist is just a violent guy, though sex is also somewhere on the table. Muggers are motivated by a general desire to harass, though getting people's purses, watches, and wallets is always somewhere on the table.

Going beyond mere assertion, the *Times* explains why oil cannot be considered the primary motivation. To bring about a regime change to grab the oil is a gamble of enormous proportions because Iraq's oil industry is in a "deplorable state," the country needs to be rebuilt, and—this will shock you—there is "uncertainty over the future." That's it. That's the whole argument, which we will now examine.

Uncertainty is a universal feature of the world, and it doesn't somehow prevent risk taking. As for rebuilding the country, the Bush administration has already said that US taxpayers would be on the hook for these expenses (though the United States would also try to rope NATO in). The contracts for rebuilding will go, inevitably, to the likes of Schlumberg Ltd. and Halliburton Corp. (Cheney, former CEO). At the very least, their investments will be guaranteed, a fact that seriously diminishes the extent to which the expense of rebuilding reduces the intensity of the oil motive.

In the story, Youssef M. Ibrahim of the Council on Foreign Relations does raise one interesting point. He says that there are risks to bringing all the Iraqi oil on the market because if one opens all valves, the price of oil could plummet, which could dramatically reduce profits. We know that Cheney thinks it should be a matter of policy that oil never fall below a certain price floor (as he told Tim Russert on *Meet The Press* July 30, 2000). One can imagine that this prospect could prove a mitigating factor. And yet, if prices can be kept above $20 and demand increases, and Bush-connected companies are doing the selling, there are still plenty of profits to be had even if the oil price plummets.

More forthright is a side bar included in the *Times* article that concerns untapped oil reserves.

> Some analysts speculate that Iraq's reserves may be closer to 200 billion barrels. Others put the number close to 300 billion. . . . Deeper and more western prospecting has yet to be done.

There's more to add:

> Even the known reserves, however, have yet to be fully developed. There are [as] many [as] 17 "giant" fields in Iraq—an oil-industry designation indicating reserves in excess of one billion barrels. Throw in a few "super-giants" and a couple dozen "large" fields and the potential is clear, regardless of who controls the country.

Can you imagine that some people might think that getting control of the oil is the primary motivation? Yet people who suggest such a thing are to be dismissed as cranks. In fact, it is far clearer that greed and profiteering are behind US foreign policy than the Wall Street scandals (notice that US foreign policy is never called a scandal).

At least in the private markets, greed must be channeled to public service in order to be realized. And regardless of what government regulators say, stock analysts face no incentive to deliberately cause their clients to experience losses. That's because we are dealing with private money and freedom of choice, which builds in a kind of accountability. Both profits and losses are privatized.

But where is the accountability in US foreign policy? The decision makers have hundreds of billions of dollars of other people's money at their disposal and all the potential gains are their own. In other words, the expenses are socialized and the profits are privatized—a perfect prescription for a scandal of immense proportions. As for the people who are killed, they are no one's assets.

When it comes to foreign policy, it should be clear that the Bush administration will do anything for a buck.

51.
Was Lenin Right?*

The connection between the war on Iraq and the desire for oil raises an important ideological consideration. Millions of college students are taught the Leninist idea that capitalist economies are inherently imperialistic. This is supposedly because exploitation exhausts capital values in the domestic economy, and hence capital owners must relentlessly seek to replenish their funds through grabbing foreign resources. It takes war to avoid the final crisis of capitalism, in this view.

College students might be forgiven for thinking there is some basis for this in the real world. In American history up to the present day, the onset of war tends to track the onset of economic doldrums. Might war be just the ticket to revive a moribund capitalist class? Recall that it was then-secretary of state James Baker who said the first Iraq war was all about "jobs, jobs, jobs." The line between the owners of capital and the warfare state has never been that clean in American history, and it has arguably never been as conspicuously blurred as it is today.

The view that sustaining capitalism requires aggressive war is usually said to originate with V.I. Lenin as a way of rescuing Marxism from a serious problem. The problem was that capitalism was not collapsing in the nineteenth century. It was growing more robust and more productive, and the workers were getting richer, not poorer—all facts that weighed heavily against the Marxist historical trajectory. The Leninist answer to the puzzle was that capitalism was surviving only thanks to its military aggression. The prosperity of the West originated in blood.

---

*January 2003

CAPITALIST IMPERIALISM

But was Lenin really the originator of the theory? Not at all. The capitalists beat him to it. As Murray N. Rothbard explains in his *History of Money and Banking in the United States* (2002), the idea began with a group of Republican Party theoreticians during the late Gilded Age, who were concerned that the falling rate of profits would end up crippling capitalism and that the only salvation was a forced opening of foreign markets to US exports. These were the brain-trusters of Theodore Roosevelt, who ended up heralding US aggression against Spain in 1898.

The fear of falling profits stemmed from David Ricardo's mistaken theory that the rate of profit is determined by the stock of capital investment. In fact, the rate of profit, over the long run, is determined by the rate of time preference in society. All else being equal, as savings rise, profits fall, which doesn't at all spell disaster for capitalism. It could in fact be an indication of a robust, competitive economy in which no business interest can count on a sure thing in the marketplace.

But the theorists of imperialism didn't believe it. Economist Charles Conant developed the theory in a series of essays beginning in 1896, including "The Economic Basis of Imperialism," which appeared in the *North American Review* in 1898. In this piece, Conant argued that advanced countries have too much savings, too much production, and not enough consumption, and that this was crowding out profitable investment opportunities for the largest corporations.

The best way to find new consumers and resources, he said, was to go abroad, using force, if necessary, to open up markets. He further said that the US industrial trusts then dominant on the landscape could be useful in promoting and waging war. This would further cartelize American industry and increase profits. Hence, said Conant, "concentration of power, in order to permit prompt and efficient action, will be an almost essential factor in the struggle for world empire."

Yes, that sounds exactly like the version of reality given to us by Lenin, only the moral judgment is reversed. While Lenin condemned imperialism for profit, Conant found it praiseworthy, an inspiring plan of action. Indeed, many of his contemporaries did too. Boston's *US Investor* argued that war is necessary to keep capital at work. An "enlarged field for its product must be discovered," and the best source "is to be found among the semi-civilized and barbarian races."

By the turn of the century, this view had largely caught on in the economics profession, with even the eminent theorist John Bates Clark of Columbia praising imperialism for providing American business "with an even larger and more permanent profit."

TODAY'S PROFITS OF WAR

Today the same creed is captured in the pithy if chilling mantra of the *New York Times* columnist Thomas Friedman: "The hidden hand of the market will never work without a hidden fist" (*The Lexus and the Olive Tree*). Lenin himself couldn't have said it better.

Joseph Nye of Harvard fleshes out the point: "To ignore the role of military security in an era of economic and information growth is like forgetting the importance of oxygen to our breathing."

Brink Lindsey of the Cato Institute puts a different spin on the same line. His goal in *Against the Dead Hand* is to convince military imperialists that international trade can be an important ally in the fight for global dominance. Instead of seeing trade across borders as the extension of voluntary exchange among individuals, he sees global trade as a weapon to use against foreign states that do not conform to the DC ideal. In Lindsey's view, foreign trade, managed by the US government through treaties and bureaucracies, is merely a way to wage the fight against terrorism "with maximum effectiveness."

Historian Robert Kagan is even more brutally clear: "Good ideas and technologies also need a strong power that promotes those ideas by example and protects those ideas by winning on the battlefield."

So there you have it: if you want to use a cell phone, you have to be willing to send your son to die for the US imperium in a war against Iraq! And if you do lose your son in battle, know that this was necessary in order to shore up US domination of the world economy. This is the creed of the neoconservatives who champion both military and economic globalization.

How far we've come from George Washington's "great rule of conduct for us, in regard to foreign nations": extend commercial relations but avoid political connections.

> Harmony, liberal intercourse with all nations, are recommended by policy, humanity, and interest. But even our commercial policy should hold an equal and impartial hand; neither seeking nor granting exclusive favors or preferences; consulting the natural course of things; diffusing and diversifying by gentle means the streams of commerce, but forcing nothing.

PEACE AND FREEDOM

With the communists and capitalists agreeing that war and profit are mutually dependent, how is a believer in peace and freedom to respond? While war can result in profit for a few, a truly free economy is incompatible with wartime profiteering. Indeed, war comes at the expense of alternative uses of resources. To the extent that people are taxed to pay for armaments, property is diverted from its most valuable uses to purposes of destruction.

The idea that commerce and war are allies is a complete perversion of the old liberal tradition. The first theorists of commerce from the sixteenth century through the eighteenth century saw that a most meritorious aspect of commerce is its link to freedom and peace, that commerce made it possible for people to cooperate rather than fight. It made armaments and war less necessary, not more.

What about the need to open foreign markets? The expansion of markets and the division of labor are always wonderful things. The more people involved in the overarching business of economic life, the greater the prospects for wealth creation. But force is hardly the best means to promote the cooperative and peaceful activity of trade, any more than it is a good idea to steal your neighbor's mower to improve lawn care on your block. Bitterness and acrimony are never good business, to say nothing of death and destruction.

In any case, the problem in Iraq is not that Iraq is somehow withholding its oil from the market. For years—even before the first war on Iraq—its oil supplies have been available to the world. In one of the great ironies of modern war history, the first Bush administration waged war, it said, to keep Iraq from withholding its oil resources from world markets. The US then proceeded to enforce a decade of sanctions that withheld most of Iraq's oil reserves from the market (thereby increasing prices and profits for US firms).

We are somehow not permitted to say this, but the solution to Iraq is at hand. Repeal sanctions immediately. Trade with Iraq. Oil prices would fall dramatically. Hatred of the US would abate. The plight of Iraq could no longer be used as exhibit A in terrorist recruitment drives. The only downside, of course, is that US companies connected to the Bush administration would not be the owners of the oil fields, but instead would have to compete with other producers in supplying consumers with oil.

Well, so be it. The idea of free enterprise is that everyone gets a chance, and no one industry or group of producers enjoys special privileges. Through competition and cooperation, but never violence, the living standards of everyone rise and we all enjoy more of the life we want to live. It's not hard to understand, except in the corridors of the Bush administration, where theorists have linked arms with Leninists in the belief that war is always good, and always necessary, for business.

52.

WAR AND THE ECONOMY*

The Mises Institute has worked relentlessly to call attention to the dangers of the recessionary environment (and the dangers of the bubble that preceded it), as well as the distraction and destruction of war. Bill Moyers, who has a show on PBS, found himself intrigued by this combination of being against the war but for a free and globally engaged commercial republic. I went on his show to talk about this, but his curiosity tells me that a primer on war and economy is needed.

Behind the current confusion of ideological categories is the longstanding canard that war is good for the economy. If what you care about is a prosperous economy, why wouldn't it make sense to spend hundreds of billions of dollars on huge industrial products like military planes and tanks? Why not employ hundreds of thousands in a great public-works program like war? Why not destroy a country so that money can funnel to American companies in charge of rebuilding it? Doesn't all of this help us out of the recession?

All these questions somehow come back to Bastiat's "Broken Window" fallacy. In the story, a boy throws a rock through a window. Regrets for this act of destruction are all around. But then a confused intellectual pops up to explain that this is a good thing after all. The window will have to be fixed, which gives business to the glazier, who will use the money to buy a suit, helping the tailor, and so on. Where's the fallacy? It comes down to focusing on the seen (the new spending) as versus the unseen (what might have been done with the resources had they not had to be diverted to window repair).

Let us never forget that the military is the largest single government bureaucracy. It produces nothing. It only consumes

---

*March 2003

resources, which it takes from taxpayers by force. Making matters worse, all these resources are directed toward the building and maintenance of weapons of mass destruction and those who will operate them. The military machine is the boy with the rock writ large. It does not create wealth. It diverts it from more productive uses.

How big is the US military? It is by far the largest and most potentially destructive in the history of the world. The United States this year will spend in excess of $400 billion (not including much spy spending). The next largest spender is Russia, which spends only 14 percent of the US total. To equal US spending, the military budgets of the next 27 highest spenders have to be added together. If you consider this, and also consider the disparity of the US nuclear stockpile and the 120 countries in which the United States keeps its troops, you begin to see why the US is so widely regarded as an imperialist power and a threat to world peace.

This is very hard for Americans to understand. We tend to think of the American state as a mere extension of our own lives. We all work hard. We mind our own business. We tend to our families and involve ourselves in local civic activities. We love our history and are proud of our founding. We are pleased by our prosperity (even if we don't know why it exists). We think most other Americans live the way we do. We think our government (if we think about it at all) is nothing but an extension of this way of life.

A deadly military empire? Don't be ridiculous. The military is just defending the country. Bush is a potential tyrant? Get real! He's a good man. Those crazy foreigners who resent the United States are really no better than those people who attacked us on September 11, 2001: they envy our wealth and hate us for our goodness. We are a godly people, which makes our enemies ungodly, even demonic. This is a short summary of a widely held view, one that those who seek a government-dominated society use to build their public-sector empire.

What most Americans refuse to face is that what the government does day to day, and in particular its military arm, is not an extension of the way the rest of us live. Government knows only one mode of operation: coercion. It does not cooperate; it coerces. Because it is constantly overriding human choices, it makes unrelenting errors, most often producing consequences opposite of the stated intention. This is no less true in its foreign operations than it is in its domestic ones.

Consider the most recent military action in Afghanistan. The Taliban was nothing but a reincarnation of the opposition tribes the US government supported when the country was being run by the Soviets in the 1980s. Back then we called them freedom fighters. When the Taliban fled the capital city last year, the US military knew where to look for them because it was the US military that assisted in building their hideouts during the last war.

What did the war do to the country? All hoopla aside, it is no freer, no more democratic, and no more prosperous. The warlords are running the country and women are still subject to fundamentalist Islamic dictate. How many civilians did the United States kill? Thousands, perhaps many thousands. During the war, every day brought news of a few dozen innocent dead, all verified by humanitarian organizations monitoring the situation. We don't have a definitive final tabulation because US forces bombed radio and TV stations and worked to keep news of the dead from leaking.

The *New York Times* reports concerning the newest proposed war: "General [Richard] Myers gave a stark warning that the American attack would result in Iraqi civilian casualties despite the military's best efforts to prevent them." Americans don't like to think about this, but it is a reality nonetheless. As for best efforts, one would have to turn a blind eye to the history of US warfare to believe it.

With regard to Iraq in particular, let us remember that the United States has waged unrelenting war on that country for 12 years, with bombings and sanctions that the United Nations says have killed millions. The entire fiasco began with the

Iraqi invasion of its former province, Kuwait. Warned in advance by the Iraqi government, the US ambassador responded that the United States took no position on the border-oil dispute.

But let's return to the economic costs associated with war. It does not stimulate productivity. It destroys capital, in the same sense that all government spending destroys capital. It removes resources from where they are productive—within the market economy—and places them in the hands of bureaucrats, who assign these resources to uses that have nothing to do with consumer or producer demand. All decisions made by government bureaucrats are economically arbitrary because the decision makers have no access to market signaling.

What's interesting this time around is how the markets seem to have caught on. The prospect of war is inhibiting recovery. The stock market is now at 1998 levels, with five years of increased valuations wiped out. The recession itself, the longest in postwar history, may have been the inevitable response to the economic bubble that preceded it, but the drive to war is prolonging it. It could get worse and likely will. Consumer confidence is falling, as is consumer spending. Unemployment is rising. The dollar is falling. Commodity prices are rising. All signs point to a man-made economic calamity.

The deficit is completely out of control. The idea of tax cuts is fine, but let's not pretend as if the bill for government spending doesn't need to be paid by someone at some point. It will be paid either through inflation or higher taxes later. In the meantime, deficits crowd out private production because they need to be financed through bond holdings. War will only make the problem worse. From time immemorial, war has gone along with fiscal irresponsibility.

War also goes hand in hand with government control of the economy. Bush has increased spending upwards of 30 percent since he took the oath of office. He has imposed punishing tariffs on steel, hardwood, and wheat. He has created the largest new civilian bureaucracy erected since World War II. He has unleashed the federal police power against the American people in violation of the constitution. All of this amounts to a war on freedom, of which commercial freedom is an essential part. This is why no true partisan of free enterprise can support war.

But what about September 11? Doesn't that event justify just about anything? Let us not forget that this was a multiple hijacking, of which there have been hundreds over the decades since commercial flight became popular. The difference this time was that the hijackers gave up their lives rather than surrender. It was a low-budget operation, and needed no international conspiracy to bring it about. It was easily prevented by permitting pilots to protect their planes and passengers by force of arms, but federal bureaucrats had a policy against this.

In any case, there is no evidence that Iraq had anything to do with 9-11. The Iraqi regime is liberal by Muslim standards and for that reason hated by Islamic fundamentalists. Unlike Saudi Arabia, it tolerates religious diversity, permits gun ownership, and allows drinking. It has a secular culture—complete with rock stars and symphony halls—that few other Muslim states have.

Yes it is a dictatorship, but there are a lot of these in the world. Many of them are US allies. The focus of the Bush administration on Iraq has more to do with personal vendettas and Iraqi oil. In waging war, the Bush administration proposes to spend twice the annual GDP of the entire Iraqi economy! The United States will spend $2 for every $1 it will destroy—the very definition of economic perversity. What's more, an attack will only further destabilize the region and recruit more terrorists intent on harming us.

Meanwhile, the prospect of war has markets completely spooked. Is this a narrow economic concern? Not in any way. Prosperity is an essential partner in civilization itself. It is the basis of leisure, charity, and a hopeful outlook on life. It is the means for conquering poverty at the lowest rung of society, the basis on which children and the elderly are cared for, the foundation for the cultivation of arts and learning. Crush an economy and you crush civilization.

It is natural that liberty and peace go together. Liberty makes it possible for people from different religious traditions and cultural backgrounds to find common ground. Commerce is the great mechanism that permits cooperation amidst radical diversity. It is also the basis for the working out of the brotherhood of man. Trade is the key to peace. It allows us to think and act both locally and globally.

What makes no sense is the belief that big government can be cultivated at home without the same government becoming belligerent abroad. What also makes no sense is the belief that big-government wars and belligerent foreign policies can be supported without creating the conditions that allow for the thriving of big government at home. The libertarian view that peace and freedom go together may be the outlier in current public opinion. But it is a consistent view, the only one compatible with a true concern for human rights, and for social and global well-being.

53.

IRAQ AND THE DEMOCRATIC EMPIRE*

As all students today know, Iraq is the country that the US invaded with the attempt to convert the state and the people from enemy to friend. On the face of it, this sounds rather implausible, of course. Good fences make good neighbors. Friendship and peace are not usually the result of insults, sanctions, invasions, bombings, killings, puppet governments, censorship, economic controls, and occupations. If this generation learns anything from this period, that would be a good start.

---

*February 2006

Earlier students thought of Iraq as the country that was forever being denounced by the Clinton administration and by Bush's father when he was president. Why? Iraq, it seems, had some crazy notion that the US might attempt an invasion at some point in the future, and thus thought it had better prepare by spending money on its military. Its weapons program, however, was quickly dismantled under pressure from the UN.

Doubtful that Iraq had really given up the idea of creating a viable national defense, the US cobbled together extreme sanctions against the country, preventing it from trading with the world. The standard of living plummeted. Middle class merchants suffered. The poor died without the essentials of life. The child mortality rate soared. The head of the US State Department told a reporter on national television that even if US sanctions had resulted in 500,000 child deaths, they were "worth it."

Jumping back earlier, the US had waged another war on Iraq. Bush Senior saw it as the war to end all aggressions, in this case an aggression of Iraq against its neighbor called Kuwait, a name that has been strangely absent from the news for the better part of 10 years. What was strange was how the US had given the green light to Saddam to aggress against its neighbor, with the US ambassador having told Saddam Hussein that the US took no position on its long-running border dispute with its former province.

Now, if we jump back still further and consider the Reagan years, students would remember a long and boring but truly bloody conflict between Iraq and Iran. It lasted eight years, between 1980 and 1988. The US favored Iraq in this war. Saddam was a friend of the US, a man on the payroll. The weapons he used in this war on Iran were provided to him courtesy of the US taxpayer, as weapons inspectors in the 1990s were reminded when they went hunting for WMDs. There is a famous photo of one of Reagan's weapons emissaries, Donald Rumsfeld, smiling broadly as he shakes hands with Saddam.

The war did not fully wreck Iraq, though many of its sons died. The country was secular and liberal by regional standards.

There were private schools, symphonies, universities, and a complex and developing economy. Women had rights. They could drive and have bank accounts. They wore Western clothing. You could get a drink at a bar or buy liquor and have it at home. Christians were tolerated. They could worship as they pleased, and send their children to Christian schools. The electricity stayed on. You could buy gasoline. It was an old-fashioned dictatorship but it was, in regional terms, prosperous.

The war between Iran and Iraq was inconclusive. But today, we've come full circle. Iraq is a wreck. The *Wall Street Journal* ran a story the other day that documented how the prevailing political influence today in Iraq is Iran's ruling Shiite political party, which hopes to add another country to those ruled by Islamic law. So, from the vantage point of 25 years, it appears that the winner has finally been decided in the great Iran-Iraq war. The side that the US favored lost.

This is increasingly the pattern in the post-Cold War world. The US spends money, invades countries, sheds blood, and becomes ever more powerful at home and unpopular abroad. In the end, no matter how powerful its weapons or how determined its leaders, it loses. It loses because people resist empire. It loses for the same reasons that socialism and its central plans always fail. Large-scale attempts to force people into predetermined molds founder on the inability of the state to allocate resources rationally and to anticipate change, as well as the ubiquitous and pesky phenomenon called human volition. Mankind was not meant to live in cages.

Why did the US win wars in the past? Because it fought far poorer governments. Today it loses because it fights populations—people acting on their own, forming their own associations, using their brains to outwit bureaucrats, and cobbling together resources from underground markets. The market always outruns the planners for the same reason that guerrilla armies usually win over regular armies. Decentralized and spontaneous associations of dedicated individuals are smarter and wiser and more committed than centralized and planned bureaucrats who follow their rule books.

This is a point well elaborated by the Austrian School of economics. The full critique of war would involve an elaboration on the work of F.A. Hayek and Murray Rothbard and their modern disciples. Time and space does not permit, so let me quickly draw your attention to the writings of Mises on this point.

In 1919, he wrote a book called *Nation, State, and Economy.* One of the many great discoveries of Guido Hülsmann was that Mises's original title is better translated in one word: Imperialism. It is a relentless attack on the idea of democratic empire, and an investigation of the role of the democratic state in foreign policy matters.

In the old world that was then passing, Mises wrote, imperial monarchs had ruled over large-scale, multiethnic, multilingual, and sometimes multireligious territories with an eye to carefully balancing the relationships among groups and avoiding policies that set group against group. It was the only policy that made their rule viable. If they failed to do this, their rule was threatened. Royal families specialized in linguistic proficiency. They adopted an air of fairness, and tended over time to liberalize economic structures in the interest of harmonizing groups.

Mises welcomed the age of democracy because he believed that political democracy was the closest analogy to applying a market principle to the sphere of civic life. But he made an important proviso. Under a democratic regime, empires would have to come to end. There could be no rule over multiethnic, multilingual, multireligious populations. Every group would need to be permitted self-determination. Democracy meant, in Mises's view, the right of groups and even individuals to chose their own state. There could be no rule over a people or part of a people without their consent.

Mises then observed a dangerous paradox. The onset of the age of democracy was also the age of the rise of socialism. Socialism requires control, not only over economic structures but also over all of civic life, including religions. The most extreme form of socialism was totalitarianism. Mises saw that socialism and democracy were based on incompatible principles. If people are given true choice in regimes, they can also choose the rules under which they live. But socialism is predicated on the supposition that people can be permitted no choice. They must live under a plan as crafted by a dictator.

Mises saw that the attempt to wed socialism and dictatorship would lead to unparalleled calamity, which indeed it did because Mises's pathway out of this problem was ignored. He mapped out his solution in his great book *Liberalism*, which appeared in 1927. Here he said that the foundation of liberty is private property. If property were protected from invasion, all else in politics follows. The state cannot be imperialistic because it cannot raise the funds necessary to fund adventures in foreign lands. On the other hand, he wrote, the more the state is given control over private property, the more it will be tempted toward imposing its rule via arms and war.

Therefore, he said, war and socialism are both part of the same ideological apparatus. They both presume the primacy of power over property. In the same way, peace and free enterprise are cut from the same cloth. They are the result of a society with a regime that respects the privacy, property, associations, and wishes of the population. The liberal society trades with foreign countries rather than waging war on them. It respects the free movement of peoples. It does not intervene in the religious affairs of people but rather adopts a rule of perfect tolerance.

I don't need to tell you that this is not the kind of regime under which we live in the United States. The state is an empire, a democratic empire. It is aggressive internally and externally. Indeed, it is the richest and most powerful government on earth and in all of human history. Along with this has come a cultural change. The founding fathers loathed and feared war. They said that nothing ruins a country quicker than the warlike spirit. It brings bankruptcy, corruption, and tyranny. George Washington warned against war, and called for trade and friendship with all nations.

The ideology of war has infected our rulers. Mises explained it in his book *Liberalism*. This is an ideology against which rational argument does not work. If you say war leads to suffering, pain, and death, they will say: so be it. Instead, writes Mises, the warmongers claim that

> it is through war and war alone that mankind is able to make progress. War is the father of all things, said a Greek philosopher, and thousands have repeated it after him. Man degenerates in time of peace. Only war awakens in him slumbering talents and powers and imbues him with sublime ideals. If war were to be abolished, mankind would decay into indolence and stagnation.

I submit to you that this is precisely the ideology that reigns in such publications as *National Review*. This is the view propounded from the lecterns at Republican gatherings. Speaker after speaker at conservative conferences echoes this very view. I've heard it again and again in private conversations among diehard Republicans.

This view that war is good for us is sheer fantasy, a dangerous and violent fit of utter irrationality. But it persists. It infects. It kills.

What view should replace the ideology of war? Mises again:

> It starts from the premise that not war, but peace, is the father of all things. What alone enables mankind to advance and distinguishes man from the animals is social cooperation. It is labor alone that is productive: it creates wealth and therewith lays the outward foundations for the inward flowering of man. War only destroys; it cannot create. War, carnage, destruction, and devastation we have in common with the predatory beasts of the jungle; constructive labor is our distinctively human characteristic. The liberal abhors war, not, like the humanitarian, in spite of the fact that it has beneficial consequences, but because it has only harmful ones. . . .

> Victorious war is an evil even for the victor . . . peace is always better than war.

The US has already lost the war on Iraq. It should pull out. When? Now. What will happen? I don't know. No one knows. What will people do when you let them out of their cages? What will slaves do when you free them? What happens when you free those who are imprisoned unjustly? I don't know the answer to these questions, and no one does. I will observe that other countries count the day that the US soldiers left as the beginning of a bright future.

I think of Somalia, which—after a Bush Senior invasion—Clinton wisely left in a lurch after violence against American soldiers. Today warlords still compete for control of the capital. The CIA factbook contains a sentence that might have pleased Thomas Jefferson: Somalia has "no permanent national government." But the rest of the country has moved on. It has prospered.

Here is more from the latest CIA factbook:

> Despite the seeming anarchy, Somalia's service sector has managed to survive and grow. Telecommunication firms provide wireless services in most major cities and offer the lowest international call rates on the continent. In the absence of a formal banking sector, money exchange services have sprouted throughout the country, handling between $500 million and $1 billion in remittances annually. Mogadishu's main market offers a variety of goods from food to the newest electronic gadgets. Hotels continue to operate, and militias provide security.

The CIA chooses the word "despite" the seeming anarchy. I would like to replace that with "because" of the seeming anarchy.

If the US leaves Iraq, a big cost will be borne by Americans. We have lost freedoms and rights. The military and spying sector has grown enormously. Big government abroad is incompatible with small government at home. To the extent we cheer war, we are cheering domestic socialism and our own eventual destruction as a civilization.

When you consider the full range of social, economic, and international planning on which it has embarked, you can know in advance that staying cannot work. Government is not God, nor are the men who run it impeccable or infallible, nor do they have a direct pipeline to the Almighty. Even if they were angels, they couldn't do it. The method they have chosen to bring about security and order is destined toward failure. But they are not angels. Their power has corrupted them, and the more absolute the power they gain, the more damage they create.

Let me state plainly too that we should end the entire "War on Terrorism" because it cannot work and it is killing us instead of them. The pool of potential terrorists is unlimited, and it has been unleashed by the very means the state has employed. Bin Laden is still on the loose, and everyone knows that there are hundreds or thousands of additional Bin Ladens out there.

But can't the state just kill more, employ ever more violence, perhaps even terrify the enemy into passivity? A bracing comment from Israeli military historian Martin Van Creveld: "The Americans in Vietnam tried it. They killed between two-and-a-half and three million Vietnamese. I don't see that it helped them much." Without admitting defeat, the Americans finally pulled out of Vietnam, which today has a thriving stock market.

Can the US just back out of its War on Terror? Wouldn't that mean surrender? It would mean that the state surrenders its role, but not that everyone else does. Had the airlines been in charge of their own security, 9-11 would not have happened. In the same way that the free market provides for all our material needs, it can provide our security needs as well.

The War on Terror is impossible, not in the sense that it cannot cause immense amounts of bloodshed and destruction and loss of liberty, but in the sense that it cannot finally achieve what it is supposed to achieve, and will only end in creating more of the same conditions that led to its declaration in the first place.

In other words, it is a typical government program, costly and unworkable, like socialism, like the War on Poverty, like the War on Drugs, like every other attempt by the government to shape reality according to its own designs. You can see the results in the fatality figures. You and I paid for those flags on the caskets of the soldiers. We paid for the war that cost them their lives. We paid for the cheaper coffins of the far more numerous Iraqi dead. We didn't do it voluntarily. The state forced us to do so, just as it is forcing Iraq to endure a dreadful occupation.

What is in the past is gone, a cost that is sunk and never to be regained. But we can control the future. Now is the time to end this ghastly undertaking in Iraq.

In American political culture, which is dominated by the competitive interest groups we call the two main political parties and their ideological compatriots, we are asked to choose between two false alternatives.

In the first, as that offered by the left and the Democrats, we are asked to think of the state as an expansive Good Samaritan who clothes, feeds, and heals people at home and abroad. They completely fail to notice that this Samaritan ends up not helping people but enslaving its clients and leaving the rest of us like the robbery victim on the street.

In the second, as offered by the right and the Republicans, we are asked to think of the state as an expansive Solomon with all power to right wrong and bring justice and faith to all peoples at home and abroad. They completely fail to notice that Solomon ends up behaving more like Caesar Augustus and his successors, sending all the world to be counted and taxed and then plotting to kill any competitive source of authority.

Are you independent minded? Reject these two false alternatives. Do you love freedom? Embrace peace. Do you love peace? Embrace private property. Do you love and defend civilization? Defend and protect it against all uses of Power, the evil against which we must proceed ever more boldly.

54.
EVEN CONSERVATIVES NEED
THE ANTIWAR MOVEMENT*

American citizens who have doubts—any doubts—about the war have been subjected to an amazing barrage of hate and threats in recent days. But if you believe the polls that show 90 percent-plus support for this war, it seems oddly disproportionate to whip up hysteria against a handful of doubters.

Rather than defend the antiwar position itself, I want to make a different argument. If you believe in freedom at all, you should hope that there are at least some doubters and protesters, regardless of the merit of their case. Even if you think this war is a great and necessary thing to teach the terrorists a lesson in American resolve, the preservation of liberty at home is also an important value.

The existence of an opposition movement is evidence that some restraints on government still exist. The government, which is always looking for reasons to increase its power, needs to know that there will always be an opposition.

The view that wartime requires complete unanimity of public opinion is not an American one—it is a position more characteristic of Islamic or other totalitarian states, where differences of opinion are regarded as a threat to public order, and where the leadership demands 100 percent approval from the people. These are also states where the head of government requires that he be treated like a deity, that there be no questioning of his edicts, that he govern with unquestioned power.

This is the very definition of despotism. Unpopular government is dangerous enough; popular government far more so. When public officials believe that there are no limits to their

---

*October 2001

power, no doubters about their pronouncements, no cynics who question their motives, they are capable of gross abuses. This is true both in wartime and peacetime. The most beloved governments are most prone to become the most abusive.

If you think that such despotism is not possible in the United States, you have not understood the American founding. Thomas Jefferson taught that American liberty depends on citizen willingness to be skeptical toward the claims of the central government. "Confidence is everywhere the parent of despotism," he wrote in his draft of the Kentucky Resolves.

> Free government is founded in jealousy, and not in confidence. It is jealousy and not confidence which prescribes limited constitutions, to bind down those whom we are obliged to trust with power.

"In questions of power," he concluded, "let no more be heard of confidence in man, but bind him down from mischief by the chains of the Constitution."

Wartime means that government is unleashing weapons of mass destruction against other human beings and their property. It is the most terrifying of all the powers of government. The war power, which means the power over life and death, can create in those who use it a feeling of omnipotence, the belief that they have absolute power, which gives rise to absolute corruption, as Lord Acton observed. This is true whether the war actions are popular or not.

Now, add to that reality an additional element: The population that supports the war power with its taxes is consumed in nationalistic fervor—to the point that nobody believes that government is capable of making a bad choice or of abusing its power. That is a sure prescription for abuse, and not only in wartime—the government enjoys this uncritical attitude, and will demand it in peacetime as well. Typically, in these cases, the abuse of peoples' rights is not decried but celebrated.

We have seen this happen in American history. Writing in the *Wall Street Journal*, Jay Winik reminds us that wartime abuse of presidential power has a long history. Lincoln imprisoned anti-war activists, including newspaper editors, judges and attorneys, and otherwise suspended all civil liberties. Wilson made it a crime to voice dissent on any aspect of the war, including the way it was financed. The jails were overrun with independent-minded people. Franklin Roosevelt did the same, and even set up internment camps for American citizens of Japanese descent.

Incredibly, even ominously, Winik writes about this in defense of the emergency powers that wartime provides. This is why we need to trade liberty for security, he says, and he implies that the Bush administration needs to go much further to meet the (low) standards set by his predecessors.

Winik's ultimate defense, however, involves a claim that is just plain wrong: "despite these previous and numerous extreme measures," writes Winik,

> there was little long-term or corrosive effect on society after the security threat had subsided. When the crisis ended, normalcy returned, and so too did civil liberties, invariably stronger than before.

It's true that the despotism subsided after the wars ended, if only because government has a difficult time trying to maintain the level of public support it enjoys during wartime once peace has arrived. But does government really return to normalcy?

In fact, what changes is our definition of normalcy. In no case after a war did the government return to its prewar size. The postwar government is always bigger, more intrusive, more draconian, more expensive, than the prewar government. It feels smaller because the government is no longer arresting dissidents. But our standard of what constitutes freedom and despotism changes during wartime. Nothing has been as corrosive of American liberty as war.

Wartime tyranny also creates an historical precedent for future violations of liberty. Every president who desires more power cites his predecessors who enjoyed similar power, just as the bloody legacies of FDR, Wilson, and Lincoln are being invoked on behalf of Bush today (witness Winik's own article).

Jefferson said in his first inaugural address:

> If there be any among us who would wish to dissolve this Union or to change its republican form, let them stand undisturbed as monuments of the safety with which error of opinion may be tolerated where reason is left free to combat it.

If you hate the antiwar movement and want to see it suppressed, you are no friend to liberty, even in peacetime.

55.
THE PAULIAN FOREIGN POLICY DOCTRINE

[Introduction to Ron Paul, A Foreign Policy of Freedom, *Lake Jackson, Texas: The Foundation for Rational Economics and Education, 2007.]*

Ron Paul has always believed that foreign and domestic policy should be conducted according to the same principles. Government should be restrained from intervening at home or abroad because its actions fail to achieve their stated aims, create more harm than good, shrink the liberty of the people, and violate rights.

Does that proposition seem radical? Outlandish or far-flung? Once you hear it stated, it makes perfect sense that there is no sharp distinction between the principles of domestic and foreign policy. They are part of the same analytical fabric. What would be inconsistent would be to favor activist government at home but restraint abroad, or the reverse: restraint at home and activism abroad. Government unleashed behaves in its own interests, and will not restrict itself in any area of life. It must be curbed in all areas of life lest freedom suffer.

If you recognize the line of thinking in this set of beliefs, it might be because you have read the *Federalist Papers*, the writings of Thomas Jefferson or George Washington or James Madison, or examined the philosophical origins of the American Revolution. Or you might have followed the debates that took place in the presidential election of 1800, in which this view emerged triumphant. Or perhaps you read the writings of the free traders prior to the Civil War, or the opponents of the War on Spain, or those who warned of entering World War I.

Or perhaps you have read the speeches and books against FDR's New Deal: the same group warned of the devastating consequences of World War II. Or maybe, in more recent history, you understood the animating principles behind the Republican takeover of Congress in 1994: a generation had turned away from all forms of foreign and domestic "nation building."

Not only does this Paulian view have a precedent in American history; it sums up the very core of what is distinctive about the American contribution to political ideas. The proposition was and is that people are better able to manage their lives than government can manage them. Under conditions of liberty, the result is prosperity and orderly civilization. Under government control, the result is relative poverty and unpredictable chaos. The proof is in the news every day.

How unusual, how incredibly strange, that Ron Paul, who has stood for these principles his entire public life, is criticized by some as a radical, outside the mainstream, and influenced by experimental ideas that are marginal at best. And why is he treated this way? Because he takes the ideas of Washington and Jefferson seriously, just as seriously as he takes the idea of freedom itself, and he does so in times when faith in Leviathan remains the dominant political ideology.

Ideology is such a powerful force that it has propped up policy inconsistency for more than a century. The left has a massive agenda for the state at home, and yet complains bitterly, with shock and dismay, that the same tools are used to start wars and build imperial structures abroad. The right claims to want to restrain government at home (at least in some ways) while whooping it up for war and global reconstruction abroad.

It doesn't take a game-theory genius to predict how this conflict works itself out in the long run. The left and the right agree to disagree on intellectual grounds but otherwise engage in a dangerous *quid pro quo*. They turn a blind eye to the government they don't like so long as they get the government they do like.

It's one thing for the left to grudgingly support international intervention. It makes some sense for a group that believes that government is omniscient enough to bring about fairness, justice, and equality at home to do the same for people abroad. In fact, I've never been able to make much sense out of left-wing antiwar activism, simply because it cuts so much against the idea of socialism, which itself can be summed up as perpetual war on the liberty and property of the people.

What strikes me as ridiculous is the right-wing view that the same government that is incompetent and dangerous domestically—at least in economic and social affairs—has some sort of Midas touch internationally such that it can bring freedom, democracy, and justice to any land its troops deign to invade. Not that the right wing is principled enough to pursue its domestic views, but I'm speaking here of its campaign rhetoric and higher-level critique of government that you find in their periodicals and books. The precise critique of government that they offer for the welfare state and regulatory measures—that they are expensive, counterproductive, and hobble human energies—applies many times over to international interventions.

But the right always seems to have an excuse for its inconsistency. In the early '50s, many on the right said that the usual principle of nonintervention had to give way to the fight against communism because this was a uniquely evil threat facing the world. We have to put up with a "totalitarian bureaucracy" within our shores (words used by W.F. Buckley) for the duration in order to beat back the great threat abroad. And so Leviathan grew and grew, and never more than under Republican presidents. Then one day, communism went away, the regimes having collapsed from self-imposed deprivation and ideological change.

A few years went by after 1990 when the right was inching toward a Paulian consistency. Then 9-11 happened, and the great excuse for Leviathan again entered the picture. Never mind that, as Congressman Paul pointed out, the crime of 9-11 was motivated by retribution against 10 years of killer US sanctions against Iraq, US troops on Muslim holy lands, and US subsidies for Palestinian occupation. No, the American Right bought into the same farce that led them to support the Cold War: Islamic fanaticism is a unique evil unlike anything we've ever seen, so we have to put up with Leviathan (again!) for the duration.

Well, Ron Paul didn't buy into it. He is unique in this respect, and this is especially notable since he has been under pressure from his own party at a time when his party has ruled the executive, judicial, and legislative branches. He stuck by his principles, and not merely as a pious gesture. His critique of the post 9-11 warfare state has been spot-on in speech after speech. He foresaw the failure of the US invasion of Afghanistan. He never believed the nonsense about how US bombs would transform Iraq into a modern democracy. He never went along with the propaganda lies about weapons of mass destruction. Nowadays, we often hear politicians say that they have changed their minds on the Iraq War and that if they had known then what they know now, they never would have gone along. Well, hindsight is child's play in politics. What takes guts and insight is the ability to spot a hoax even as it is being perpetrated. In any case, they have no excuse for not knowing: Ron Paul told them!

The freedom to trade internationally is an essential principle. It means that consumers should not be penalized for buying from anyone, or selling to anyone, regardless of their residence. Nor should domestic suppliers be granted anything like a monopoly or subsidized treatment. Nor should trade be used as a weapon in the form of sanctions. Ron Paul has upheld these principles as well, which makes him an old-fashioned liberal in the manner of Cobden and Bright and the American Southern tradition. He has also rejected the mistake of many free traders who believe that a military arm is necessary to back the invisible hand of the marketplace. For Ron Paul, freedom is all of a piece.

Ron Paul's singular voice on foreign affairs has done so much to keep the flame of a consistent liberty burning in times when it might otherwise have been extinguished. He has drawn public attention to the ideas of the founders. He has alerted people to the dangers of empire. He has linked domestic and foreign affairs through libertarian analytics, even when others have been bamboozled by the lies or too intimidated to contradict them. He has told the truth, always. For this, every American, every citizen of the world, is deeply in his debt. In fact, I'm willing to predict that a hundred years from now and more, when all the current office holders are all but forgotten, Ron Paul's name will be remembered as a bright light in dark times.

We can't but be deeply grateful that Ron Paul's prophetic words have been collected in this book. May it be widely distributed. May its lessons be absorbed by this and future generations. May this treatise stand as an example of how to fight for what is right even when everyone else is silent. May it always be regarded as proof that there were men of courage alive in the first decade of the third millennium. May public and intellectual opinion someday rise to its level of intellectual sophistication and moral valor.

SECTION 3: 9–11

56.
WHAT NOT TO DO*

Suddenly, after the attack, all of our wealth and all of our freedoms are up for grabs, and not only by foreign terrorists, but by our own government and its uncritical cheerleaders. Is there a limit to how much liberty can be compromised in the name of security? How much spending Congress should authorize? How much money and credit the Federal Reserve should create? How much business can be regulated?

Apparently not. But why not? A government unconstrained by law, tradition, or public opinion is nothing short of despotic. Not everything can be justified in the name of punishment, prevention, and safety: not conscription, not the elimination of privacy, not killing innocents, and not the use of nuclear weapons that necessarily violate the tenets of just war. Yet one US senator, no less, has called for the death of innocents on grounds that terrorists don't distinguish between military and civilian targets. In other words, we are being told to fight terrorism by becoming terrorists ourselves.

Robert Higgs, author of *Crisis and Leviathan*, has shown how government grows the most during times such as these. In a

*September 14, 2001

299

usual wartime situation, the government massively expands and then falls back only partially after it is over. This creates a ratchet effect that guarantees a relentless march of the state. Every new spending program creates a precedent said to apply in peacetime. How often have we heard calls for a "Marshall Plan" to solve this or that social issue?

The present circumstances are even worse than wartime, where at least there is a starting point and an ending point (though Clinton's wars have clouded even this). A war against terrorism, already begun in the 1980s and so far spectacularly unsuccessful, promises to be perpetual because of the endless number of conceivable threats. We'll never know if we are winning or losing the war since something as monstrously huge as the recent attack could happen anytime.

It is proposed that we be on permanent war alert, which means that we must permanently trade our liberty for a promised (but undelivered) security. Bush's requested $20 billion, make that $40 billion and rising, for antiterrorist measures is just the beginning, but think for a moment of just how much money that is. That's the annual budget of a very mature federal agency, more than twice the total spent by all the world's citizens going to the movies, and more than the entire GDP of Panama and Slovenia combined.

The US government already spends nearly $10 billion and employs nearly 1,000 people to work on counterterrorism exclusively, and it has gained us nothing. Are we really supposed to believe that quadrupling this budget will somehow work to prevent future attacks? The money so far has done nothing but saddle the American people with more armed federal agents and invasions of privacy. It's a sad commentary that many Americans, for now, say they are willing to shell out more in taxes and give up commercial freedoms. It is even sadder to note that the purchased security won't actually be delivered.

So far we haven't even been spared the commentator who pops his head up to observe, after a natural disaster, that at least the government-directed rebuilding effort will be good for the economy. One might think that the sheer scale of the losses would be too immense for that classic Keynesian fallacy to rear its head. But no: writing in *Slate*, Timothy Noah informs us that "we live in a very wealthy nation that responds to horrible disasters by spending large sums of money." This spending will, he predicts, "provide a meaningful Keynesian stimulus to a national economy."

Must we recount Frédéric Bastiat's parable of the broken window? The story goes that a boy throws a rock through a store window, and everyone is justly sad. Suddenly, Timothy Noah's nineteenth-century equivalent shows up to say, hey, this is actually great! Now the glazier will be paid to fix it, and he in turn will buy a suit, and the process will multiply until everyone is actually made better off. What this forgets is the alternative uses of the resources that are spent in rebuilding: the unseen costs of property destruction.

And speaking of unseen costs, what about the alternative uses that might have been made of the $40 billion (for now) to be spent on counterterrorism that will go to hiring more government employees to boss everyone around? This kind of spending multiplies the damage already done by the terrorists, destroying more wealth and channeling more resources from social needs into political ones.

There have been many other equally absurd actions, all of which amount to compromising our personal and commercial liberty. The first impulse of the government in all times of crisis is control and coercion. So it was no surprise that all planes, private and commercial, were forcibly grounded, including those carrying overnight packages. But this action has already bankrupted Midway Airlines, and others will follow in the United States and Britain. If it gets worse, so will the pressure to subsidize them.

New regulations are being imposed that will dramatically increase the costs associated with air travel, some of them (like the elimination of curbside check-ins) making no sense whatsoever. The presumption is that the airline industry itself has no incentive to prevent hijacking. Well, perhaps if airline crews had not been barred (decades ago) from carrying weapons, this never would have happened. Leave it to the government to prohibit owners of airlines from defending their own property (and customers) when it is most vulnerable and thus necessary.

Perhaps, too, if the airlines weren't so busy obeying preposterous government demands (like asking every passenger if our bags have been with us the whole time) and otherwise doing things the federal way, they could have designed some serious antihijacking measures that didn't also attack the paying customers. Government "security" crowds out real security provided in the commercial marketplace.

The coercion generated by the crisis first showed up in the harassment of gasoline retailers, who, trying to conserve resources in the face of a wildly gyrating spot-market price for gas, raised prices. To threaten them and investigate them gives us a clue into what government will do with its new powers: not go after difficult-to-find criminals, but the easy-to-find innocents who are just trying to make do.

Then there's monetary policy, the means by which the government taxes when the legislative process seems too cumbersome. Thus the Federal Reserve injected $38 billion one day, another $70 billion the next, and established a $50 billion swap line with other central banks the next. Now that's power. Not all of this new money will make its way into the economy; at least, that should be the hope. To destroy the purchasing power of the dollar in response to the destruction of the US financial district is a heck of a "response" to terrorism.

As for the draft, someone please explain how conscripting America's young men and women into the military—forcibly taking them away from their jobs and schools—is going to prevent more attacks like we saw September 11. It's a power grab, of course. The government is using this occasion to do what it could only have dreamed of doing last week.

Civil liberties are already being curtailed. The government's invasive "carnivore" software is being shopped around the nation's leading Internet Service Providers, to permit the feds to spy on all email communications. Until now, the ISPs resisted. But in the aftermath of the new Bush "antiterrorism" act passed by the Senate, they will not be allowed to say no.

As regards the mainstream print media, they are their usual selves: allowing their pages to be effectively enlisted in the war effort without complaint. Hence, the *Wall Street Journal* and the *New York Times* are both whooping it up for bombing anything and everything, on the theory that yet another display of rampant imperialism will deter future attacks and not actually have the reverse effect. By pursuing this course, we are made less secure, of course.

What, then, should the government do in this time of crisis? Less, not more. It was the US foreign policy of unyielding empire that incited these attacks in the first place. It's hard to say when the turning point was. It might have been 1990, when the United States gave tacit approval to Iraq to invade Kuwait and then bombed Iraq back into the stone age for doing so. It might have been the war on Serbia, or the bombs in Sudan, or the destruction of the Chinese embassy, or any number of other foreign adventures.

Most likely, the turning point was May 12, 1996, when Madeleine Albright, then US ambassador to the United Nations, explained to Lesley Stahl of CBS that 500,000 dead Iraqi children, killed by US sanctions, was morally justified to get Saddam. "We think the price is worth it," were her exact words, words that were mostly unreported here but which rang out throughout the Arab world. She was then made Secretary of State. That was five years ago. We continue to bomb Iraq, often on a daily basis, and the sanctions are still on. We should not do unto others what we do not want them to do unto us.

There's never a good time to give up liberty. But when everyone else is calling for despotism to fight despotism, it's the best time to stand up and say: We will not be moved. We need more, not less, liberty.

57.
FORGOTTEN VICTIMS OF 9-11*

In all discussion of 9-11, one year later, much attention is given to the firefighters, police, and emergency workers whose services, as employees of the public sector, were called on that day. You may hear about the innocents who died on the airplanes that were hijacked and used as missiles. The people you won't hear about are those who were specifically targeted and murdered.

They were, after all, working for the private sector. They were traders and merchants, people working in the field of economic enterprise. In an ironic tribute to their value, these people were targeted because the terrorists hoped to cripple the US economy. It would appear that the terrorists understood something that even our own elites do not understand.

If you find that observation shocking, consider the current campaign against business. Though Republican, the Bush administration has followed the FDR model in subtly and not-so-subtly blaming the private sector, specifically those in finance and accounting associated with large enterprises, for the current recession and the gutting of pensions that resulted from falling stock prices.

These people have been scapegoated for the downturn in the business cycle, just as the terrorists scapegoated the New York financial sector for what they see as the belligerence of US foreign policy. Not understanding the resilience of American enterprise, the terrorists hoped to put a big dent in American prosperity.

US government elites, however, have for a year attacked the same class of people while overestimating the extent to which

_____

*August 2002

financial markets can be hamstrung, hindered, and harassed without consequence.

True, the campaign has so far been limited to those individuals and institutions that can readily be accused of "fraud" even though most of the issues under consideration are complicated matters of accounting principles that no jury is competent to adjudicate. Make no mistake, however, the merchant class as a class is under fire, just as it has been throughout history during periods of economic downturn.

Congress, of all institutions, has hauled business executives in front of them to accuse them without trial, asking questions so asinine that they can't possibly be answered with a straight face. Greenspan himself has blamed the "infectious greed" of the business class for the downturn in the markets.

Most outrageously, Bush has drawn an analogy between the 9-11 terrorists and the American business class! That was the subtext of his remark that "In the aftermath of September 11, we refused to allow fear to undermine our economy and we will not allow fraud to undermine it either." Thus did he promise "No more easy money for corporate criminals. Just hard time. . . . This law says to every dishonest corporate leader, you'll be exposed and punished. The era of low standards and false profits is over."

But look at the names of the businesses that suffered destruction and death in the 9-11 attacks. They were Deutsche Bank, Fiduciary Trust, Kemper Insurance, Lehman Brothers, Morgan Stanley Dean Witter, Cantor Fitzgerald, Oppenheimer Funds, Credit Suisse First Boston, and others involved in banking, finance, insurance, accounting, management, and the craft of trading generally.

These are the companies that invest our savings, provide insurance, trade currencies, and coordinate prices across borders and markets. They are not perfect. They are not all-knowing. And during this bear market, many of them have lost money. But it is they who take the risk to find entrepreneurial opportunities in markets of all sorts. Even today, as in ancient times, their craft is wrongly considered ignoble and perhaps even inherently dishonest. And yet, they are the people who work daily to sustain prosperity and improve the lot of mankind.

After they were so cruelly attacked on 9-11, the federal government stepped in to make two great promises, both of which turned out to be lies. First, the feds assured us that they would bring to justice those who brought those attacks about. They have not done so. They have violated liberties and stepped up Leviathan, but Osama and his co-conspirators remain at large, and one wonders whether the government prefers it this way in order to keep us all constantly afraid.

The second great promise the government made was that it would protect us and American prosperity from further attacks. And true to form, the same people have spent the last year attacking business, casting aspersions on traders and those in the financial industry, rounding up executives, and deliberately obscuring the difference between boom-market accounting and outright fraud.

Let us not forget that all this began with a multiple hijacking. And what has the government done to prevent that in the future? It has vastly increased the inconveniences for average travelers, which has in turn bankrupted several airline companies (also private enterprises). These companies are still not allowed to arm their pilots to protect their planes—an entire year later! Meanwhile, the United States is engaged in a foreign policy that might as well be designed to incite further attacks.

What lessons have we learned since 9-11? As usual, nothing. What should we have learned? First, that enterprise has its enemies and these enemies have no hesitation about using violence to achieve their ends, whether that violence comes from terrorism, the Justice Department, or the sidearm of the officially empowered regulator. Second, we should have learned that we cannot trust the government to give us justice or provide us security.

During this anniversary, you will hear many tributes and much discussion of the meaning of it all. Keep track, if you can, of all the times when you hear mention of the occupations of those who died in the World Trade Center, the vocations to which they dedicated their lives. I wonder whether you will find any examples at all.

And yet it remains true that those who understand the contribution of enterprise to civilization must mourn the lost lives of those who worked in the World Trade Center. We grieve for their lost vocations as well, and we owe it to them to appreciate anew their contribution to society.

58.

COUNTERTERRORISM (BY GOVERNMENT) IS IMPOSSIBLE*

At last the topic of 9-11 has shifted onto productive ground. Thanks to the efforts of former counterterrorism official Richard Clarke, some thought is being put into the government failures behind the attacks. "Your government failed you," he says. Precisely, and in many more ways than he or anyone else at these hearings is willing to say.

Here is the problem. The core failure goes way beyond anything the current government managers—however inept, distracted, or corrupt—can correct. If you tell your dog to make you dinner, for example, you can observe later that the dog failed to do so, and have great regrets about this. But what you learn from this experience and how you proceed are the crucial questions. Does the dog need better tools, more scoldings, and a professional trainer? Better to observe that the dog is not the right one for the job. In the same way, the government is not the

---

*March 2004

right one for the job of providing security for the American people.

The conclusion of the commission investigating the policies leading up to 9-11 will be the same as from every government commission: a recommendation that the government should have done more and should do more in the future. Both Clarke and his critics presume that the war on terrorism is something that the government can fight, and the debate is over whether the government had done enough prior to 9-11 to sort through intelligence findings, name al Qaeda as the key problem, and anticipate the attacks.

Bush's critics are thrilled to hear Clarke restate what has long been known: the Bush administration was obsessed with Iraq to the exclusion of the radical Islamic threat.

There can be no question about this administration's Iraq fixation. The Bush regime had it in for Iraq for a whole range of reasons, from personal vendettas to oil to regional political issues and probably a few others we are not privy to. It certainly cries out for explanation why this poor country, ruled by a man the US government had long backed, suffering under sanctions for a decade after an unjustified war, should be invaded and occupied even though it represented no threat to the United States.

Clarke believes Iraq was a distraction, and he is surely right. He also believes that more should have been done sooner to counter genuine terrorist threats, that the attacks on Afghanistan should have taken place earlier, that Bin Laden should have been taken out earlier, that the military and the spooks should have taken more liberties in zapping the bad guys before the bad guys zapped us.

The solution implied in this approach is something no American should favor. It implies not less warmongering but merely a different form of imperialism, focused on one country instead of another, this set of intelligence data instead of that, while not even addressing the question of why the United States might be the subject of attacks at all. It is even possible that more

Clarkeian-style counterterrorism would have inspired more attacks sooner, but we'll never know since there are no controlled experiments in the relationship between politics and the real world.

And despite all the partisan wrangling about the Clarke message and the hearings in general, the upshot is a message that perfectly accords with something that every bureaucrat and politician wants to hear: that government needs a freer hand, that it did not do enough, that it needs more resources, that it should not be hamstrung in any way. What are government commissions for, except to announce such findings and create a cover for Congress and the White House (whoever happens to occupy it) to demand ever more money and power?

The real question to ask is whether it could have been any other way. Say the US had killed Bin Laden. Cheney is of course correct that this would not have prevented 9-11. Even if it had, there would have been other attacks of a different sort. Or say the US had entirely destroyed al Qaeda (whatever that would mean): Albright is correct that the ideology behind al Qaeda's existence is still everywhere to be found because it represents not a peculiar conspiracy by a few, but a response to US policy in general.

The government can spend many years and billions of dollars preventing attacks that have already occurred by doing things it might have wished it had done years or decades ago. But note that there has been no discussion at all of the actual policies that everyone knows inspired the attacks and made them easier to carry out.

Just to mention a few: the stationing of troops in Saudi Arabia, the sanctions against Iraq, the continuing intervention in the ever-lasting Israel-Palestine conflict, the propping up of secular dictatorships all over the Arab world, the raising up and funding of Islamic radicals to counter Soviet influence in Afghanistan, and the regulatory prohibitions in the United States against permitting airlines to manage their own security issues. The US government cannot pursue all these policies and then react in shock when it turns out that some people exploit them with violent intent.

Many observers of these policies predicted that something along these lines would take place. You don't need to be a "counterterrorism" bureaucrat to see it. The response to the events of 9-11 around the world was very telling. While the world felt awful for America, most everyone (except Americans) believed that something like this was inevitable. As for who was responsible, the enemies of the United States have become countless. The government's response was to make ever more enemies, which is what the recent US policy in Iraq has done.

In other words, the only real way to prevent terrorism is to do less in the way of government policy and more in the way of private provision and trade, which would be far easier to do if the warfare state would stop fomenting trouble all around the world.

How can the market provide security? This gets us into another huge area, and nothing I could write in a column would fully convince anyone of such a radical thesis, so let me merely refer you to the book, *The Myth of National Defense*, edited by Hans-Hermann Hoppe, which shows that security is not a unique good that must be provided by the state. (Even if you don't own it, there is no good excuse not to read it: mises.org/etexts/defensemyth.pdf.)

Let me mention just one issue that has impressed many people who are following the hearings: that of information overload. There are so many bits of intelligence data that are flying in and out of government offices, how can policy makers possibly assess the relative seriousness of various threats, much less prepare coherent responses to them?

Contrary to what the government implies, this is not a problem unique to the public sector. A typical multinational corporation faces an information problem just as serious: data flying from every country concerning a million different topics and conditions, every one of which could have a profound effect on profitability the very day it is received.

How do corporations deal with the problem of information overload? They rely on market signaling and the decentralized planning of millions of private individuals to provide guidance, and they depend heavily on the minute-by-minute feedback mechanism as provided by prices. The government has no such institutions at its disposal, neither to convey information, nor assess its accuracy, nor provide ongoing feedback on how it responds to conditions.

The lesson we should take from 9-11 is that the government cannot protect us. It is utterly inept, and no changes in policy as recommended by a commission or present or ex-government officials are going to change that.

59.

AN INEVITABLE BOG*

Let's just say the postal system were private, and delivering packages of anthrax to government offices. Imagine, then, how dramatically different the spin would be. The carrier companies would be catching hell for not having the proper security measures in place, and for obviously "putting profits ahead of safety." All political pressure would be for nationalizing the mails. Surely this is the only way to assure total protection!

But, of course, the post office has always been nationalized, before Nixon renamed it an "independent" government-chartered faux-corporation to lose more money than ever. Has government involvement in the mails protected anyone from infection? No. Does the post office have any system in place to assure its customers it is not delivering packages laced with disease? No.

---

*November 2001

If the mails were private, companies would compete on speed, price, and even safety. You might be loath to open anything from a disreputable company. But under the present system, there is only one supplier. On certain types of packages, consumers have no choice but to send and receive using the government's service, which offers no guarantee of anything.

Precisely because it is a government operation, the post office isn't on the hot seat, just as the government's failure to provide security wasn't blamed for 9-11. There's this absurd presumption that government is always better at providing security than the market, and when the government proves to be terrible, the presumption is that any system would have failed under the circumstances, but that government failed less than others would have. What a leap of faith!

Here's a concrete example of market-provided security—based in the use and defense of private property—that relates directly to 9-11. On July 6, 1954, back before the FAA decided to disarm pilots, an armed teenager forced his way onto an American Airlines DC-6, with 58 passengers on board, on the tarmac at Cleveland airport. When it became clear that he had every intention of hijacking the plane, the captain, William Bonnell of Fort Worth, Texas, took out his little .38-caliber Colt and blasted him. (The story appears in the *Houston Chronicle*.)

The story had no real impact at the time, just as robberies prevented by private gun ownership never make the news. That's the way the market provision of security works: it means routine checking for every contingency. We lock our houses and cars even when we feel no grave threat that we will be robbed. We have alarm systems on our houses, maybe only because it means lower insurance rates. Even grocery stores use monitors in parking lots and store aisles, not because the management believes thieves and hoodlums are everywhere, but just to be on the safe side.

That's the market at work, which is not to say that market provision of security is perfect. The key difference between it and government is that it responds to violations of property and to the threat of such violations with proactive measures. It has every incentive to do so. The most the government can do is to keep issuing its preposterous demands for us to go on "the highest state of alert"—with no other information and no attempt to assess the reliability of whatever "intelligence" they claim to have.

[Note: What the heck is this "highest state of alert" anyway? To hear the Justice Department talk, you'd think the entire nation had been through drills and learned all the proper responses. Instead of helping us prepare for attacks, then, the government denies us information that might actually help (if such information exists).]

Bizarre is the only way to describe the proposals to put government in charge of security at airports. If the post office has no means of preventing the delivery of disease, and the government's jails can't keep out drugs, why would anyone believe the feds can improve the already federally supervised security at airports? The only real benefit will be for public-sector unions, who will recruit more dues-paying members, and for those who want to acculturate us to more regimentation.

Not only has the government botched the provision of security; it has botched the war. Whether it's bombing Red Cross buildings and mud huts with civilians inside, inspiring people to emigrate to Afghanistan in order to fight, or failing to find Bin Laden (or even cough up indisputable evidence that he was involved), the war has so far been a typical government failure—not unlike the War on Drugs.

No surprise that headlines in the US and the UK this week observe the same downtrend in public support for the war effort. Though support is still high, majorities are no longer willing to say that the war is going well, or predict that it will end well. As the stories in the *New York Times* and the *London Observer* have emphasized, the key is not the raw polling numbers but the trend, which suggests that public support is weakening.

Bin Laden is still at large, for one thing. And the status of the other nine on the FBI's "most wanted" list doesn't inspire confidence. Many of them have been at large for years, right here in the good old US of A. What makes anyone believe that the same government that can't catch its own fugitives is going to nab characters like Bin Laden in some godforsaken hell between the border of China and the Caspian Sea?

There are always those who say that the reason for the failure is that government isn't going far enough. We didn't spend enough on welfare for the War on Poverty, we haven't cracked enough skulls during the War on Drugs, we haven't given public schools enough money in the War on Illiteracy, and we haven't dropped enough bombs or used enough troops in the War on Terror.

In same way, after 72 years of Soviet socialism, you can still find ex-apparatchiks who say that socialism was never really given a chance. Some people will never give up their faith in power.

60.

THE MEANING OF SECURITY*

Let's think about the word security, which has been in the news lately because the Bush administration seeks a major shift in the way funds are spent in Iraq. It wants $3 billion moved from spending on reconstruction to spending on "security." There's a political science lesson in that usage.

The reason for the shift, of course, is the obvious unraveling of anything resembling civilization in Iraq: bombings, killings, mini-wars are everywhere. Whole regions of Iraq are lost to US control, and not even Baghdad is holding. Of the $18 billion

---

*September 2004

Congress allocated for public works, the Bush administration argues that it makes sense to divert some to bring a measure of public stability to the country.

But what are we really talking about when we say "security"? It is money taken from you and me to be spent to force the Iraqi population to submit to the puppet government that rules only because of the United States. It is money to pay for more police, weapons, bullets, bombs, spying, arresting, torturing, jailing, maiming, and killing.

The theory is that more fear and more fear-inspiring bloodshed will tame the guerrillas and stop them from plotting more bombings, shootings, killings. The money will buy compliance, and pay the bills of those who use force to try to bring it about. Many people would be happy for an end to violence, to be sure, but the primary purpose is the protection of the state from rebels.

Submission and compliance: that is what is meant by the term security in the state's lexicon. It is an interesting choice of words. Its use in public life dates at least to the advent of Social Security, a tax scheme that promises to put you on welfare in your old age in exchange for paying 14 percent of your income to support current retirees who constitute the wealthiest demographic slice of the American population. Even in this case, the term security meant compliance, as shown by the tendency of recipients to back ever more redistribution.

Now we have the Department of Homeland Security, a gargantuan agency that administers foreign and domestic spying, sends hither swarms of agents to harass us at airports, conduct drills in the event that the government decides that martial law is the only option, and generally suppress any and all signs of insurrection wherever they might appear. Here too the term security means submission, control, compliance, obedience, and stability for the state.

Who is this security trying to secure? We are told it is for our own benefit. It is government that makes us secure from terrible threats. And yet, if we look closely, we can see that the main beneficiary of security is the state itself.

We all understand this intuitively. Let's say you know that someone is after you—an ex-spouse, for example—and threatens your very life. Would you call the Department of Homeland Security and expect a response? No, the DHS is there to protect the state, as evidenced by the comparatively energetic response that a threat to the president's life would elicit.

Of course, there is a need and demand for authentic security. We all seek it. We lock our doors, deter criminals with alarms, arm ourselves in case the alarms don't do it, prepare for the worst in the case of natural disaster, save for the future, and construct our professional lives in ways that minimize the chance of disadvantageous turns of events. This is what security means to us in the real world.

It is not unexpected that the state would seek the same thing: security not for us but for itself and its employees. The state has a special reason to desire security: its agents are always a minority of the population, funded by eating out their substance, and its rule is always vulnerable. The more control it seeks over a population, the more its agents are wise to watch their backs.

Where does that leave the rest of us in our demand for security? In the world of ideas, a vigorous debate is taking place about the extent to which private enterprise is capable of providing security, not only as a supplement but as a full replacement for state-provided security.

Advocates of fully privatized security point out that in the real world, most of the security we enjoy is purchased in the private sector. Vast networks of food distribution protect against starvation, private agents guard our homes, insurance companies provide compensation in the event of unexpected misfortune, and the locks and guns and gated communities provided by private enterprise do the bulk of work for our security in the real world.

In our community, we spent days preparing for what was expected to be the terrible hurricane Ivan. It didn't do much damage here, but in all the preparations, this much is clear: no one counted on the government to do anything to protect us. And no one counts on the government to do any reconstruction either. We depend entirely on our own efforts, while post-disaster clean up would have been done entirely by private contract.

The message of this school of thought is that liberty and security (real security) are not opposites such that one must choose between them. They go together. Liberty is the essence of the free enterprise system that provides for all our material needs, that helps us overcome the uncertainties and contingencies of life.

As for the public agencies, how do they act in a crisis? They are reduced to sending out warnings to "stay alert" and otherwise blowing big alarms as if no one can look outside their windows, listen to the radio, or check the web. This is pretty much all Homeland Security does with its laughable system of color-coded alerts. They also order us to leave our homes, search us, and threaten us with arrest if we protest.

The truth is that government has less ability to protect us in an emergency than we have to protect ourselves. And despite all the propaganda you hear about brave public workers, the same was true during 9-11. The bottom line is that it represented the greatest failure of state security in a generation. That is the real lesson from that day.

Iraq too demonstrates a lesson concerning public and private security. When it is politically feasible, the high muck-a-mucks in Iraq choose to use private security firms to protect themselves. This was the major undertaking of its mercenaries when the US civilian government was running matters. How ironic that even the state chooses private contractors when it can. When it seeks genuine security, it too buys it on the free market.

Americans have something in common with Iraqis: experience has told us that when the government promises to bring us security, it means only that it wants more control over our lives so that the state can enjoy longevity and peace at our expense. The real choice isn't between liberty and security; it is between our security and the state's.

61.
A Tribute to Trade*

[This column is dedicated to the memory of the friends and associates of the Mises Institute who died at the hands of the terrorists who destroyed the World Trade Center.]

The sight of New York City's twin World Trade Center towers falling to the ground, the result of an act of deliberate aggression, seems to symbolize two points that seem entirely forgotten today: the magnificent contribution that commerce makes to civilization, and just how vulnerable it is to its enemies. If the enemies of capitalist commerce are hell-bent on the destruction of the source of wealth, there are few means available to prevent it.

From the two towers soaring 1,300 feet above the city, a person on the 110th floor enjoyed a panoramic view stretching 55 miles: a broad vision of human civilization. Much more important for the flowering of civilization is what went on there: entrepreneurship, creativity, exchange, service, all of it peaceful, all of it to the benefit of mankind.

What kind of service? Germany's Deutsche Bank occupied four floors. The financial firm of Morgan Stanley took 20 floors, and at the time of the explosion, the firm was hosting a meeting for the 400 members of the National Association of Business Economists. Fred Alger Management, a training ground for

---
*Setepmber 11, 2001

young traders and stock analysts, occupied the 93rd floor. Bond dealers for Cantor Fitzgerald took up floors 101 through 105. Mass Mutual was on the 33rd floor.

Fiduciary Trust, a wonderful money management company, employed 500 people who worked on five floors at the very top of the building. Other companies there included Network Plus, Harris Beach & Wilcox, Oppenheimer Funds, Bank of America, Kemper Insurance, Lehman Brothers, Morgan Stanley Dean Witter, Credit Suisse First Boston, and Sun Microsystems.

Here were the brokers who invest our savings, trying their best to channel resources to their most profitable uses. Here were insurance companies, which provide the valuable service of securing our lives and property against accidents. Here were many retailers, who risk their own livelihoods to provide us with goods and services we as consumers desire. Here were lenders, lawyers, agents, and architects whose contributions are so essential to our daily lives.

Some of us knew men and women who are now dead. But most of them will remain anonymous to us. Whether we knew them or not, they were our benefactors nonetheless, because in the commercial society, the actions of entrepreneurs benefit everyone, in mostly imperceptible ways. They all contribute to the stock of capital on which prosperity itself is based. They work daily to coordinate the use of resources to eliminate waste and inefficiency, and make products and services available that improve our everyday lives.

Think especially of the remarkable people in that place who facilitated international trade. They daily accomplished the seemingly impossible. Faced with a world of more than two hundred countries, and hundreds more languages and dialects, with as many currencies and legal regimes, and thousands of local cultural differences, and billions of consumers, they found ways to make peaceful exchange possible. They looked for and seized on every opportunity that presented itself to enable human cooperation.

No government has been able to accomplish anything this remarkable. It is a miracle made possible by commerce, and by those who undertake the burden of making it happen.

We often hear platitudes about the brotherhood of man. But you don't see it at the United Nations or at the summits of governments. There you see conflicts, resolved usually by the use of other people's money taken by force. But at the World Trade Center, the brotherhood of man was an everyday affair.

It didn't matter if you were a small rug merchant in Nepal, a fisherman off the Chinese coast, or a machine manufacturer in the American Midwest, the people who worked here put you in contact with others who valued what you did and what you could give to others. Consent and choice, not conflict and coercion, were at the core of everything. Their watchword was contract, not hegemony.

True, the objective of all these merchants and traders may have been their own personal betterment, but the effect of their work was to serve not just themselves but everyone else as well. Because the beneficial effects of trade are not just local but national, and not just national but international, the inhabitants of these buildings were in many ways the benefactors of all of us personally. The blessings we experienced from their work came to us every time we used a credit card, withdrew money from the bank, bought from a chain store, or ordered something online.

In short, these people were producers. Frédéric Bastiat said of them: they are the people who

> create out of nothing the satisfactions that sustain and beautify life, so that an individual or a people is enabled to multiply these satisfactions indefinitely without inflicting privation of any kind on other men or other peoples.

Yes, they earned profits, but for the most part, their work went unrewarded. It was certainly unappreciated in the culture at large. They are not called public servants. They are not praised for their sacrifices to the common good. Popular culture treated these "money centers" as sources of greed and corruption. We are told that these people are the cause of environmental destruction and labor exploitation, that the "globalists" inside the World Trade Center were conspiring not to create but to destroy. Even after all the destruction wrought by socialism, capitalists must still bear the brunt of envy and hatred.

The impulse to hate the entrepreneurial class shows up in myriad ways. We see it when franchise restaurants are bombed, as they frequently are in France. In the United States, the government works to "protect" land from being used by commerce, and increasing numbers of our laws are built on the presumption that the business class is out to get us, not serve us. The business pages more often report on the villainy, rather then the victories, of enterprise. Or take a look at the typical college bookstore, where students are still required to read Marx and the Marxians rather than Mises and the Misesians.

All the enemies of capitalism act as if its elimination would have no ill consequences for our lives. In the classroom, on television, at the movies, we are continually presented a picture of what a perfect world of bliss we would enjoy if we could just get rid of those who make a living through owning, speculating, and amassing wealth.

For hundreds of years, in fact, the intellectual classes have demanded the expropriation and even the extermination of capitalistic expropriators. Since ancient times, the merchant and his trade have been considered ignoble. In fact, their absence would reduce us to barbarism and utter poverty. Even now, the destruction of the property and people at the once-mighty towers of the world has already impoverished us in more ways than we will ever know.

Those who understand economics and celebrate the creative power of commerce understand this higher truth, which is why we defend the market economy at every opportunity. That is why we seek to eliminate the barriers that governments and anticapitalists have erected against the businessmen's freedom.

We see them as the defenders of civilization, and so we seek to guard their interests in every way we know how.

We mourn the lost lives of those who worked in the World Trade Center towers, which are no more. We mourn their lost vocations. We owe it to them to appreciate anew their contribution to society.

As Mises wrote,

> No one can find a safe way out for himself if society is sweeping towards destruction. Therefore everyone, in his own interests, must thrust himself vigorously into the intellectual battle. None can stand aside with unconcern; the interests of everyone hang on the result. Whether he chooses or not, every man is drawn into the great historical struggle, the decisive battle into which our epoch has plunged us.

PART IV: THE MARKET

"Markets do not exist as a 'policy'; they are the de-facto result of respecting rights to person and property."

Section 1: Capitalism (and Mercantilism)

62.
The Millennium's Great Idea*

Thank goodness this bloody century, the era of communism, national socialism, fascism, and central planning—in short, the century of government worship—is coming to an end. May we use the occasion to re-pledge our allegiance to human freedom, which is the basis of prosperity and civilization itself, and to repudiate every ideological force that opposes it.

The first blows struck by the enemies of liberty in this century were World War I and the Bolshevik Revolution. These two events broke the hearts of an entire generation of classical liberals, because they interrupted centuries of progress toward peace and freedom. These men understood something that we do not today: that the moments in the history of mankind characterized by comfort and security (to say nothing of prosperity) are sadly rare.

The truth is that, for the masses of men, the history of the millennium has been one of hunger, famine, and disease. In

*December 1999

325

twelfth-century England, for example, a deadly famine occurred every 14 years. From the thirteenth to the seventeenth centuries, famine characterized every 10 years. These episodes killed tens of thousands, and forced average people to eat dogs and tree bark.

Not that daily life without famine was comfortable. For the masses of men, houses were tiny, with a hole in the thatched reed roof for smoke. The town pump was the only water supply. Sewage disposal was primitive, and outbreaks of scurvy, leprosy, and typhus were common and expected. People pronounced themselves blessed when their child lived past age one, while few adults lived past age 30.

The first break in this long history of misery came with the rise of commercial society in Spain and Northern Italy, and then the industrial revolution in Britain. People flocked from the countryside to the factories. We're told that conditions were deplorable, and hours long and hard. But compared with what? The alternative for most people was the life of a beggar or prostitute—or rural starvation.

Too little attention is paid to the heroic owners of the first factories. They were usually from a humble lot, and they undertook enormous risks, while pouring profits back into the business. Their factories opened only over the opposition of the entrenched elites. Their only intellectual backers were the classical-liberal economists, who saw that their efforts represented freedom and prosperity for the common man.

What was being produced in these factories? Not goods for the nobility, but clothing and equipment used by average people to improve their daily lives. As Mises said, this was the first time in history that mass production was undertaken for the masses. (If you read nothing else this next year, see Mises's treatment of the industrial revolution on pages 613–19 in the Scholar's Edition of *Human Action*).

The population of England doubled in the century following the industrial revolution—proof enough that it dramatically expanded living standards. In our own times we have also seen an extraordinary flowering of enterprise wherever and whenever freedom has been permitted. Consider that in 1900, worldwide life expectancy averaged 30 years. Today, it averages 65 years. As Nicholas Eberstadt has argued, this is what accounts for the astonishing increase in global population.

But what is the fundamental cause? Economic development, which has brought food, good nutrition, and sanitation as well as medicine to the world. And look at us today, taking Wal-Mart and Wendy's for granted, as if they always existed and always will. We are irritated when the grocery runs out of prime rib roast, and we won't touch lettuce that is wilted. We should remember that we are only the third or fourth generation in world history to have access to these things year-round.

And what, in turn, is the cause of economic development? That much-reviled institution called capitalism, a word that means nothing more than the freedom to own property, to trade, and to innovate. Capitalism has proven to be the most spectacular engine of progress known to man, and its expansion the greatest idea of the millennium. Every material comfort we enjoy today we owe to the free economy, the least understood and most assaulted foundation of civilized life.

63.
THE LEGITIMACY OF CAPITALISM*

Why does freedom need a relentless intellectual defense? Because of statements like the following:

> the legitimacy of global capitalism as the dominant system of production, distribution, and exchange will be eroded even further, even in the heartland of the system; while there are villains aplenty, it is the dynamics of the system of

---

*July 2002

deregulated, finance-driven global capitalism that is the central problem.

The words happen to be written by pop econo-sociologist Walden Bello, but the sentiments have been echoed all across the left, right, and in-between. Certainly Bello's conviction that the problem is with the market system reflects the views of every bureaucrat currently regulating the capital markets, and probably two-thirds of tenured professors in this country.

Capitalism needs a conscience, says Bush, because otherwise it will be consumed by the "destructive greed" of businessmen. Greenspan concurs, adding that when this greed is "infectious," it destabilizes markets. "This cowboy capitalism must stop," adds Maxine Waters, further urging Bush and Greenspan to apply a regulatory "conscience" to quarantine "infectious greed."

Yet Bush didn't go far enough in his speech, say the nation's editorial pages. He should have gone "after the evils of capitalism" itself, says the San Francisco *Chronicle*, in the same way that Clinton went after racism even when it emanated from Sister Souljah.

After all, the corporate scandals demonstrate that the Seattle protesters (smashing store fronts, looting, and rioting against the market) were "prophetic," writes lefty columnist Sean Gonsalves. He hopes their plans to hamper the market can proceed without "some F.A. Hayek or Milton Friedman fanatic drowning" them out.

Regulating financial markets is only a start. Government spending is exploding. Protectionism is on the march. The police state is making huge inroads against the ability and responsibility of individuals and communities to provide for their own security and privacy. Politicians are clamoring to put businessmen behind bars, on the belief that this will stop the fall in stock prices.

If you think about it, the hysteria is astonishing, even terrifying. The market economy has created unfathomable prosperity and, decade by decade, century by century, miraculous feats of innovation, production, distribution, and social coordination. To the free market, we owe all material prosperity, all leisure time, our health and longevity, our huge and growing population, nearly everything we call life itself. Capitalism and capitalism alone has rescued the human race from degrading poverty, rampant sickness, and early death.

In the absence of the capitalist economy and all its underlying institutions, the world's population would, over time, shrink to a fraction of its current size, with whatever was left of the human race systematically reduced to subsistence, eating only what can be hunted or gathered. Even the institution that is the source of the word civilization itself—the city—depends on trade and commerce, and cannot exist without them.

And this is only to mention the economic benefits of capitalism. It is also an expression of freedom. It is not so much a social system but the natural result of a society wherein individual rights are respected, where businesses, families, and every form of association are permitted to flourish in the absence of coercion, theft, war, and aggression.

Capitalism protects the weak from the strong, granting choice and opportunity to masses who once had no choice but to live in a state of dependency on the politically connected and their enforcers.

Must we compare the record of capitalism with that of the state, which, looking at the sweep of this past century alone, killed hundreds of millions of people in its wars, famines, camps, and deliberate starvation campaigns? And the record of central planning of the type now being urged on American enterprise is perfectly abysmal.

Let the state attempt to eradicate anything—unemployment, poverty, drugs, business cycles, illiteracy, crime, terrorism—and it ends up creating more of it than would have been the case if it had done nothing at all.

The state has created nothing. The market has created everything. But let the stock market fall 20 percent in 18 months, and what happens? The leading intellectuals discover anew why the Bolshevik Revolution was a pretty good idea, even if the results weren't what idealists might have hoped. We are told that we must rethink the very foundations of civilization itself.

In every society, there are greed, fraud, and theft. But let these vices rear their heads in a socialist society—though the norm is a continual and brutal struggle for power—and the fact goes unnoticed or is attributed to the remnants of capitalist thinking. Let these vices appear in a largely free economy, and the cry goes out: take away the freedom to trade and put the state in charge!

The advocates of regulation may protest: we have no plan to eradicate the market economy and replace it with socialism, but rather to improve it, make it transparent, make it honest, save it from itself. This is the line now being pushed by the likes of John McCain, who protests that he favors free markets but opposes "crony capitalism." He says that it will take massive government oversight to bring about "trust and transparency," which are essential to market economies.

Let's leave aside the evidence that the economic downturn and even the accounting scandals are a consequence of government meddling with credit and regulation of industry and the financial markets. A more fundamental question for McCain or anyone who agrees with him is: do you believe capitalism is soiled by the sins of individuals, in which case no social system measures up because they are all inhabited by sinful individuals, or do you believe that there is a sin at the very root of capitalism itself that can and must be suppressed by the state?

Of course we know the answer. After all, if we are only talking about the sins of individuals, the market has been brutal in its punishment. To the same extent that the credit-fueled bull market overlooked old-fashioned concerns like corporate revenue, the market is now on a witch-hunt against any firm that prettified its books. And this is all to the good. Whether the scandals result from greed, error, or just bad forecasting, the markets do not care: bankruptcy is the result. No institution, certainly not government, has a greater incentive to fix itself than the market.

If you believe, however, that there is a sin at the heart of capitalism, it makes no sense to permit the market to police itself. The possibility of such a thing is ruled out *a priori*, which is a habit of mind as endemic to the interventionist as to the full-fledged socialist. It is a very dangerous mindset, too, because once the regulators are unleashed to "perfect" the market economy, there is no end to the number of blemishes the political class will discover and attempt to correct.

The end result is to hobble and cripple markets to the point that they cannot do what they are supposed to do. At best, you end up with economies like we see in Europe today: bureaucratized and hamstrung, lacking in innovation and opportunity, burdened by unproductive welfare states, and riddled with political corruption. This in turn infects the culture by encouraging an attitude of dependency, one wholly contrary to the American spirit.

It seems absurd to have to say it: the legitimacy of capitalism is not in question. Were it not for the mysterious persistence of anticapitalist bias, it would be perfectly clear to everyone that the only institutions that should be seriously questioned today are the regulatory state and central banking, the first of which is inhibiting recovery and the second of which caused this mess in the first place.

Let's return to the original question: why does freedom need unrelenting economic defense?

Consider Ludwig von Mises's description of the intellectual culture of 1931, as the world sunk further into economic depression:

> The capitalistic economic system, that is the social system based on private ownership of the means of production, is rejected unanimously today by all political parties and governments. No similar agreement may be found with respect to what economic system should replace it in the future. Many, although not all, look to socialism as the goal. They stubbornly reject the result of the scientific examination of the socialistic ideology, which has demonstrated the unworkability

of socialism. They refuse to learn anything from the experiences of the Russian and other European experiments with socialism.

Concerning the task of present economic policy, however, complete agreement prevails. The goal is an economic arrangement which is assumed to represent a compromise solution, the "middle-of-the-road" between socialism and capitalism. To be sure, there is no intent to abolish private ownership of the means of production. Private property will be permitted to continue, although directed, regulated and controlled by government and by other agents of society's coercive apparatus. With respect to this system of interventionism, the science of economics points out, with incontrovertible logic, that it is contrary to reason, that the interventions, which go to make up the system, can never accomplish the goals their advocates hope to attain, and that every intervention will have consequences no one wanted. ("The Causes of the Economic Crisis: An Address")

After Mises wrote this, fascism tightened its grip in Italy, and the Third Reich began its program of extreme interventionism, militarism, and protectionism in Germany. The New Deal came to the United States, and the entire era ended in world war and holocaust. How much has changed, really, in 71 years? The hatred of markets must be countered by defenses of freedom in every generation. Our lives depend on it.

64.

ART, FAITH, AND THE MARKETPLACE*

Beginning next week, on Ash Wednesday, we will all be witness to the largest mass act of arts/humanities consumerism since the last *Harry Potter* book. Mel Gibson's movie

---

*February 2004

The Passion will be released. It is widely believed to be the most powerful film representation of Christ's crucifixion ever made.

Churches all over the country are organizing to distribute tickets and see the film. Is this sacrilege? The conventional wisdom, left and right, might suggest so. In many states, local laws restrict what you can buy and sell on Sunday, for religious reasons. Catholics still take it on the chin for trafficking in indulgences hundreds of years ago. Christmas and Easter are said to be debased when they are "commercialized."

Why no complaints that anticipation for *The Passion* partakes of a similar sin? For one thing, the conventional wisdom has held that religious movies aren't moneymakers. When Mel sunk $25 million of his own money into the project, people said he was crazy. But it is slowly dawning on people that the potential market for this film is darn close to unlimited. Might this become at once the most religiously pious and financially successful film ever made? It might, which does indeed raise the issue of religion and commerce.

Is it wrong to make lots of money off the religious sentiments of others? Is it bad to profit from trafficking in piety? It should be clear that these are loaded questions. Anyone who is excited about the film can generate an easy response. Gibson made the film because he cared about the topic. The actors and crew joined the effort because they too cared. People are willing to pay to see it because they care about it. Some people make money, but that's fine. Making money is better than losing money.

In short, there's really no issue here because everyone is benefiting and no one is being debased. This much might be clear to people who think about the problem a bit, but let's explore. Why does the issue of the morality of profit come up at all? Profits are calculated in terms of money, which is a tool for allowing us to engage in transactions beyond barter.

With money, we don't have to bring a chicken or a piece of software to the theater and bargain with the owner, who then has to find things to trade with the distributor, who then has to find stuff that the producer likes, and on and on. Instead, we all use money, which allows us to calculate and put a price on various goods and services for which we would otherwise have to find direct users. Money is simply a tool, though one essential to a developed division of labor, and therefore prosperity. It can be a means for accomplishing great things (saving people from lives of misery) or evil things (30 pieces of silver), but it is still essential to an economy beyond the level of primitive autarky.

When voluntary exchange results in tremendous quantities of money landing in the possession of a single person or group of people, it can only signal one thing: that the good they traded was highly valued by others. In this sense sky-high profits are a sign of social service, and the higher the profits, the more we can say that this money's owner served society. Profits are not ill-gotten gains, but signs of successful activities on behalf of the needs and wants of others. In a free market, this is universally true.

Profits serve also as a signal for other producers to come into a certain line of work. It doesn't matter whether those who chase profitable undertakings are in it "for the money" or whether they passionately believe in doing the most economically useful activities in society. The greediest motive and the most humanitarian one both yield the same result: profits attract resources in their direction. Eventually, of course, new entries into an otherwise unchanging market drive down profits until they are very low, which is why business must constantly improve and cut costs to stay ahead.

If there is a tendency for the rate of profit to fall over time, what is the source of high profits? In a word: entrepreneurship. This is the act of correctly anticipating a yet unmet consumer desire and making a judgment that this desire can be met in an economically viable way. Good entrepreneurial calls yield above-average profits, while bad calls net losses in a process that signals over time how best to go about making good judgments about the future. Sometimes the least plausible judgments yield the highest return.

That a movie about a 2,000-year-old event could generate the amount of public interest that this one has was certainly an entrepreneurial judgment. If the movie is good and audiences are willing to shell out to see it again and again, and rent it later, it could turn out to be the greatest entrepreneurial judgment in the history of film. For one thing, Gibson certainly went his own way with this one, depending on none of the established channels for making movies. If this movie is a blockbuster, there is going to be wailing and gnashing of teeth all over Tinseltown.

Also, by the logic of economics, you can know that the high profits associated with this film are going to attract new entries into this genre. We are going to see movies about many episodes from the gospels, made very much on the model of this one and seeking to serve the same audience. Thus will we have the capitalist marketplace serving religious ends—something we are often told is impossible.

For decades and centuries, many Christians have condemned commerce on grounds that it doesn't serve godly ends. In fact, there are no ends (both good and evil) that commerce cannot serve. Money changed hands to bring about the crucifixion. But money also changed hands to buy the tomb, and to bring about this movie.

If you like *The Passion*, and you like Mel's vision in having seen a need where others did not, and the saga of the film and all the obstacles inspires you, remember that none of this would be possible without the institutions of the market economy. To make a movie like this requires more than a good story and courage. It also requires private property, market exchange, investment capital, flexible wages, distribution networks, discretionary income, freedom of association, and sophisticated financial systems to keep track of it.

Go see *The Passion*, and if you are among those who are always yammering about the evil of commerce, stop it.

65.

CAPITALISM AND THE BURGER WARS*

If you love bad news, devote your life to studying government. You'll learn about the colossal waste of NASA, the diseases spread by the school-lunch program, the lies of the FBI, the corruption subsidized by foreign aid, and the debauchery of the military base.

So where can we turn for good news? To private enterprise, of course, where efficiency, hard work, and creativity still count for something. In markets, the old ideals of public service still survive, with people working hard to bring us great products and services at prices we can pay, and without waste. Here the average guy is sovereign, and people fall over each other to put excellence first.

The glories of private enterprise are most evident in the marvels we take for granted. For example, free enterprise created the marvelous, if much derided, institution of fast food. If there were a bureau of hamburger production, they'd be as scarce as budget cuts. As it is, citizens of every social and economic standing have daily access—in minutes—to a balanced meal denied to kings only two centuries ago.

This is no small feat, but one of many millions of miracles of the marketplace. The great challenge of economies from the earliest times was to get all people, not just the rich, access to food. Otherwise, a large and growing population could not be sustained. Only the advent of capitalism, particularly in America, made this possible, and fast food has played a key role in our times in making it so.

Anthropologists note that throughout human history, one key sign of prosperous times is the wide consumption of beef

---

*July 1997

(which requires far more land and other resources than crops). It's no surprise that America distinguished itself in world history for being the first society in which beef was available to one and all, no matter how poor, especially through the hamburger.

And what a glorious thing the hamburger is. It combines meat, grains, cheese, and vegetables into a simple, delicious package for quick and enjoyable consumption. It seems so easy, yet the efficient production of the hamburger, in all its details, is of infinite complexity. Only the coordinative powers of a market economy could possibly produce it.

Without the freedom of contract and capital accumulation, the right of private property, stock markets, and the price system, there would be no way to bring together the thousands of production processes needed to make a hamburger—from farming, ranching, and the manufacturing of thousands of individual capital goods from branding irons to refrigerators.

This is why the fast-food burger is rightly seen as a symbol of freedom around the world, and why the citizens of former socialist countries crave it more than any other American export. Living under communism, beef was for only the super rich and well connected. A delicious, cheap, widely available beef sandwich is an unimaginable dream come true.

Even at the retail level, consider the way capitalism works to everyone's benefit in the fast-food industry. To attract more business, McDonald's is slashing the price of a Big Mac (that's "two all-beef patties," etc.) to 55 cents. That's one-fourth of its current price and only a few pennies above the cost of its ingredients.

Moreover, the company will serve it in 55 seconds, or you get it free. This discount harks back to 1955, the year McDonald's began to revolutionize how people eat, in America and all over the world. In time, the company will offer the same deal on other favorites like the Quarter Pounder. And this is despite the dollar having lost 83 percent of its value since 1955!

Why is this huge company, with sales of $31.8 billion and 42 percent of the fast-food burger market, doing this? Not because anyone ordered them to do so or because the management swells with compassion for humanity and its need to eat cheaply. McDonald's would love to raise its prices. But it can't, so long as it needs to strike back against competitors making serious inroads into what it sees as its territory.

Burger King won the hearts of many by offering a Whopper that weighs more than the Big Mac. It's also tapped into the huge market for breakfast that McDonald's pioneered with the Egg McMuffin. It turns out that consumers are also impressed by Burger King's Croissanwich. Then there's the "problem" of Wendy's. Sales are growing by 7 percent per quarter, because consumers like the old-fashioned atmosphere, larger burgers, and ketchup that comes in cups instead of aluminum baggies.

It was, of course, a huge error for McDonald's to do away with its wonderful Styrofoam boxes on crazy eco-grounds. And like all large companies, it has an institutional tendency to want to rest on its laurels, a temptation the free market does not allow anyone to indulge.

Americans tend to take all this scampering for consumer loyalty for granted, but think what it implies on a deeper economic level. It shows who's really in charge of the free enterprise system. It's not the moguls who own or manage the company or the franchises. It's not even those who make the food.

No, the king of the market for fast hamburgers is the consumer. With his decision to buy or not to buy, he shapes the market and determines the range of qualities and prices of goods and services. And it is he who will decide the winners and the losers in the burger war. No matter how big a company is, or how vast its market share, all is lost without the vote of the little guy with the spare change.

Under no other system of economics (forget politics) does so much depend on the individual choices of the average fellow. He can be as fickle or finicky as he wants; there is no penalty for him either way. Meanwhile, the private company can't complain; it can only respond. It is enslaved to the whims of the buying public, which is exactly as it should be.

History is littered with businesses that despised this system because they grew tired of competing. Instead, they enlisted the state to gain a leg up, bypassing the competitive marketplace and the will of the public. This is how we came to have antitrust laws, trade protection, business subsidies, loan guarantees, and government-enforced cartel arrangements.

Thankfully, the fast-food industry is still largely governed by market forces, as the burger wars show. The profit and loss system functions here as well as anywhere. This system turns double-entry bookkeeping into the crucial means for the public to communicate its desires to those who provide the goods we depend on every day. If you don't like the Whopper, you don't have to call Burger King's corporate headquarters. You merely refrain from buying it.

Neither are any of these competitors free to waste resources in pursuit of consumer dollars. They must scrimp and save, cutting costs at every corner. And they must find the most efficient way of getting consumers what they want without ever sacrificing quality.

The result is a vast, efficient, and productive process that serves all of society. And it happens without costly elections, bipartisan commissions, ethics-in-hamburger laws, regulators, bureaucrats, special prosecutors, or any of the other trappings of government.

So successful is this system that its fiercest critics are reduced to complaining of the supposed "cultural decline" it brings about, as if the ability of everyman to buy a burger is a grave threat to civilization. This aesthetic critique of capitalism is about all that's left of the socialist lie.

What, then, have been the cultural effects of the fast-food industry? In fact, they have been wonderful. It has rescued us from socialist puritans who hate cows and want to permanently ban beef from the American diet. It has provided jobs to millions of young people and taught them the work ethic. It has single-handedly kept alive the great American birthday party. Above all, it has showed us that eating well in good times and bad does not have to be the exclusive privilege of the well-to-do.

We take it all for granted, but make no mistake: without the institution of capitalism that makes fast food possible, the vast majority of the human population would be reduced to hunter-gatherer status in short order.

Is there a way to bring the workings of the market to bear on now-frustrating sectors like education, mail delivery, utilities, public safety, and the courts? Of course. The government merely needs to get out of the way, and let the market do for these services what it has done for the great American habit of eating on the run.

66.
In Praise of Failure*

The stories are now legendary: internet hotshots going from riches to rags in a period of months, infallible stock-pickers with their reputations in tatters, and stock prices of established companies off 75 percent from their highs. The business press is now talking openly about the possibility that the bull market is over. We may be in for a long period of disappointing returns and falling net worth of individual portfolios heavily invested in stocks.

Maybe. In any case, everyone seems to agree that the dot-com shakeup on Wall Street is not all bad news. It has made individual investors more skeptical of Internet hype, and venture capitalists more careful about where they put their money. If a web venture is not attracting customers, and its expenses continually outstrip its revenues and ability to raise money, it must reorganize or shut down. Any other option would require

---

*November 2000

wasting resources on business projects that the market has shown to be of marginal worth.

Let's broaden the lesson. When people think of capitalism, they think of wealth and profits. But one of the main features of the market economy is its ability to generate losses and produce business failures. And just as some envy-filled politicians can't sleep well knowing that profits are distributed unequally, others can't bear the thought of business failure. In fact, both profit and loss have social and economic merit and should be allowed to take their market-driven course.

Agitation for laws against sudden plant closings were a staple of political rhetoric in the 1980s. We endured 70 years of bellyaching that "family farms" are being out-competed by corporate monoliths and foreign imports. Politicians still roam the land haranguing us about the catastrophic transformation of the industrial Midwest into the "rust belt."

But none of these trends produce disaster, any more than the failure of an Internet startup causes social convulsions. The misery is sector-specific and temporary. The market adjusts because the free economy permits people to adjust to change on the upside and downside.

Immense damage can result from the attempt to stave off inevitable losses. Protectionism is the classic example. Businesses losing money attempt to shield themselves from foreign competition by keeping artificially high the prices consumers pay for goods and services. These higher prices are a form of taxation, and the protected industries are receiving the revenue. "Counter-cyclical" fiscal and monetary policies also backfire, the most famous example being the Hoover administration and the New Deal that followed, which, as Murray Rothbard showed in his classic study, actually prolonged America's Great Depression.

Antitrust is another example. It is a form of regulation that comes to the defense of a marginal firm that is being out-competed by a more profitable firm. This is why nearly all antitrust cases begin with one business accusing another of malfeasance.

Perhaps the best example of industries that have failed is in the public sector. The second half of the life of the Soviet economy can be seen as an elaborate effort to keep failing industries alive. And in the United States, the quality and efficiency of public schools have dropped every year for many decades, and yet they are not permitted to go out of business. The same is true for all government "services," which survive only because they aren't subject to market judgment.

This is one of many reasons why converting Social Security taxes into a stock-market subsidy would be a big error. Anything over which the government claims an interest tends to be protected from losses, and that is particularly true of programs that affect powerful interest groups. Social Security funds invested in the stock market would be shielded against the kind of declines that have hit dot-coms in recent months. This would be a step toward socialism.

And yet with the internationalization of stock and money markets, politicians have found that shielding companies and sectors from losses can produce painful results. Instead of producing profits, the attempt produces economic stagnation that does damage and only puts off the inevitable. International capital flows away from sectors and countries that are hiding behind walls of protection and interventionism.

Now, the left is oddly celebratory about these new trends among dot-coms. It's ideological perversity: the left demands socialist profits and capitalist losses. But this is no better than the Business Roundtable's demand for capitalist profits and socialist losses. Both are inconsistent with the capitalist economic framework of freedom and responsibility.

And why do businesses fail? Many reasons. Their owners and managers fail to properly discern market conditions and consumers preferences, or they fail to anticipate changes in resource availability and tastes. Poor internal management can do a company in, and so can aggressive competition from companies who were drawn to a market segment in hopes of sharing in the profits.

One kind of unjust loss is that produced by political intervention. Companies saddled with absurd class-action lawsuits alleging "discrimination" end up closing operations that might otherwise have survived. Then there's the outrageous attempt by the courts to bankrupt the tobacco and firearms sectors. This produces accounting losses, but it is the moral equivalent of burglary or arson.

"Greed is right," said Gordon Gekko in the movie *Wall Street* (1987). "Greed works. Greed clarifies, cuts through and captures the essence of the evolutionary spirit." Fine. But the same can be said of business losses and failures. They are right. They cut through and clarify. And as much as profits, they capture the essence of a healthy market economy.

67.

THE BLESSINGS OF DEFLATION*

Let's say you set out on a Saturday shopping trip, drive up to the mall, and see a sign that says "50 percent off everything!" That's great news, right?

Or let's say you are in the market for a new car, and the sticker shock you experience is that cars are cheaper than they used to be. Amazing and wonderful!

Or let's say you are paying for your daughter's college education and find that you have set aside more money than is necessary because the price of tuition and books is lower than you expected. Glory be!

Or let's look at it from the point of view of business. You are a manufacturer and your main expense is steel parts. After many years, even decades, of rising prices for ball bearings and other machine parts, your costs suddenly decline. The cost of

---

*May 2003

replacing assets is dramatically reduced. That leaves more for investment, marketing, paying employees, and enticing investors with dividends. It is a win-win situation for everyone.

So far, "deflation" seems like a glorious thing. But wait, says conventional wisdom. Consumers and businesses may benefit, sure, but what about sellers? They always desire the highest price possible for their products. If Dell had its way, every computer would cost $1 million, and they would certainly charge that if they could sell the same number of computers at this price as versus $1,000. By the same token, consumers want to pay exactly $0 for what they buy. It is the interplay between these two ideal worlds that yields the market price.

If businesses have been required by virtue of competitive pressure to sell at ever-lower prices, how can they make a buck? By becoming more efficient. Anyone who has ever worked in a business knows that efficiency is something that businesses do when they have to. A monopolist is facing no competition (think of a government toll road) and so can charge high prices and maintain awful inefficiencies year after year. A business in a competitive environment cannot.

The computer industry itself provides the best illustration. Prices have plummeted even as sales have soared. Computer makers and retailers have profited handsomely. And this is not a unique case. The same has happened to appliances, which have gone down in price dramatically over the years even as sales have risen higher and higher. Why? Because the companies have gotten better and better at doing what they do, and have thereby been able to make profits even in the face of continual price declines.

Thus we see that there is no radical disconnect between the interest of consumers (who always want lower prices) and overall economic health. What's good for consumers is good for everyone. You can only marvel at the many economists and commentators who try to convince the public that deflation is a very scary thing. In doing so, they enjoy the cachet associated with generating a counterintuitive conclusion, but in this case, it is simply wrong. The first intuition that bargains are a great thing is precisely the right one. In discerning economic theory, sometimes common sense turns out to be all you need.

And yet, many experts still say we should "worry about falling prices" because they represent a "destructive force" (according to Martin Wolk at MSNBC, for example). He explains as follows: "As prices keep going down, money grows more valuable." So far so good!

But he goes on to say that this is actually a bad thing because it creates "an enormous disincentive for consumers and businesses to spend money. Economic activity slows, unemployment rises and demand continues to decline." Well, but that presumes that consumers have something to gain by forever stocking up on dollars and never buying anything, which is absurd. It's true that falling prices create incentives to save, but so long as the preference of consumers is to save instead of spend, that can only prepare the way for a future of economic growth. Consumers save for a reason, namely, to spend later.

Wolk's next point concerns the implications of deflation for debt. Deflation makes it "far more difficult to pay back existing loans." It's true that loans are paid back in dollars that are more valuable than the ones borrowed. But that is part of the risk one takes when deciding to borrow in the first place. If we all had perfect foresight, our behavior would change substantially. But that is no case for pressing the pause button on economic affairs. What deflation does is provide a disincentive to borrow and an incentive to use current savings for purposes of investment. It means a reward for well-capitalized companies and individuals—a good thing all around.

Now we get to the crux of the matter: the Great Depression. The assumption is that falling prices somehow caused the economy to crumble. In fact, it was the after-effects of the boom combined with massive government intervention that caused the depression. The only silver lining in the entire period of the 1930s was precisely the falling prices that made the dollar count for more. Falling prices (a falling cost of living) are what Murray

Rothbard has described as the "great advantage" of recessions. If you can imagine the Great Depression without falling prices, you have conjured up an image that is far worse than the reality.

Ask yourself whether during economic downturns, you want your money to grow or shrink in value? If your future job security is in doubt, do you want to pay more or less for goods? If your savings are meager, do you want them to have more or less purchasing power in the future? If you answer these questions rationally, you can see that deflation is wonderful for everyone, and the saving grace of a period of economic contraction. Throughout the nineteenth century, prices fell in periods of economic growth, which is precisely what one might expect. This is all to the good.

As Rothbard has said,

> rather than a problem to be dreaded and combated, falling prices through increased production is a wonderful long-run tendency of untrammeled capitalism. The trend of the Industrial Revolution in the West was falling prices, which spread an increased standard of living to every person; falling costs, which maintained general profitability of business; and stable monetary wage rates—which reflected steadily increasing real wages in terms of purchasing power. This is a process to be hailed and welcomed rather than to be stamped out.

If we must have recessions, make them deflationary recessions. What's far worse is the phenomenon of the inflationary recession that Keynesians are always trying to foist upon us. For the same reason that deflation is a good thing, rising prices during a recession are the worst possible thing, because they provide a disincentive to save and invest for the future. They encourage present consumption and thereby gut the capital base necessary for future growth. They prolong suffering in every way.

Thus can we see that the widely approved prescription to prevent deflation, namely inflation, is the worst possible path. But this is precisely what the Fed has endorsed as a matter of policy. It is hardly surprising that the central planners managing our lives would adopt the exact policy that will make us so much worse off.

Fortunately, the free market contains mechanisms that can work around attempts by the Fed to inflate. It could be that the banks have a hard time foisting new money on people and instead work to protect their balance sheets. Businesses too, stung by economic contraction, might avoid going further into debt, no matter how cheaply they may be able to borrow. In this case, prices could fall whether the Fed wants them to or not.

In economics, it is a good rule that what is good for individuals and families is also good for the economy. Everyone wants a bargain, which is to say a low price. Sadly, in our present age of inflation, lower prices mostly affect specific products and sectors. May the joy we take in falling prices for electronics be expanded to anything and everything we buy. Let the commentators fret and worry about what their fallacious macroeconomic models tell them. The rest of us can sit back and watch our standard of living rise and rise.

Sadly, I doubt we will see any deflation. Even based on the last ten years of data, overall price increases are still the norm.

In fact, since 1913 and the founding of the Fed, the dollar has lost 95 percent of its value. It is far more likely that this robbery will continue rather than for our lost purchasing power to be restored to its rightful owners: you and me.

68.
ARE MARKETS BORING?*

William F. Buckley and Irving Kristol recently explained why they are not drawn to consistent free-market logic, and why they have never been shy to advocate various forms of statism: they find market thinking rather dull.

---

*June 2004

The psychology of the antimarket left can be a puzzle, but even more confounding is the mentality of the antimarket right. There are agrarians, medievalists, and nationalists, and, above all, the neoconservatives, who dread the market as much as any socialist from days of yore. Their critique differs, but all complain about the strictures that economics places on the policy imagination.

In fact, that is one of the merits of economics.

Because there is no danger of an imminent takeover by agrarians or medievalists, let us look at neoconservative ideology, especially through the eyes of its two key founders, Kristol and Buckley. It is this deviation from libertarian theory that has become the most present menace to sound economics and the world economy, if only because they have political power.

The reason the neocons reject freedom and peace, they recently revealed, is that they find the framework of market-oriented thought intellectually boring—an objection that deserves to be addressed after some background on the neocons and their perspective.

Buckley was the transitional figure from the pre-1950s Old right to the Cold War New Right. As the first neoconservative, it was he who somehow provided the intellectual gloss to cover the division between the incompatible ideas of war and peace that emerged in the early years of the Cold War. It was he who made the impossible seem possible: erecting (in his words) a "totalitarian bureaucracy within our shores" while maintaining domestic liberty and free trade.

Back then, the libertarians rallied around liberty and property. They might have countenanced a military buildup as a temporary measure, but they saw peace as the goal and the foundation of civilization. Buckley, in contrast, advocated the creation of an imperial foreign policy and saw war as a defensible policy goal—a vision obviously incompatible with a market order he otherwise claimed to support.

Whereas Buckley had left his intellectual roots in the Old Right, Irving Kristol moved over from the Trotskyite left by embracing the military machine and its role in the world, while accepting markets only with a litany of reservations. In any case, what animated his imagination was not enterprise but the militarization of American foreign policy, and American life.

Where does this leave the program of the old liberals from Jefferson to Mises? Free markets, free trade, and peace with all nations become clichés to invoke in service of a nationalist agenda that, in its worst incarnations, aspires to run the world. So much for freedom-minded conservatism of the pre-war variety, as articulated by the likes of Hayek and Mises in Europe and Chodorov, Mencken, and Garrett, among many others, in the United States.

Political scientist Corey Robin spent some time with Buckley and Kristol over the last year, and wrote up the results (*Washington Post*, May 2, 2004). Professor Robin was taken aback to discover their hostility to freedom as the animating ideal of society—a hostility that many of us have long known about, but which, until recently, was the best-kept secret about conservatism. Buckley told Robin that he finds conservatism's emphasis on the market to be uninspiring.

It "becomes rather boring," Buckley said. "You hear it once, you master the idea. The notion of devoting your life to it is horrifying if only because it's so repetitious."

In the same way, Kristol says that the goal of economics is and should be world political power. The role of the United States is "to command and to give orders as to what is to be done. People need that." Both, according to Robin, view concerns over money and economy as petty and bourgeois, not exciting enough to animate a serious life of the mind.

It is unfortunate that Buckley believes that markets are dull and that Kristol believes that controlling people and giving orders are what people need and want. But they leave unexplained why it is that the world must adapt to their personal sense of what fulfills them emotionally. What they are really saying here is that market logic restrains their thinking and acting in ways that they do not like. In this case, it would be far better to have them playing with video games than with real life.

And yet there is a certain valid point they are making here about how economics diminishes the role of would-be philosopher kings, just as gravity reduces the ability of magicians to make things float. Economics is part of the ungoverned structure of reality that even the smartest people cannot change. Economics hems in the state even as it illuminates the nearly unlimited possibilities for the use of the creative imagination within a framework of property protection and free exchange.

Economics tells us how enterprise creates seeming miracles all around us. But it also tells us that real resources don't grow on trees, that all government spending must take a bite out of the private sector in some way. Economics tells us that all attempts to control prices and wages will lead to shortages and surpluses, and that any intervention causes trouble. It tells us that you can't expand the money supply without creating distortions—among a thousand other points that contradict government wishes.

From the political point of view, economics seems like a series of strictures against doing things that politicians naturally want to do and intellectuals want to tell them to do. So it is no wonder that intellectuals and politicians resent market logic. And yet, economic logic is not a fiction.

These two are hardly the first to reject market logic on grounds that it is restrictive for the state. But this is somewhat like rejecting walls around you because they contain your person. You can deny walls all you want, but attempting to walk through them is going to end with unfortunate consequences.

Economic logic is intellectually constraining in another sense. To the extent that you move away from market means, you leave the sphere of voluntarism and enter the sphere of coercion. Markets do not exist as a "policy;" they are the *de-facto* result of respecting rights to person and property. It is impossible to move away from market means without violating rights. Since markets, trade, and voluntarism are the basis of civilization itself, to reach for something else means to move toward de-civilization and the rule of the brute.

Understood this way, it is intellectually irresponsible to say: "Markets are fine, and I favor and defend them, but we also need war and command structures to make the world exciting." Is the contradiction not obvious? War and command structures are the very opposite of markets. To say you want both is like a doctor who says: "I like healing people and finding cures for disease, but, to keep life from becoming dull and uneventful, we also need to create diseases and make people sick."

That still leaves the question: are markets dull?

A major contribution of the Austrian School was to move economics out of the realm of self-interest maximization into the study of the whole of human material life. Economics is not just about stock markets, corporate comings and goings, and household finance. Still less is it the study of greed. It is about the whole of our material existence, which includes literature, art, science, health, music, leisure, sports, and all voluntary associations within society.

In short, economics is no more or less boring than life itself. The minimum requirement for anyone who aspires to be a social-science intellectual is that he or she find society itself fascinating. The next hope is that the person desires to see society thrive in peace and prosperity. If the neoconservatives sincerely desire this, they must reject war and militarism, which only crush what markets create. They must reject the sorcerers of violence and destruction in favor of the philosophers of peace and freedom.

69.

DO FOOD MAKERS WANT TO KILL YOU?*

Freedom can stand or fall on issues large (wars, depressions, natural disasters) or small (a hundred thousand regulations that manage our daily lives). Regulations on food labeling count among the small issues. It is a tricky issue for market advocates because bad labeling might actually count as breach of contract and thereby require legal intervention of some sort.

As Murray Rothbard writes,

> if A sells B breakfast food, and it turns out to be straw, A has committed an illegal act of fraud by telling B he is selling him food, while actually selling straw. This is punishable . . . [by] the legal code of the free society that would prohibit all invasions of persons and property.

But conceding that small point does not mean that regulators should be permitted to regiment all aspects of food production, which is where we are headed.

At issue is the theoretical presumption itself. Can market forces manage issues of food labeling or must regulators be involved? Many politicos on Capitol Hill are under the impression that food manufacturers are neglectfully poisoning the 6 to 11 million Americans who have food allergies by sneakily failing to point out on labels that the food contains deadly ingredients. So here we have the ultimate paranoid-socialist fantasy at work: business rakes in profits through fraud while people die!

So in order to protect life and limb, the House and Senate have passed the "Food Allergen Labeling and Consumer Protection Act" that requires manufacturers to say whether their food contains milk, eggs, peanuts, tree nuts, fish, shellfish, wheat, or soy. This legislation was supported by the FDA and

---

*July 2004

the DHHS, two bureaucracies you know have your health foremost in mind. This is supposedly going to save 250 lives per year, and protect millions from sickness.

It passed on a voice vote. If anyone opposed the bill besides Ron Paul, the press certainly hasn't said anything about who he is. And yet there is every reason for a freedom lover to be against this bill, and something very fishy going on with its seeming absence of opponents.

When it passed, it was heralded by one and all, as if it represented another small step in the march of history toward fairness, justice, and truth. The news stories treated it as a victory for consumers over rapacious and even murderous food makers who lie, lie, lie over the ingredients in their products. Thank goodness for government, we are supposed to believe, because it protects the interests of the little guy against blood-sucking corporate snack kings.

But think about this. It is rather implausible that anyone selling food would somehow be reluctant to say that this or that product contains milk, eggs, peanuts, or whatever. This is not information anyone would have a reason to hide. These are not ingredients that somehow gross out consumers, or chemicals that producers would just as soon people not know about.

Perhaps the amounts are too small to mention, but still end up deadly to consumers who have particular allergies toward them? Perhaps so, but then a bit of education is all that is necessary, for no one has a greater incentive to insure the safety of their products than food makers. It is contrary to good business to risk the lives of those who consume your products.

Doubt it? Think back to every food panic you can remember. Nothing makes people more hysterical and resentful than the idea that a particular food is not nourishing but rather deadly. One dramatic death is enough to throw an entire hemisphere into mania. It doesn't take much thought to realize that food manufacturers are rather disinclined to want this level of bad press for themselves. Death is bad for business. So is sickness.

But you might say that the manufacturers are not aware of the danger that some people face from food allergies. Really? Who has more of an incentive to stay constantly on top of the latest information concerning such matters: the makers of food or Congress? Not even the regulators have a reason to stay on top of these matters. It is the makers and sellers of food themselves who have the greatest stake in being aware of what consumers need to know.

Nor is the food allergy niche too small: every food retailer has an incentive to market specifically to this group to stay ahead in a business with very thin profit margins. Even if the manufacturers are not quite on the ball, grocery stores don't want to sell food that kills people, and for many years the major chains have been working with food-allergy groups to send out alerts on products that might contain small traces of listed foods.

Not only that. The FDA has been sending out press releases on this subject for years, and the Federal Register published a regulation back in 1992! And anyone who knows something about the FDA knows that it is the last institution to hear about such matters. As with most regulatory agencies, it sends out press releases and mandates long after the private sector has already dealt with the issue. This is the routine aspect of all safety regulation: retailers and manufacturers discover the problem, issue the recall, manage returns and compensation, while the FDA and various safety commissions send out press releases for the media to run.

If it is really necessary for Congress to force (that is what legislation is about) food makers to confess that they use eggs or peanuts or whatever, in order to prevent people from dying who would otherwise croak on a crumb, if it is really essential that the coercive apparatus of the state—which George Washington compared to a fire and the whole liberal intellectual tradition warns is up to no good—be put to use in this way, if this is really necessary, then there is no case for freedom at all. If government needs to do this, it needs to do everything. If the market fails here, it fails everywhere, and we need the total state.

So far from being a small nonissue, the food allergy regulation bill is a test case. To support it is implicitly to support the full regulation of economic life by politics. To believe that the market works—especially in the case of an issue and sector that any idiot can see is perfectly capable of managing itself—is to undermine the core principle that freedom manages society and government is just not necessary.

How does the market respond? By making ingredients explicit or providing incentive for producers to produce special products that meet the needs of special dieters. Another market response is the development of trade associations that certify products for special needs, such as that offered by the National Nutritional Foods Association. There are probably hundreds or thousands of such organizations.

Now, the food-allergy regulation advocates say that it is far more complicated than this. A case cited at FoodAllergyInitiative.org says that two people were rushed to the hospital because an older brother discovered that the package of a Rice Krispies Treat said it might contain nuts, but once contacted the company said, well, actually, there are no nuts in the R-K Treat. The kids left the hospital. The grave matter here is that the "family suffered an unnecessary scare and trip to the emergency room." The legislation supposedly gets rid of this problem by forcing manufacturers to be more specific and eliminate weasel-phrases like "may contain."

In this case, the problem was caused by the regulation itself. The company that made the snack would not have sensed the need to add that it "may contain" peanuts if not for fear of regulators who punish the failure to disclose. What the anecdote does is suggest the need to tighten the screws further: you must say what is in your product and you must be sure that whatever you say might be in your product had darn sure better be there!

Now we are getting to the heart of the issue. As you read about this subject ever deeper, you find that the issue isn't really ingredients. It is the small traces of peanuts or some other substance that might be in food resulting not from a recipe but from the equipment used in manufacturing plants. Small traces of peanuts might be floating in the air or tiny particles of milk product might be remaining in a large mixer, as it moves from making one product to another. What the new regulation demands is that even these small particles be either completely eliminated or the label needs to say what is in there—and if it says it is there, it had better darn sure be there.

What we are talking about here is extreme cleaning, extreme attentiveness, and extreme disclosure—not merely the elimination of negligence or inattentiveness but the addition of difficult processes in manufacturing itself. Most of the product recalls impacting on allergies deal with such issues: animal crackers that contained traces of milk, a frozen vegetable that contained traces of eggs, a packaged turkey product that included just a bit of milk. And so on it goes.

Now, it might appear that such an idiosyncratic diet that would demand such extreme measures is best served by companies that specifically cater to such needs, as with the many religions that have special food requirements and sustain large sectors of food makers who specialize in dealing with them. Perhaps, then, the food-allergy is best handled in this way. Why impose such strictures on the whole of the market?

In handling such issues, the largest manufacturers are in a far better position to absorb the expense of complying as compared with the smaller ones. That is not to say that the small companies openly argued against the legislation. Who is going to come out for the right to kill allergy sufferers? No, just as with the whole history of product regulation, especially in Republican administrations, the large producers run roughshod over the small ones by harnessing market pressure towards safety to a solution that imposes legal penalties on smaller and start-up competitors.

This is not a small factor in the history of economics. It is how the regulatory state came about, from the Progressive Era to our own. Regulation then as now is a form of mercantilism that benefits some at the expense of others. And the some who benefit are not the consumers. This labeling bill won't help those with food allergies so much as reduce their own level of attentiveness to what they eat, giving them a false sense of confidence. It could thereby lead to more deaths, followed by more regulation.

Economic life needs to be regulated but the question is: by what and how? It can be regulated privately so that consumer needs and producer behavior are coordinated and all types of innovation are rewarded, or it can be regulated by the state, which uses its mandate to reward friends, strangle innovation, raise costs, and give us all a false sense of security. It is the market process of competition and consumer service that serves us all, even those with highly specialized needs. The government serves only itself and those with clout enough to get the state to do their bidding.

70.
IN PRAISE OF SHODDY PRODUCTS*

The average family will spend about $1,000 on Christmas gifts, and much of what we buy might be described as rather shoddy. It is prone to break and wear out. Kids' gifts might not last the day. Our new clothes might not make it to next season. Our electronic stuff might break down in a year. Our kitchen gadgets might snap and break. Household gifts of all sorts just aren't what they used to be. The spines of our books will snap, our yard equipment will need replacing by summer's end, and our tools will break rather than last for generations as our granddad's did.

---

*December 2004

Many commentators have noted that kitchen appliances, and many other things, just don't seem to last the way they used to. In the old days, you got a blender as a wedding gift and your daughter would use it when she came home from college. These days we are lucky if a blender or hand mixer lasts a few years. The same seems true of washers and dryers, lawn mowers and edgers, clothing, electronic equipment, and even homes.

Some people blame China, others Wal-Mart, others the Web, and still others just think it is a sign of the times when civilization is sinking into a hole in preparation for Armageddon. Regardless, that this trend is awful is rarely questioned. So let us question away.

Paradoxically, this pervasive shoddiness is not a bad thing but a sign of rising wealth. It is a sign of prosperity that we prefer the new to the repaired. As consumers, we show a preference for throwing away and replacing rather than being stuck with a dated gizmo or unfashionable item. What's more, our preference for shoddiness over durability is not wasteful at all, but merely a reflection of the market's ability to adjust to consumer demand with resource supply. In making ever more shoddy products manufacturers are doing what is best for all of us.

To begin to understand why, consider that in 1,000 years, the pyramids will still be standing but your subdivision will likely be long gone. Does this indicate that the ancient world was a better and more prosperous place because it made structures that will last and last? Clearly not. Durability is only one value among many competing values in the production and consumption process, and it is very likely to decline in the order of priorities as wealth increases.

One of the many targets of antimarket thinkers in the 1950s was so-called "planned obsolescence"—the practice of manufacturers to design their products to wear out and break down at a certain point in the future. In this conspiracy view, this practice would thereby cause consumers to have to go out and buy a new and very similar item. Clever manufacturers would couple this planned obsolescence with a cosmetic change masquerading as an improvement to fool the consumer into thinking that he got his money's worth, when in fact he was really being ripped off, paying twice for what should have only been bought once.

There are bad assumptions here. First, the model assumes that the manufacturers are far more clever than the consumers, who are treated as some sort of passive victims of powerful capitalist interests. In fact, in the real world, it is the manufacturers who are clamoring to keep up with the ever-changing, discriminating, cheap, and fussy consumers, who dump products and switch to others for reasons both rational and mysterious. The full-time job of entrepreneurs is to discern the values, find an economical way to serve them, and even to anticipate them.

Second, the model makes an odd normative assumption that products should last as long as possible. In fact, there is no preordained market preference for how long goods should last, as the pyramid example illustrates. It is probably possible to make a car or a toothbrush that would last 100 years. But is it desirable? Consumers prefer lower price, the newest technology, and different amenities other than longevity. As materials have fallen in price, it makes more sense to replace the good than to create it to last forever. Do you want a $200 blender that lasts 30 years or a $10 blender that lasts five years?

Whatever consumers prefer in the long run is what dominates the market. How can we be sure? Competition. Let's say all manufacturers make blenders that die in five years only, and this fact is widely loathed. One manufacturer could beat the competition by providing a product that emphasizes longevity over other features. If consumers really value longevity they will be willing to pay the difference, and many people do.

For many things, it makes economic sense for them to last only until the next improvement comes along. Imagine if a computer manufacturer produced a machine that was advertised as a lifetime computer, the last computer you will need as long as you live, complete with software that will similarly last forever. Anyone with savvy would be skeptical, realizing that this is the last thing you want. Far from being a rip-off, then, obsolescence is a sign of rising prosperity.

In times of massive and frequent technological improvement, it would be sheer waste for manufacturers to dump resources into making products last past their usefulness. In computers, for example, to make them durable enough to last more than six years would be a big mistake in today's environment. The same could be true of house longevity. Everyone knows that old houses can be charming but bears to grapple with in terms of heating, cooling, plumbing, wiring, and everything else. The efficient solution might well be to level a house and rebuild rather than attempt an upgrade.

This would only be a waste if you push longevity ahead of technological improvement. Individual consumers are free to do that, but we have no basis for declaring this value set as fixed and unchanging. We do not live, nor do we wish to live, in a world that is static, where development never occurs, where what exists has always existed and always will.

So it is with clothing and furniture and other goods. As people have more disposable income and it rises over time, people want to be able to replace what they wear to accord with changing tastes. A society in which clothes are forever mended, electronic parts are forever fixed, and existing products are forever bucked up to go another mile is not necessarily a rich society. To be able to toss out the broken and torn is a sign of rising wealth.

It is common for people to look at a hollow door or a composite-wood desk and say: what cheap and shoddy products these are! In the old days, craftsmen cared about the quality of what they made! Now no one cares and we end up being surrounded by junk!

Well, the truth is that what we call high quality from the past was not available to the masses to the same extent it is today. Homes and cars might have lasted longer in the past, but far fewer people owned them than in today's world, and they were far more expensive (in real terms).

In a market economy, what is called quality is subject to change according to the preferences of the consuming public. Whether products should last a lifetime (such as fine jewelry) or a day (fresh bread) cannot be determined outside the framework of a market economy. No central planner can say for sure.

If your book falls apart, your clothes collapse in tatters, and your washing machine suddenly keels over, resist the temptation to decry the decline of civilization. Remember that you can replace all these items at a fraction of the price that your mom or hers bought them. And you can do so with minimal fuss and trouble. And it is very likely that the new versions of the old products that you buy will have more bells and whistles than the old.

You can call this planned obsolescence if you want to. It is planned by producers because consumers prefer improvement to permanence, availability to longevity, replaceability to repairability, motion and change to durability. It is not waste because there is no eternal standard by which we can measure and assess the economic rationality behind the use of resources in society. This is something that can only be determined and judged by individuals using resources in a market setting.

Of course a person is free to live in a drafty stone house, listen to music on a Victrola, wash clothes with a washboard, tell time with a sundial, and make one's clothes from flour sacks. Even now this is possible. One is free to be completely obsolete. But let us not equate this status with wealth, and let us not aspire to live in a society in which everyone is forced to prefer the permanent things to the cheap, improving, and widely available things.

71.

THE SUPER–RICH TAX THEMSELVES*

In a man bites dog story, some of America's richest men have joined together to oppose one of the best ideas in years: cutting or repealing the estate tax. Investor Warren Buffett, Bill's dad William Gates, anticapitalist speculator George Soros, lefty ice-cream magnate Ben Cohen, at least two Rockefellers, and many others, have signed an ad that decries the proposed tax cuts on many spurious grounds.

Gates in particular says that if he had time he would found and run an organization called Millionaires for the Estate Tax. Coming from a man who heads a foundation with $20 billion to burn, that is an interesting comment. He is purporting to speak for people with a small fraction of the wealth he has at his disposal. The existence of billionaires is a wonderful testament to the glories of the capitalist system, but let us not forget that many of them are loony tunes on issues outside their core business.

This coalition says an estate tax repeal will decrease charitable giving, as if people only give to charity to escape the tax. Wrong. The effect would be the reverse. As wealth grows across generations, there would be more money to give away. Indeed, after having sapped (at least) half a trillion dollars in capital from the economy this century (Joint Economic Committee, 1998) estate taxes have declined and exemptions increased at the same time charitable giving has gone way up.

More important to these people is the moral argument. They say that inheritance elevates privilege above merit. But this is a false distinction that asserts an egalitarian view of merit. It is also very dangerous because it puts government instead of the private sector in charge of deciding who merits what.

---

*February 2001

There are many things we don't "merit" by their definition: good parents, loving homes, quality education, family connections, and the like. We didn't choose or "earn" those. Should the government take them away in the name of equal opportunity? Scary stuff. A broader and more correct definition of merit would see it as connected with justice, and it is not just that government should tax family earnings away in one generation or many.

I suspect that the super-rich are not giving their real reasons for opposing the repeal of estate taxes. It may at first look like these men are going against their self-interest to favor estate taxes. In fact, the super-rich have a personal interest in preventing others from joining their ranks. With estate taxes they can afford, they still stay at the top of the heap. Without them, their social and economic position will be continually threatened by upstart dynasties.

Buffett and Soros are very gifted men. They have the special talent to create vast sums of wealth in their own lifetimes. But not everyone has such talent. Others need the extra help that family money provides. Far from increasing opportunity, then, estate taxes block opportunity for people who have less entrepreneurial talent than these one-generation wonders. By advocating such taxes, these men are trying to establish a monopoly of wealth at other people's expense.

There's also a strange psychology at work among the super-rich. They may be successful entrepreneurs, but none of these men is a convinced capitalist. Most of them give to left-wing causes that seek to undermine the market economy. Lacking any real education in market economics, they feel a sense of guilt for their earnings.

Despite their wealth, they have imbibed the dominant culture's ethic of egalitarianism and decided to promote it as a means of expiating their alleged sins. No surprise here, since these men read the papers and see the daily attacks on their wealth. They watch television where they are personally vilified as robber barons.

These leftist attacks begin to take a toll. Now, no one would care if they decide to purge their guilt by dumping all their money on private charities. But they want to vacuum other people's bank accounts. That's where their intellectual errors become positively destructive.

What's more, we shouldn't be surprised that the rich are leading the charge for estate taxes. This is the way it's always been. At the turn of the century, it was Andrew Carnegie, one of America's wealthiest men, who argued most passionately for an estate tax. In a series of articles in the *North American Review*, he said that all wealth should go to the community at the end of a man's life. Clearly he confused the state with the community.

Carnegie also argued that inheritance is bad for kids. It makes them lazy and un-enterprising. We all know of cases where this has proven true. But there are many ways around this problem: setting up trusts that allocate the money according to certain preset conditions. Even if that weren't true, whether one family's kids are indolent or enterprising isn't the business of government.

And as economist Alexander Tabarrok argues in a paper written for the Mises Institute,

> the adage says that wealth corrupts; perhaps, but wealth has no monopoly in this regard. It is easy enough to lead a worthless and parasitical life without an inheritance; I have seen neither argument nor evidence which suggests having an inheritance increases this possibility. ("Death Taxes: Theory, History, and Ethics")

In fact, Tabarrok notes the tendency of people who bequeath vast sums of wealth to also bequeath a sound moral and educational inheritance as well.

In a capitalist society, the institution of inheritance is more than a moral institution; it is part of the process whereby wealth is transferred to those who can best use it to serve the wishes of consumers.

The most important reason that people save is the hope of providing a better life for their children. A society that punishes that impulse with taxes is foolish. It is draining energy from the single most powerful engine of capital accumulation. If the super-rich don't want their kids to get their money, fine. Donate every penny of it to someone else. But they are wrong to block others from exercising a free choice.

72.

THE STEEL RIPOFF*

In its dealings with foreign nations, the United States generally tries to maintain the moral high ground in its pronouncements and policies. But by slapping a 30 percent tariff on foreign steel, the US government has hit rock bottom in hypocrisy and favoritism, and everyone knows it.

The idea here is to help one inefficient, bloated, and pampered industry at the expense of all US consumers of steel, including US businesses, and all producers in Europe, Asia, Brazil, and Australia. This is brazen protectionism, deeply harmful all around, not to mention morally repugnant.

It is also a terrible example to the world. What business will the United States have telling Latin American governments to curb mercantilist policies that privilege state-connected businesses and punish everyone else? What moral authority remains for the United States to tell Japan that its system of crony capitalism must come to an end? Who will pay a whit of attention to any US president who decries subsidies and industrial planning in other people's countries?

The repercussions are already being felt via damaged relations in Latin America and Europe. The World Trade Organization will likely give the green light for retaliation. Russia has

*March 2002

already banned imports of US chicken, and protectionist lobbies all over the world are rushing to take advantage of the opportunity.

This is bad economics all around. President Bush said the tariffs are merely designed to allow the US steel industry "to adjust to surges in foreign imports." In fact, the tariff does exactly the opposite. It permits the industry to refuse to adjust to reality. It allows US industry to continue to overproduce, overpay, and do so with outdated, inefficient, and costly methods. It postpones the day when steel must deal with the reality that other nations have dreamed up better and cheaper ways of doing things.

As for the implication that this is just designed to get steel through a temporary period of tough times, that is pure rubbish. There has been no flood of imports. Less steel is imported today than five years ago. But the facts don't matter, apparently. Ever since the artificial boost that steel received from World War II, the industry has gone through many rounds of "temporary" tough times. It has been rescued again and again, with tariffs, quotas, loan and pension guarantees, union privileges, and a hundred other gimmicks that stand in total opposition to the idea of free enterprise, all to keep a clean coat of paint on the great artifice.

The tradition that gives rise to such bailouts at everyone's expense is Soviet to the core. The theory of the Politburo central planners was that so long as everyone was employed doing something, especially if that something involved making big machines to boost industrial production, all was well. Never mind that the stuff they were making was super costly and unmarketable outside the confines of the Soviet state. It seemed to work for a while, and then one day everyone looked around to discover that the world had passed them by.

So it is with US steel, which has long thrived at its current size due to its connections to government. The Bush administration is doing its best to keep a failing system and a failing industry pumping along, no matter the cost to other US businesses and consumers. Some economists say the costs approach $8 billion, but that figure is spurious because the opportunity costs (what might otherwise be done with the resources were they not consumed by economically unviable projects) are essentially incalculable.

In economic terms, tariffs are indistinguishable from taxes. They take people's property by force by requiring businesses and consumers to pay far higher prices for goods than they would otherwise pay in a free market. To that extent, they harm the prospects for economic growth. If anyone says otherwise, he is ignoring hundreds of years of scholarship and the entire sorry history of government interference with international trade.

And then there's the question of trade war. No government in the world today takes a principled stand for unilateral free trade (the only policy consistent with free-trade ideals). Every government is looking for a good excuse to adopt the policies of autarky, taxes, protection, and industrial subsidies. Bush's steel tariff hands an excuse to the world. We can only hope that some enlightened leaders will stop short of full-scale trade war.

Finally, some people claim that propping up the steel industry is necessary because the nation is at war and war requires steel. Thus, American consumers need to be ripped off to support the munitions manufacturers. But notice that the bomb manufacturers themselves must also pay higher prices for steel, so they aren't being helped. Steel tariffs only make it more costly to build the same weapons the US would otherwise produce in the absence of the new tax.

As for the war excuse generally, it could also be cited in defense of complete autarky since there's hardly a producer or consumer good in existence that war planners can't find some use for. When policymakers start talking this way, look out. Most hot wars begin in trade wars. Witness the current war on terrorism, which began with a mass murder driven by revenge against persistent US trade sanctions.

Bush's new tariffs create more enemies and antagonize friends at the very time when the United States ought to be doing its best to win friends and influence people in the direction of freedom. Let there be no talk of the "fairness" of these tariffs. Here's a better description of them: a shameless act of mass thievery.

73.
THE BRIDGE OF ASSES*

Senator Kennedy says that minimum wage laws are essential to make sure that no working person lives in poverty, which is a strange thing to say, if you think about it. The reason a person works is precisely so that the person will not live in poverty. The minimum wage law does nothing but specify the floor below which a person may not work, and thus it can only, on the margin, increase the likelihood of poverty. If the key to eliminating poverty were more severe laws, why not forbid people from working for less than $100 per hour?

Economic libertarians focus on the fallacy of minimum-wage legislation because the issue serves as a window through which to observe the very soul of a policy worldview. It is the *pons asinorum* of the relationship between economics and politics. If the free market works—meaning the existence of exchange under private property and contract enforcement—then there is no need for such laws; indeed, such laws do violence to the market. If, on the other hand, we need such laws to guard against exploitation and to boost living standards, there is every reason for all-around central planning.

If economic libertarians can convince someone to give up support for the minimum wage (and such laws enjoy massive

*October 2003

public support), the rest falls into place. After all, the wage is but a price for labor services, a price that works like any other in the sense that it is subject to the laws of supply and demand. The employer wants to pay zero, while the employee wants $1 million per hour. The actual market wage results from economic forces that turn these seemingly irreconcilable demands into a cooperative contract that benefits everyone.

So it is with all economic transactions. The buyer wants to pay zero and the seller wants the highest price possible. But reality intervenes to curb these initial impulses. Economic actors are constantly faced with limited means, including money and time. Because of these limits, actors face competing demands. This competition between alternative uses of resources brings into play certain dynamics that cause the seller to realize that he can't charge too high a price and the buyer to realize that he can't pay zero.

In the labor contract, the seller is the laborer hawking his labor services, while the employer is the buyer purchasing such services. If you want to understand the psychology of the employer faced with a hiring decision, imagine your attitude as you shop in any retail outlet. You examine the goods and compare the benefits you will receive from paying what the seller is asking in exchange. You want to economize on resources—an impulse that is praiseworthy because it leads to minimizing waste. Why should we expect any less of the employer, who similarly wants to economize?

Now, again, it is always true that the buyer wants to pay less than the seller is offering, while the seller always wants more. So too in the labor contract: the seller of the labor services (no, the laborer does not actually sell himself, so let's hear none of this rhetoric about how you can't put a price tag on people) always wants more, while the buyer of labor services always wants to pay less (employers are not unusually miserly; they are no different from any buyer in the marketplace). The wage is nothing but a compromise between these two demands in light of existing realities.

What are the existing realities? There are many. There is the quality of the services to consider. Will this person make a contribution to the overall profitability of the firm, if not now then after a period of time? How much of a contribution will the person make compared with how much employing the person will cost in terms of others' time and company resources? Will the person stick around so that it is worth putting in the time to train the person? Does the person in question have a history and the credentials that minimize the risk to the employer? Is this person likely to be litigious and bring lawsuits crashing down on the company?

Another major factor that weighs on the buyer's decision is the reality that the seller (the laborer) faces a huge range of buyers to whom his or her services could be offered. There are always competing demands on time. The employer must make an offer good enough to draw the potential employee away from whatever other things he or she might otherwise be doing, whether it is working for someone else or just lazing around the house.

To make the contract work, it is essential that both parties to the exchange have maximum flexibility. If the worker is brilliant and experienced, he can viably put a high price on his services. If he has to change occupations and is trying to gain new skills, is just starting out in the workforce, or is disabled in some way, he may need to start the bargaining process with a much lower than average wage offer. He might even want to begin with an unpaid apprenticeship. In fact, he might want to begin with a "negative wage"—that is, arranging for a parent or someone else to actually pay the employer to hire the person.

Now, let's return to the minimum wage. Most of the discussion concerning these laws focuses on the impact on the business owner. But the really important point concerns the effect on the worker. It amounts to the government coercively limiting the price that the seller of labor services can offer on the market. It says to the worker, in effect: you may not offer too low a price for what you have to offer or else the government will show up and crack some skulls. Thus it doesn't do any favors to the worker; instead it removes the control that the person has over the conditions under which he or she may offer to work.

The worker who decides to start a new career or is just beginning in the marketplace thus faces a limited range of options. There are conditions under which it could amount to shutting the person out of licit employment altogether and instead force the person to work in the underground economy. It could force him to be unemployed and be permanently shut out of the marketplace so that labor data don't even reflect his existence. It could impose on him the mandate to only work in professions that earn a higher income now rather than pursuing some other line of work that may pay less in the short run on the bet that it will eventually pay much more in the long run.

In discussions of the minimum wage, the question always arises: does it lead to unemployment as measured by the data? What follows is a blizzard of studies, some showing that unemployment goes up after the laws are passed, some seeming to show no change, and even some seeming to show that unemployment goes down. What all these amount to is an elaborate and fallacious leap that purports to show that because one event followed another, the latter event must have necessarily been caused by the former. Human engagement in a market setting is actually too complicated to be captured by such statistical manipulations.

What these studies cannot show are the invisible effects of such laws. How many jobs were held onto because the minimum wage limited the workers' options? How much extra productivity was required of marginal workers because the employer was forced into hiring people who might otherwise produce less than they are paid to produce? How many people have moved out of mandatory high-wage areas into areas where wages are more flexible? How many workers might otherwise be hired were it not for the existence of minimum wages?

We can know via logic that the minimum wage leads to less hiring at rates below the minimum wage than there would otherwise be in absence of the laws. There should be no question that this is the case, since this is precisely what the laws are supposed to do. This is why unions are the top advocates of minimum wage laws even though very few of the union rank-and-file earn the minimum wage. Clearly, they are trying to keep a lock on the job market and limit competitive pressure from low-wage workers. Can all of these forces be illustrated in the politicized "studies" trotted out to show that the minimum wage causes no harm? Not in any way. In an economy driven by the choices of human beings, statistical data cannot reveal all.

The debate over minimum wage laws goes to the very core of how we view the relationship between economics and politics. Politicians who enact these laws imagine themselves as central planners magically bringing compassion and high living standards into being with the stroke of a pen. People who support the laws have a flawed view of the market process that sees exploitation behind all exchange relationships. Unions that back them are selfishly using the political process to enrich themselves at others' expense.

Only economic libertarians understand the actual reality: the minimum wage is a violent imposition on the freedom of association that harms all of society in the long run. The United States has been blessed by the fact that pressure to increase the minimum wage has been resisted at the federal level for many years. If we care about reducing unemployment and retaining the conditions for future prosperity, we had better not make the mistake of increasing it. If Congress had any economic sense, it would repeal all these laws forthwith.

74.
CAN THE MARKET DELIVER LETTERS?*

Like all government operations (public schools, domestic security, tax collection), the Post Office has to continually reform itself to avoid a complete public-relations meltdown. Thus did the Post Office become the Postal Service some 30 years ago. The name change was supposed to indicate how its management was going to be less like government and more like business.

But what institution defines business? It is not in the name. It is not an attitude or even managerial strategy. The core of business is private ownership. It is this institution that makes trade and competition possible, which in turn establishes prices and valuations, which in turn make possible rational economic calculation. Without private ownership, a government operation—whether a Soviet factory or the US Postal Service—lacks the essential means to act like a real business.

When the Post Office was reformed, it did not become privately owned, and its core service was not opened to direct competition, so its managers never confronted real risk nor faced the prospect of real loss. And so, by bureaucratic accounting standards, it still loses money and tries to make up for its failure by penalizing its customers with worse service and higher prices.

An even better idea might have been to actually make it a business—as in capitalists and entrepreneurs using their own money, or selling stock, to compete to provide services to the public, finding financially viable and efficient means for delivering letters. It is as simple as allowing private investors to take possession of all post offices, trucks, planes, and equipment, while repealing all restrictions on entering the mail market.

---

*December 2002

After all, anyone who says private enterprise can't deliver mail, given the amazing achievements of the market economy relative to Stalinist-style bureaus, has no plausible argument left.

Well, one argument keeps reasserting itself: the need for universal service, which is to say, the need for letter delivery to cost the same amount no matter where something is delivered. Private enterprise, say critics of privatization, will invariably charge more for out-of-the-way places as versus close-by places.

The answer to that objection is that the need for one price is without economic justification, at least *a priori*. It could be that private enterprise would end up charging a single price for delivery, the way long-distance services have benefited from charging a single per-minute charge. But it doesn't have to be this way. It would stand to reason that some delivery routes could command a higher price than others.

In any case, it is up to the consumers to decide. Under private enterprise, no one is forced to pay anything to anyone. Despite all the perfunctory gestures toward friendliness, the Postal Service does not serve consumers first. It serves its union, the government, and itself.

In any case, even the Postal Service doesn't take its universal price standard too seriously. It applies it only to domestic mail, but all other services and international mail service build in price discrimination. And if you add an additional ounce in weight, the price goes up. And notice that the one-price rule on first-class domestic mail does not mean one price for all time. It keeps going up every few years.

Who is to say it is more fair to have a single price that is always going up rather than a variety of prices that are stable or go down (as the price of most communications have done in the last two decades)? Who is to say it is fair to have a single (rising) price on letters within the United States, but not to Canada or Mexico? These price rules are so silly that they actually illustrate the problem with government mails: they are run by bureaucrats, not capitalists.

The proposition that government must enjoy a monopoly on letter delivery flies in the face of all experience. Even on matters of the security of the mails, private enterprise would do a better job. When the anthrax threat was everywhere last year, the government mails were powerless to stop it or otherwise screen the mail. Imagine how much better private enterprise would have been at the same job. And then the USPS has the gall to cite anthrax as an excuse for increasing the price of stamps!

The letter statutes that make it a crime to deliver a nonurgent letter for profit are still in force. Private enterprise has ingeniously gotten around the problem, through dozens of delivery services, overnight letters, and glorious email. By doing so, private enterprise has kept communications up to modern standards, even as the Postal Service continues its ancient-world practice of dragging sacks from place to place and accumulating losses year after year.

That brings us to the Bush administration's commission to look into Postal Service reform. Serving on it will be a variety of big names to look into the question of how to make the postal service viable in the age of email. Some people are celebrating this step as visionary. But come on: Do we really need this? It's like a commission to look into how to make the IBM Selectric viable in the age of Microsoft Word, or looking into how to save the market for horse-drawn carriages in an SUV age.

The consumer has already spoken. The Postal Service is an antique. Sell it, or let it fend for itself. Maybe there is something worth saving, but let entrepreneurs sort it out. We don't need a commission to tell us what we already know. The Postal Service needs to go.

Maybe we will all be pleasantly surprised, and the Bush administration's panel will recommend a complete sell off. And yet the Bush administration has made one thing perfectly clear: this is not what is intended. Undersecretary of the Treasury Peter Fisher told a news conference: "This is not a stealth project to privatize the Postal Service."

The right response to that comment is: forget stealth! Make that the goal! Surely the Bush administration would not face catastrophic political consequences for telling the truth on this matter. What could be the downside? Letter carriers, being part of a powerful labor union, tend to support and vote for Democrats anyway.

Another possible reform will be to allow the Postal Service to set the price of its own stamps rather than have to appeal to government for every increase. No doubt, this would be sold as a market reform. Recall that during the 1980s, the Soviets tried the same thing, allowing its factory managers to set their own prices. But without private ownership, the freedom to set prices becomes the freedom to loot! It's not price control to require the Postal Service to get its stamp-prices approved; it is a restriction on bureaucratic power.

Fundamental, not cosmetic, change is necessary. Why doesn't the Bush administration act? Because the real reason for the government mail that hardly anyone wants to talk about is this: the government wants to maintain a foothold in our essential communication infrastructure. In the high-tech revolution, it has lost much of that foothold. The government controls no viable Internet Service Providers and it has found it difficult to monitor emails, IMs, and all the other forms of communication available.

It may make economic and even political sense to let private enterprise do the whole of the job of delivering letters. But, from the point of view of our government managers, it would mean surrendering a certain amount of power and authority over the population. And no one in Washington is in any mood to do that.

75.

The Economic Lessons of Bethlehem*

At the heart of the Christmas story rest some important lessons concerning free enterprise, government, and the role of wealth in society.

Let's begin with one of the most famous phrases: "There's no room at the inn." This phrase is often invoked as if it were a cruel and heartless dismissal of the tired travelers Joseph and Mary. Many renditions of the story conjure up images of the couple going from inn to inn only to have the owner barking at them to go away and slamming the door.

In fact, the inns were full to overflowing in the entire Holy Land because of the Roman emperor's decree that everyone be counted and taxed. Inns are private businesses, and customers are their lifeblood. There would have been no reason to turn away this man of aristocratic lineage and his beautiful, expecting bride.

In any case, the second chapter of St. Luke doesn't say that they were continually rejected at place after place. It tells of the charity of a single inn owner, perhaps the first person they encountered, who, after all, was a businessman. His inn was full, but he offered them what he had: the stable. There is no mention that the innkeeper charged the couple even one copper coin, though given his rights as a property owner, he certainly could have.

It's remarkable, then, to think that when the Word was made flesh with the birth of Jesus, it was through the intercession of a private businessman. Without his assistance, the story would have been very different indeed. People complain about the "commercialization" of Christmas, but clearly commerce was

---

*December 2001

there from the beginning, playing an essential and laudable role.

And yet we don't even know the innkeeper's name. In two thousand years of celebrating Christmas, tributes today to the owner of the inn are absent. Such is the fate of the merchant throughout all history: doing well, doing good, and forgotten for his service to humanity.

Clearly, if there was a room shortage, it was an unusual event and brought about through some sort of market distortion. After all, if there had been frequent shortages of rooms in Bethlehem, entrepreneurs would have noticed that there were profits to be made by addressing this systematic problem, and built more inns.

It was because of a government decree that Mary and Joseph, and so many others like them, were traveling in the first place. They had to be uprooted for fear of the emperor's census workers and tax collectors. And consider the costs of slogging all the way "from Galilee, out of the city of Nazareth, into Judea, unto the city of David," not to speak of the opportunity costs Joseph endured having to leave his own business. Thus we have another lesson: government's use of coercive dictates distorts the market.

Moving on in the story, we come to Three Kings, also called Wise Men. Talk about a historical anomaly for both to go together! Most Kings behaved like the Roman Emperor's local enforcer, Herod. Not only did he order people to leave their homes and foot the bill for travel so that they could be taxed. Herod was also a liar: he told the Wise Men that he wanted to find Jesus so that he could "come and adore Him." In fact, Herod wanted to kill Him. Hence, another lesson: you can't trust a political hack to tell the truth.

Once having found the Holy Family, what gifts did the Wise Men bring? Not soup and sandwiches, but "gold, frankincense, and myrrh." These were the most rare items obtainable in that world in those times, and they must have commanded a very high market price.

Far from rejecting them as extravagant, the Holy Family accepted them as gifts worthy of the Divine Messiah. Neither is there a record that suggests that the Holy Family paid any capital gains tax on them, though such gifts vastly increased their net wealth. Hence, another lesson: there is nothing immoral about wealth; wealth is something to be valued, owned privately, given, and exchanged.

When the Wise Men and the Holy Family got word of Herod's plans to kill the newborn Son of God, did they submit? Not at all. The Wise Men, being wise, snubbed Herod and "went back another way"—taking their lives in their hands. (Herod conducted a furious search for them later.) As for Mary and Joseph, an angel advised Joseph to "take the child and his mother, and fly into Egypt." In short, they resisted. Lesson number four: the angels are on the side of those who resist government.

In the Gospel narratives, the role of private enterprise, and the evil of government power, only begin there. Jesus used commercial examples in his parables (e.g., laborers in the vineyard, the parable of the talents) and made it clear that he had come to save even such reviled sinners as tax collectors.

And just as His birth was facilitated by the owner of an "inn," the same Greek word "kataluma" is employed to describe the location of the Last Supper before Jesus was crucified by the government. Thus, private enterprise was there from birth, through life, and to death, providing a refuge of safety and productivity, just as it has in ours.

76.
THE FAITH OF ENTREPRENEURS[*]

Ludwig von Mises didn't like references to the "miracle" of the marketplace or the "magic" of production or other terms that suggest that economic systems depend on some force that is beyond human comprehension. In his view, we are better off coming to a rational understanding of why markets are responsible for astounding levels of productivity that can support exponential increases in population and ever higher living standards.

There was no German miracle after World War II, he used to say; the glorious recovery was a result of economic logic working itself out through market forces. Once we understand the relationship between property rights, market prices, the time structure of production, and the division of labor, the mystery evaporates and we observe the science of human action making great things happen.

He is right that understanding economics does not require faith, but there are actions undertaken by market actors themselves that do require faith (and Mises would not disagree with this)—immense faith, faith that moves mountains and raises up civilizations. If we accept the interesting description of faith by St. Paul ("evidence of things unseen") we can understand entrepreneurship and capitalist investment as acts of faith.

Everyone who is in business understands this. It requires a thousand daily acts of seeing the unseen future to be in business. The reality of the marketplace is that the consuming public can shut you down tomorrow. All they need to do is to fail to show up and buy.

This is true from the smallest business to the largest. There is no certainty in any business. Nothing is a sure thing. Every

---

business in a market economy is a short step away from bankruptcy. No business possesses the power to make people buy what they do not want. All success is potentially fleeting.

Success does yield a profit, but that provides little comfort. Every bit of profit you take for yourself comes out of what might otherwise be an investment in the development of the business. But neither is this investment a sure thing. Today's smash hit could be tomorrow's flop. What you perceive to be a solid investment could turn out to be a short-term craze. What you see, based on past sales, as having a potential mass appeal could actually be a market segment that was quickly saturated.

Emperors can rest on their laurels but capitalists never can.

Sales history provides nothing but a look backwards. The future is never seen with clarity but only through a glass, darkly. Not only is past performance not a guarantee of future success; it is no more or less than a data set of history that can tell us nothing about the future. If the future turns out to look like the past, the probabilities still do not change, anymore than the probability of the next coin toss landing on heads increases because it happened previously five times in a row.

Despite the utter absence of a road map, the entrepreneur-investor must act as if some future is mapped out. He or she must still hire employees and pay them long before the products of their labor come to market, and even longer before those marketable products are sold and turn a profit. The equipment must be purchased, upgraded, serviced, and replaced, which means that the entrepreneur must think about today's costs and tomorrow's and the next day's *saecula saeculorum*.

Especially now, the costs can be mind-boggling. A retailer must consider an amazing array of options concerning suppliers and web services. There must be some means of alerting the world to your existence, and despite a century of attempts to employ scientific methods for finding out what makes the consumer tick, advertising remains high art, not positive science. But it is also an art with high expense. Are you throwing money down a rat hole or really getting the message out? There is no way to know in advance.

The heck of it too is that there are no testable causes of success because there is no way to perfectly control for all important factors. Sometimes not even the most successful business is clued into what it is, precisely, that makes its products sell more as compared with its competitors. Is it price, quality, status, geography, promotion, psychological associations people make with the product, or what?

Back into the 1980s, for example, Coca-Cola decided to change its formula. The result was a catastrophe as consumers fled, even though the taste tests said that people liked the new better than the old.

If the historical data are so difficult to interpret, think how much more difficult it is to discern probable outcomes in the future. You can hire accountants, marketing agencies, financial wizards, and designers. They are technicians, but there are no such things as reliable experts in overcoming uncertainty. An analogy might be a man in a pitch-black room who hires people to help him put one foot in front of the other. His steps can be steady and sure but neither he nor his helpers can know for sure what is in front of him.

"What distinguishes the successful entrepreneur and promoter from other people," writes Mises,

> is precisely the fact that he does not let himself be guided by what was and is, but arranges his affairs on the ground of his opinion about the future. He sees the past and the present as other people do; but he judges the future in a different way.

It is for this reason that an entrepreneurial habit of mind cannot be implanted through training or education. It is something possessed and cultivated by an individual. There are no entrepreneurial committees, much less entrepreneurial planning boards.

The inability of governments to engage in the entrepreneurial act of faith is one of many reasons why socialism cannot work. Even if a bureaucrat can look at history and claim that his agency could have made a car, drywall, or a microchip, that same person is at a loss to figure out how innovations in the future can take place. His only guide is technology: he can speculate about what might work better than what is presently available. But that is not the economic issue: the real issue concerns what is the best means given all the alternative uses of resources to satisfy the most urgent wants of consumers in light of an infinity of possible wants.

This is impossible for governments to do.

There are thousands of reasons why entrepreneurship should never take place but only one good one for why it does: these individuals have superior speculative judgment and are willing to take the leap of faith that is required to test their speculation against the facts of an uncertain future. And yet it is this leap of faith that drives forward our standards of living and improves life for millions and billions of people. We are surrounded by faith. Growing economies are infused with it.

Mises forgive me: this is a miracle.

SECTION 2: ECONOMICS & ECONOMISTS

77.

WHAT ECONOMICS IS NOT*

The most common misunderstanding about economics is that it is only about money and commerce. The next step is easy: I care about more than money, and so should everyone, so let's leave economics to stockjobbers and money managers and otherwise dispense with its teachings. This is a fateful error, because, as Mises says, economics concerns everyone and everything. It is the very pith of civilization.

This is a confusion sown by economists themselves, who postulate something called "economic man" who possesses a psychological propensity to always behave in ways that maximize wealth. Their mathematical models, predictions, and analysis of policy are based on this idea.

In the real world, however, we know this not to be the case. The world as we know involves profit seeking but also extraordinary acts of charity, sacrifice, nonpecuniary giving,

*February 2006

and voluntarism (though I dislike that term since all commercial exchanges are voluntary too!).

How to account for these? The Austrian approach to economics dispenses with the idea of "economic man," or rather broadens the meaning of economics to include all action, which takes place in a framework of scarcity. Scarcity requires that we economize on something in all that we do, even when wealth is not the motivation. For this reason, Austrians analyze acting individuals, not maximizing prototypes.

Why is this important? A common complaint against the free market is that it needs to be supplemented by laws that restrict the power of materialism unleashed. The market does "greed" well, people admit, but we need government to provide charity, order, law, and restraint of all sorts, as if these areas lie outside the domain of economics.

The truth is that a theoretical structure that explains stock markets but not charity auctions, chain stores but not church attendance, savings rates but not child rearing, has no claim to be a universal theory at all.

Murray Rothbard defined the free market as integral to an entire theory of a free society that is ordered and developed through the cooperative action of all its membership. That action is not conditioned on profit seeking only, but on the institutions of ownership, contract, and free association.

Economics, then, is a science that is rooted in a larger understanding of what used to be called the liberal order. The central claim of this understanding is that society—just like the smaller subset often called "the economy"—needs no central manager to thrive.

And just as economic structures are best managed by property owners and traders, the entire society contains within itself the capacity for self-management. Any attempt to thwart its workings through the coercion of the state can only create distortions and reduce the wealth of all.

Anyone familiar with current economics texts and journals knows that this is not the view that they promote. They are still stuck in an era where bureaucrats imagined themselves as smarter than the rest of us, where central bankers believed that they could end the business cycle and inflate just enough to cause growth but not ignite inflation, where antitrust experts knew just how big businesses should be.

But can government managers know how to manage daily decisions on production and allocation better than property owners? Can they improve on the agreements, innovations, and rules created by acting individuals? They have neither the intellectual equipment nor the incentive to do so. They are blind to the realities of our lives and incapable of doing more for us than we can do for ourselves, even if they had the incentive to do more than rob and coerce us.

How is it that the economics profession has come to overlook these points? Murray Rothbard believed it was partially due to the decline of the general treatise on economic theory, systematic books that begin with fundamentals and trace cause and effect through the whole range of human action.

These books were common in the nineteenth century. Thank goodness that Mises wrote his amazing work *Human Action*, and Rothbard wrote his elaboration on Misesian economics in the form of *Man, Economy, and State*. The Mises Institute publishes both.

You know what? They are still being read, teaching each new generation of economists through the work of the Mises Institute. And not just in the United States: we receive regular progress reports from study groups in China, Latin America, Eastern Europe, and Africa. A universal theory is once again having a universal impact.

78.

ECONOMICS: THE WEATHER–VANE PROFESSION*

The economics profession has made a sharp turn to the left as was evident at the last meeting of the American Economic Association. Gone was any praise of tax cuts and private property, or criticism of federal spending and regulation. Instead, there were reassertions of Keynesian falsehoods, mathematical treatises with no economic content whatsoever, and an attempted (and mistaken) extension of economics into sex and religion.

This left turn took place, as it has in the past, because most economists are lapdogs of the state. Paid directly or indirectly by government, they seek their advancement through government, consider government jobs to be the pinnacle of their profession, and are ever attentive to their master's voice.

When Reagan was in the White House, supply-sideism was in vogue. If most economists didn't become disciples of Arthur Laffer, Jude Wanniski, and George Gilder, they were at least interested in incentives. The less-statist Rational Expectations and Monetarist Schools also became popular.

Now, however, with Bush's neo-Keynesians in control of national policy, academic after academic defends government spending and deficits, and attacks tax cuts and "market failure." Few write about privatization or deregulation.

Economists are buttressed in their attitudes by the national media, which are also pro-government. Any economist who wants to be "fit to print" had better stay in step with the *zeitgeist*.

---

*March 1992

Not that this is anything new. Contrary to myth, Franklin D. Roosevelt did not embark on his statist New Deal because of Keynesian economics. Keynes's *General Theory* wasn't published until 1936, when the New Deal was already three years old. (Mussolini's program was FDR's actual prototype.)

Nor was it a coincidence that the model that came to dominate the profession was the policy of nearly every industrial power (including Nazi Germany, whose economics Keynes praised in his Introduction to the German edition of the *General Theory*).

Not until Western governments began to run deficits as a matter of course did economists discover the benefits of red ink; most economists were not in favor of central bank manipulation of the economy until the Federal Reserve was established; and there was no profession-wide consensus on the virtue of redistribution until the income tax amendment.

Shifts to the left are made easier these days by mainstream analytical models, which are radically unsound. For starters, they bypass questions of private property, legal institutions, and differences among people. For this reason, the popular schools of the 1980s were not solidly free market. While they improved the old Keynesian aggregations, none—Supply-Side, Rational Expectations, nor Monetarist—challenged the Keynesian framework.

No Keynesian model allows economists to question the notion of government management, or that it can improve on the free market by making business more competitive, wages more flexible, prices more responsive, and money flows more rational. This is part of the reason that economists of almost all stripes have continued to dance to the Keynesian tune, changing only partners.

There is only one school of economic thought that refuses to dance: the Austrian. We want to fire the conductor, break the instruments, tear up the sheet music, and lock the ballroom.

Only the Austrian School is based on economic law, on real human beings acting in a world of scarcity, and on the natural order of liberty. That is why we know, and can demonstrate, that government intervention must always damage the market.

From Carl Menger's day to our own, Austrian School economists have condemned the errors of government, no matter what the politicians wanted, no matter what the risk to careers.

Austrians remain a minority in the profession (the courageous are always a minority), but a bigger minority than at any time since the 1930s; we have an astounding number of good professors and students. But meanwhile, the welfare state grows. What to do?

We cannot rely on politicians, although we should try to elect the rare good one. Most economists are useless as well. That is why we need the public, guided by the right intellectuals. As Ludwig von Mises pointed out, economics is far too important to leave to the economists. Everyone should know at least the basics.

At the second annual meeting of the John Randolph Club in January, Club President Murray N. Rothbard laid out a strategy for involving the public. Certainly the inchoate sentiments already exist. Who doesn't despise bureaucrats and politicians? What normal American really thinks they should run our families, regulate our businesses, and spend our incomes?

Most Americans are angry and resentful at the present state of affairs, and who can blame them? What other emotions should we feel as society, subverted by socialist egalitarianism, collapses around us? It is our job to point out the villains: state managers and their pet welfare recipients: underclass, foreign, and corporate.

Instead of trying to persuade the politicians of some marginal scheme, we need to show the public how the trillions extracted from their wallets are spent, and on whom. Once done—and it is no small task—we could begin an authentic revolution against Washington, DC. Then we need not worry about the economics profession. It will be following along nicely.

79.

KEYNES RULES FROM THE GRAVE*

Everyone is at work on a "stimulus plan" for doing something about the recession. But the much-publicized disagreement between the Republicans and Democrats is not about economic theory as such. There has been no critical thinking applied to the subject of why the recession, the longest in the postwar period, continues. Rather, the disagreement is about which levers to pull when, and who should get the benefits.

All this is evidence that Keynes rules us from the grave. Popularized and reduced to sound bites, the fallacies are far easier to detect than in Keynes's impenetrable prose from his 1936 treatise that first resurrected ancient fallacies and garbed them in the language of science.

The underlying idea in the Keynesian tradition is to attribute the length of the recession to insufficient effective demand, so it is up to government to give the economy a kick-start, change public psychology, spend money on anything and everything, stop the money hoarding and start the buying, inflate a bit here and there, drive down interest rates, run deficits for a while, and fool the workers into thinking they're getting raises while their real wages are falling.

That's the traditional mix of policies that has been employed during every recession between the early thirties and the current day. Bush clearly subscribes to this view. After his meeting with a group of economists who should know better, he said a feature of his plan is that it "recognizes that money in the consumers' pocket will help grow this economy." In fact, the White House says that the first principle of its economic program is to "encourage consumer spending."

---

*January 2003

Just think about this. Let's say that every one of us emptied our bank account today and just bought something. And let's say we used all our assets and leveraged them to the hilt to borrow as much money as possible, and then spent that. What would happen? Well, shelves would empty and prices would go up and the business pages would roar with approval.

But what about tomorrow? There would be no savings left to fund new projects after this little boomlet. Products on shelves would languish. Long-term projects would have no customers. We would have spent ourselves straight into recession again. This plan boosts the economy in the same way that an amphetamine boosts one's mood. It's an illusion that must end.

There is no evidence that this path has ever worked to pull an economy out of recession. And if you look at consumer debt, it seems that my little allegory of spending mania isn't far from the reality.

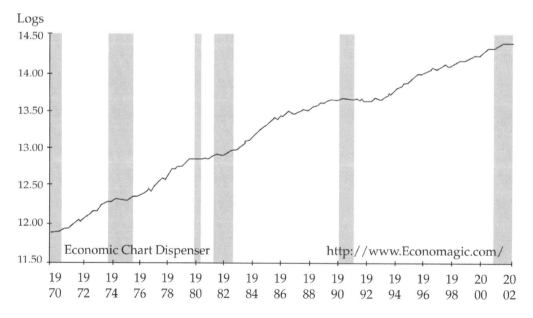

Consumer Credit Outstanding: Total; Millions of Dollars; NSA

Personal consumption figures have topped any in history but still no recovery:

Personal Consumption Expenditures; Billions of Chained 1996 Dollars

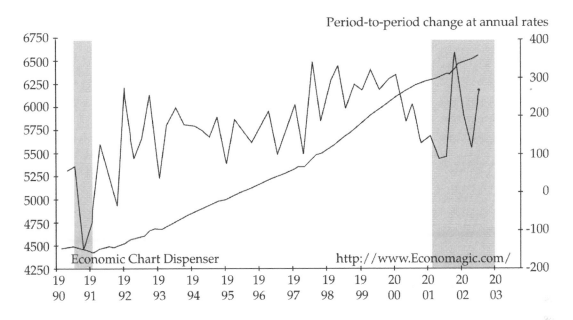

While any nonsocialist should cheer a tax cut (though if government keeps spending ever more money, it has to come from somewhere) let's not pretend that the Bush administration is driven by the desire to free the economy from the taxman's shackles. If every dime saved by taxpayers were put into savings accounts, the administration would consider its plan a failure. The idea is to get people to spend ever more money. Perfunctory tax cuts are the type of Keynesian policy Republicans like because it dovetails nicely with GOP slogans about small government.

The idea of eliminating taxes on dividends in particular is designed to boost demand for the stocks that pay them (typically older companies with more political connections). And where is the money that will flow to stocks coming from? Most likely from investments that currently yield interest payments—at least that's the theory. If the purpose were merely to boost the business sector and eliminate double taxation, that could be accomplished by a reduction of corporate taxes, an idea that was ruled out early on.

Another idea that made a brief appearance in late December was to create a payroll tax holiday. The Democrats favored this idea because it would benefit their constituents, but the

Republicans rejected it out of hand, proving once again that they have no general interest in making government cheaper for average Americans. The idea was quickly dropped when everyone realized the dangers associated with creating a precedent that would allow people not to pay a tax. After all, if a tax holiday is good for the economy, why not make it permanent?

But will draining savings and boosting spending cure what ails us? No, because the US economy is, in fact, not suffering from some blight of insufficient aggregate demand. It is suffering from the malinvestments of the previous boom, when the capital-goods sector expanded disproportionately to what savings could justify, an imbalance brought about by the Federal Reserve's loose money policies of the late 1990s.

But you won't read about this in the literature of the Keynesians who still rule the roost in Washington. For further proof, look at the headlong rush to extend unemployment benefits on into the future. This is completely contrary to what economic reality should dictate. In a recession with unemployment, wages need to fall in real terms. But an ironclad tenet of Keynesian economics is that this must never be allowed to happen. By this one error, the Great Depression in the United States and Britain was prolonged by many years.

There are several undeniable realities of a recessionary environment. Wages tend to fall. Businesses tend to be liquidated. Resources are withdrawn from investment and put into savings. Consumers spend less. Stock prices fall. All of these tendencies may seem regrettable but they are necessary to bring all sectors back into realistic balance with each other. It can only do harm to fight these developments—via policies that promote debt and gin up the business sector—as Japan has done for 10 years and Washington is doing again today.

Even if the first stimulus held out the prospect for success, Washington has worked for 18 months to cripple economic growth through mind-boggling spending, aggressive protectionism, and attacks on the personal liberty that undergirds free enterprise. The prospect of war and all it entails is the Sword of

Damocles threatening American prosperity (not an additional spending boost, as the Bush administration seems to believe). All this drains power and resources from the private to the public sector, the last thing an economy in recession needs.

Might the economy be in recovery mode had Washington not engaged in these destructive acts? Perhaps. It is a general rule of public policy that when government acts to fix a problem, it makes the targeted problem worse and creates a few more in the process.

By all means cut taxes! Anytime, anywhere! But one must also cut spending if the goal is to reduce the overall burden of government (and that is clearly not the goal). One must also be prepared for the possibility that citizens will save this money, as they probably should, rather than spend it. In the current DC hysteria, however, it is Keynesianism and not clear economic thinking that rules.

80.
MYTHS OF THE MIXED ECONOMY*

The planned economy was all the rage in 1937, when Prentice-Hall published a 1,000-page tome on *The Planned Society: Yesterday, Today, Tomorrow: A Symposium by Thirty-Five Economists, Sociologists, and Statesmen.* The "question that confronts us today is not if we shall plan, but how we shall plan," wrote Lewis Mumford in the Foreword. All the contributors—Keynesian, socialist, communist, and fascist—agreed with that point, including such luminaries as Sidney Hook, Benito Mussolini, and Joseph Stalin.

But the book was honest. It linked Stalin and Keynes, fascism and the New Deal. The plans were not identical, of course,

---

*August 1992

but all agreed on government "rationality" as versus the "chaos" of the free market.

Most of the authors advocated the "mixed economy," Mises's name for an admixture of capitalism and socialism. Such a combination, he showed, is necessarily unstable, and our own mixed economy is tilting towards statism, with such regulatory disasters in the last few years as the Clean Air Act, the Americans With Disabilities Act, and the Civil Rights Act.

Today, no part of the economy is left untouched by the President's budget and the swarm of regulatory agencies. Buttressed by most of the economics profession, the regulatory state today rules and ruins America. Communism lost, but social democracy won.

In the American mixed economy, it is the job of the planner to: ensure "full employment" (as federal policies create joblessness); encourage technological innovation (not through markets, but through subsidies); ensure a "fair" distribution of wealth (rewarding parasites and punishing the productive); manage international trade (though it needs no more management than domestic trade); and keep "public goods" out of private hands (even though public ownership must always be less efficient than private).

The planner has taboos as well. He must never mention private property, praise the coordinative function of prices, criticize pressure groups unless they're anti-big-government, be cynical about the uses of power, call for a tax cut, or identify the real source of prosperity as the free market.

Charles Schultze, President Carter's chairman of the Council of Economic Advisers, not only adheres to these rules and taboos in his new book *Memos to the President*, he sets them out for every policymaker to follow in the future.

In the entire work, he has not one good word to say about the market, private property, or the price system. His central assumption is that the government must manage the economy to prosperity. According to Schultze, we should believe that: the Federal Reserve protects the dollar, when our money has lost 93 percent of its value since the Fed was established; the Fed can cure business cycles, when every decade or so, it causes a serious economic setback; the government can create full employment, even as it causes unemployment with such welfare measures as the minimum wage and civil rights; the government can develop new technologies, even though bureaucracy is a proven technology killer; we can trust the government to improve our standard of living, though our standard of living has fallen for nearly 20 years; the government protects us from monopolistic capitalists, even while government creates and sustains destructive monopolies from the post office to the schools; regulatory agencies do protect us from dirty air, unsafe drugs, and lead poisoning, while everywhere government is biggest, from Moscow to DC, life is dirty and unsafe.

Naturally, mainstream economists—the useful idiots of the interventionist state—advise presidents on economic policy. Today, these economic planners see their primary task as "keeping supply and demand in balance." That doesn't mean allowing the market to work, of course, but rather pushing and releasing buttons on the planning machine.

There are two views on how to do this, one mainstream and one rival. The mainstream view says that a decrease in overall demand causes economic downturns, and so demand should be increased by government spending and money creation. This is supposed to make up for the deficiencies of the private sector.

The rival view says declines are caused by a fall in overall supply, caused by any number of factors, including an irrational fear of investment. So, boosting overall demand through spending or inflation only exacerbates the troubles.

The second view has better policy implications, but both are misguided. They assume that there is something called overall demand conglomerating the values of consumers and producers alike. This obscures the real economy.

The obscurantist aggregations don't stop with "supply" and "demand." The planners also discuss such categories as capital and investment as if they were homogeneous, representing these very diverse groupings as single letters in their macroeconomic models.

Both views also assume that government managers are smarter than the market. Imagine that you had to plan the household finances of your next-door neighbor, with little or no information about their income, tastes, and talents, all of which can and do change. Yet the planners have been trying to do this for decades, to the entire economy.

To explain their way out of this problem, the planners separate the "micro" economy from the "macro" and claim the decisions of individuals have nothing to do with the overall picture. It's true that no one individual can, for example, change the net rate of savings in the economy, but there would be no net rate of savings without individual decisions.

It is out of the millions of decisions of real people that the economy is created, and it is the job of the economist to understand and explain how that happens, not to encumber it.

The planners of the mixed economy like to talk about supply and demand as if they needed the government to coordinate them. Yet supply and demand describe the natural pattern of economic behavior in the absence of government interference.

If there is a chicken plague, the price of eggs will soar. The consumer doesn't have to read the "Chicken Health Update" to know that he should economize on eggs. The price tells him that, and he can then look for substitutes.

Conversely, if Frank Perdue genetically engineers a super-chicken that lays many more eggs than the normal bird, the price of eggs will plummet. But the consumer doesn't need to read "Techno-Poultry Weekly" to know that. He need only look at the price.

In a free market, there is no need for planners to bring supply and demand into line. The daily transactions of millions of consumers do so, leavened by the risk-bearing entrepreneurs. It is the mixed economy itself that creates the demand for economic planners to run it. Massive deficits destabilize the economy, leading to calls for government to stabilize it.

The "entitlement" programs are interventions as well. Government spending may increase the demand for some goods and services, but it drains resources from the private economy just as surely as taxes. Yet the "opportunity costs" of confiscating these resources never factor into the planners' models.

How much does the mixed economy cost us? We can't know. Despite the well-intentioned attempts of some economists to figure it out, no one can know the effects of technologies never created; firms never started; people never hired; others hired by government fiat; central bank-created recessions; and higher prices from taxes, regulations, and government-generated demand. We can only know that the effect is gigantic, harmful, and growing.

Government intervention can be criticized on a number of other grounds that the mixed-economy planners do not mention:

- First, politicians and bureaucrats are self-interested. In the private sector, self-interest works to the common good. In the public sector, it means expansion of the government's budget and power, which attacks the common good.

- Second, the market can sometimes anticipate the planners, negating the effects of government action. If the Federal Reserve increases the money supply, the market can take account of the likely inflationary effects and prices will rise sooner and higher than the managers thought.

- Third, intervention increases the incentive to evade the law, thereby enlarging the less-efficient and societally unfortunate underground economy.

- Fourth, intervention distorts the price system and the interest rate, which work to coordinate the use of resources. Price controls and regulations cause misallocation, and Fed-lowered interest rates cause businessmen to make bad investments.

- Fifth, intervention undermines the division of labor, preventing people from doing the tasks they are most suited for because regulation prevents employers from hiring on merit.

If the mixed economy is such a disaster, why do we have one? Because it enables the well connected to loot the rest of us in a social democracy disguised as "democratic capitalism." To get away with the looting, the mixed-economy state attacks all countervailing institutions: families, neighborhoods, businesses, private schools, and charitable and religious organizations. The results are the barbarism and increasing poverty we see all around us.

The Planned Society didn't mention that, but it is the inevitable outcome of what it recommended, and what the US government practiced in 1937, and today.

81.

A Marxoid "Oops"*

When a congressman cites the Constitution, I'm glad to hear it mentioned, but I know he's subverting it with every vote he casts. That's how I felt when left-wing economist Robert Heilbroner said in the *New Yorker* that "Mises was right" about socialism.

Ludwig von Mises was never able to get a paid academic post in the United States. He was shut out of American economic journals, and boycotted and ridiculed by the establishment—all because he told the truth, without fear or compromise, when it wasn't fashionable to do so.

---

*November 1990

Heilbroner, however, has never been anything but fashionable. A professor at the New School for Social Research, his lecture fees are high and his books sell well, especially his history of thought, *The Worldly Philosophers*, which glorifies Marx and Keynes and never mentions the Austrians.

Like John Kenneth Galbraith, Heilbroner has gotten rich by attacking capitalism. And also like Galbraith, every time he writes a book, the reviews in the top media read like sales copy.

In his *New Yorker* article, Heilbroner mentions the debate of the 1920s and 1930s on the workability of socialism. Mises started it by saying, in his 1920 article on "Economic Calculation in the Socialist Commonwealth" and 1922 book *Socialism*, that socialism was impossible. For more than two decades, the left sought to refute this, and the conventional wisdom held—until the collapse of Communism in 1989—that Mises had been wrong.

Now Heilbroner says Mises was right: "no Central Planning Board could ever gather the enormous amount of information needed to create a workable economic system." Although true, that was not Mises's point. His critique was far more radical: that an economy couldn't function properly, i.e., economically, without a free price system. Socialism in particular couldn't work because there are no free prices for its commonly owned means of production.

Mises also made an even more significant point for those of us in the West: free prices are what makes an efficient economy possible. Therefore, every step away from the free market subverts economic calculation. Mises's arguments about socialism therefore also apply to the American economy of today.

Therefore Heilbroner's misstatement serves a purpose. If he really believed that Mises was right, he could hardly endorse "socialist capitalism" as the answer to our problems.

As late as 1970, Heilbroner was apologizing for Stalin. Sure, old Joe made mistakes, usually "self-defeating" ones, poor guy, but "we must bear in mind that industrialization on the grand scale has always been wrenching, always accompanied by economic sacrifice, and always carried out by the more or less authoritarian use of power." This is Stalin as the Soviet Henry Ford.

Also in 1970, Heilbroner ridiculed Mises (without naming him) as the reactionary dolt who claimed "in the first days of chaos following the Russian Revolution" that "socialism was . . . 'impossible.'"

Ha ha, said Heilbroner. The USSR has grown "roughly twice as fast as the United States," and Soviet socialism "continues to produce at good rates."

In the midst of a government-caused depression in 1978, Heilbroner had the answer: "a powerful, and I think irresistible, force for planning the economic process"—"a general sticking of the public nose into private life."

In 1980, Heilbroner praised Communism for "the immense material and cultural improvement that these regimes have brought to their peoples." History cannot be pushed back. "In our times and henceforth, change is upon the world, in large part inspired and guided by Marxism itself. The task now is to understand it."

He endorsed world government as necessary for economic justice in 1988, since "the nation is in some way the ultimate barrier that has to be transcended before something like social-ism may be reached."

Like other rich leftist intellectuals, Heilbroner is a trimmer. Even his *New Yorker* piece is all mea and no culpa. He wasn't wrong when he disagreed with Mises; the times have changed.

Mises was right at the wrong time. This is in contrast to Heil-broner, who was right then and right now.

Heilbroner, like all leftists, doesn't believe in economic law. What worked in 1920 may not work in 1990, but might work again in 2000. Socialism may not be feasible now, but that doesn't tell us anything about the future—if it comes back into fashion in Manhattan salons.

In Eastern Europe, the Baltics, and Russia, Heilbroner—like Galbraith—is scorned as an apologist for totalitarianism, while interest is high in the unabashed capitalists like Mises, Hayek, and Rothbard.

But in the United States, the situation is less encouraging. What conservative or libertarian could be published on Mises or any other subject in the *New Yorker*? In intellectual America, now as in the past, only the left is respectable—whether it repents its sins or not.

82.

STILL THE STATE'S GREATEST LIVING ENEMY*

The more time you spend with Austrian economists or libertarian intellectuals, the more you realize that Murray Rothbard's influence has been underestimated. No, his name is not a household word (yet) but his influence is felt in another way: those who read him experience what amounts to the intellectual challenge of their lives. Whether that means adopting his paradigmatic approach to political economy, elaborating on a feature of his system, or attempting a refutation, once read, Rothbard seems inescapable.

Mises.org documented, on the tenth anniversary of his death, the way in which his influence is increasing, and dramatically so ("The Unstoppable Rothbard," January 7, 2005).

It is also a good time to revisit Justin Raimondo's spirited and compelling biography of Rothbard, *Enemy of the State*, which came out on the fifth anniversary of his death. This

*April 2005

neglected book reconstructs postwar intellectual history with attention to Rothbard's contribution. The author himself was a player in many of Rothbard's post-1970 ideological struggles so the reader can enjoy a box seat at some of the most exciting debates of the period.

Rothbard's principles were, of course, consistent from the time he first put pen to paper, and they made him a lightning rod for controversy and the standard by which all pro-liberty thought is measured to this day. But it was often the application of the principles, as much as the principles themselves, that earned him passionate detractors and defenders. His enemies were also driven crazy by his unfailing good humor: he was completely unflappable, always found joy in smashing evil, and somehow always won in the end.

Rothbard was the architect of the body of thought known around the world as libertarianism. This radically antistate political philosophy unites free-market economics, a no-exceptions attachment to private property rights, a profound concern for human liberty, and a love of peace, with the conclusion that society should be completely free to develop absent any interference from the state, which can and should be eliminated.

Rothbard worked his entire life to shore up this ideological apparatus—in economic theory, historical studies, political ethics, cultural criticism, and movement organizing. As Raimondo says, no biography can be complete without coming to terms with the simultaneous occurrence of all these professional contributions—a tough job when you are dealing with a legacy that includes 25 books and tens of thousands of articles.

This is an outstanding account of his life that valiantly struggles to treat them all between two covers, though in the end even Raimondo too must specialize, in this case on Rothbard the cultural-political commentator and organizer.

"If ever the antipode of the Court Intellectual existed," Raimondo writes, "then surely his name was Murray Newton Rothbard." Even today, radical thinkers are tolerated insofar as they stick to high theory. But this was not Rothbard's way. He never remained aloof from the passing scene: I've seen 30-page private memos from Murray written weeks before elections evaluating candidates in even the smallest House races (this was at a time when politics mattered more than it does now). It was in his application that he instructed us, not only in the ideals we should seek, but also in the all-important area of how we might go about achieving them, and do so without compromising ideals.

Applied Radicalism

In 1952, for example, Rothbard (at the age of 28) was very concerned about what was happening to the American Right as it had existed between the wars. The old isolationist, classical-liberal, anti-New Deal forces were being shoved aside in favor of a new breed of Cold Warriors agitating to use the state against Russia, our ally in war only a few years earlier. How could conservatives champion small government and also call for vastly expanded nuclear weapons and a US global empire? He kept asking the question but wasn't getting satisfactory answers. Barely beginning his career as an economist and public intellectual, he flew into the opposition mode.

"What we really have to combat is all statism, and not just the Communist brand," Rothbard wrote in a column appearing in the periodical *Faith and Freedom*. "Taking up arms against one set of socialists is not the way to stop socialism—indeed it is bound to increase socialism as all modern wars have done." China should be recognized. Nuclear weapons should be dismantled. Not one dime should be spent building the US empire. As for the "captive nations" problem, Rothbard suggested that the United States free its own: Hawaii, Alaska, and Puerto Rico!

The election of 1956 pitted Dwight Eisenhower against Adlai Stevenson, both of whom offered statist domestic policies. (Sound familiar?) But Stevenson was against conscription and less pro-war, and thus garnered Rothbard's support, the moral priority being the prevention of another massacre of young men. Rothbard even worked the phones from the Stevenson campaign headquarters in Manhattan. His turn against the Republicans got him tossed off the *Faith and Freedom* masthead, led him to appeal leftward for allies, and sparked a lifelong war with William Buckley and the mainstream of the conservative movement.

Very little changed throughout his life. He was radically in favor of free markets and radically opposed to war, a wholly consistent opponent of the welfare-warfare state. But in the intellectual-political history of 1952–1989, there was no place for such a person. Official opinion required philosophical inconsistency, and the segmentation of intellectual camps followed the same course.

So Rothbard often had to make political decisions by weighing the foreign-policy question against a candidate's domestic program. Let's fast-forward 40 years, for example, to the presidential elections of the 1990s. Pat Buchanan challenged George Bush for the Republican nomination, saying that Bush had made two unforgivable errors: he waged an unjust war against Iraq and he raised taxes. Did Rothbard cheer Buchanan? You bet. And he worked overtime trying to get Buchanan up to speed on broader economic issues while defending him against the wrong-headed charges of the left.

But Buchanan lost the nomination, and refused to pursue a third-party option. Rothbard then turned to Perot as the candidate worth rooting for, and on the same grounds: Perot blasted Bush's war and his taxes. Then Perot suddenly pulled out. That left Bush and Clinton, whose foreign policy was no different from Bush's but whose domestic policy was worse.

Rothbard then rooted for Bush against Clinton. His very controversial column appeared in the *Los Angeles Times*, and it garnered more hate mail than Rothbard had ever received in his life. Many libertarians (not famous for strategic acumen or catching the subtleties of such matters) were shocked by his noninterest in the Libertarian Party nominee. But by that time, Rothbard was convinced that the LP was running a presidential campaign in name only, that it was a clique devoted not to real political education but to organizational maintenance.

Had Rothbard become a Republican? Far from it: two years later, he blasted Newt Gingrich in the *Washington Post* even before the new Republican Congress under Newt's leadership had assembled. Had he become a Buchananite? Take a look at his 1995 piece, reprinted in *The Irrepressible Rothbard*, in which he predicts that in 1996 Pat would concentrate on protectionism to the exclusion of every other important subject. He was getting trapped into "becoming just another variety of 'Lane Kirkland Republican'." That article sent the Buchananites through the roof. But it foreshadowed the fall of yet another promising political force.

The point that few people could fully grasp about Rothbard was his complete independence of mind. He had one party to which he was unfailingly loyal: the party of liberty. All institutions, candidates, and intellectuals were measured by their adherence to that standard and their ability to promote it. Neither did he make (as the old conservative cliché has it) "the perfect enemy of the good," as his argument for Bush over Clinton demonstrates. He was always eager to prevent the greater evil in the course of advancing human liberty.

Indeed, Rothbard was a tough-as-nails strategist and thinker, one who was breathtakingly creative as an intellectual force but refused blind devotion to conventional wisdom or any institution or individual that promoted it. Such a man is bound to make enemies. Hardly a day goes by when I don't run across some wild misunderstanding of his life and work, some outrageous calumny spread by those who know he can no longer answer them, some baseless theory claiming to be an extension of Rothbardian ethics, or, worse, a wildly distorted presentation of history that misrepresents Rothbard's role in some political affair.

CONVENTIONAL CRITIQUES

It's usually best to not pay attention to these trivialists. As Raimondo points out, "he was a giant among pygmies, too large to be consumed by the struggle with his errant followers."

There's no reason why today's Rothbardians should be consumed by the claims against him either. And yet, a main virtue of this book is precisely that it debunks a room-full of myths about the man, and it does so not with conjecture, but with primary documentation. Let's consider a few.

He wasn't consistent.

Raimondo produces letters and articles from his earliest writings showing that he had mapped out most of his life's work. That goes for his attachment to Austro-free-market theory, his anarcho-capitalism, his devotion to natural rights, his love of the Old Right political paradigm, his optimistic outlook for liberty, his hatred of war, his essential Americanism, and even his reactionary cultural outlook. The ideas were all developed throughout the course of his life, but the seeds seemed to be there from the beginning. The attacks were too. Ralph Lord Roy's 1953 book *Apostles of Discord* blasted some early Rothbard articles as dangerously supporting "unregulated laissez-faire capitalism." Exactly. He learned, he developed, he elaborated, but he never made a fundamental shift.

He wasn't original.

Rothbard never claimed complete originality, as his attackers imply. His economic theories came from the work of Ludwig von Mises, his political-ethical views from the Jeffersonian-Thomist tradition, his foreign policy from the American Old Right, his anarchism from the Tucker-Nock American tradition of political radicalism. What Rothbard did was draw them together into a complete and coherent apparatus, and anchor them, as had never been done before, to a complete theory of private property. This is his unique contribution, and Raimondo demonstrates it. Austrian economics and libertarian theory might not have survived into the twenty-first century but for Rothbard's work. And that doesn't count his hundreds of micro-discoveries along the way. Yes, he was original, and he always underestimated the originality and power of his ideas.

He was just an ideologue.

Rothbard wrote volumes and volumes of economic history and economic theory having nothing expressly to do with libertarian theory, or political advocacy, except to the extent that they dovetailed with the rest of his research program. Raimondo also skewers the claim that Rothbard turned to non-mathematical Austrian economics because he didn't know math. Absurd! His Columbia undergraduate degree was in mathematics, with highest honors. He rejected the use of math in building economic theory on strict methodological grounds.

In any case, even as he was engaged in political polemics in the 1950s and early 1960s against the Buckley takeover of the right, he was writing *Man, Economy, and State,* as well as long scholarly pieces for the economic journals. He was accused of pamphleteering early on, but his scholarship kept pace with his journalism, as if there were two or three Rothbards working continuously.

He had no lasting influence.

As you read Raimondo, you are struck by how far and wide this man's influence extended (and extends!) in the worldwide classical liberal movement. He was the founder of the Center for Libertarian Studies, the founding editor of the *Journal of Libertarian Studies*, the founder of the first Austrian School economics journal, the inspiration behind the Mises Institute, the muse at the *New Individualist Review*, the leader of the split in YAF, the motivator behind the whole libertarian movement, the recruiter for Mises's seminar, the person who named the Cato Institute, and much more.

His speeches appeared in amazing places, from Joe McCarthy rallies to the floor of Congress. His "Circle Bastiat" provided the intellectual infrastructure for decades of growth in the movement. The world today is populated by Rothbardians, and they are wielding surprising influence.

He should have stuck to high theory.

The implication here is that Rothbard would have had greater influence had he not reached out to popular audiences. That's nonsense. Like Mises, Rothbard believed in waging a multi-front battle. But Rothbard himself granted that his course was not wise, if what he sought was professional advancement. As he explained in a letter to Robert Kephart:

Bob, old and wiser . . . heads have been giving me similar advice all my life, and I'm sure all that advice was right. . . . When I was a young libertarian starting out, I was advised by Leonard Read: "Only be critical of bad measures, not of the people advocating them." It's OK to criticize government regulation, but not the people advocating them. One big trouble with that is that then people remain ignorant of the ruling class, and the fact that Business often pushes regulatory measures to cartelize the system, so I went ahead and named names. . . .

Then, when I became an anarchist, I was advised, similarly: "Forget this anarchist stuff. It will injure your career, and ruin your scholarly image as a laissez-faire Austrian." I of course didn't follow that perfectly accurate advice. Then, come the late 1950s, I was advised by friends: "For god's-sakes, forget this peace crap. Stick to economics, that's your scholarly area anyway. Everybody is against this peace stuff, and it will kill your scholarly image, and ruin you with the conservative movement." Which of course is exactly what happened. And then: "Don't attack Friedman directly. Just push Austrianism." And "don't push Austrianism too hard, so you can be part of one big free-market economics family."

So you see, Bob, my deviation from proper attention to my career image is lifelong, and it is too late to correct at this point. I'm sure that if, in Ralph [Raico]'s phrase, I had been "careful," and followed wise advice, I would now be basking in lots of money, prestige, and ambiance. . . . Why did I take the wrong course? . . . If there had been lots of libertarians who were anarchists, lots who were antiwar, lots who named names of the ruling elite, lots attacking Hoover, Friedman, etc., I might not have made all these choices, figuring that these important tasks were being well taken care of anyway, so I may as well concentrate on my own "positioning." But at each step I looked around and saw indeed that nobody else was doing it. So then it was up to me.

He quit doing serious economics after the early 1960s.

This accusation seems to credit the greatness of *Man, Economy, and State* and *America's Great Depression* from the early 1960s, but suggests that he peaked in these years and went downhill from there. This charge can only be sustained by failing to carefully examine his 100-page bibliography. He wrote for the *International Encyclopedia of the Social Sciences* in 1968, and his articles "Lange, Mises, and Praxeology," "Freedom, Inequality, Primitivism, and the Division of Labor," and "Ludwig von Mises: Paradigm for Our Age" appeared in 1971, and in 1972 he had chapters in several scholarly books on World War I, Herbert Hoover, and economic method. So it goes in 1973, the year he wrote a long piece on method for a volume devoted to phenomenology (oh, yes, he also came out with *For A New Liberty* that year), and several more articles for economic journals.

And in 1975, the first and second volumes of *Conceived in Liberty* came out—a detailed narrative history of the Colonial period. A year later, fully eight long scholarly pieces appeared, as well as another volume of *Conceived*. On and on it goes throughout his career (including his studies of Fetter's interest rate theory in 1977), his three seminal pieces on Austrian theory for the first post-Mises books on Austrian theory, his introduction to Mises's *Theory of Money and Credit* in 1981, his eight large scholarly pieces on economic theory in 1987 (including his many entries in the Palgrave, etc. etc.), culminating in his two-volume *History of Economic Thought*, which Raimondo regards as his crowning achievement.

He abandoned radical libertarianism after the early 1970s.

This is the opposite charge from the one made above, made by people who were irritated that he did not keep writing *For A New Liberty* again and again. But in fact, Rothbard kept plugging away on extending the libertarian framework, with pieces throughout the 1970s (one on punishment is cited and extended in Randy Barnett's new book on libertarian legal theory). "Society Without a State" appeared in 1978, "Quest for the Historical Mises" appeared in 1981, and, most importantly, *The Ethics of*

Liberty appeared in 1982. "World War I as Fulfillment"—one of his most radical pieces ever—appeared in 1989, and, of course, throughout the 1980s, he was blasting away at Ronald Reagan's foreign and domestic policy (a time when many ex-libertarians were cozying up to the government).

He didn't do any serious scholarly work after the late 1970s.

This is another related charge, and it is equally as absurd. Take a look at Edward Elgar's *Logic of Action*, a two-volume collection of his scientific writing appearing in that publisher's Economists of the Century series. Most of the pieces come from the 1980s and 1990s, when he was, if possible, more productive than he had been during any other period. Also, see above.

He allowed Libertarian activities to distract him from scholarship.

This line is repeated by those who were actively involved with his struggles over the leadership of the Libertarian Party. Certainly those battles consumed his enemies. There are even times when these activities threaten to consume Raimondo! But, as he points out, during the worst of the battles (1979–1983), Rothbard wrote and published *The Mystery of Banking* and *The Ethics of Liberty* "in addition to several major scholarly articles, and was simultaneously researching a book on the Progressive era in American history" (manuscript in the archives of the Mises Institute). "How he managed this level of productivity while engaged in this increasingly acrimonious dispute is a testament to the scale of his intellectual gifts," Raimondo writes.

Some respond: but if he hadn't been involved in these petty political struggles, how much more might he have produced! This is a fallacy. For Rothbard, activism of this sort was a habit, a means of relaxation, a source for diverting his energies in order to replenish them for the heavy lifting he had to do. It is as silly to imagine "what might have been" as it is to think what the average person could accomplish at work if he never had to sleep. By the way, Rothbard also spent countless hours reading about chess, attending classes on music and architecture, watching his beloved soap operas, and keeping up with sports.

Are we to say that these "distracted" him, or should we say that they made him a well-rounded person?

He left libertarianism to become a leftist in the 1960s.

Raimondo's book puts all this in perspective, at long last. The upshot: Murray never became a leftist. Again, his views never changed. His "New Left Period" had nothing to do with hippies; it was an attempt to seek soldiers for the libertarian cause within the ranks of the left because it was here you found the ant-statism of the day: the complaints about federal police, the antidraft protests, the antiwar sentiment, war revisionism, the praise of civil disobedience, and all the rest. Murray worked to find the best parts of the New left and steer its leadership to a pure position. It didn't work, though it didn't entirely fail either. In any case, it was the best hope he had at the time.

He departed libertarianism during his paleo period.

Again, Murray never left libertarianism. He did leave the Libertarian Party and its surrounding movement (including the DC crowd trying to ingratiate itself with the state) in 1989. I was there when Murray was hooted down during a convention when he rose to speak on behalf of his candidate for party chairman. Yes, it's true: outrageously, they booed him because his candidate was too bourgeois and too middle class, despite being politically radical. Recall that 1989 was the year the Cold War ended, and a new opening appeared to achieve Rothbard's dream of bringing about a middle-class revolution against the state. He saw that the Libertarian Party was not the vehicle for doing this. Might his judgment have changed later?

In later years, he sucked up to the right.

This is a very odd claim given that most of his popular writings from the 1990s, as collected in *The Irrepressible Rothbard*, consist of attacks on the mainstream of right-wing individuals and organizations, particularly the welfare-warfarism of the neoconservatives. This claim also fails to understand a point that Raimondo hammers again and again: foreign policy was a top concern for Rothbard. He saw that the left was becoming committed to "humanitarian imperialism" after the destruction of the Soviet Union, while the grass-roots right was becoming isolationist on foreign policy. He sought to encourage this trend.

In the meantime, a dozen articles in mainstream venues have taken notice of the very rise of isolationist sentiment that Rothbard noted earlier than anyone else. To a surprising degree, he was responsible for turning a trend into a movement, especially among a new generation of scholars and political activists who had no intellectual investment in Cold War political opinion. As for his Confederate sympathies, he was calling Lincoln the "butcher of the South" in the early fifties, just as John T. Flynn, Mencken, and Nock did in earlier generations.

He was a great theorist but a terrible strategist.

Also absurd. Raimondo demonstrates the acuity of his strategic thinking even in some of his most controversial moves to reach out to the left and reach out to the right. In its time, each move made sense and fit with the overall strategic plan. In fact, one of Rothbard's seminal contributions was developing libertarian strategy. Moreover, Raimondo also shows that his detractors, who were always anxious to sell out to the powers-that-be, invariably flamed out. Raimondo only takes issue with one strategic judgment Rothbard made over a particularly bitter LP nomination fight, but even here he provides the reader with enough information to see it from Rothbard's point of view.

He loved Khrushchev and was objectively pro-communist.

This accusation circulated in the 1960s and resurfaced in Bill Buckley's bitter and malevolent obituary of his old nemesis. "Rothbard physically applauded Khrushchev in his limousine as it passed by on the street," wrote Buckley. Nonsense. What was at issue was Rothbard's refusal to join the ridiculous *National Review* campaign to whip up a protest against Khrushchev's visit to the United States (taken, we now know, over the vociferous objections of hard-liners in the Kremlin). Raimondo quotes Rothbard noting that Buckley and Co. are always eager to extend their hand to any other "Bloody Butcher" in the world, including "Winston Churchill, Bloody

Butcher of the refugees of Dresden, and countless others." Rothbard refused to join Buckley's call for "a totalitarian bureaucracy within our shores" to fight the Cold War, and for that, Buckley never forgave him. (A must read: the epilogue skewering Buckley's obit point by point.)

He broke with former friends.

The implication behind this attack is that Murray was a nasty guy who liked to stab people in the back. Raimondo shows that Rothbard's legendary breaks—including those with Rand, with Cato, with the LP, with the Buckleyite Right, etc.— were of two types: people stabbing him in the back or Rothbard getting fed up with a long series of despicable sellouts. There were no other kinds of breaks, and, actually, the reader will be surprised at how long-suffering Rothbard proved to be, especially considering the characters and nonsense he was confronted with.

It may seem a petty point, but Raimondo's book very ably demonstrates this long-suppressed truth. Moreover, he shows that Rothbard was often the victim of campaigns against him, whereby former associates tried to wield their influence to suppress his writings. A very special treat is the truth about the Cato-Rothbard split, in print for the first time: Rothbard couldn't take the growing conventionalism of the outfit. Obviously, Rothbard's instincts were borne out by later events: he would have left anyway when Cato started backing vouchers, new long-range bombers, forced savings, etc.

He talked Karl Hess into not paying taxes, thereby ruining his life.

This charge, which first emerged in an early draft of Hess's autobiography and has otherwise circulated for years, is outrageous on the face of it. Murray cheered on every tax revolt, but he never counseled anyone to be a personal martyr. You can do very little work for liberty from jail, he used to say. Raimondo brilliantly quotes from an old book of Hess's describing the moment he became a tax protester, and it had nothing to do with Rothbard's urgings and everything to do with Hess's penchant for making bad judgment calls out of anger.

He became a Buchananite.

When Pat Buchanan criticized Bush's war and tax increases, and was smeared as an anti-Semite, Rothbard rose to his defense. He also worked to turn Buchanan into a consistent libertarian, or at least to make him into the model of what he claimed to be: an Old Right isolationist constitutionalist. Raimondo points out that Rothbard was frustrated that he did not achieve his goal.

Further, he points out that Rothbard "chided Buchanan for being a classic case of the old adage that some people (especially politicians) often concentrate on those issues in which they have the least expertise; in Buchanan's case, this is undoubtedly the realm of economics." Special credit goes to Raimondo for pointing this out, since he is personally far more favorable to Buchanan than Rothbard was from 1992 forward.

He abandoned libertarianism for the Christian right.

How tedious! Rothbard wrote for conservative Christian publications in the early 1950s and onward because he saw in Christianity a devotion to law and morality, not of state but of transcendent origin. Early memos even have Rothbard praising Catholicism for its implicit universalist anarchism as opposed to the nationalist-statist strains in Protestant history. Moreover, Rothbard showed how the demands of the rank-and-file Christian right were mostly libertarian: keep government out of our churches, families, communities, and schools. Even today, libertarians have yet to understand the potential for strategic alliances here.

He worshiped Mises.

Absurd. Raimondo quotes affectionate letters about Mises, and demonstrates that Rothbard saw Mises as the greatest living economist. But he also worked to improve Mises in many areas, including utility theory, the economics of law and intervention, public goods, and many other areas, giving rise to the claim that . . .

He departed from Mises.

Raimondo further shows that Rothbard was far and above Mises's leading expositor and defender, in economic theory and policy. They had a warm relationship. Mises, moreover, had the greatest respect for Rothbard as a man and an economist.

He changed his view of immigration.

Actually, Rothbard held the same position his whole life: there is no right to immigrate (as he writes in *The Ethics of Liberty*) but rather immigration should be by invitation, not invasion, as consistent private-property rights economics would dictate. In the exact opposite of what a market policy would be, the state forbids invited people to immigrate, but invites millions with no invitation from property owners.

He refused to learn from others.

Throughout his life, Murray read voraciously and never stopped learning from the good scholarship of those working in many fields. He was always on the cutting edge of the newest valuable literature, drawing the attention of libertarian scholars toward recent discoveries in historical scholarship, economic theory, and philosophical reflection. He also acquired knowledge during his forays with diverse ideological groups: from the left, he came to fully appreciate the power of protest and from the right, he came to fully appreciate the political implications of cultural institutions as well as the moral necessity of decentralized politics. Moreover, he was ever-anxious to credit those around him for insights, as a quick glance at his footnotes indicates.

Meanwhile, the scholarly branch of Rothbardianism is so huge, interdisciplinary, and international, I can no longer keep up with it. And his books keep coming out, selling well, and staying in print. Books, articles, dissertations, and more: Rothbard lives today as never before.

Enemy of the State goes way beyond documenting the life and work of Rothbard. Raimondo argues for Murray's strategic judgment in a huge range of political and ideological controversies. He also explains why Rothbard was so hated and attacked during his lifetime: he was the victim of envious and unprincipled types who couldn't stand his willingness to speak truth to power. And yet Rothbard always maintained his cheerfulness, productivity, and optimistic outlook. Raimondo rightly gives much credit for this to Murray's wife of almost 40 years, JoAnn. He called her, in a dedication, "the indispensable framework," and indeed she was.

Reading it, you can't help but thrill at how this book will affect a new generation of readers, giving them a fresh perspective on postwar intellectual and political history and also inspiring them to radical thinking in defense of human liberty. Even if you have never heard of Murray Rothbard, you will be drawn to his life, his mind, his spirit. To understand his times and ours, you must read this book.

As Raimondo concludes:

> Whether it is exercised upon the minds of this generation, or the next, the liberating force of Rothbard's ideas is gathering momentum. He built a monument to liberty, a mighty edifice that towers over the horizon and cannot be ignored—a challenge and a reproach to the guardians of the status quo, and an inspiration to the revolutionaries of tomorrow.

SECTION 3: BANKING & THE BUSINESS CYCLE

83.
THE CASE FOR THE BARBAROUS RELIC*

We flatter ourselves, in this technological age driven by financial innovation and mind-boggling efficiencies, that we know more than any previous generation. But there is lost knowledge, among which is the knowledge of what sound money feels and looks like, what it does, who makes it and why, and how it holds its value.

So let us revisit Robert Louis Stevenson's classic story, *Treasure Island*, and the climactic scene where the pirates and their companions have finally found their treasure and prepare to haul it away. The narrator reports as follows:

> It was a strange collection, like Billy Bones's hoard for the diversity of coinage, but so much larger and so much more varied that I think I never had more pleasure than in sorting them. English, French, Spanish, Portuguese, Georges, and Louises, doubloons and double guineas and moidores and sequins, the pictures of all the kings of Europe for the last

---

*November 2005

419

hundred years, strange Oriental pieces stamped with what looked like wisps of string or bits of spider's web, round pieces and square pieces, and pieces bored through the middle, as if to wear them round your neck—nearly every variety of money in the world must, I think, have found a place in that collection; and for number, I am sure they were like autumn leaves, so that my back ached with stooping and my fingers with sorting them out.

There is more to learn about real money from this paragraph than in most money and banking texts. Here we discover that money is international. It matters not what nation-state or private party mints it. Money can come in all shapes and sizes. It has enduring value for hundreds of years. It can be put in a vault and found by anyone in the future and retains its value. Its merit as money is not dependent on the existence or persistence of any single government.

The regimes that minted the coins may be long forgotten but the money they made stays as a permanent part of the economic landscape until it is melted. What this suggests is independence for the people who have, hold, and use the money. They are not roped into any regime as such. They go about their economic affairs as independent people. Their money, which cannot be destroyed by the actions of a central government or a central bank, testifies to their status as free people.

And what is it made of? Gold, silver, or any precious metal, something or anything that will cause a back to ache and the fingers to hurt from sorting them out. Money is heavy, robust, durable, divisible, enduring. It is treasure. It is worth hiding when one is in trouble and worth hunting for if one stumbles upon a map to guide you there. As to when it was minted and by whom, it doesn't matter. Money lasts. Money is true. It transcends the generations. It transcends the nation. It transcends the state.

As for any money minted or printed in the last 50 years, some of it may have value as a collectible but its value would vanish to near zero if it were melted. As for the paper, it would be truly worthless. One can imagine the scene in *Treasure Island* had they opened the trunk to discover wads of paper currency from defunct governments. Let's just say the story would have ended very differently. It might have looked more like that scene in Lawrence of Arabia where the warriors trek hundreds of miles across the desert for treasure only to find crates full of paper cash, which the plunderers promptly throw to the wind. Lawrence wisely departs the scene on a horse, promising to return with real money.

Incidentally, I do think there is a point to buying children coins for presents. Just to hold an older coin of gold and silver imparts a lesson of sorts. It illustrates the reality of a history that is different from our present. I've never seen a child disregard a nice gold or silver coin. They keep it in a safe box, show it to their friends, and reflect on the sense of personal empowerment they experience from owning it. Children know what treasure is, even if central bankers do not.

Today we think of money as something to possess for instrumental purposes but something otherwise created and managed by the government to keep the economy going.

The new Fed chairman, Ben Bernanke, was grilled at his Senate confirmation hearings as if he were a magician who could pull rabbits or squirrels out of his hat, depending on his mood that day. All the questions related to whether he would tend to prefer the rabbit of employment to the squirrel of inflation. The goal of these politicians was to prod him into admitting that squirrels are far more preferable than rabbits, and if he would just admit it and swear to it, they would give him a free pass and let him perform, while Congress and president provide the necessary smoke and mirrors.

And by the way, Bernanke also promised to keep the Fed completely free from politics.

> I assure this committee that, if I am confirmed, I will be strictly independent of all political influences and will be guided solely by the Federal Reserve's mandate from Congress and by the public interest.

When ex-Fed chairman Arthur Burns arrived at the Bonn airport as ambassador to Germany, a reporter asked him how he could have agreed to Nixon's desire to inflate so massively? The Fed chairman must do as the president wants, he answered, or the Fed would lose its independence.

Here is a rule of thumb. If an institution has a dot-gov in its web address, as in FederalReserve.gov, it is not independent and it is not free of politics.

One politician summed up the Fed's mandate this way: "guiding the economy to create broadly shared prosperity."

Herein we find the perfect summary of what is wrong with Washington's view of economic life. It imagines the economy to be guided by the Fed, and that prosperity is created by its printing press. Bernanke, however, was not in a position to correct the record, for he has himself spoken about the wonderful and limitless power of the Fed to create as much money as it wants to.

Thus spake Bernanke to those worried about deflation:

> The US government has a technology, called a printing press (or, today, its electronic equivalent), that allows it to produce as many US dollars as it wishes at essentially no cost. By increasing the number of US dollars in circulation, or even by credibly threatening to do so, the US government can also reduce the value of a dollar in terms of goods and services, which is equivalent to raising the prices in dollars of those goods and services. We conclude that, under a paper-money system, a determined government can always generate higher spending and hence positive inflation.

What awesome power! Are we really supposed to believe that a government that possesses the ability to create unlimited amounts of money will wall off the institution that does the creating from any political influence? Surely not. The independence of the Fed is just a mask that the government uses so that it can avoid taking responsibility for any downside that comes about from the Fed's awesome power.

I suppose that if I had a counterfeiting machine, I too would want it kept out of the house and run by someone I could appoint who would nonetheless swear to be completely independent if caught in the act.

The Bernanke hearing was a despicable display in more ways than we can count. That there is a direct relationship between inflation and employment was never questioned, even though that relationship does not exist as a matter of history or economic law.

To use the printing presses to drive down unemployment is to risk not only inflation but also radical economic instability and business cycles that can end in the worst of all worlds. And the idea that low unemployment—as a symbol of a growing economy—needs constant infusions of paper money inflation from the Fed is belied by the whole of the nineteenth century, as well as by economics.

What did Bernanke and his examiners agree on? They agreed that the Fed should be all-powerful in matters of macroeconomics. They agreed that there should not be any ironclad rule for the conduct of monetary affairs, but rather that smart guys ought to wing it day by day to achieve the right mix of policy options. And they all agreed that the prevention of deflation, meaning a fall in the general level of prices, ought to be the number one priority. So when you hear that Bernanke favors "low inflation," remember that the emphasis is on the noun and not its modifier. It means that he prefers any amount of inflation to a condition of deflation.

Why the hysteria against deflation? We are faced with a real puzzle here. In the whole of the private sector, the number one focus of retailers these days, particularly those dominant retailers such as Wal-Mart and Home Depot, is low prices. This they emphasize above all else because they know that this is what consumers want.

And yet in the public sector, we find exactly the opposite: an ironclad promise that prices will not be low but rather will be continually rising. So if Wal-Mart's slogan is "Always Low

Prices," the slogan of the Fed and the government should be "Always Higher Prices."

The question is why. Why is it that Congress, the Fed, and the presidency all agree that deflation is something to be avoided at all costs?

The experience of the Great Depression looms large, but as Murray Rothbard has shown, low prices were just about the only good economic trend that was happening throughout the 1930s. Imagine if you had all the same disasters occurring—all inspired by bad economic policy—but with high prices on top of it all! Here is a test. We all know people who lived through it. Ask them today if they would have been better off if all goods and services had been two or three or ten times more expensive.

No, the trouble with the Great Depression was not low prices. Nor were low prices and wages the cause of the economic downturn. As Rothbard further showed, the downturn was a correction of a previous inflation, a macroeconomic version of the dot-com bust, and one that was made ever worse by governmental attempts to fix the problem. As for the Fed, it did not pursue a policy of benign neglect but rather desperately attempted to inflate the money supply and was unable to do so.

The real blame for the Great Depression lies with precisely the policy that Bernanke favors, that is, a steady and relentless increase in the money supply to keep the economy humming while not sparking price increases that are politically objectionable. This inflation targeting is precisely the problem since it sends false signals to capital-goods investors and borrowers, skewing the production structure forward in time to a greater degree than underlying savings can support.

Not knowing what the Austrian School says, Congress and the Fed might believe that a policy of low-grade inflation is the best protection against depression. But I don't believe that this is why they favor such a policy. Nor do I think that the desire to boost employment is the reason, since there is no evidence for anything like a long-run tradeoff between inflation and unemployment.

The reason the government—and here I speak of Congress and the presidency—favors a loose monetary policy, a discretionary rule at the Fed, and ongoing low-grade inflation is the most obvious one of all. It pays the bills.

In other words, the reason is no different from that of private counterfeiting. They like to have money without having to work to get it. That is essentially what the Federal Reserve provides the government. It doesn't have to worry about its bond rating collapsing or its credit standing falling. It doesn't have to bother with taxing people. It can hide the costs of government in the complications associated with monetary affairs.

Looking back at the history of inflations in the United States, we can detect a single event that, more than any other, prompts the government to engage in inflationary finance. I wish I could report to you that inflationary finance was a modern invention of the modern regime with its endless wars and welfare expansions.

Sadly, America was born in monetary sin, so to speak. The Continental Congress financed the Revolutionary War with paper money, beginning in 1775.

The currency was supposed to be retired in seven years with a pro rata tax levied by the states. But once the government got the hang of the magic of war finance, it forgot about the pledge and endlessly expanded the currency. Between 1775 and 1781, the Continental went from trading on par with one dollar in specie to being nearly worthless.

It was a tragic incident because it benefited all the worst people in this young country, the very group that later pushed for the Constitution to replace the Articles, and backed the creation of the first central bank, to enrich themselves. In some way, this war, which was undoubtedly just and involved a meritorious secession from a distant government, was the beginning of the end, precisely because it unleashed a horrendous inflation and schooled a new governing elite in the benefits of inflationary finance.

It has been war that has been the driving force in monetary depreciation throughout history. If Bush had been forced to raise the hundreds of billions that he has spent on his Iraq caper through taxation, his supporters would be far less supportive, and his policy more honest. Instead, he has been able to count on the inflationary finance of his friends at the Fed to make it all possible. Monetary policy has been the handmaiden of empire in other ways too, as the dollar is used as political leverage against nearly every country in the world from Argentina to China to Russia.

Fiat currency engenders conflict of all sorts, unbalances the economic structure, and puts everyone's savings at risk. It is for this reason that Alan Greenspan once wrote that the cause of freedom is bound up with the cause of the gold standard.

Should our monetary system be reformed so that it is based on a pure gold coin standard? Yes it should. This would be the single best reform we could make for the cause of freedom. Its commercial benefits include stability, predictability, and honesty in finance. Its moral benefits include a financial system that does not reward living beyond one's means. From the point of view of government, a gold standard would tie the hands of the state. They could wish and long for wars, welfare, foreign aid, bailouts, subsidies, and graft, but unless they could raise the money by taxing, all their talk would be pointless. That is a country I want to live in.

For years I've heard people suggest that the Mises Institute come up with a detailed plan for how the conversion would work. In fact, there are many models to choose from, from Joseph Salerno's to Murray Rothbard's to George Reisman's to Ron Paul's own legislation, which has been before the House for some two decades. What is lacking is not a plan. It is the political will. It would require that the government recognize the error of its own ways, agree to limit its power and influence, abolish the Fed, and return the control over economic structures back to the people. And you wonder why the movement for a gold standard struggles!

But let me just clear up a few myths about gold. It is not the case that under a gold standard, we would all find ourselves in the position of that young man in *Treasure Island*, with aching backs and throbbing fingers. Banks would continue to exist and compete on a sound basis. All financial services would continue to exist just as they do now, from credit cards and bankcards to PayPal and stock portfolio checking and all the rest. Indeed, we would see an explosion of financial innovation under the gold standard because so many of the uncertainties associated with inflationary finance would be a thing of the past.

Money would become truly international, or would tend in that direction as more countries decided to make their currencies as good as gold. And if we managed the transition properly, government would have no monopoly on the production of money. This would be something handled by the private sector, as suppliers competed based on beauty and design and reliability. In an ideal world, all currencies in the world would be different names for precious metals, all interchangeable with each other based on weight and fineness.

If that sounds complicated or unreasonable, or even completely unviable, let us remember that all forms of freedom seem impossible in the midst of despotic control.

Many intellectuals and officials in Russia and China couldn't really imagine how society would work if people were permitted to live and work and move where they wanted. To them it sounded like chaos. Germans can't imagine how society would survive without strict laws on when retail shops can open and close. And people in Britain went into a panic recently on the suggestion that pubs be permitted to stay open longer than usual.

In our own country, we can't imagine the legalization of drugs, the elimination of the minimum wage, the abolition of Society Security, or not bombing someone every two years. These things seem crazy to us because we have adapted to statism. So it is with money. We are used to the idea that government should run the monetary system. And that's why when we say we favor the gold standard, people think we are nuts. But today in China or Russia, anyone who favors a return of travel and moving restrictions is considered dangerous and deranged—which is precisely how I feel about anyone who says that government ought to be given full control of a nation's monetary institutions!

So I ask you to imagine how the world worked before the advent of central banking and before our permanent state of inflationary paper currency. Imagine if the money you made and saved were as good as gold—a truly independent medium of exchange that was not subject to political manipulation, confiscation, or depreciation. The wizards at the Fed would not control our destinies, Congress's appetite for spending would be curbed, and the president would be a bit more cautious about embarking on wars that would cost political capital. It would be the world of *Treasure Island*, where the only criminals we would need to worry about owned ships, not fleets, and where the pirates sang ditties about rum, not national anthems to the glory of the state.

84.
THOSE BAD OLD BUTTONED-UP DAYS*

Anything dismissed as "Victorian" these days is bound to be virtuous and rare, yet so compelling to decent people that a mere mention scares the pants off libertines. I'm talking, of course, about sound banking, which the *Wall Street Journal* dismisses in an editorial as "Victorian Finance."

"The Victorians were people, you recall, who upon discovering the little secret of sex, thought the human race was about to vanish," says the *Journal*. "Likewise, our modern Financial Victorians have discovered the little secret of credit."

---

*September 1991

The Victorians were merely realistic about sex, as we are not about credit, but the wages of sin are about to be paid.

After the S&L-bank orgy, Americans no longer believe in financial promiscuity. That's why, says the *Journal*, a belief in 100 percent reserves and "worries about 'too much leverage' or 'too little capital' creep out of heavily curtained conference rooms and into daily conversations." A "modern economy runs on credit. And credit runs on fractional reserves." Without them, banks would have "nothing to lend."

Except on the point that people are worried, the *Journal* is wrong about everything, including the most important: the Mises Institute's conference room doesn't have any curtains. But I can't blame the editorialist. The entire establishment is white knuckling it these days.

If enough people realize the banks are a house of cards, it will be 52 pick-up. When a very small percentage of depositors demanded their money, it closed the giant Bank of New England. Every other big bank is in similar condition, protected from the same fate by an increasingly ephemeral "confidence," with the Federal Reserve as tender of last resort. But here's the real "little secret" of our age: the Fed can't bail out more than a few big banks without hyperinflation. Thus the *Journal*'s distress. The government is coming to the end of its rope, and it's around the neck of the banks.

All these troubles can be traced to the legal doctrine of fractional reserves, which says that your liquid bank deposits are owned not by you, but by your bank, to do with as it pleases. When people realize this, it scares them. They want their money to be there when they need it, not in some deadbeat real estate project or Third-World politician's pocket.

As Murray N. Rothbard and every other free-market economist before the Progressive Era argued, there are two functions in honest banking: warehousing money as versus loaning it out. When a customer deposits his cash for a fixed term—by purchasing a CD, for example—the bank can properly loan it out for one day less, with prudential reserves against loan losses. But a demand deposit is different.

Under the terms of the contract, demand deposits are to be available any time the customer wants them. In a sound system, the banks keep 100 percent reserves for their demand deposits. Anything else is fraud, as the best of the Founding Fathers argued—if I may be forgiven for harking back to pre-Victorian times.

As the libertarian Tom Paine said, money in a bank is "the property" of the man who "deposits cash there." He "can draw the money from it when he pleases. Its being in the bank, does not in the least make it the property of the stockholders."

Accompanying unsound banking is fiat paper money. The only "proper use for paper," wrote Paine, is "to write promissory notes and obligations of payment in specie upon." But when a government "undertakes to issue paper as money, the whole system of safety and certainty is overturned, and property set afloat." It is "like putting an apparition in the place of a man; it vanishes with looking at it, and nothing remains but the air."

Paper money, wrote Paine, "turns the whole country" into speculators.

> The precariousness of its value and the uncertainty of its fate continually operate, night and day, to produce this destructive effect. Having no real value in itself it depends for support upon accident, caprice and party, and as it is the interest of some to depreciate,

the "morals of the country" are destroyed with "new schemes of deceit. Every principle of justice is put to the rack, and the bond of society dissolved."

No matter how often—or maybe because of how often—we are told that the bank apparitions are solid, we still want 100 percent reserves, witness the extreme reluctance to leave more than $100,000 in any one account. What is deposit insurance but an attempt to provide 100 percent reserves by another name?

Unlike real 100 percent reserves, however, it allows the banks to profit from what Paine called "vice and immorality."

It's true that eliminating deposit insurance under a paper-money, fractional-reserve system like ours would bring chaos, but that is what's coming anyway. Substitute hard money for paper, make the dollar an unchanging weight of gold, and we would have a real market system.

Note: so-called deposit insurance cannot be privatized. Banks, as entrepreneurial ventures, are not insurable, except against poolable risks like fire and theft. No businessman can purchase insurance against failure, and in a free market, neither would any bank. Deposit insurance is merely a government subsidy to the banks, and as such, illegitimate. Without it, banks would be subject to market forces like every other business. They would have no privileges or immunities beyond the rule of law.

"Paper money appears," said Paine, to cost "nothing; but it is the dearest money there is." More bank credit inflation, which the *Journal* advocates to turn "bad credits into good credits," is no different; it causes economic distortions, future recession, and illegitimate transfers of wealth, all to bail out a group that deserves opprobrium, not welfare for the well connected.

Human nature is the same today as in the Victorian era, and so are the laws of economics. The only solution to the bank crisis is the old solution, which every good economist advocated before our wanton century: honest money and honest banking. Now all we need is a Tom Paine to lead that revolution.

85.

THE POLITICAL BUSINESS CYCLE*

It's September 1992 and Federal Reserve chairman Alan Greenspan announces a big increase in the discount rate and bank reserve requirements. Interest rates and unemployment increase, the economy goes into a deeper recession, and Bush is defeated. But Greenspan has no apologies: as a nonpartisan servant of the public, his policies must "focus only on what's good for the economic health of America. The boom was hurting our country; we had to purge the malinvestments to make way for long-lasting growth."

That scenario is about as likely, of course, as Madonna joining Mother Theresa. Greenspan will do what Fed chairmen always do: the White House's bidding. Thus he has artificially lowered interest rates for most of 1991, leading to more economic troubles after the election.

The first economists to examine thoroughly the political business cycle, Stephen Haynes and Joe Stone, found "strong four-year cycles in unemployment and inflation, with peaks and troughs consistent with the four-year electoral cycle" from 1951 through 1980, the last year they looked at.

Why isn't this as big a scandal as the October Surprise? It almost was, in the early 1970s, when Richard Nixon appointed Arthur F. Burns, beloved economist and party hack—the Greenspan of his time—as chairman of the Fed's board of governors. In making the announcement, Nixon said, "I respect his independence. However, I hope that independently he will conclude that my views are the ones that should be followed." The audience applauded, and Nixon turned to his old friend. "You see, Dr. Burns, that is a standing vote for lower interest rates and more money." It was the only vote needed.

---

*October 1991

In August 1971, with price inflation running at 4 percent, Nixon severed the dollar's final tie to gold and imposed price and wage controls. Under that stunningly opportunistic cover, Burns hiked money growth from 3.2 percent in the last quarter of 1971 to 11 percent in the first quarter of 1972, the election year. The economy boomed, prices were artificially restrained, and Nixon was reelected in a landslide. After the election, he removed some of the controls, price inflation soared to 12 percent, and Burns stepped on the monetary brakes, bringing on a recession.

Such economic offenses are more difficult to prove these days, since Burns abolished the practice of taking detailed minutes of the meetings of the Federal Open Market Committee.

Recorded or not, however, Greenspan also does the president's bidding. After all, as Arthur Burns once explained to a German reporter, "If the chairman didn't do what the president wanted, the Federal Reserve would lose its independence." Steve Axelrod, former staff head of the Open Market Committee now making his fortune on Wall Street, told me that was "the most damaging statement ever made by anyone connected with the central bank." Damaging, of course, because true.

The Fed serves two masters, the government and the big banks. In matters of the government's core interests, i.e., elections, it calls the tunes—not that it gets any opposition from the big banks on inflating.

At its inception, the Federal Reserve's proponents said it would be above politics. Thus its "independence." But this has always been disinformation. The Fed is the quintessentially political agency in DC.

Not that Fed policy is the only way Washington, DC, gets its way. For example, politicians also have fiscal policy at their disposal, which is to say they can spend more of our money on public works, welfare, etc. And trade regulators can wipe out whole classes of imports to create boomlets for select domestic manufacturers.

All these strategies seem to improve the economy, only later turning out to be deadly. By then, the politicians are safely reelected.

The cost in human suffering of the political business cycle and related political manipulations is incalculable—but we can know that most Americans are poorer, and most businesses shakier, than they would be without government central banking, high spending, and regulations.

86.
Y2K and the Banks*

The Y2K computer bug isn't like a natural disaster or mass disease. It is a technical problem with a technical fix that can be overcome with work and time. However, and without speculating about the ultimate fallout from the problem, the bug has exposed a very real and deep infraction that has long plagued the US banking system.

Thanks to long-ago government interventions that redefined a bank deposit as a loan, modern banks only hold a fraction of the demand deposits in people's cash accounts. The rest is used as the basis for extending and pyramiding loans. If too many depositors demand their cash at once, which is their right, it would trigger a bank run, which in turn would lead to the so-called contagion effect, and runs on other banks.

Under this scenario, since most banks these days are considered "too big to fail," the Fed would have to run the printing press full time or they would go belly-up immediately. The result would be a dramatic deflation followed by hyperinflation.

Banks genuinely fear that this will be the result of public nervousness over Y2K. In February, a Southern California office

---

*April 1999

of GTE suggested that its customers hold a month's salary in cash during the transition to the new millennium. The banking industry went bonkers, denouncing GTE for breaking silence on the question and attempting to reassure the public that extra cash holdings were unnecessary.

The point is this: whether or not it is prudent to withdraw money from the bank, why should the suggestion alone be enough to drive the industry into paroxysms of fright? It is one thing to desire someone's business. It is quite another to regard the perfectly reasonable actions of your customers as a mortal and systemic threat to the well-being of society as a whole. To understand why takes us to the heart of the great secret of modern banking.

Under genuinely sound banking, in which the money you deposit at the bank is held for safekeeping while you draw down your funds as you see fit, it wouldn't matter at all how many people withdrew funds or when. The analogy here is the grain elevator, which is used solely for storage. Every customer of the elevator is free to withdraw the full quantity of his grain at any time because the proprietor must keep 100 percent reserves on penalty of fraud.

So it is under the gold standard, in which sound banking could be divided into two kinds. With deposit banking, you retain full title to your gold and only use the bank as a storage warehouse. Paper money was a ticket that acknowledged your ownership of the gold. The tickets were accepted because the bank was trusted. Free-market competition ensured that reputable banks would not fudge their holdings and loan out what did not belong to them; indeed, banks would hold 100 percent reserves. With loan banking, on the other hand, the depositor surrenders his right to withdraw his money at any time and instead transfers title to the bank itself, which is then free to extend loans and earn (and pay) interest on the money.

Under today's fiat money, fractional reserve system, all banking is treated as loan banking, and, with some accounts, banks hold no reserves whatsoever. As Murray N. Rothbard frequently reminded us, under the old rules of accounting, all modern banks are technically bankrupt all the time.

The only factor that suppresses that fundamental reality is consumer confidence. Deposit insurance, an institution designed to shore up a bankrupt system, contributes to the sense of confidence. Even small depositors' actions, like withdrawing a bit more cash, undermine that confidence.

Despite the appearance of stability and soundness, then, the foundations of modern banking are actually extremely precarious. It would only take the right kind of crisis, or perceived crisis, to throw the entire system into chaos.

Bank runs and the threat of bank runs serve a heroic function in a free society. They spur banks on to be more careful in the conduct of their business. We need more, not fewer, of them. The right to withdraw one's funds from the bank is not only an essential part of freedom; it is a way of reminding banks that they are part of the matrix of voluntary exchange in a market economy, even if they do benefit from huge subsidies from the Federal Reserve.

87.

BANK PRIVACY HYPOCRISY*

One of many pastimes of government bureaucrats is forcing foreign banks to cough up tax information on US citizens. This is a disaster for the cause of privacy, the right of contract, and freedom itself. If the campaign, which has been going on for years, finally succeeds, it will mean the end of bank privacy for Americans. It also devastates foreign economies that see a comparative advantage in offering secure banking to people from around the world.

A priority for totalitarian states is to smash the ability of citizens to escape the reach of government, particularly in their

---

*July 2001

personal finances. The government wants money more than anything else, and the bigger the government, the more willing it is to use unseemly and evil tactics to get it. The US government claims to be the model for free societies but in its attacks on citizens banking outside its borders, it is acting in the tradition of the worst despots.

Adding to the outrage is the typical hypocrisy, insisting on a standard for other countries that the US government will not apply to itself. And this is where the subject of bank privacy gets really interesting. It turns out that many citizens of governments around the world like to use US banks because they can be trusted not to steal the money and also because the US doesn't share tax information on foreigners with their governments. In other words, the United States, and particularly Florida, is a tax haven for many foreign peoples.

Now, this is a good thing, something of which we can be proud. It is the best tradition of freedom to provide a safe harbor from grasping governments wherever they may be. But where does the US government get off denouncing every tax haven in the world and strangling any other government that permits private banking? The hypocrisy is obvious, and the way to end it is to allow other countries to be havens from US laws in the same way the United States is a haven from other governments' laws.

The Clinton administration, in its final scary days, had the idea that it would deal with the evident hypocrisy by forcing US banks to cough up information on foreigners who do their business here.

This is consistent with the Clinton philosophy: the first and only purpose of any citizen anywhere is to serve the state. To the extent that the US government can facilitate this, the Clinton regime believed, it should do so in every possible way.

But here's the trouble. With the regulation poised to go into effect, many domestic banks started to complain. If we start to report interest income earned by foreign depositors to their governments, bankers worried, these people might just take their money elsewhere.

Florida Governor Jeb Bush was particularly incensed about the idea and made his position clear to Treasury Secretary Paul O'Neill. Bush wrote him that the proposed regulation

> would place US banks at a competitive disadvantage relative to banks in the Caribbean and Europe . . . and would seriously hamper the ability of US banks to continue to attract foreign deposits.

How much money is at stake? One Miami banker said that if new disclosure regulations are imposed, the city of Miami alone would see the withdrawal of $15 to $20 billion from the banking system. These are depositors who fear that their governments will persecute them for the crime of making money and not giving their governments a cut. These are governments that hate free enterprise and wealth, or regard any pot of money as the state's for the taking. Of course, all governments are kleptocracies, but these regulations imposed on US banks would make life for foreign despots even easier.

It is very likely that the Bush administration will reverse the Clinton administration's regulation and permit US banks to continue to withhold information about interest-bearing accounts from foreign governments. The administration might just seek to strike a deal with Britain just as it currently has a deal with Canada. This would be a terrible thing, but it is not as bad as the goal of the Clinton administration to turn the entire world-banking sector into a huge tax-collection cartel.

In the cause of freedom and privacy, the United States should go further to permit other countries around the world to become tax havens from those oppressed by US taxes, in the same way that the United States is a haven from other governments. The more countries compete for depositors' money, the better off we are. And economist Richard Rahn is exactly right that providing privacy in the age of Leviathan is a wonderful service that consumers seek and that all banks would provide if the government would leave them alone to do so.

We all go to great lengths to keep our finances private. We have passwords on our online accounts. We worry about the security of online orders. Websites purchase very expensive software to make this possible. There's a national movement on to prevent business from using any knowledge they have of health or purchasing habits. Americans love their privacy.

But you know what? None of the corporations or colleagues we worry about can legally steal our money. That is a power reserved to governments alone. Hence, if privacy from others is important, it is hugely important for the cause of liberty that we have it from government. The existence of the income tax itself dealt a deadly blow to privacy, which is just one more reason the income tax should be scrapped.

Another problem is that the banking system has become something of an adjunct of the state, thanks to the Federal Reserve System. Once the large banks sought a government-backed lender of last resort, the game was over: as the decades have passed, they are more and more used by their benefactor, the state, to achieve the aims of the political class at the expense of their customers.

There was a time in American history when any banker who turned over information to the government would be seen as traitorous and evil. It's hard to blame the banks today for the problem because they are coerced as much as the rest of us. But let us not ever forget the ideal: a complete separation between banking and the state. May all the world be a tax haven.

88.

UNPLUG THE MONEY MACHINE*

When antisocialist, post-Soviet reformers of the Baltic states sought to reign in government power, they looked to solve the money problem first. Moscow held unlimited power to flood their economies with cheap money, and to fund itself as

---

*February 1995

an imperial power lording it over other peoples. That had to end before the market economy could be restored.

Republicans should follow this lead if they want to solve our problem with big government. Richard Nixon thought that going off the gold standard would be good for himself politically. But his reckless action made possible, even inevitable, the explosive expansion of government spending, debt, and intervention that followed.

Alan Greenspan, then an independent economist, warned that the remnants of the gold standard were all that stood between the American people and Leviathan. He was right, of course, but now, as chairman of the Federal Reserve, he exercises the power over the economy he once told all freedom lovers to loathe.

From time to time, James Grant, the Austrian School journalist of *Grant's Interest Rate Observer*, prepares a prospectus on the US government. He's not trying to market US debt to his subscribers, but to make a more profound point: no sane person would buy US debt if the issuing agent were judged by market standards of creditworthiness. It is only the central bank's power to buy debt, to be the "lender of last resort," that leads people to buy and hold in perpetuity.

When Orange County went bankrupt, the market worked as it is supposed to. It evaluated the bonds, saw that something was fishy, and dumped them all at once. The Orange County government, like the fabled tulip bulb industry in Denmark, was bust. Now, if Orange County had a Federal Reserve, its powerful treasurer could have fueled the growth of county government until the next millennium.

That's nothing to brag about. It's not alchemy at work, but a highbrow version of old-fashioned counterfeiting. A central bank agrees to create as much money as is necessary to cover every potential monetary claim. This allows for miles-high pile-up of debt and the unlimited creation of new money. The Fed, in particular, has a variety of tricks in its bag: requiring banks to keep fewer savings for outstanding loans, lowering the rate charged to member banks for overnight purchases, and outright purchase of Treasury securities.

Much of our country's economic and cultural decline dates from 1972, and the Fed is a primary cause. A 1972 dollar is now worth about 29 cents, thanks to the central bank's power to create money out of thin air and "insure" deposits with a promise never to run out of printer's ink. People who saved for their retirement then know now that they are not even close to being prepared now.

The increase in nominal prices and wages has not harmed everyone proportionately. The government is much richer than it was, and look who's poorer: savers, families, small businessmen, workers, and the rest of the middle class. We've been clobbered by the Fed's printing presses. The essentials of life—education, health care, housing—have all become much less affordable.

The destruction of the gold standard—which really began with the founding of the Fed in 1913—has allowed the government to fund an entire class of reliably left-liberal voters, and agitators to push for more programs.

The growth of government made possible by fiat, Fed-controlled money has created a policy culture in which everything is permissible. Every good and service comes under a myriad of regulations. Every business and local government obeys countless mandates. No one in public life talks of substantial budget cuts on the order of $500 billion, which ought to be only the beginning.

The Fed is indeed mischievous, and in more ways than even gold bugs know. The central bank has recently thrown itself into the social engineering business. Its regulatory arm won't approve bank mergers unless the banks have paid tribute to the underclass by overlooking poor credit histories.

The gold standard was once a dam holding back the floods of statism, but it was blown up by a multigenerational conspiracy of self-interested politicians and special interests. It wasn't just the central government that benefited. Large bankers themselves appreciate the profits and power that come with the ability to expand money and credit beyond what real savings could ever support.

A form of the gold standard was called for in the 1980 Republican platform, although Ronald Reagan did nothing to give us one (though he deserves credit for creating the US Gold Commission that enabled Ron Paul and Jesse Helms to bring back American gold coinage). The point is this: Republicans in those days at least understood the importance of reining in the power of the Fed-bank-government cartel to create unlimited amounts of fiat money.

The then-prominence of supply-siders brought some attention to the issue of monetary reform. But their preferred solution—a watered-down version of the already diluted Bretton Woods system—would not have defined the dollar in terms of gold, or allowed domestic convertibility. Instead it would have resurrected something weaker than the system that fell apart in the early 1970s, suggesting that even supply-siders are unwilling to learn from history.

Since the 1994 election, the Republican elite hasn't breathed a word challenging the enormous power the Federal Reserve exercises over the economy. For the backbenchers, anyway, let's hope it's because of ignorance, and not because they're owned by the large banks or want the Fed to fund their pet legislative projects, just as it funded Democratic ones in the past.

At least one trend points in the wrong direction: the Republican leadership doesn't want to force the Fed chairman to testify before the Banking Committee anymore. That's too bad since it removes one source of accountability, if a small one, from an otherwise unaccountable entity.

Some Republicans operate on the theory that the more "independent" a central bank is, the less it is tempted into inflationary policies. The view is a conventional one and derives largely from the empirical example of Switzerland and Germany.

The problem with purely empirical analysis is that it ignores cause and effect. The Germans and Swiss have relatively sound money not because the central bankers are independent, but because the economic and political culture won't allow inflationary schemes of the sort we're saddled with. The central banks would lose all credibility if they tried.

There can be no such thing as a thoroughly independent central bank in the way the corner grocery store is independent. Politics determines a central bank's decisions, as does the desire to increase bank profits. We're just not supposed to notice or talk about it in polite company.

If the Republicans really wanted to challenge Leviathan, they would strangle the Fed, its very lifeblood. If we dismantled the Fed and made our money good as gold again, it would matter a lot less who sat in the White House or in Congress, for they would have much less power to harm us even if they wanted to.

Forget the balanced-budget amendment: the gold standard is what big government types really fear. That so few want to unplug the government's money machine tells us more about the governing elites, including the Republicans, then we are perhaps willing to face.

89.
THE DOT-COM FUTURE*

Owners of dot-com stock funds regret ever having heard of the Internet. Webmasters who dropped out of school to get rich quick are crawling back to their guidance counselors to be readmitted. Companies that laid many miles of fiber-optic cable wonder whether they made a huge error.

---

*July 2001

Lost in all the talk of the tech meltdown, however, is any distinction between where the Internet has succeeded and where it has failed. Neither has there been much sensible analysis of why the run-up and fall-off of Internet stocks were as dramatic as they were. Let's take the second question first.

The Internet boom is often chalked up to capitalist man's tendency toward maniacal waves of overreaction. A new technology appears on the horizon, the theory goes, and people run like lemmings until they find themselves falling off a cliff into the sea (although I'm told that, in real life, lemmings don't actually do that). Such is life under a system that rewards greed before need, they say. Perhaps we need government to make us more responsible?

The trouble with the lemming metaphor is that it has nothing to do with economics. New technologies are always available for the taking for commercial applications, and have been since ancient days. Technology by itself is not inherently valuable. The key question is whether the technology is profitable relative to other projects. It is the job of entrepreneurs to exercise judgment about whether their use will really pay off in the long run.

Hence, it is not new technology alone that spawns hysteria in a market economy. In a typical market setting, some people are enthusiasts and others are skeptics. Where some see profits, others see losses, and whoever ends up right wins (until something else comes along). It's not a perfect system, but it prevents lemming-like behavior from becoming the norm.

The necessary ingredient that turns new technologies into market manias is excess supplies of credit that can be burned up by speculators. There's only one institution in our society that makes such credit appear to be free for the taking: the Federal Reserve. It alone has the power to make money appear out of thin air. Working through the banking system, it can pump money into and out of the economy and bring about all kinds of zany behavior.

Sure enough, when you look at the Federal Reserve policy of the late 1990s, you find dramatic inflation of the core measures of the money stock (M2, M3, and MZM [M1 no longer has much meaning because of financial deregulation]). These core measures hit bottom in 1995 and then began a straight upward climb until peaking in early 1999. By 2000, a long fall in the rate of increase was evident in all three, until earlier this year, when the Fed turned on the spigots once again. Why can't the Fed keep going indefinitely? That way lies hyperinflation.

This pattern closely tracks the run-up and subsequent collapse of Internet stocks. Because of the loose money policies of the Fed, venture capitalists enjoyed a huge increase in funds available for investment. What they may or may not have known is that the funding was an illusion created by the central bank. It wasn't based on savings (which actually fell during the same period), and the investments they made were not based on a realistic assessment of firms' earning potential.

Investors weren't so much blinded by technology as drowned in seas of cash, freshly created by the Federal Reserve system. Many projects that might have been worth trying out expanded too fast too quickly and ended up squandering the phenomenal infusions of cash.

It was inevitable that the illusion would dissipate; it was only a matter of timing. Some of the skeptics figured it would happen in 1997 and 1998, and when the crash didn't occur, they were called troglodytes who didn't understand that risk had been repealed in a new era of cyberspace. But once the Fed stopped feeding it, the tech boom did indeed come to an end.

There is a psychological element to the story. In the late 1990s, speculation abounded about the advent of a new economy and a new world, even new modes of being, brought on by the new age of cyber-living. Today, all such talk is regarded as a sign of insanity. Just as 'Net promoters were once hep and happening, 'Net debunking is now all the rage.

Just as inflationary finance creates manias, the slump can create exaggerated reactions in the other direction. Regardless of Webvan and Salon.com and other famous failures, the Internet has permanently changed the way free enterprise works. Because of the speed at which information travels, the economy is more efficient than it was. Web traffic, despite the dot-com collapse, is higher than ever. Particularly in areas of news and research, the Web continues to be an unparalleled success.

And while it is fashionable to cite the unreliability of the Web for information, this, too, is sorting itself out. There are reputable and disreputable sources of information on the Web, just as there are in the print media. What a surprise: consumers themselves are figuring out ways to tell the difference. What the establishment doesn't like is that *The New York Times* can no longer pose as a national organ of truth because the full story is only a click away.

It's not only dot-coms that are failing. Print publications, particularly those dealing with public affairs and other boring topics, are failing left and right. It turns out that for those who keep up with politics, the Web continues to be a dreamland of information and commentary. It's also wonderful to see the way the Web is shaping up to work much like the old economy, with mergers and big players playing a decisive role in driving innovation and profits.

Far from having discredited capitalism, our experience with the Web so far is that it underscores the structures of the free-enterprise economy and vastly outcompetes any services offered by government. To the extent anything should be discredited today, it is the Federal Reserve with its policy of distorting reality and delivering false signals to market players.

And let it never be forgotten that without government backing, the Federal Reserve would be just another marble building in an imperial capital. It certainly wouldn't have the frightening power to spur global manias.

The lesson: Don't blame the market; place the blame exactly where it belongs, with our masters in DC who prevent free enterprise from bringing discipline to the monetary system.

90.

BLAMING BUSINESS*

Forget gridlock and partisanship, the US Senate has found something besides attacking other countries to agree on: attacking business right here at home.

No one can accuse these guys of being soft on crime, so long as the alleged crime occurs within the private sector, and involves the always-vulnerable businessman.

Should supposedly defrauding shareholders be a distinct crime punishable by up to 10 years in prison, thereby replacing the existing system in which defrauding shareholders falls under the category of mail and wire fraud? Yes, said the Senate in a 100-to-0 vote.

Should the government prohibit companies from docking the pay of employees who scheme with government investigators? Yes, 100 to 0.

Should the period of time in which investors can file lawsuits against companies to recoup losses due to alleged securities fraud be extended? Yes, 100 to 0.

Should it be easier to prosecute people for altering or destroying their records when a government agency is investigating a corporation, even if the investigation isn't yet official? Yes, 100 to 0.

Should all penalties of all sorts be expanded? Yes, 100 to 0.

John "The Bomber" McCain caught the reigning fascistic spirit of the moment: "Until somebody responsible goes to jail for a significant amount of time, I'm not sure these people are going to get the message."

---

*July 2002

The message is: all the crooks are in business, and only great government can save us.

The proposals to crush, thrash, smash, and otherwise slam business are raining down hard, with Republicans joining with Democrats in sheer demagogic hatred of the capitalist system itself.

None of this has to do with a conviction that WorldCom and Enron and the rest really committed fraud in the usual sense. The problem with these companies (and they are not typical) is that they took part in a more general fraud called the New Economy: the idea that the Federal Reserve can create limitless prosperity through money creation and lower interest rates.

Had these companies' forecasts of infinite product demand, and thus infinitely increasing stock prices panned out, nobody would be complaining. But the Fed's boom turned to bust, as it must, and the political parasites had to find some way to deflect the blame.

Remember the scale of what we are dealing with. By the late 1990s, tens of millions of people had grown accustomed to checking their online holdings daily, and watching them grow. Regular citizens became day-traders. Folks were exuberant as their portfolios rose to double and triple expected figures. Visions of early retirement and the lush life danced in their heads.

Everyone was a financial genius.

But by this year, these same people have seen their once-fat portfolios grow shockingly skinny. While people can deal with stock-market losses, they cannot understand how in a mere 12 to 19 months, trillions could have vanished, and their exuberant visions too.

There is something intuitively correct about the average person's suspicions. It doesn't make sense that so much could be wiped out so quickly, and people are right to assume that powerful people are rigging the game. The business cycle isn't an act of nature. It is brought about by shady characters working behind the scenes.

So Washington is attempting to turn public anger away from the guilty—the Federal Reserve and the politicians who cheered on its credit run-up—to business. All this hot air about corporate fraud is designed to permit people to believe that their portfolios were looted by CEOs with shredding machines.

You say: nobody is stupid enough to believe that!

Think again. In the early 1930s, this was precisely the view promoted by FDR and widely believed among the general public. This was also the import of Bush's antibusiness rave on Wall Street, which Republicans celebrated and Democrats denounced for not going far enough. This is why the Senate is passing stupid resolutions and voting on bad legislation, which will muck matters up further in predictable and unpredictable ways.

Not even Wall Street experts have a clear fix on why markets fall, other than some general lack of confidence that plays on itself. Not one in a thousand would identify the loose credit of the 1990s as the cause of the boom, and fewer still could explain how that boom unraveled and why.

Every economic downturn in modern history has been accompanied by a boom-time accounting scandal, leading to more regulation. This is why ignorance of economics—in particular Austrian economics—is so dangerous. Something about the business cycle seems fishy, even crooked, but precisely what does not flow from intuition alone.

It's time to buy copies of Gene Callahan's smart and funny *Economics for Real People* for your friends and family, and your stockbroker and congressman too. Knowledge may be the only way to stop the government from blaming everyone but itself for the meltdown nobody but it brought about.

91.

DEFINE IT AWAY*

People made fun of Gerald Ford's buttons that said "WIN"—
meaning "Whip Inflation Now." The buttons and the
accompanying propaganda campaign implied that consumers'
bad vibes were the cause of inflation. Ha, Ha.

Now, the White House, members of both parties, and their
court economists have done Gerry one better. Lacking any strategy for getting rid of inflation, they intend to redefine it. Their
new formula will show prices going up more slowly. This will
help the government, but for anyone trying to keep tabs on
unceasing monetary destructionism, it's a terrible, even dangerous, idea.

Redefining the Consumer Price Index will have large and
immediate repercussions. Thanks to a Nixon-era change, Social
Security benefits are increased automatically by inflation. The
higher prices go, the larger the checks. A deliberate dumbing
down of the CPI is a way of saving money. That—supposedly—
is why Republicans support it.

Cutting spending in times of $1.7 trillion budgets is, of
course, a moral obligation. But there are better ways. Why not
cut or eliminate cost-of-living adjustments themselves? It turns
out that the American Association of Retired Persons opposes
this direct route, but won't oppose changing the inflation rate.

A seedier side to this scheme has to do with taxes, and
Republicans are hush-mouthed about it. If government statistics reveal less inflation, the tax brackets won't adjust to price
movements. The difference between actual and official inflation
will net billions for the government. And here we see a secret
purpose: to extract more wealth from the American people in
ways they won't detect.

---

*February 1996

From the taxpayer's point of view, then, the proposed change means higher taxes, better disguised, although the Republican supporters of the plan won't tell you that.

To drum up support, backers are quick to reassure us that all good economists say the current CPI understates the real inflation rate. But if economists could know the real inflation rate, there would be no need for a CPI. We'd only need to consult the financial fortunetellers.

In the old days, only Austrian School economists criticized government economic data. They refuted the idea that economic activity can be accurately quantified and they debunked the gizmos economists use to pretend it can.

But nowadays, there's a raging debate on the CPI. Every theory is shot down by someone else, and on seemingly solid grounds. There are hundreds of formulas and strategies for determining the direction and range of price movements. There's the "geometrical" formula, the "harmonic average" formula, and the "arithmetic" formula currently in use. Moreover, everyone has an idea of what should and shouldn't be in there and how much it should count.

Why so much debate? Because every attempt to discover an inflation rate is necessarily flawed. We can't just measure inflation the way we measure the height of a tree. Prices reflect too many variables. We can't be sure what accounts for changes. It makes no sense to lump together price changes for incomparable goods.

Nor is there a "price level" in the sense that there's a sea level, and the desire to make it stable (monetarism was the most elaborate) is a futile exercise. Let's say: liver transplants are going up in price, computers are going down in price, and milk remains the same. What can we conclude about movements in the overall price level? Honestly speaking, nothing.

There is no "average" price for goods and services because there are no "average" buyers of goods and services. There are only specific consumers who purchase specific products and services. People who buy college tuition for five children experience a different "inflation rate" than twenty-something techno-hermits.

Neither is there a definite "inflation rate" waiting to be unveiled. Even when the government is goosing the money supply, inflation affects different goods and sectors at different times and to varying degrees.

All that said, we do need some way to gauge the effects of monetary policy on prices. The index number, for all its faults, is about the best we can do. The CPI, like all index numbers, is generated by comparing the data from one "basket" of goods in period A with the data from the same basket in period B, and formulating the change.

The results will be fraught with errors. To retain some modicum of honesty, we must adhere to two rules. The formula must be inclusive of many goods, sectors, regions, etc., and it must be consistent. The best and practically only way to render an index number utterly useless is to change its definition in mid-course.

That, of course, is precisely what the politicians are planning to do, and not because the current CPI is wildly inaccurate. The problem, if anything, is that it is revealing the wrong thing: that prices keep going up. What the government wants is a measure—any measure—that shows less inflation.

The Federal Reserve always promises that it's working to bring down inflation, but, as Murray N. Rothbard shows in *The Case Against the Fed*, it never does. Since the Fed came into being, the dollar's value has plummeted to less than a nickel, and even at a 3 percent inflation rate, prices will tend to double every 25 years.

Now we can tell why the Fed supports the CPI change. It wants to cover its crimes by appearing more successful at "battling inflation." What the Fed doesn't want to talk about is the real cause of inflation: not greedy consumers, avaricious workers, or price-gouging corporations, but the central bank itself, with its power and practice of creating money out of thin air.

If the government and the Fed really want to lower inflation, there's an easy way to do it. Stop the printing presses with a gold standard. With no artificial increases in the money supply and a growing economy, prices would tend to fall over the long run. The norm in the computer industry would become economy wide under sound money.

A truly inflation-free economy would spur savings and growth, be free of business cycles, restrict government power, and restore living standards. To reduce inflation by defining it away, on the other hand, is like eliminating debased coinage by readjusting the scales. It's something only government would do.

92.

WHAT MADE THE NEXT DEPRESSION WORSE[*]

How inevitable is the continuing expansion of the domestic and international economy? Barring a major war and a major depression, and a policy response that repeats the errors of traditional countercyclical policies, I would say that continued world economic expansion is likely.

For an Austrian all too aware of how governments can foil prosperity, that may sound like an optimistic prediction. But consider. With the fall of socialism, the world economy has opened up as never before. New technologies have wrought new efficiencies. Private enterprise has become ever better at mass marketing to the benefit of everyone. The division of labor is expanding internationally. No matter how hard the government

---

[*]April 2005

continues to try, it just can't seem to throttle the extraordinary power of the market economy.

And yet we cannot bar every contingency, particularly for the United States. The economy is not depression proof. If the government and the Federal Reserve are willing to work hard enough, they can kill off even the most robust economic expansion. From an Austrian perspective, the likely scenario is that the Fed will attempt to forestall recession via credit expansion, which distorts production structures and makes the recession even deeper.

I seriously doubt that our economic managers have learned enough about economics to avoid this fate. We still must grapple with the problem of the business cycle, which is a feature of the market economy insofar as it is fueled by fiat money managed by a central bank.

Let me begin, then, with some background on the Austrian business cycle theory. At the start of the Great Depression in Europe, the Austrian School, then still centered in Vienna, was well positioned to explain the cause and offer a way out. Mises's first statement of the core of the theory had been widely circulated in his 1912 book, *The Theory of Money and Credit*. It was still considered the definitive work. In this book, he explains how interest rates are not arbitrary constructs or prices of money dictated by central banks, but rather an integral part of the market economy, coordinating productivity, investment, and savings.

When these signals are manipulated by the central bank, they convey bad information to producers about the availability of resources. Producers invest for a longer time horizon than exists in the real economy and their clusters of errors create what appears to be a sharp rise in productivity and growth. But the boom turns to bust in the passage of time, as consumers run out of resources and projects are left unfinished. The low-interest rate policy had a good run of it, but eventually reality returns and the bad investments are washed out of the system.

But here is a complicating factor. Since the Great Depression, governments have hardly ever permitted recessions to take their market-driven course. Instead, they tend to pile artificial booms on top of economic busts, which can lead to very odd results. The examples are all around us.

The last economic crisis we faced was five years ago. The central banks of the world began to inflate by driving interest rates down to historically low levels. Adjusted for inflation, interest rates have been negative in Japan, Europe, and the United States since early 2004. This proves very attractive for borrowers, and leads to reckless lending, waves of entrepreneurial errors, and sector-specific inflation.

Contrary to conventional wisdom, we have more to fear from the political response to recession than we do from recession itself. That's because the response usually consists in pumping ever more money and credit into the economy.

Part of the problem is intellectual. In the Great Depression, for example, people observed that banks were failing and immediately concluded that the problem was not enough liquidity. They observed that consumers were not spending and assumed they needed more money. They observed that businesses were having their credit lines cut and thought that more credit was needed.

As Murray Rothbard has shown, this was the path chosen by both Hoover and FDR in the early years of the Great Depression. And though it did not work, the inflationist remedy remained the policy response of first resort. In every case, the solution is the same: plug in the printing presses and let them perform their magic. Alan Greenspan, for example, has the reputation of an inflation hawk but consider that he has turned to the printing presses in every crisis that has come about during his tenure.

What is unseen is the hidden cause of the crisis, which is in the past. It is the expansion of money and credit that leads to imbalances that eventually turn booms to busts. What people have done in concluding otherwise is to confuse cause and effect, something akin to concluding that puddles of water on the ground are causing it to rain. To carry the analogy further, these same people might attempt to drain all puddles as a way of stopping the rain. We can laugh at such absurdities, but these fallacies are a common strain among social scientists trying to understand the business cycle.

In Mises's day, the rise of positivism meant a new fashion for collecting data and eschewing all forms of deductive theory. So despite many years of work, and growing acceptance of Mises's own theory, it was not only difficult to explain cause and effect, it was difficult to get even economists to look beyond the here and now to see the underlying causes. This was the first serious indication among the Austrians that the battle for the future of economics would in part be a battle over economic methodology.

Does good economics consist in collecting and manipulating data, organizing them in a manner to measure the extent to which any two random economic phenomena collide in time and thereby concluding that this statistical correlation can serve as a proxy for causation? This is the theory that led people to believe that it was a burst of technology that caused the dot-com boom, or that the dot-com bust was God's way of smiting greedy CEOs.

Really, this approach to business cycles is no more scientific than the approach a primitive witch doctor takes to healing, but at least the witchdoctor has to take some responsibility for whether the patient lives or dies. The economists just wash their hands and walk away.

In the United States, the Great Depression presented similar difficulties. There were very few economists here who understood the theory, and so a void was left for Keynes, who told the government everything it wanted to hear. He said the core problem lies with too little money, too little government spending, too little central management of investment. After many decades of hearing economists tell how government should curb its appetite for power, this new message was much welcome. Corrupt politicians the world over celebrated!

Benjamin Anderson and Henry Hazlitt battled it out in the early 1930s, but they too confronted an establishment anxious for fast solutions to endemic problems, and the rise of an economic profession that was increasingly impatient with deep theoretical understanding. What sold in the intellectual world then was superficiality. So Keynesian solutions were tried, and failed, in a repeated pattern from the 1930s until our own times.

Only the Austrians seem to be willing to take a careful look at not only what is seen but also what is unseen. Mark Thornton has shown that it was only the Austrians who seemed to understand that something had gone very wrong in the mid- and late-1990s, and foresaw that the dot-com boom was essentially unsustainable.

As a result, more people are paying attention to the Austrian theory now than ever before. In fact, a leading post-Keynesian was recently accused by a colleague of being an Austrian, and he quickly denied it. But then he added: "The Austrian theoretical framework seems to be the only tool at hand. And when all you have is a hammer. . . ."

I always imagine what Mises would say if he heard these words, nearly 100 years after he first came up with his explanation for the business cycle. How such knowledge would have brought him solace in those difficult years of total Keynesian dominance. It goes to show that if you are willing to wait and be patient, the truth will win out in the end. Mises believed in this principle. We should too.

I've already mentioned what the world economy has going for it: the expansion of the division of labor, technological advance, and economies that are opening up to trade and investment. The dollar is still the dominant currency the world over, which gives the US economy in particular a competitive advantage. We have been able to enjoy the comparative nirvana of low-priced consumer goods while depending on foreign markets to absorb the dollars created domestically.

But related to this last point, let's talk about the downside. The falling dollar on international exchange portends an ominous change for the US economy. The factors that permitted the United States to export inflation have come under challenge. The Euro can be a viable competitor to the dollar in the future. With shrinking demand for dollars, the United States could find itself with genuine inflation on its hands. There are already signs of this on the way, with rising commodity prices and oil prices.

As Antony Mueller has pointed out, the three most essential price systems of the modern economy are unusually sensitive to political manipulation: the oil price, the interest rate, and the exchange rate. This doesn't mean that the Fed and the government can dictate them but it does mean that these prices respond especially rapidly and dramatically to political error.

It would be very easy to drum up a scenario in which the US economy falls into a tailspin, with the dollar losing its position as the world standard, interest rates soaring, housing prices collapsing, inflation taking off, and the economy left with few means of recovery given the high debt load and low savings rate of the American family. Whether and to what extent this is a likely scenario I do not know, but it does seem clear that until something is done to stop the spending and debt generated by Washington, DC, there will be a high price to pay.

Now, in my ideal world, the United States would take the path long recommended by the old liberal tradition. We would have free trade with the world, establish a gold standard that defined the dollar as gold, end central banking, and bring about completely free domestic markets. This is the Austrian version of utopia, and it has two key advantages: it would bring about the most productive economy in the history of the world, and it would also serve as the best guard to freedom.

Tragically, however, the Bush administration has brought us no closer to that ideal. Instead it has pursued a huge range of interventions in the market process that may seem uneventful now but could matter far more should the economy once again fall on bad times.

Economic downturns are precipitated by credit expansions and contractions but monetary policy cannot alone account for the length, breadth, and shape. This is inspired by other factors. The Hoover and FDR interventions in the early stages of the Great Depression made matters worse by preventing a downward wage correction, by interfering with the right of Americans to engage in foreign trade, by bailing out bankrupt banks, and otherwise inhibiting the operations of the market.

In those days, politicians waited for economic downturns before wrecking the market. Nowadays, they are glad to intervene for any reason anytime. Republicans are no better than Democrats in this regard, despite the former's professed love of free enterprise.

I here offer what I regard as Bush's top ten economic errors, which might be the very errors that will make the next depression far worse than it needs to be.

Number Ten: Martha Stewart Jailing. This was just a disgrace. This great entrepreneur was guilty of nothing but being beloved, famous, and rich. When the Justice Department couldn't get her for insider trading, of which she was not guilty under any conceivable definition, the government changed the charges to obstruction of justice, which really comes down to being willing to defend yourself. If you claim you are not guilty, you open yourself up to prosecution for being wrong. The real point of this case, I believe, was to put a great American entrepreneur in her place, and inspire fear and loathing across corporate America. This isn't just my opinion. This was a point made by the *New York Times*, in the hope that her jailing would intimidate the whole of the American business class.

Two additional points behind this fiasco. The original case concerned an anticancer drug that was made by the company in which she held stock, ImClone. The corporate stock took a dive after the FDA barred the drug, but later tests revealed that the drug was everything the company said it was.

Also, in sweet revenge, Martha Stewart handled herself in jail with great dignity and now goes on to greater heights in her commercial endeavors. All power to her, but the costs are still there: investors are more cautious, corporate America is more cautious, and ever more live in fear of their DC masters. A fearful and oppressed business class is a very bad omen for continued economic expansion.

Number Nine: Unrelenting Protectionism. The Bush administration began its campaign for old-fashioned protectionism with a disgraceful tariff on steel that did nothing to help the industry but much to harm American business by vastly raising the costs of steel. After incredible protest, the Bush administration finally declared victory and repealed its tariff, but only while adding more tariffs and protections for timber, shrimp, clothing, and a hundred other items in the US Trade Representative's daily operations, all of which have the same theme: the rest of the world had better buy our stuff, but the US government has no obligation to stop taxing American consumers to benefit well-connected US companies.

I'm especially concerned about the Bush administration's obsession with what it calls intellectual property rights. I'm as sorry as the next guy that merchants on the streets of Beijing are selling illicit copies of *The Incredibles* and the complete ninth season of *Friends*. But I do not believe it is the job of the US government to go abroad with the goal of slaying these particular monsters.

The problem is even more significant with technology and pharmaceuticals. Patents are government grants of monopoly privilege. They are a bad enough policy at home but it amounts to an egregious form of imperialist mercantilism to use the foreign policy powers of the US government to enforce them.

Number Eight: The Social Security Reform Hoax. Genuine privatization would be a grand idea. But that is not what the Bush administration proposes. Not anywhere close. They are proposing to partially convert the existing tax-and-spend system into a forced savings program. This is not choice but rather a species of socialism. The forced investments would be fed to approved funds with approved companies and be guaranteed a rate of return.

So in the end, Bush-style privatization would partially socialize the most important sector of the American capital markets, and we aren't talking about small change. And how would this transition be funded? Bush has suggested that he would be willing to lift the FICA cap, which would mean the worst tax increase in US history. Debt, taxes, inflation—take your pick. The costs are in the trillions.

Number Seven: Government Spending. You will notice that Bush has lately been talking like a budget cutter. He is going to rein in government spending, he says. Well, I suppose everyone has known about the great uncle who swears he is going to cut back on his drinking but somehow keeps ending up at the dry-out farm. He is the first president since John Quincy Adams not to veto a single bill during his first term in office. Total federal government spending is up by 30 percent in his first term, which is three times the rate of growth wrought by that bad old big spender Bill Clinton. Since 2001, the government has hired an additional 140,000 civilians for its ranks.

In an anomalous manner, government revenue has been falling for some six years. Now, the response in a household to this type of trend would be to cut back. But the government has the exact opposite response. It has become more profligate even as its revenue stream is not producing what it might have expected. But beware: the bills will be paid somehow someday. All we know for sure is who will be doing the paying.

Number Six: Failure To Repeal the AMT. There have been no shortages of warnings about the Alternative Minimum Tax. This sneaky little prosperity killer will snag another three million taxpayers this year, and another 30 million by the end of the decade. Now, this all results from some tiny change in the tax law that dates back to the Nixon years, which means that no one alive is willing to take any responsibility for it. But no one in Washington is complaining about it either, the Republicans least of all. Bush was in a good position to stop the nonsense, but did nothing about it. Not only that: Bush's latest budget actually rescinds some exemptions that Congress had granted in recent years.

Number Five: Prescription Drug Benefit. This is the largest expansion of federal welfare since the Great Society. New estimates put the cost at $700 billion over 10 years but we might as well round up and say an even trillion. To think: when Congress voted on it, they believed it would cost only $400 billion. Now I'm always a bit amused by these claims that Congress is shocked! shocked! that a government program costs more than it was supposed to.

I find it even more befuddling why Congress would be all for a program that only costs $400 billion but draws the line at $700 billion. This is like a burglar leaving the last bit of jewelry in a safe on grounds that to take it too would be akin to theft. In any case, this program is a calamity. And so we have, in the name of allaying high drug prices, a vast artificial increase in demand. There were other ways to lower the costs of drugs but because it might mean denying pharmaceutical companies some revenue, the Bush regime decided instead to socialize their profits.

Number Four: Failure to Rein in Fannie/Freddie. We may very well have a housing boom on our hands. Housing prices have doubled in some markets from 2001 through 2004. The median price of a single-family home has risen from $145,000 to $183,600. The boom is caused by artificially low interest rates but facilitated by two federally chartered private institutions that are effectively too big to fail. They have doled out mortgage welfare for so long and to so many, that most Americans no longer know what it means to have to scrimp and save for a house.

But price hikes cut both ways: they are great for the seller but terrible for the buyer. Most of us fall into both categories, so we develop a dependency relationship with price hikes. We need to learn to think of rising prices as something unnatural and unwelcome. Entrepreneurial profit is a great thing, but constantly rising prices on this scale suggest a market distortion. If a depression comes, and the industry has to be bailed out, or if mortgage rates rise dramatically in the near future, we will have a calamity on our hands.

Number Three: Signing and Enforcing SOX. At the end of the dot-com bust, some people in Washington developed the idea that corporate America is run by crooks who spend all their time cooking the books. Now: imagine politicians in Washington complaining about anything run by crooks who cook the books! In any case, their answer was a series of show trials for CEOs and CFOs that completely overlooked how the business cycle had changed accounting standards.

That was followed by the passage of the Sarbanes-Oxley Act, which gave the federal government complete supervisory authority over the accounting of every publicly listed company and enforced criminal penalties against CEOs and CFOs who sign off on any audits the government disputes.

The costs have been unthinkably large: in the hundreds of billions. Accountants report spending nearly all their time complying with it, and some critiques have compared this bill with FDR's National Industrial Recovery Act, given how much it empowers government to manage affairs that were once left to the discretion of the private sector.

And don't you just love the theory behind these regulations, which supposes that large publicly listed companies have no strong incentive to keep good books?

It only takes a moment's thought to realize that the investor class is the most sophisticated watcher of business, and business has every incentive to provide whatever information is needed or wanted by investors. It was the markets, not government, that discovered the anomalies at Enron and the high-profile cases. All government regulations end up doing is forcing companies to waste resources complying with edicts rather than serving stockholders and consumers.

Number Two: Markets By Force. As a lover of free markets, I'm embarrassed that the Bush administration has said that part of its goal in invading Iraq and bringing total chaos and massive death to that country was to give them a capitalistic economy. In fact, the Bush administration still enforces price controls on gasoline in Iraq, still forbids free trade, still excludes free enterprise communication and airline companies from setting up shop, and still refuses to allow Iraqis control over their own oil. However, even had US forces really brought about free enterprise in Iraq, militarism and war are not the right way to do it. The way to bring markets to the world is not by war and force, but by trade and example.

I suggest we take with a grain of salt all claims by the Bush administration that it is seeking to expand markets around the world. If it really sought to expand markets, the place to begin is right at home. Instead, we've seen the opposite. It is closing markets, harassing successful entrepreneurs, and hobbling enterprise through high regulations.

Number One: the Appointment of Ben S. Bernanke, formerly of the Fed, to be the chairman of the Council of Economic Advisers. Please listen to his words from a speech given in 2002—given in the context of trying to settle down people's fears of the economic future:

> The US government has a technology, called a printing press (or, today, its electronic equivalent) that allows it to produce as many US dollars as it wishes at essentially no cost. By increasing the number of US dollars in circulation, or even by credibly threatening to do so, the US government can also reduce the value of a dollar in terms of goods and services, which is equivalent to raising the prices in dollars of those goods and services. We conclude that, under a paper-money system, a determined government can always generate higher spending and hence positive inflation.

Well, these comments certainly do calm fears that deflation is in our future. But what he seems incredibly sanguine about is the effects of inflation. Already, inflation amounts to a daily robbery of the American consumer. Even in these supposedly low inflation times, price indexes have doubled since 1980. What this means is that one dollar in 1980 purchases only 50 cents worth of goods and services today. There are no long lines at gas stations and we aren't panicked for our future, but we are still being robbed, only more slowly and more subtly than in the past.

The Bernanke appointment is certainly a wake-up call for anyone who has a benign view of the Bush administration's economic priorities. Indeed, we might as well say that, long-term, this could be the most egregious decision that the Bush administration has made.

An inflationist Keynesian and an aggressive advocate of printing-press economics, Bernanke is the sort of crank who becomes famous in history for having destroyed whole countries. He is utterly and completely dedicated to the idea that paper money will save the world, with no downside. I shudder for our future if he becomes head of the Fed. Yet this appointment is probably a pathway to Greenspan's job, as it was for Greenspan himself.

Now, I'm not predicting another depression any time soon. But I will say that if one comes, all these Bush policies are going to make a depression less easy to recover from. They all work to make the economy less responsive to human ingenuity, harm the manner in which prices convey accurate information to entrepreneurs, and make it more difficult for individuals to put their financial houses back in order.

But just because the depression isn't here yet, let us not wait to decry all these policies for what they are: violations of free-market ethics and the true spirit of American enterprise.

The beauty and glory of economic science are that it consists in a series of laws and principles that do not change according to time and place. The prescription for prosperity and stability and human economic flourishing is always and everywhere the same: freedom of association, freedom of contract, freedom of enterprise, freedom to trade across borders without penalty, sound money redeemable in something besides paper, private property rights, wages and prices that adjust by market conditions, and a legal structure that shores up these institutions rather than undermining them.

If the United States were to establish such conditions, my cautious optimism about the future of world economic health would turn to wild enthusiasm, because the country would once again become a beacon of liberty to the world, in precisely the manner that the best thinkers among the founding generation imagined it would be.

Section 4: Natural Disasters

93.
War on Gougers?*

Just as the script dictates, cries of "gouging" are now heard across the land.

"I think a lot of it is pure greed," a consumer told the *New York Times*. Another said, "If there's a chance of the oil companies' driving up the prices, they'll do that." Another: "I don't blame the government, I blame the gas companies." Still another: "They are going to get all the money they can out of us."

In covering economic issues, journalists have a way of quoting the most ignorant possible statements by consumers. And you watch: these statements will, in turn, be followed by statements from officials warning gas stations and oil companies against raising prices too much. A poor station owner will be singled out by a local newspaper and might eventually face some sort of federal charges for economic crimes.

Of course gas station owners and oil companies want to make a buck. So does everyone else, in good times and bad. They want to charge the highest price possible consistent with

---

*2003

the highest profit. At the same time, consumers want to pay the lowest price possible. It is in the marketplace that these differences are sorted out in the glorious and peaceful institution of voluntary exchange, where a meeting of minds takes place and society's needs are met.

For hundreds of years, thanks to the insights of economic science, we've known a lot about the forces that push prices in a range of different directions. We know that producers will offer more supply at a higher price than a lower price, and we know that more consumers will buy more at a lower price than a higher price. We know that all of this happens without the guiding hand of government. Students are taught this in Economics 101 (whether they remember it is another matter).

What we do not know is the precise weighting of factors that go into why prices increase at any particular time. The bits of information that are built into the price of anything are too diffuse and vast. For the same reason that no price on the market can be completely unpacked and dissected, it is also impossible for any outsider to know what the price of anything "should" be. That is why the market price exists in the first place: to provide an evaluation of the value of resources relative to their availability, their desirability, and the costs associated with delivering them.

Ah, prices! How we take them for granted! In fact, they are guides to the conduct of life itself. What should you have for dinner? Should you take that vacation or not? Should you buy or rent? Should you supplement your wardrobe or not? Should you heat your house till it's warm and cozy or just wear a sweater indoors? All these decisions are made based on the price of things. They are what make rational daily living possible. Without them, all would be chaos.

But somehow, in a time of crisis when prices leap around in various directions—doing their job to coordinate supply and demand and conserve resources to overcome the uncertainty of the future—all this wisdom is forgotten. Consumers suddenly look at their retailer as the enemy and the government starts taking names. The worst part is that it is precisely during times of market uncertainty and change that prices are needed more than ever to coordinate resources.

When the oil price rises, it suggests more supply is needed. More precisely, it sends two signals: to consumers it says conserve, and to producers it says invest. If nothing else changes, and people follow the price signals, the price will end up falling as consumers cut back purchases and producers bring more product to market. Putting a price ceiling on oil will short-circuit this mechanism, causing producers to offer no more than is currently available (or even less), and consumers to continue buying as much as they always have. Again, if nothing else changes, the result will be shortages, which the government will attempt to rectify through ever more stupid policies.

In the case of the oil price, there is an additional complication. Many people in powerful positions are dead-set against a lower oil price. The environmentalists are nervous about lower prices because they fear it will lead to more gas consumption and SUV purchases. This is one reason (not love of caribou) that they oppose opening up more public lands for drilling.

In government, we've had sanctions against Iraq that have artificially kept supplies off the market, driving up the price. This is something the Bush administration, closely connected with the oil industry, approves. David Frum reports in his account of his time with the Bush administration that Bush himself is a passionate opponent of lower oil prices. Frum once suggested that Bush call for lower prices to help consumers. Bush looked at him like he was nuts, and pointed out that lower prices are the source of all the problems.

Max Boot, current fellow at the Council on Foreign Relations and former editor of the *Wall Street Journal* opinion page, provides further evidence that this is the case:

> For that matter, would our government really want a steep drop in prices? The domestic oil patch—including President Bush's home state, Texas—was devastated in the 1980s when

prices fell as low as $10 a barrel. Washington is generally happy with a range of $18 to $25 a barrel.

Even as far back as the 2000 presidential race, Richard Cheney told *Meet the Press*, "we need a national energy policy." He explained that prices can be too high but that they can also be too low ("no one will invest"). He was asked, "what is the correct price of oil," and Cheney mumbled on about the need for price stability.

These are very dangerous attitudes based on remarkable ignorance of the forces of economics. No one can know in advance what the correct price of anything should be. If prices fall, it would indeed signal producers to offer less. Some producers, maybe even most, would go out of business. This is precisely what should happen.

There is no way for government to plan better than the market, especially for unusual market disturbances, which is why Soviet-style programs like the Ford administration's "Strategic Petroleum Reserve" are so ridiculous. They work as subsidies to the oil industry even as they keep supplies on the market artificially low. Knowing that the government may, at any time, unleash all this pent-up supply on the market, producers face a diminished incentive to drill and process oil for consumption.

But to the average consumer, none of this matters. They see only the price meter on the gas pump, and get mad at the poor fellow behind the counter who processes their credit cards. Then they go running to the government for help. This is the worst possible outcome.

Remember that fellow who said, "I don't blame the government"? Well, he should. And if the government intervenes to force the price down and shortages result, he will have even more reason to do so.

94.
WEAPON OF MASS CREATION*

You can learn so much about human nature, the workings of society, and the functioning of markets by looking at the aftermath of a natural disaster. It is a fascinating laboratory for observing how society functions under the worst conditions.

If you have ever been through a natural disaster, and paid attention to how the preparation and clean-up take place, you know precisely what I am referring to: the splendid creative power of human energy to cooperate to overcome the most astonishing barriers.

Such settings can teach us so much about politics and economics. If society can function in these radically abnormal settings, if markets can work well, we discover so much about the power of the same forces and institutions to manage under normal conditions.

Florida has been through four hurricanes this year, and the damage has been overwhelming. Contrary to what you read in various newspapers, this destruction is not a good thing for the Florida economy. People who have read Bastiat's story of the boy with the rock, as told by Henry Hazlitt in his book *Economics in One Lesson*, marvel at how others still haven't learned the lesson. In the midst of destruction, someone will always raise a voice to defend the view that the destruction has a wonderful upside, that the rebuilding will stimulate rebuilding.

My favorite example this season comes from *USA Today*. The headline read: "Economic Growth From Hurricanes Could Outweigh Costs" (September 27, 2004). The story read as follows:

> Economists tallying the numbers expect the hurricanes will be neutral in their effect on the US economy, or may even give it

---

*October 2004

a slight boost, particularly because of an expected reconstruction boom in the already red-hot construction industry.

Then comes the inevitable quotation from a naïve economist, who pretends to have highly specialized if counterintuitive knowledge: "It's a perverse thing," said Steve Cochrane of Economy.com. "But from an economic point of view, it is a plus."

Tell you what: let's not put Mr. Cochrane in charge of national economic policy. We might find man-made disasters hitting all of our communities in order to help us. Maybe instead of sending all those bombs overseas, they could be dropped right here at home, so as to spur a massive rebuilding boom. It's a perverse thing, he might say, but it's for our own good.

If you understand why people believe that, you can understand why there exists something called Keynesian economics, which postulates that everyone can be made better off by letting the government rob people and give money to bureaucracies to spend. You can also understand how it is that people cheer on inflation and taxation as productive devices. You can see why so many are still under the impression that war is an economic stimulus, and that Iraq will somehow be better off with billions in reconstruction spending rather than by not having had its towns and cities blown up in the first place.

In short, if you can understand why people celebrate a hurricane's productive power, then you can understand how it is that people think that Leviathan as we know it today is an institution to celebrate and adore, and why we should build on its marvelous successes like Social Security, public schooling, the War on Drugs, and the War on Terror.

These same people should also celebrate other institutions such as crime waves for their productive power. After all, when people have things looted from them, they must then go out and buy more things, which stimulates more production and so on.

Conversely, if we are to realize that hurricanes are, after all, not a good thing for Florida or anywhere else, we have taken the first step toward seeing what is wrong with all forms of what Mises called destructionism. This is the ideology that sees some merit in undoing, demolishing, reversing, or hobbling the march of human enterprise. Who would favor such an ideology? Many of the same people who think hurricanes and wars are good for us.

At first, destructionism would seem perverse and easy to refute. In fact, destructionism has a hold on the public mind. It was unleashed in the twentieth century and it continues to play a huge role in public affairs today. It is the ideology that celebrates confiscatory taxation, punishing regulation, aggressive war, and the daily acts of public administration that destroy wealth.

Natural disasters are something human society has to cope with, and the market has found brilliant ways of doing so. Government, on the other hand, is a man-made disaster that is sustained only by the ideological ignorance of the population that somehow believes that because destruction is officially sponsored by the law and the legislators, or otherwise endorsed by the democratic process, that it yields great good or forestalls great evil.

In the same way that society has learned to deal with natural disasters—and this is part of the miracle of human creativity I will address—we have also learned how to deal with the persistent presence of government, in ways that have surprised government's biggest critics.

But let us begin with the time before the natural disaster to see how the market handles these settings. Long before the storm appears in the high seas, the market institution of insurance has assessed the risk and offered to bear that risk for people at a price.

Homeowners with a mortgage are required to insure their houses, and insurance companies must make an assessment of the risk associated with the location and the likelihood of disaster. If the risk is high, the premiums are high too, and so people will not build there. The homeowner himself does not need to know the risks; that information is conveyed in the price, and he responds accordingly.

Of course, the presence of government-provided insurance foils this market system and ends up creating hazards, which is exactly what federal flood insurance (created in 1968) does. It subverts the market process and encourages irrational decision-making. This is the only reason that people in large numbers build on flood plains and islands that are ripe targets for hurricanes. Nonetheless, the operation of the private insurance market does the bulk of the work to guide rational building patterns.

When the news appears that a hurricane is coming, the first reaction of the population is to stock up on provisions, and who is there to provide but private enterprise. Indeed, we take it all for granted. It is not government or bureaucracies that make available many days in advance such items as dry goods, batteries, flashlights, water, generators, and all the rest. It is the free market, and, yes, these firms make money in the process, by providing a service people want.

So plentiful were bottled water and canned tuna and batteries in Auburn the week before Hurricane Ivan that panic buying subsided very rapidly. It dawned on people that a dozen stores were going to have plenty available for everyone. Order came about because consumer expectations fell in line with resource supply. People were calm not because government told them to be or because they believed that public authorities would care for them. Rather, people had confidence that private enterprise would supply what they demanded, regardless of the conditions.

When the hurricane actually hit, government offices were closed, but Wal-Mart and Lowe's and Kroger remained open throughout, with vast quantities of extra provisions on hand. When it became clear that the hurricane had passed, restaurants opened within minutes. Tree cutting services were everywhere. Handymen were hawking their wares.

The main concern of everyone is electricity, a service provided not by private enterprise, but by a monopoly under the supervision of government. For some reason, everyone knows that power goes out in a storm. The providers know this; consumers do, too; and so does the press. Everyone lives with it. No one questions it. The wind blows, the rain comes, the lights go out, and we wait until regulators deign to turn them back on.

Imagine such a service as provided purely by private enterprise. Surely the first order of business would be to create an energy flow that managed to stay on during an emergency. The problem would be overcome by entrepreneurs and capitalists, chiefly because the consumer is king. With electricity, however, we all just accept the fact that it goes down in a storm and we must wait for the bureaucracy to supervise its restoration.

When private enterprise fails, we don't hesitate to complain, demand, and even sue. But when government fails at its most essential duty of keeping the lights on, most people don't even bother to complain. I should add that this is a very serious matter, one that often involves life and death.

Electricity is a common example of what used to be considered a public good, one that private enterprise, it was said, could not provide or for which competition would be wasteful. Of course we now know this claim to be ridiculous—just look what private enterprise has done with cell and wireless technology. The main barriers to reliable energy provision are the government monopolies that keep private enterprise out.

Nonetheless, private enterprise has done its best to get around the restrictions. Large stores like Home Depot are fully prepared with enough private generators to power their stores, and home generators are ever more common.

As a side note, it is certainly true the Post Office will do everything possible to deliver your mail in a storm, or at least we have developed a general expectation that the service will not be dramatically worse in a storm than it is while the sun is shining. Perhaps that is not saying much. But I'm sure you are relieved to know that, no matter what the weather, the government can get to you to deliver a message.

You will notice that natural disasters tend to be far less deadly in wealthy, capitalist countries than in poor socialist ones. The press invariably attributes this to building codes, as if socialists had never thought of that. Now, nothing strikes me as more absurd than the assumption that only government cares if your own house can withstand an earthquake or tornado. The people who live there, the banks, the insurers, the builders— none of them have any interest in solid construction and so the regulators have to be involved. That's the theory anyway, and it is ridiculous.

Moving on in the parade of folly, let me say a few words about price gouging. Nowadays, every state and most towns have strict rules against raising prices to too great an extent during a storm. This shuts down an important rationing mechanism when it is needed most, and also prevents the market economy from signaling consumers concerning dramatic shifts in the relative value of available resources and services.

In saying this, I have no doubt that there are unscrupulous people out there waiting to exploit a human emergency to make vast sums of money. And yet, this a far better option than what is the actual choice: not cheaper service but no service at all. I assume that everyone would prefer the option of a high price, whether or not you buy, to no good or service at all. A temporarily high price also serves the function of signaling other entrepreneurs and capitalists about market disequilibria. It permits a faster market clearing.

There are few things as disgusting as prosecutions of gouging cases. The owner of a gas station, believing that he might be able to sell gas for $5 per gallon, for however brief a time, will risk life and limb to get to his shop to open it for travelers. That is his passion and vocation. Take him to jail for engaging in voluntary exchange and you have violated a human right. Tell that same person that he is not permitted to sell at a higher price, and there will be no gas available. That is our choice: what some people call gouging—or no goods and services. Government, as we know from the case of electricity, prefers the latter.

Another way in which government prevents people from responding rationally to a crisis is through mandatory evacuation orders, premised on the idea that government officials know what is better for you than you know yourself. In the aftermath of one of these orders, the newspapers are always shocked to see that some people might have taken advantage of the evacuation, stayed behind, and helped themselves to the property of others. I suppose nobody in government had really thought about the message that a mandatory enforced evacuation sends to criminals: something along the lines of COME AND GET IT!

A regulation that Murray Rothbard found to be particularly egregious is that which prevents people from returning to their homes after a natural disaster. It is particularly cruel because immediately following the storm is when the real wonders of human cooperation come into play. Every resident from the smallest renter to the owner of the largest landed estate examines the space outside his or her door and assesses what needs to be done. There is no expectation that someone else should be responsible for it. The locus of control and responsibility is clearly defined.

Mother Nature acted, but it is property owners who must respond. And so they do, starting with what is theirs. But it does not stop there. We also help our neighbors in need. Anyone with a chainsaw gets busy, starting again with his own property and extending services out to neighbors. Heroic efforts take place all across the community, the town, the county, and the state.

Private enterprise is there too, with building materials, tree cutting services, plumbers, and repair services of all sorts. If it is something you need or want, it is available. One by one, hour by hour, the damaged area is cleaned up, at least that part of it that is privately owned. If you have gone through this in the past, it is truly a marvel to behold the power and productivity of thousands and tens of thousands of people caring for their own and helping out neighbors. In my own observation, it seems to take less than a day to do more than half the clean up. What we observe in these cases is not just the free market at work but the whole workings of human society, people cooperating commercially and charitably toward their mutual betterment.

What we see in this case is something that nearly all the social science literature claims cannot happen. The economists doubt that prices and wages can respond quickly enough to re-equilibrate supply and demand according to new conditions. Not only do we see this happening in real life; we actually observe private enterprise attempting to anticipate change that is coming and to be prepared before it happens. And keep in mind that this is true during times of emergency and crisis, not just during normal times.

Contrary to the claims of social democrats from time immemorial, that markets are fine from day to day but not during exceptional events, we find that markets love nothing more than a challenge that offers a profit opportunity. Where government sees only devastation, markets see possibility.

We see this happen in war-torn areas, where the merchant class struggles against impossible odds to provide. We see this in American cities with areas so violent that most people would try desperately to avoid even driving through. But the merchant class sees a chance for providing a service, and so risks life and limb.

All over the world where the risks are high and the barriers seemingly insurmountable, we see private enterprise providing and serving others. This is true of the smallest peasant money changer to the largest multinational corporation. Commerce does what others are unwilling to do. And it is hardly ever given credit.

But we should not single out commerce as a special case within society. It is the conviction of the liberal intellectual tradition dating back to the Middle Ages that society contains within itself the capacity for internal self-management. This is in contrast to the claims of the sociology literature, which posits that human society is riddled with conflict between groups: races, ages, ethnicities, and abilities. The sociologists have sliced and diced the human population to such an extent that it would seem impossible for anyone to get along at all, and certainly not in times of emergency.

But a natural disaster shows precisely the opposite, that there are many paths to human cooperation. It can take commercial forms or it can take the form of charity, and within each of those we see thousands of variations of forms. In the end, society works to accomplish amazing things by bringing together the individual efforts of every person and property owner, and it does it all without central command or coordination.

Let's return to the scene of the hurricane. Within a week after a natural disaster, we find that most places have restored normalcy and order and even beauty. All that is left to do involves plantings and more fundamental building projects of various sorts. But the settings have been fully prepared. The recovery is well on its way. This is the great surprise that greets us in the aftermath of the storm. People love to brag and talk and go on about all the horrors created by natural disasters, but the truly marvelous and newsworthy thing is not the disaster but the wonderful manner in which it is repaired: by voluntary human effort.

The public parks, the school grounds, and the land claimed by the state are usually cleaned up in far longer time. But these days this is for a reason that goes beyond the usual bureaucratic incompetence. Every community seeks disaster assistance, money that usually ends up in the hands of local governments where officials pass it out to their friends. The newspapers cooperate in this creation of phony disasters in the hope of getting big bucks from the likes of the Federal Emergency Management Agency.

The morning after Ivan, our local paper headline in massive type: DEVASTATION. It showed a picture of a man carrying sticks across his lawn, an awning from a burger joint flipped up due to wind, and a tree that had tipped over onto someone's porch. This was not exactly the kind of devastation that would take hundreds of millions of taxpayer dollars to fix. But everyone knows that after the storm, all official institutions have to play up damage as much as possible in order to gain the attention of federal authorities.

The whole enterprise of disaster aid has become one of the great rackets of modern government. Today we have the disgusting spectacle of senators and presidents coming to visit weather-injured places, as if they have within their capacity the ability to size up damage and make provisions for making it all correct. We are supposed to believe that they know more about the proper course of action than insurance adjusters and property owners.

If we had honest politicians, they would say:

> Of course I'm sorry about what happened to that beach in Florida, but my presence there would only distract from the essential work being done by owners and their insurers. I don't know anything about the topic, and even if I did, I would not want to steal from some to give to others to realize my political priorities.

I'm reminded of the classic story of how Congressmen Davy Crockett was denounced by a constituent for having voted to pay for the rebuilding of Georgetown after a fire. He never did it again. These days, I suppose, we would be grateful for such a modest response by the Congress. We would be glad that the entire apparatus of the Leviathan state had not begun a global War on Arson and arrested anyone carrying matches.

Like dictators and führers, politicians always come to the scene of a natural disaster carrying a wad of cash. William Anderson documents that this scam really took off during the Clinton presidency, but these days government sits through every natural disaster with bated breath, hoping for a chance to do what it does best: grab power and hand out other people's money to friends of the state. As for the actual rebuilding, it is done by private enterprise, and in a timely and efficient manner. It is the social means (to use Oppenheimer's phrase) that rebuilds and restores, not the state.

I have taken you through all of this in order to illustrate a larger point about how private enterprise and the social means respond to every manner of exogenous shock that attempts to derail the path of progress. The biggest barrier of all, something far more costly than all the natural disasters combined and even great criminal acts such as that which occurred on 9-11, is government itself. It daily interferes with the path of progress through taxes, regulations, distortions such as subsidies and price controls, as well as wars and trade barriers. It is helpful to think of the way free enterprise responds to government: it's the way society responds to a natural disaster. Yes, some people get rich off government. But taken as a whole, it is a disastrous cost on society that must be overcome.

Government is not productive. It is not creative. It does not bring blessings. Government spending drains resources from society, taking from those in whose hands it has the highest value and putting into the hands of people who serve the state. Regulation forestalls choice. Taxation loots from people the reward of work and productive endeavor.

Most destructive of all is war, and yet it is war that people are most likely to credit with bringing prosperity. But as Mises says,

> War prosperity is like the prosperity that an earthquake or a plague brings. The earthquake means good business for construction workers, and cholera improves the business of physicians, pharmacists, and undertakers; but no one has for that reason yet sought to celebrate earthquakes and cholera as stimulators of the productive forces in the general interest.

Of course, he wrote that in 1919. Today, I'm sure we would have no problem finding people who say such preposterous things.

Austrians are unique in having great clarity about the damage caused by government. And yet sometimes even Austrians have a tendency to underestimate the power of free enterprise to overcome obstacles to serve the world and bring prosperity to the multitudes. I doubt that even the most ardent fan of free markets would have imagined that ex-Red China could be transformed in such a short period of time, that Eastern Europe would undergo a total upheaval toward prosperity in a mere 10 years, that New York could so quickly bounce back after 9-11, that the recovery after the dot-com bust would be so rapid.

Alone among schools of economics, Austrians understand the dangers of credit expansion of all sorts, how even small interventions can cause terrible dislocations, how the downside of government policies is overlooked by just about everyone. To explain and articulate the downside is our comparative advantage. This is one reason that Austrians tend to be better at anticipating the bust than seeing the boom. To explain the fact of ongoing destruction is not the same as having perfect predictive power concerning the creative response by producers and entrepreneurs.

Austrians have had their fair share of gloom-and-doomers among financial economists, and they have been right more times than we realize. Mark Thornton has a new study out that examines what economists were saying during the height of the dot-com boom. He found that Austrians were just about the only ones who saw that it had to come to an end. And many called the timing exactly right. This was at a time when most everyone else saw nothing but endless price increases for securities in our future.

But being able to see the downside should not make us blind to observing the astonishing ways in which private enterprise is able to adjust itself so well in the presence of government intervention. Despite living with the largest governments ever created in the history of the world, the free market has been able to work around them to be the source of the second greatest technological revolution of the last 500 years, namely that which has taken place between the invention of the microchip and the commercialization of wireless technology. We live today with technology that would have been unimaginable even five years ago.

Let me just give an example of this. It is within the power of any of us in this room to have delivered to a family member living anywhere in this country just about any CD, book, clothing, or food item that they may desire, by express to their door by noon tomorrow, merely by clicking on a few buttons from any one of the laptops located in this room, and to track that package on its way to delivery through live websites. All of this takes place within the framework of the market matrix. If you take a trip to your local wireless dealer or office supply store and have a look at the technology that is out there these days, you observe an amazing array of astonishing gizmos that have been created, perfected, marketed, and employed outside the radar screen of government.

There was a time when something like the Food and Drug Administration or the Consumer Product Safety Commission could claim to keep up with all the products we use. But today the consumer markets are moving so fast and with such power that government can't possibly keep up. When it gets involved in an antitrust suit involving technology, we can only marvel at the sheer ignorance with which government regulators and judges approach these topics. Truly government today is living decades behind the rest of the world, on the belief that its old-fashioned methods of coercion and propaganda can competently deal with a digital world of wireless and instant everything.

Communications technology is the most obvious example. Government once aspired to control all the command posts in society, among which was the technology that permitted people to talk to each other and pass on information. Government still attempts this, with its ridiculous post office and public utility monopolies. But the private sector has moved way beyond this. We have email, cell phones, instant messaging, Google, and amazing technologies that combine all of these to produce an alternative communication infrastructure that lives and thrives outside the ability of government to manage it. Hillary Clinton complained that the web lacked much-needed gatekeepers. Well, that was years ago. The would-be gatekeepers are still nowhere to be seen, and we are none the worse off.

We should never forget, in the midst of all our warnings about government power, that government is deeply incompetent, and laughably so. Consider the attempts by the World Trade Organization to presume to manage global trade. The WTO was created in 1995 as a follow-up to the failed attempt in 1948 to create a Keynesian-style command center for the management of the world economy. Today, the WTO, at its least intrusive, serves as little more than a dispute resolution panel— a service that would otherwise be provided by private enterprise. The idea that it serves as some sort of planning board for the world economy is utterly laughable, not because the WTO would not relish that role, but because it would be impossible for it to do so.

The WTO came about in 1995, about the period when world trade began to blossom as it had not in 100 years. China was solidly on the path toward its present renaissance. East Asia was becoming a hugely viable market. Latin America was entering onto a new path of integration. Most importantly of all, Eastern Europe and Russia had opened up.

The economy is global now, and there is no going back. The division of labor has vastly increased and all the world's population is involved in the great task of creating and producing to meet human needs. Where does this leave government? Doing what it has always done: looting people, starting wars, and generally being a pain in the neck. It continues to grow like a tumor on the world, but private enterprise has consistently outrun the ability of government to chase it and tackle it. It is this market—

the very institution based on human liberty that we are so dedicated to defending—that is also our main weapon against the state.

Now, I'm not arguing that technology can somehow make government irrelevant. I'm sorry to report that many governments in the world retain weapons of mass destruction. The biggest government of all has the most weapons, and this government in question is the only one that has ever actually employed a nuclear weapon against civilians. Instead of naming that government, let's just call it Government X.

Government X has decided that it should be the world's only superpower and that it should stand in judgment over all countries in the world. It has decided that it alone has the right model of culture and politics, and that it is a snap to make carbon copies of itself in far-flung places through a few well-placed bombs.

At least, this was the view of the regime in charge of Government X only a year and a half ago. It reflected a kind of hubris and even insanity. Had that regime been successful in its wars against two other governments, let's call them Y and Z, we might have had cause to be gravely pessimistic about the future of warfare, as Government X marched through the entire alphabet of countries and changed their regimes to copies of the high-tax social democratic militarism so well practiced by Government X. But this is not the case. Military history has few failures as colossal as the war of Government X against Governments Y and Z. And while we are right to feel great sadness for the terrible loss of life on all sides, we should not regret that the empire was denied success. These wars were nothing but cases of government intervention gone terribly wrong, unnatural disasters visited upon the populations of all the countries involved.

And yet we overcome. World trade proceeds apace, and production continues, not because of the order brought to the world by government, but in spite of the disorder brought to the world by government. The market has not only taken on the burden of confronting nature itself, which erects so many obstacles to the well-being of the human population, but government as well, which is the largest obstacle to progress ever known in the history of civilization.

One reason natural disasters alarm us is that there seems to be very little we can do to alter their course. Anti-hurricane intellectuals can do very little about changing the direction of an Ivan or Jeanne. However, intellectuals can alter the course of unnatural disasters such as government. Governments themselves are products of ideas, mostly bad ones, and they can be curbed and dismantled by other ideas.

It is essential that we, as lovers of liberty, constantly warn about the dangers presented by the state. But it is also our job to constantly say, in as many ways as we can, that it does not have to be this way. The state is not the foundation of society, it is not the source of our security, it does not bring about prosperity, and it does not protect us. Government instead stands outside of society and lives off its proceeds, and does so for its own benefit and not that of society. To understand this and impart this message to the current generation of students that benefits so enormously from the blessings wrought by the market are surely tasks worthy of all our efforts.

This afternoon I have spoken at length about crisis and destruction and the response. I've done so because of something I've noted from the students who now come to us for Mises University and read our materials. The events of 9-11 have shaped the current generation of students. These students do not remember the ideological wars that we older folks grew up with, which pitted communism against capitalism.

Today, the essential question is whether government or the market is the essential source of our security and justice. To those students who have accepted the claims of the state, that justice comes through war, and that the state must abolish all that came before in the name of providing future protection—to these students, the state is the heroic institution of our time. It has become for them, tragically, the source of social salvation.

On the other hand, the event also raised up a new generation of very thoughtful, highly active, and analytically rigorous students who have seen through the propaganda. They have seen how the state so cynically used a tragedy and crisis of its own creation in order to fasten a kind of despotism on a country with a libertarian heritage, and how this response has made us less safe and wrought vast amounts of destruction. That dreadful day forced a choice on an entire generation: to follow the path of power wherever it leads, or to rethink all the assumptions that dominate the intellectual climate of our time.

Those of us in the Misesian tradition of thought are very fond of intellectual combat and delineating the differences between our way of thinking and that of our adversaries, whether they are on the right or the left or somewhere in between. At the very core of the difference is one's view of the viability of human cooperation apart from state intervention. If you can understand how a small community can recover from a hurricane without the aid of government, or if you can understand how a magnificently productive global economy can grow and thrive and provide for billions, without the aid of a global state, then you understand a very critical point. It is this: society and all its works can thrive without central management by a coercive apparatus. If people have liberty, property, and law, they have the basis of what it takes to make a civilization. Anything that compromises those institutions is a force for de-civilization.

After a natural disaster hits, we open our doors to see a space desperately in need of clean-up. With regard to government in the world today, we see something very similar. Let us open our doors and look without flinching at the terrible mess that the state has made of our world. To those who say this is beautiful and productive, let us explain why this is not so. Let us point to wars and poverty, mass sickness and disease, and explain their cause. Let us stand up to those who would celebrate destruction and show that it is unnecessary and terribly tragic. And let us not despair when we see a world torn asunder by the state, but rather see the evidence of invention and creativity that surrounds us, and look for every opportunity for rebuilding.

95.

THE STATE AND THE FLOOD*

Ludwig von Mises wrote, "No one can escape the influence of a prevailing ideology," and Gulf Coast residents know precisely what it means to be trapped—ostensibly by a flood but actually by statist policies and ideological commitments that put the government in charge of crisis management and public infrastructure. For what we are seeing in New Orleans and the entire Gulf Coast region is the most egregious example of government failure in the United States since September 11, 2001.

Mother Nature can be cruel, but even at her worst, she is no match for government. It was the glorified public sector—the one we are always told is protecting us—that is responsible for this. And though our public servants and a sycophantic media will do their darn best to present this calamity as an act of nature, it was not and is not.

Katrina came and went with far less damage than anyone expected. It was the failure of the public infrastructure and the response to it that brought down civilization.

The levees that failed and caused New Orleans to be flooded, bringing a humanitarian crisis not seen in our country in modern times, were owned and maintained by the Army Corps of Engineers. The original levees surrounding this city below sea level were erected in 1718, and have been variously expanded since.

---

*September 2005

But who knew that a direct hit by a hurricane would cause them to break? Many people, it turns out. Ivor van Heerden of Louisiana State University, reports *Newsday*,

> who has developed flooding models for New Orleans, was among those issuing dire predictions as Katrina approached, warnings that turned out to be grimly accurate. He predicted that floodwaters would overcome the levee system, fill the low-lying areas of the city and then remain trapped there well after the storm passed—creating a giant, stagnant pool contaminated with debris, sewage and other hazardous materials.

Newsday goes on:

> Van Heerden and other experts put some of the blame on the Mississippi River levees themselves, because they channel silt directly into the Gulf of Mexico that otherwise would stabilize land along the riverside and slow the sinking of the coastline.

He is hardly some lone nut. *National Geographic* ran a large article on the topic last year that begins with a war-of-the-worlds scenario and reads precisely like this week's news from New Orleans. It is the Army Corps of Engineers that has been responsible for the dwindling of the coastline that has required the levees to be constantly reinforced with higher walls. But one problem: no one bothered to do this since 1965. That's only the beginning of the problems created by the Corps's levee management, the history of which was documented by Mark Thornton following the last flood in 1999.

Only the public sector can preside over a situation this precarious and display utter and complete inertia. What do these people have to lose? They are not real owners. There are no profits or losses at stake. They do not have to answer to risk-obsessed insurance companies who insist on premiums matching even the most remote contingencies. So long as it seems to work, they are glad to go about their business in the soporific style famous to all public sectors everywhere.

And failure of one structure has highlighted the failures of other structures. The levees could not be repaired in a timely manner because roads and bridges built and maintained by government could not withstand the pressure from the flood. They broke down.

And again, it is critical to keep in mind that none of this was caused by Hurricane Katrina as such. It was the levee break that led to the calamity. As the *New York Times* points out:

> it was not the water from the sky but the water that broke through the city's protective barriers that had changed every- thing for the worse. . . . When the levees gave way in some critical spots, streets that were essentially dry in the hours immediately after the hurricane passed were several feet deep in water on Tuesday morning.

Indeed, at 4 p.m. on Monday, August 29, all seemed calm, and reports of possible calamity seemed overwrought. Two hours later the reports began to appear about the levee. A period of some 12 hours lapsed between when the hurricane passed through and when the water came rushing into the city. There is some dispute about precisely when the levees broke. Some say that they were broken long before anyone discovered the fact, which is another outrage. There was no warning sys- tem. There is no question that plenty of time was available between their breakage and the flooding to enable people to make other arrangements—and perhaps for the levees to be repaired. People were relieved that the rain subsided and the effects of Katrina were far less egregious than anyone expected.

That's when the disaster struck. The municipal government itself relocated to Baton Rouge even as the city pumps failed as well. Meanwhile, the Army Corps of Engineers apparently had no viable plan even to make repairs. They couldn't bring in the massive barges and cranes needed because the bridges were down and broken, or couldn't be opened without electricity. For public relations purposes, they dumped tons of sand into one breach even as another levee was breaking. But even that PR move failed since most helicopters were being used to move people from spot to spot—another classic case of miscalculation. Many bloggers had the sense that the public sector essentially walked away.

But the police and their guns and nightsticks were out in full force, not arresting criminals but pushing around the innocent and giving mostly bad instructions. The 10,000 people who had been corralled into the Superdome were essentially under house arrest by the police who were keeping them there, preventing them even from getting fresh air. A day later the water and food were running out, people were dying, and the sanitary conditions becoming disastrous. Finally someone had the idea of shipping all these people Soviet-like to Houston to live in the Astrodome, as if they are not people with volition but cattle.

After evacuations, the looting began and created a despicable sight of criminal gangs stealing everything in sight as the police looked on (when they weren't joining in). Now, this scene offers its own lessons. Why don't looting and rampant criminality occur every day? The police are always there and so are the hoodlums and the criminals. What was missing that made the looting rampage possible was the bourgeoisie, who had either left by choice or had been kicked out. It is they who keep the peace. And had any stayed around to protect their property, we don't even have to speculate what the police would have done: Arrest them!

Now, in the coming weeks, as it becomes ever more obvious that the real problem was not the hurricane but the failure of the infrastructure to work properly, the political left is going to have a heyday. They will point out that Bush cut spending for the Army Corps of Engineers, that money allocated to reinforcing the levees and fixing the pumps had been cut to pay for other things, that we are reaping what we sow from failing to support the public sector.

The ever-stupid right will come to the defense of Bush and the Iraq War that has completely absorbed this regime's attention, pointing out that Bush is actually a big and compassionate spender who cares about infrastructure, while demanding that people recognize his greatness, along with all the other pieties that have become staples of modern "conservatism."

But this is a superficial critique (and defense) that doesn't get to the root of the problem with public services. NASA spends and spends and still can't seem to make a reliable space shuttle. The public schools absorb many times more—thousands times more—in resources than private schools and still can't perform well. The federal government spends trillions over years to "protect" the country and can't fend off a handful of malcontents with an agenda. So too, Congress can allocate a trillion dollars to fix every levee, fully preventing the last catastrophe, but not the next one.

The problem here is public ownership itself. It has encouraged people to adopt a negligent attitude toward even such obvious risks. Private developers and owners, in contrast, demand to know every possible scenario as a way to protect their property. But public owners have no real stake in the outcome and lack the economic capacity to calibrate resource allocation to risk assessment. In other words, the government manages without responsibility or competence.

Can levees and pumps and disaster management really be privatized? Not only can they be; they must be if we want to avoid ever more apocalypses of this sort. William Buckley used to poke fun at libertarians and their plans for privatizing garbage collection, but this disaster shows that much more than this ought to be in private hands. It is not a trivial issue; our survival may depend on it.

It is critically important that the management of the whole of the nation's infrastructure be turned over to private management and ownership. Only in private hands can there be a possibility of a match between expenditure and performance, between risk and responsibility, between the job that needs to be done and the means to accomplish it.

The list of public sector failures hardly stops there. The outrageous insistence that no one be permitted to "gouge" only creates shortages in critically important goods and services when they are needed the most. It is at times of extreme need that prices most need to be free to change so that consumers and producers can have an idea of what is needed and what is in demand. Absent those signals, people do not know what to conserve and what to produce.

Bush was on national television declaring that the feds would have zero tolerance toward gouging, which is another way of saying zero tolerance toward markets. If New Orleans stands any chance of coming back, it will only be because private enterprise does the rebuilding, one commercial venture at a time. Bush's kind of talk guarantees a future of mire and muck, the remote possibility of prosperity and peace sacrificed on the altar of interventionism.

Moreover, every American ought to be alarmed at the quickness of officials to declare martial law, invade people's rights, deny people the freedom of movement, and otherwise trample on all values that this country is supposed to hold dear. A crisis does not negate the existence of human rights. It is not a license for tyranny. It is not a signal that government may do anything it wants.

This crisis ought to underscore a point made on these pages again and again. Being a government official gives you no special insight into how to best manage a crisis. Indeed the public sector, with all its guns and mandates and arrogance, cannot and will not protect us from life's contingencies.

It used to be said that infrastructure was too important to be left to the uncertainties of markets. But if it's certainty that we are after, there is a new certainty that has emerged in American life: in a crisis, the government will make matters worse and worse until it wrecks your life and all that makes it worth living.

PART V: WHAT TO DO

*"Adhere to principle, even if only to bug those
who hate you for your principles!"*

96.

THE MAL-INTENTS*

Virtually every opponent of big government concedes his opponent's good intentions. But why? The destructive effects of foreign and domestic intervention are so clear that statists must be motivated, at least in part, by malice.

Communists, everyone would concede, were full of envy and hatred for the bourgeoisie. The gulag satisfied this in part. But what about the garden-variety welfare statist?

The US welfare state has spent $3.5 trillion in its various wars on poverty, yet by every measure, the underclass is worse off, and more socially menacing, than ever before. Economics tells us there's a direct connection. So why does welfare persist?

First, welfare has dramatically expanded the size and the reach of the federal government, and therefore the psychological compensation of state managers, as well as the number of jobs available in the public sector. (Some welfare-state proponents credit the very existence of the black middle class, for example, to these jobs.)

Second, the welfare state has been a massive drain on the middle class. If your first value is envy, and you seek to destroy private property and the middle-class family, you love the welfare state.

---

*June 1993

Third, the welfare state makes children less dependent on their parents, elderly parents less dependent on their grown children, and each generation less able to pass on its wealth to the next. If you don't like the independent family and its structure of authority, then this effect is welcome as well.

When Hillary Clinton or Donna Shalala or Janet Reno talk about helping children, they mean controlling them. Thanks to the welfare state, there has been a dramatic shift in children's legal (and sometimes emotional) allegiance from their parents to the state.

This further devalues children in the minds of potential parents, thus resulting in fewer kids, which is no unintended consequence. After all, when Al Gore condemns human population growth (because it might affect the numbers of gnat catchers and pileated woodpeckers), and Bill Clinton seeks to make government-funded abortions as easily available as fast food (except that you have to pay for a hamburger), a picture emerges. It's people, especially new people, and families, especially those that are internally loyal, that our rulers in Washington hate.

Another example of statist mal-intent is inflation. The public may not want their money taxed away in this fashion by the central bank, but inflation does have its beneficiaries. It is a major revenue source for the government itself, which also benefits from the depreciation of its debts. Large bankers and government contractors also profit, while union members, welfare recipients, and government employees get automatic cost-of-living raises. And egalitarians approve of the fact that inflation rewards short-term (underclass) thinking rather than long-term (upper-class) thinking, thereby decreasing the natural hierarchy of the market. And big private debtors like inflation because they can prosper at the expense of property owners.

William Greider, a top Clintonian journalist and political theorist, wrote a book a few years ago called *Secrets of the Temple: How the Federal Reserve Runs the Country*, in which he defended the late

1970s inflation on exactly these grounds. Such sentiments are secret teaching among left-liberals.

The Clintons and their healthcare hatchet man, Ira Magaziner, want to impose price controls on the medical industry. Do they know that price controls create shortages? Of course. On the other hand, shortages create demands for further government intervention, and therefore a larger and more powerful public sector.

When the Stanford academic who designed the "managed competition" health-care model spoke on National Public Radio recently, he admitted his system had problems: people won't be able to choose their own doctors; they will get fewer services; and they will pay more. What then is the virtue? Everyone will get the same benefit package. Bums will be made the equal of the productive in the care they receive.

Environmentalism is openly ill-intended, at least as far as people are concerned. Environmentalists expressly want to make us poorer. For example, they want us to stop driving our cars. That's why they keep ratcheting up emission standards despite scientific evidence that the "ozone threat" is bunk, and smaller, lighter cars are more dangerous. They keep increasing the gasoline tax to force us to drive less. And they tax us more and more to build collectivist mass-transit systems that no one wants to use voluntarily.

Even laws forcing the disabled on employers can have a secret ill-intent. Precious few disabled people will actually be made better off, for what they gain in "access" they will lose in growing public resentment. Of course, unscrupulous lawyers benefit, and so do all the opponents of business autonomy. They get, as one Tennessee bureaucrat recently admitted, a perverse pleasure from seeing small businessmen crawl.

The same goes for other civil rights laws. They all demand that no one discriminate "on grounds of . . . " (fill in the blank) or be punished. But who is the arbiter of motivations? The government, of course, and the special interest groups responsible for the legislation. That's why every civil rights bill has collapsed into a numbers game. It is only through counting the number of approved victim groups in private business or the academy that government can determine if actions are approved or unapproved. That is part of the motivation, along with redistribution, which by definition is ill-intended, like other forms of theft.

Calling our opponents well intentioned grants them the moral high ground, when they are actually gutter-dwellers. What else can you call those who seek to replace private property with government subservience, family allegiance with bureaucratic dictate, the rule of law with administrative fiat, business autonomy with centralized tyranny?

The consequences of government intervention used to be called "unintended." After witnessing socialism crash and burn in the Soviet Union and Eastern Europe, and seeing the consequences of statism at home—our cities wrecked, our economy mangled, our families weakened, our currency debased—it's time to wise up.

97.

WHAT WE MEAN BY DECENTRALIZATION*

The *Kelo* decision, in which the Supreme Court refused to intervene in the case of a local government taking of private property, touched off a huge debate among libertarians on the question of decentralization.

The most common perspective was that the decision was a disaster because it gave permission to local governments to steal land. Libertarians are against stealing land, and so therefore must oppose the court decision.

---

*July 2005

And yet stealing isn't the only thing libertarians are against. We are also opposed to top-down political control over wide geographic regions, even when they are instituted in the name of liberty.

Hence it would be no victory for your liberty if, for example, the Chinese government assumed jurisdiction over your down-town streets in order to liberate them from zoning ordinances. Zoning violates property rights, but imperialism violates the right of a people to govern themselves. The Chinese government lacks both jurisdiction and moral standing to intervene. What goes for the Chinese government goes for any distant government that presumes control over government closer to home.

How is the libertarian to choose when there is a conflict between the demands of liberty and strictures against empire? The answer is not always easy, but experience and the whole intellectual history of liberalism suggest that decentralized gov-ernment is most compatible with long-run concerns for liberty. This is why all the Founders were attached to the idea of feder-alism: that the states within the union were the primary govern-ing units, and the Bill of Rights was to protect both individuals and the states from impositions by the central government— even when liberty is invoked as a justification.

Just so that we are clear on this last point: the purpose of the Bill of Rights was to state very clearly and plainly what the Fed-eral Government may not do. That's why they were attached to the Constitution. The states, under the influence of skeptics of the Constitution's limits on the central power, insisted that the restrictions on the government be spelled out. The Bill of Rights did not provide a mandate for what the Federal Government may do.

You can argue all you want about the Fourteenth Amend-ment and due process. But a reading that says it magically transforms the whole Bill of Rights to mean the exact opposite of its original intent is pure fantasy.

Back to the libertarian presumption in favor of decentralization. There are several reasons for it.

First, under decentralization, jurisdictions must compete for residents and capital, which provides some incentive for greater degrees of freedom, if only because local despotism is neither popular nor productive. If despots insist on ruling anyway, people and capital will find a way to leave. If there is only one will and one actor, you cannot escape.

Second, localism internalizes corruption so that it can be more easily spotted and uprooted. Along the same lines, local government corruption can be rather benign by comparison; it is easier, on a middle-class budget, to pay off the zoning board than to bribe the State Department.

Third, tyranny on the local level minimizes damage to the same extent that macro-tyranny maximizes it. If Hitler had ruled only Berlin, Stalin only Moscow, and FDR only Washington, the effects of their demented policies might have been contained. This is not only a utilitarian consideration. It means that evil people are prevented from violating the rights of people outside their jurisdiction.

Fourth, no government can be trusted to use the power to intervene wisely. With such power, central governments will always invoke good motives even when they are a mere mask for power grabs (as when the US military invaded Iraq, for example). The typical path goes this way. An intervention takes place that might be celebrated by good liberals, such as the Lochner decision (1905) by the Supreme Court that invalidated New York's labor regulations. But once that power is gained, it is used to put a legal imprimatur on central planning and prevent local governments from finding an escape (the central planning of World War I was Lochner's daughter).

Fifth, a plurality of governmental forms—a "vertical separation of powers," to use Stephan Kinsella's phrase—prevents the central government from accumulating power. Lower governments are rightly jealous of their jurisdiction, and resist. This is to the good. In fact, the whole history of liberty is bound up with the glorious results of competing institutional structures, no one of which can be trusted with complete control.

To be sure, this does not mean that libertarians must be agnostic on the question of what government should look like. Law should protect person and property against invasive force. This principle applies in all times and in all places. But that does not mean that there must be a single lawgiver and enforcer. To maximize the chance that good law will prevail over bad, over the long haul, and to prevent power grabs from the top, we need a multiplicity of legal forms.

Murray N. Rothbard had a nice phrase that he used to summarize this position: universal rights, locally enforced.

Those two principles are frequently in tension. But if you give up one of the two principles you risk giving up liberty. Both are important. Neither should prevail over the other. A local government that violates rights is intolerable. A central government that rules in the name of universal rights is similarly intolerable. Heaven on earth is universal rights, locally enforced. No, it's not here yet. That's why libertarians exist, to work for the ideal.

Now, there is another form of decentralization you often hear about. It comes from those who regret globalization in all forms, including multinational corporations and the like. They complain about the centralization of life in the modern age and long for simpler times. Here's the problem: the kind of centralization they regret is a result of voluntary decision-making in the marketplace. It is freely chosen centralization. Their plans for scaling back would require massive coercion and bring about an economic calamity.

In matters of private association and market economics, libertarians can make no *a priori* decision concerning the best means to organize. Rothbard was a defender of multinational corporations and global trade, but he also saw that too much integration in the production structure is bad for business. Firms lose the ability to calculate their profits and losses when they are responsible for too great a degree of internal production for their own capital goods.

How does this impact the organization of other institutions in society, like church, extended family, civic associations, and ideological movements? Is centralization best or is decentralization best? The answer must be left to experience. The Catholic Church is centralized doctrinally but decentralized managerially. The family in the American context is not centralized between generations. Grandparents are there to dote, not rule. Civic associations take many forms, from national organizations to local ones.

Rothbard himself, in the course of experience, changed his view on the best method for organizing ideological movements. Early on, he was attracted to the idea of top-down management, with cadres and followers and cells of every sort. He saw that this worked for the Communists, so why not for the libertarians? He was right to say that nothing in libertarian theory prohibits top-down management insofar as it is voluntary and rooted in private property.

But later on in life, he changed his mind and wrote that he found serious problems with this model, and they are related to the same problems that appear with political centralization. In the *Libertarian Forum*, August 1981, he writes:

> I would like to take this opportunity to admit my previous error in calling for an ultra-centralist model for the [Libertarian Party]. Several years in the [LP] have soured me on centralism permanently. Putting the rule of the Party, or of the movement as a whole, into the hands of one man or of one tight group is a recipe for disaster. First, it means that if a few people sell out to opportunism, the rest of the movement is dragged along with it. But second, and more generally, even if the Machiners were a bunch of wonderful people, since they are not omniscient they are bound, as are all of us to make mistakes. And just as the mistakes of a government-controlled economy can ruin a nation, so the inevitable mistakes of a tight ruling clique can ruin a party or a movement. I still think it absurd to think of decentralism as "the libertarian"

form of organization. How we organize is not a matter of libertarian principle, so long as we do not violate the non-aggression axiom. But it appears that neither radical decentralism nor ultra-centralism will work in any organization. . . . [M]oderation and balance should be our organizational mode.

How right he is! Imagine if the only forms of ideology available to us were those offered by Washington, DC organizations, with their hyper-policy focus and tendency to kowtow to the state. In intellectual life, we need a vast multiplicity of forms in order to check corruption and compromise. Even in the libertarian movement, we need diversity and experimentation, not centralization, command, and control.

In the organization of business, ideas, and life itself, Rothbard recommends balance and moderation. So we might articulate two Rothbardian principles. In public affairs, we need universal rights, locally enforced. In private and economic affairs, we need neither centralization nor decentralization, but moderation and balance, trial and error. To me, these formulations represent the height of good thinking, good law, and the good society.

98.

SECEDE?*

When a famous conservative told me ten years ago that "the United States is too big," and only "breaking it up into 35 different countries" would preserve a free and decent society, I was shocked. Today, leaving aside the exact number of successor states, I wonder if he wasn't right.

Certainly secession is sweeping the world, much to the dismay of the State Department and the Council on Foreign Relations. Secession freed many subject peoples of Moscow and

---

*June 1993

Belgrade. In Italy, the powerful Lega Nord political party advocates separation from the rapacious central government in Rome, and from welfare areas of Southern Italy.

Russia itself may now break up, since Moscow continues to hold many nations subject within the "federation." Belgium should be two countries, one for the French-speaking Walloons and one for the Flemish-speaking minority. Quebec may leave English-speaking Canada. And the African artifices of colonial cartographers may dissolve as well.

In almost every African country, a dominant tribe oppresses all the rest. Why shouldn't each people have sovereignty? In fact, why shouldn't the whites of South Africa have their own homeland as well?

In the United States, meanwhile, the central government gets more tyrannical and expensive by the day. Is it time to think about bidding it adieu?

Certainly, secession from Britain made a lot of sense. Whenever "any Form of Government becomes destructive" of the inalienable rights granted by the Creator, writes Thomas Jefferson in the Declaration of Independence, "it is the Right of the People to alter or abolish it, and to institute new Government." When a "long train of abuses and usurpations" shows "a design to reduce them under absolute Despotism, it is their right, it is their duty, to throw off such Government."

"Every man and every body of men on earth, possesses the right to self-government," Jefferson wrote elsewhere, and in 1786, he even defended Shays's tax revolt, which was suppressed by federal troops. To Jefferson, "the tree of liberty must be refreshed from time to time with the blood of patriots and tyrants."

That same year, he wrote to James Madison advocating secession for what were then the western states, after Congress had proposed to make them fewer and larger. "This is reversing the natural order of things," he wrote. "A tractable people may be governed in large bodies; but, in proportion as they depart from this character, the extent of their government must be less."

Thirty years later, Jefferson wrote: "If any State in the Union will declare that it prefers separation" over "union," "I have no hesitation in saying, 'let us separate'."

Not everyone agreed. In his farewell address, George Washington—who had been horrified by Shays's rebellion—condemned "every attempt to alienate any portion of our country from the rest."

Still, the freedom to secede was accepted by many American political leaders. In 1848, even Abraham Lincoln endorsed it:

> Any people anywhere, being inclined and having the power, have the right to rise up, and shake off the existing government, and form a new one that suits them better. This is a most valuable—a most sacred right—a right, which we hope and believe, is to liberate the world.

"Nor," said Lincoln,

> is this right confined to cases in which the whole people of an existing government may choose to exercise it. Any portion of such people that can, may revolutionize, and make their own, of so much of the territory as they inhabit.

But when he became president, Lincoln called secession the "essence of anarchy." Not because of slavery, but because of taxes. Tariffs were the major source of federal revenue and like all taxes, a powerful tool of the special interests. In this case they were used to protect Northern manufacturers from foreign competition at the expense of Southern agriculture, and to fund Northern public works projects.

Surpassing even the "tariff of abominations" of 1832, Lincoln doubled tariffs when he entered office to their highest rate in American history, threatening to impoverish the South, which imported almost everything.

In his 1861 inaugural speech, Lincoln told the South it must pay taxes. He would use, if necessary, "bloodshed or violence" against the seceding states "to collect the duties and imposts," but for no other purpose.

The secession had to be stopped, a Union newspaper in Boston editorialized, because the South would be a low-tax nation with a "revenue system verging on free trade." If "only a nominal duty is laid upon imports" in Southern ports, the "business of the chief Northern cities will be seriously injured."

Woodrow Wilson too seemed to support secession for all peoples, when he said in 1918, "no people must be forced under sovereignty under which it does not wish to live." But a year later, he backed off: there were too many nationalities! "When I gave utterance to those words, I said them without the knowledge that nationalities existed, which are coming to us day after day."

Although Wilson talked endlessly about self-determination, he was actually against the break-up of unified states. He would have agreed with Eleanor Roosevelt, who asked, while US representative to the United Nations, "Does self-determination mean the right of secession? . . . Obviously not."

Sometimes tyrants, knowing the appeal of secession, have used it as a ruse. In 1931, for example, before the Chinese Communist Party came to power, it guaranteed the "right to complete separation from China" to various nationalities including "Mongolians, Tibetans, Miao, Yao, Koreans, and others living on the territory." After the Party took over, its promise went the way of Lenin's similar lie. But when China is freed from communism, as it will be, we can expect to see many regions, including the more prosperous Canton, separating from the hated Peking.

Centralized states like the United States resort not only to military force to prevent secession, but also to spending. The cash continues to flow unless a state shows even the slightest inclination to independence. Even on minor matters like the drinking age, seatbelt laws, and speed limits, the feds threaten to cut off all funds unless the state legislatures capitulate, which they soon do.

Yet why should Palm Springs taxpayers subsidize Appalachian welfare? Or Appalachians subsidize Arkansas farmers? Or Alaskans build public housing in Atlanta? Why should Texas, once an independent nation, have to take orders from anyone? Jefferson's test for a justified secession was "a long train of abuses and usurpations." Today's train makes George III's look like a caboose.

As long as the states are held under the federal thumb, they will never be able to experiment with free markets. National labor, tax, environmental, civil rights, and regulatory codes will not allow it. Wisconsin, for example, had to seek Washington's approval to try a very minor welfare reform.

"No people and no part of a people shall be held against its will in a political association that it does not want," wrote Ludwig von Mises. Otherwise economic freedom would suffer along with political freedom. For Mises, international cooperation was as important as domestic cooperation, but this was achieved through free trade, not unified politics.

Is secession the only hope for restoring freedom of all sorts? Perhaps, if we are not content indefinitely to be a "tractable people."

99.

WHAT SHOULD FREEDOM LOVERS DO?*

How can one combine professional life with the advancement of liberty? Of course it is presumptuous to offer a definitive answer since all jobs and careers in the market economy are subject to the forces of the division of labor. Because a person focuses on one task doesn't mean that he or she isn't great at many tasks; it means only that the highest productive

---

*April 2004

gains for everyone come from dividing tasks up among many people of a wide range of talents.

So it is with the freedom movement. The more of us there are, the more we do well to specialize, to cooperate through exchange, to boost our impact by dividing the labor. There is no way to know in advance what is right for any person in particular. There are so many wonderful paths from which to choose (and which I will discuss below). But this much we can know. The usual answer—go into government—is wrongheaded. Too many good minds have been corrupted and lost by following this fateful course.

It often happens that an ideological movement will make great strides through education and organization and cultural influence, only to take the illogical leap of believing that politics and political influence, which usually means taking jobs within the bureaucracy, is the next rung on the ladder to success. This is like trying to fight a fire with matches and gasoline. This is what happened to the Christian right in the 1980s. They got involved in politics in order to throw off the yoke of the state. Twenty years later, many of these people are working in the Department of Education or for the White House, doing the prep work to amend the Constitution or invade some foreign country. This is a disastrous waste of intellectual capital.

It is particularly important that believers in liberty not take this course. Government work has been the chosen career path of socialists, social reformers, and Keynesians for at least a century. It is the natural home to them because their ambition is to control society through government. It works for them but it does not work for us.

In the first half of the twentieth century, libertarians knew how to oppose statism. They went into business and journalism. They wrote books. They agitated within the cultural arena. They developed fortunes to help fund newspapers, schools, foundations, and public education organizations. They expanded their commercial ventures to serve as a bulwark against central planning. They became teachers and, when possible, professors. They cultivated wonderful families and focused on the education of their children.

It is a long struggle but it is the way the struggle for liberty has always taken place. But somewhere along the way, some people, enticed by the prospect of a fast track to reform, rethought this idea. Perhaps we should try the same technique that the left did. We should get our people in power and displace their people, and then we can bring about change toward liberty. In fact, isn't this the most important goal of all? So long as the left controls the state, it will expand in ways that are incompatible with freedom. We need to take back the state.

So goes the logic. What is wrong with it? The state's only function is as an apparatus of coercion and compulsion. That is its distinguishing mark. It is what makes the state the state. To the same extent that the state responds well to arguments that it should be larger and more powerful, it is institutionally hostile to anyone who says that it should be less powerful and less coercive. That is not to say that some work from the "inside" cannot do some good, some of the time. But it is far more likely that the state will convert the libertarian than for the libertarian to convert the state.

We've all seen this a thousand times. It rarely takes more than a few months for a libertarian intellectual headed for the Beltway to "mature" and realize that his or her old ideals were rather childish and insufficiently real-world. A politician promising to defang Washington later becomes the leading expert in applying tooth enamel. Once that fateful step is taken, there are no limits. I know a bureaucrat who helped run martial law in Iraq who once swore fidelity to Rothbardian political economy.

The reason has to do with ambition, which is not normally a bad impulse. The culture of Washington, however, requires that ambition work itself out by paying maximum deference to the powers that be. At first, this is easy to justify: how else can the state be converted except by being friendly to it? The state is our enemy, but for now, we must pretend to be its pal. In time, the dreams are displaced by the daily need to curry favor. Eventually the person becomes precisely the kind of person he or she once despised. (For *Lord of the Rings* fans, it's like being asked to carry the ring for a while; you don't want to give it up.)

I've known people who have gone this route and one day took an honest look in the mirror, and didn't like what they saw. They have said to me that they were mistaken to think it could work. They didn't recognize the subtle ways in which they themselves were being drawn in. They recognize the futility of politely asking the state, day after day, to permit a bit more liberty here and there. Ultimately you must frame your arguments in terms of what is good for the state, and the reality is that liberty is not usually good for the state. Hence, the rhetoric and finally the goals begin to change.

The state is open to persuasion, to be sure, but it usually acts out of fear, not friendship. If the bureaucrats and politicians fear backlash, they will not increase taxes or regulations. If they sense a high enough degree of public outrage, they will even repeal controls and programs. An example is the end of alcohol prohibition or the repeal of the 55 mph speed limit. These were pulled back because politicians and bureaucrats sensed too high a cost from continued enforcement.

The problem of strategy was something that fascinated Murray Rothbard, who wrote several important articles on the need for never compromising the long-run goal for short-term gain through the political process. That doesn't mean we should not welcome a 1-percent tax cut or repeal a section of some law. But we should never allow ourselves to be sucked into the trade-off racket: e.g., repeal this bad tax to impose this better tax. That would be using a means (a tax) that contradicts the goal (elimination of taxation).

The Rothbardian approach to a pro-freedom strategy comes down to the following four affirmations:

(1) the victory of liberty is the highest political end;

(2) the proper groundwork for this goal is a moral passion for justice;

(3) the end should be pursued by the speediest and most effi-
cacious possible means; and

(4) the means taken must never contradict the goal—whether
by advocating gradualism, by employing or advocating any
aggression against liberty, by advocating planned programs,
by failing to seize any opportunities to reduce State power, or
by ever increasing it in any area.

Libertarians are not the first people who have confronted the
question of strategy for social advance and cultural and political change. After the Civil War, a large part of the population of
the South, namely former slaves, found themselves in a per-
ilous situation. They had a crying need to advance socially
within society, but lacked education, skill, and capital. They
also bore the burden of pushing social change that permitted
them to be regarded as full citizens who made the most of their
new freedom. In many ways, they found themselves in a position somewhat like new immigrants but with an additional burden of throwing off an old social status for a new one.

The Reconstruction period of Union-run martial law invited
many blacks to participate in politics as a primary goal. This
proved to be a terrible temptation for many, as the former Virginia slave Booker T. Washington said.

"During the whole of the Reconstruction period our people
throughout the South looked to the Federal Government for
everything, very much as a child looks to its mother." He
rejected this political model because "the general political agitation drew the attention of our people away from the more fundamental matters of perfecting themselves in the industries at
their doors and in securing property."

Washington wrote that "the temptations to enter political life
were so alluring that I came very near yielding to them at one
time," but he resisted this in favor of "the laying of the foundation of the race through a generous education of the hand, head
and heart." Later when he visited DC, he knew that he had been
right. "A large proportion of these people had been drawn to

Washington because they felt that they could lead a life of ease there," he wrote. "Others had secured minor government positions, and still another large class was there in the hope of securing Federal positions."

As it was in the 1870s it is today. The state chews up and either eats or spits out those with a passion for liberty. The extent to which W.E.B. DuBois's Marxian push for political agitation has prevailed over Washington's push for commercial advance has been tragic for black Americans and for the whole of American society. Many obtained political power, but not liberty classically understood.

We can learn from this. The thousands of young people who are discovering the ideas of liberty for the first time ought to stay away from the Beltway and all its allures. Instead, they should pursue their love and passion through arts, commerce, education, and even the ministry. These are fields that offer genuine promise with a high return.

When a libertarian tells me that he is doing some good as a procurement officer at HUD, I don't doubt his word. But how much more would he do by quitting his job and writing an exposé on the entire bureaucratic racket? One well-placed blast against such an agency can bring about more reform, and do more good, than decades of attempted subversion from within.

Are there politicians who do some good? Certainly, and the name Ron Paul is the first that comes to mind. But the good he does is not as a legislator as such but as an educator with a prominent platform from which to speak. Every no vote is a lesson to the multitudes. We need more Ron Pauls.

But Ron is the first to say that, more importantly, we need more professors, business owners, fathers and mothers, religious leaders, and entrepreneurs. The party of liberty loves commerce and culture, not the state.

100.

STRATEGIES FOR THE BATTLE AHEAD*

Government is once again the Grinch stealing Christmas, with family income still in long-term decline. But this year, the government's tight control of the economy, its blunt attacks on our liberties, and its appetite for power have everyone up in arms, sometimes literally.

But wasn't the 103rd Congress a "failure" because it didn't pass enough legislation? If only.

During the last days of the session, at the urging of the Clinton administration, the Senate scarfed up another 6.6 million acres in southeastern California and labeled it "protected." Protected against what? Terrorists, invaders, the homeless? No, private property and economic development.

The land must be protected because "tens of thousands of people come," said an alarmed California Senator Diane Feinstein, speaking of the desert. "The scarring is enormous."

Thanks to her bill, all this land is now owned by the central state, not without historical precedent. The Soviets collectivized land during the Bolshevik revolution. But at least they didn't ban agriculture.

One of the miracles of capitalism is its ability to turn deserts into useful areas. No system but free enterprise could have made Las Vegas thrive. The same applies to much of the Southwest. Now we are supposed to believe that development, meaning human prosperity, is evil and a "threat" to sand, spiders, rats, and snakes.

The land-nationalizers frequently contradict themselves. They also warn of overcrowding and overpopulation. But if we are really concerned about too many people in too small a

---

*December 1994

space, we should open up these "protected" lands so people can do something with them, whether building another Las Vegas or showing off nature at a profit.

As we all know, however, the federal government can't get enough, so it takes ever more, like a parasite devouring its host. What's strange is that the California state government—which has to be at least a little more responsive to voters—would let the feds get away with this land grab. One clue is an unheralded bill that passed that very day, doubling federal payments to states with heavy concentrations of government land, and indexing the payments to the inflation rate.

Property rights groups fought Feinstein for at least a year, but at the end of the session, amidst the pay-offs and the logrolling, they were powerless to stop the outrage.

That doesn't mean they're giving up. They're angrier than ever, as is every liberty-loving American, and even more determined to topple Leviathan. In this cause, some strategies are successful, others fail, and still others are a wash. As we enter the new year, it's a good time to examine some of these strategies, and evaluate their relative merits.

Vote Republican.

The elections proved this to be a popular strategy. But polling also suggests the much-ballyhooed Republican "Contract With America" did not inspire much enthusiasm. That's probably because the "contract" included 10 major pieces of legislation. How about a party that promises to repeal 10 laws, or maybe abolish 10 agencies?

Electing new Republicans to the House and Senate throws out bad guys, and that's great. But we are also right to be skeptical about their replacements. After the fiasco of the 1980s—lots of talk about cutting government while massively expanding it—the Republicans have lost credibility.

Support a Third Party.

The number of third parties is increasing rapidly, and that's great. Even if the new parties don't stand for all the right ideas, they can help break up the two-party cartel that enables the power elite to control government. An additional advantage: with a third party, you don't waste your vote in a rigged system; a third-party candidate who gets any significant number of votes sends a very powerful message.

Even so, third-party politics is still politics, and the political grind offers little hope for stopping America's decline.

Abjure the Realm.

For serious pessimists, there's no hope for reversing our course. We might as well drop out, take care of our families and ourselves, and forget the rest of society. I understand the point. At the same time, as Mises wrote,

> no one can find a safe way out for himself if society is sweeping towards destruction. Therefore everyone, in his own interest, must thrust himself vigorously into the intellectual battle.

The battle for civilization would have been lost long ago if people had refused to fight. Things are bad, but we would be in a gulag by now if our forebears had not decided to sacrifice, even their lives, for the cause of liberty. Dropping out is a luxury none of us can afford right now. When the realm is repaired, only then can we safely abjure it.

Localize.

Some people figure that influencing the central government is impossible, so why not make a difference where they can? They throw themselves into local politics, working to repeal regulations, taxes, and zoning ordinances. This is praiseworthy, but it addresses a smaller problem while leaving an immensely larger one untouched. Local and state governments can never be what they ought to be, so long as they are controlled by centralized tyrants.

Join the Militia.

After the Brady Bill, citizens from Petoskey, Michigan, to Stuart, Florida, are forming militias and volunteering their time to drill in these historically grounded and truly American self-defense associations. This is a magnificent development, and one that scares the striped pants off the bureaucrats. The Founders won their liberty with militias, and our right to them is guaranteed by the Second Amendment. Today, there are more than 1,000 informal militias, with more being formed every day. Americans are taking power into their own hands, thereby making total tyranny much less likely.

Enter the Underground.

Business is so hamstrung these days by mandates and regulations that many owners and managers have decided to forget about compliance, and do business as if the government weren't there. Many independent working people agree, and so the underground is huge and growing, in cities and rural areas. Drugs are an unfortunate part of it, but the vast majority of underground participants supply licit goods and services, often more efficiently than the official economy.

Secede.

The government and the media still tell us that the "Union" is sacred, but Americans aren't buying it anymore. Every chance they get, people are seeking to erect more political barriers among themselves. Suburbs want to leave cities, counties want to leave states, islands want to leave the mainland, and Montana and other states have serious secessionist sentiments. America was founded through secession from Britain. Who now wouldn't like to secede from Washington, DC?

Move.

More and more people are renouncing their citizenship and choosing to live in places they believe have higher prospects for liberty, or lower prospects for tyranny. It's an understandable impulse, but the emigration option should be left for a real emergency. Even today, there's no place like America. And if too many people who understand the problem leave, our side will be seriously weakened.

Wait.

Is liberty an historical inevitability? Some think so, especially with the turn of the millennium approaching. According to this strategy, we should wait until the tide turns or the pendulum swings. But this ignores a central fact: history is made of human choices, so nothing is inevitable. The next century may indeed be a time of decentralization, de-politicization, free markets, sound money, and individual and community liberty. But surely we have no guarantee of that, especially if good people do nothing to bring it about. The next century could be even worse than this one.

Cultivate Sound Ideas.

It's not fashionable to put your faith in ideas. We are supposed to believe that only self-interest and political power move history. But this confuses proximate with ultimate causes. When you read the Founders, you are struck by their wide and deep learning in philosophy, law, religion, history, and economics. The revolution they fought, and the liberty they established, was a product of this learning, and of the commitments that grew from it.

We all remember the person who led us to reject statist claims. For college students who face political indoctrination in every class, and much of their time out of class, one professor can make the difference. Sometimes it's one book, one publication, one conference, or even one lecture. It makes so much sense that it feels like a mental fight switch.

Nothing apart from ideas can create this sensation. And nothing is as affecting. When we are given a really useful intellectual tool, such as an understanding of government and the market, we carry it for the rest of our lives.

From time to time, I meet even regulators or lobbyists for regulation who have read Mises, or encountered an article put out by the Mises Institute. They tell me how much they enjoyed it, and although they continue to do their jobs, it is with less enthusiasm. We have informed their conscience, and someday we may find them on our side.

Are ideas sufficient? No, but they are the essential starting place. Truth won't always win, as we all know too well. But error has consequences that we can count on. The central state has made a mess of our economy and our society, and every day, that mess is more and more apparent. Now, more than ever, we need a body of thought that can turn what the media call "cynicism" into a new way of looking at the world.

We can make a difference. In the long run, we are certain to. In the process, we make plenty of people angry, and we can expect nothing else. As a minister once put it, light cannot be extinguished by any amount of darkness, while darkness can't stand the least amount of light.

It is the right ideas cultivated in the right people that will eventually bring down the oppressors and allow the flourishing of liberty and prosperity once again. At the Mises Institute, we dedicate our lives to that cause, and we are so grateful that you make that possible.

101.
THE UNITED FRONT AGAINST LIBERTY*

Defenders of liberty are prone to despair, perhaps always, and certainly since the end of the eighteenth century, when the hopes of the last Enlightenment generation were dashed as the French Revolution descended into tyranny and war, and the American Revolution was betrayed by a centralizing coup against the Articles of Confederation.

Then, as now, the evidence that our side was losing the battle seemed overwhelming. Old-style liberalism lost defenders, not because the idea of a free society was false, but because the cause seemed hopeless.

So it is in our time, when wars and party politics are forever on attack against the individual and the common good. (There is nothing incompatible about the two.)

---

*December 2001

The mistake is to believe that somehow our efforts are in vain, that liberty stands no chance in the battle of ideas, that the situation would not be even worse without our efforts. This is precisely what the enemies of liberty seek, so libertarians must be the last to grant them satisfaction. Adhere to principle, even if only to bug those who hate you for your principles!

Nonetheless, a crisis on the current scale always reduces our ranks. Because of this thinning, in every generation the idea of liberty must be reasserted by those with the vision to see through the fog, and rediscovered by the young and courageous.

"Most men are accessible to new ideas only in their youth," wrote Mises. "With the progress of age the ability to welcome them diminishes." This is why we put so much of our efforts into education. Only victory in the battle of ideas will secure a future of freedom.

Just as the prevalence of murder and theft is not a reason to abandon the fifth and seventh commandments, so the constant tendency of the state to grow provides no reason to jettison the libertarian ideal. After a murder, we don't say: that's it, making the case against murder is hopeless! No, we see the violation of the moral rule as evidence for the need to constantly reassert the right to life. So it is with liberty: without the state, there would be no need to constantly push for the right to freedom.

But discouragement is not the only reason people abandon the cause of freedom. Often, people just get tired of being attacked for holding the very unpopular view that liberty offers a better way. The criticisms can be brutal, but they are no different in character from what they have always been. The fundamental tactic is to question our motives, and to disparage our cause as only another special interest. By exposing the supposed malice behind the motive, they believe they have made their case.

This year alone, the Mises Institute has been accused of being on the wrong side of many political fashions. It has been charged with standing up for price gougers and profiteers; promoting the interests of large corporations and monopolists; currying favor with the Chinese, the Iraqis, and the Taliban; providing an intellectual cover for racists and "neo-Confederates;" working as a shill for Wall Street; justifying moral deviancy; favoring pollution; signing up with the Christian Right; having our heads in the clouds; putting our heads in the sand; and of being in the pay of big banks and multinationals, among a thousand other claims.

LewRockwell.com has been similarly charged with every manner of treachery. I have received many ominous emails, some even threatening death. Every angry correspondent seems to believe that he has discovered my special interest, which includes all the above plus a few more, like being in the pay of drug merchants, stumping for Ultramontanists, and "providing cover for the Jews."

I've left out many accusations because they become tedious after a while. The accusations have about as much substance as those of the 1930s Marxists, who believed that winning arguments was all about exposing your opponents as apologists for capital. It is a dishonest tactic that stems from a sincere belief that nobody could possibly be involved in political commentary without a secret desire to reward some group at the expense of everyone else. Exposing this interest, the Marxists believed, is identical to undermining the credibility of the argument.

But liberty is not the demand of a special interest. It is a plea for the good of the entire society. This makes it unique in politics. Think of the debate over the stimulus package. One side wanted special breaks to help the capital sector, combined with subsidies for the same. The other side wanted special breaks for the working class, combined with subsidies for the poor. These two sides, the only ones involved in the debate, fought it out for months before reaching an impasse.

This shouldn't surprise us. Mises wrote in 1927 that the origin of all modern political parties and ideologies represents a reaction to the claim of old liberalism, that no group should be allotted a privileged legal status. The ideologies then were socialism and fascism, and each rejected the liberal idea. Today, the options are more insidiously respectable—left- and right-social democracy—but no more compatible with the old liberal ideal.

The true friends of freedom—the ones who believe in it as a matter of hardcore principle—are always few. We have been reminded of this in recent days. The much-vaunted civil libertarians of the left can be counted on to defend the rights of every antibourgeois segment of society, except when that segment crosses the state to which the left owes its primary loyalty. Thus did these civil libertarians recently see the light on the need to censor and spy on anything the state deems politically deviant. So too with the political right, which sponsors and promotes treatises on the need for traditional morality and isn't at all troubled when the state murders thousands of innocents in the course of a war.

Through it all, the libertarian theme has been the same: liberty for everyone, state privileges for no one.

This is a message that no faction within the apparatus of the ruling class wants to hear. No matter how divided the factions are among themselves, they form a united front against the libertarian idea, which is the one thing they find most intolerable.

All members of the ruling class—as well as their intellectuals and wannabes—are pleased to see any rhetorical weapon used against us. There are two reasons for this: intellectual and political.

Intellectually, our contemporaries cannot conceive of a movement that seeks not the triumph of a special interest, but only the common good. They simply cannot believe that anyone who doesn't have some axe to grind would be involved in intellectual affairs. Idealism, they think, belongs in monasteries, not public affairs.

The second reason, discussed often in the work of Murray Rothbard, is political: the triumph of liberty against power would undermine their own special interest, so they fight this prospect with everything they have.

In times of crisis, in particular, we are reminded of just how unified the ruling class is, and how it is willing to put aside internal bickering for the sake of preserving power and its ability to shuffle wealth around. This is why, for example, after September 11, the ruling class was so united in its call for war: nothing solidifies power against liberty like a war, and the state never misses a chance to use events to confer moral legitimacy on what it would like to do anyway. There were many horrible aspects to September 11, but that it seemed to provide a rationale for the dramatic expansion of the state, for its killing and looting, is the one least questioned.

To sign up with the party of liberty is to take a principled step. It means rejecting the dominant strain of politics of our time. What is that strain? That the state ought to be used to promote the agenda of some special interest, whether it be those who benefit from welfare, regulation, inflation, war, or the consolidation of the police state generally.

The party of liberty rejects all of this, not because we have a special interest but because we stick by the most unpopular claim of all: that society ought to be organized so that it benefits everyone in the long run. There is only one system that does so, and that is the natural order of liberty. That's why we believe in it, and why we will neither give up the ideal, nor yield the slightest in the face of attacks.

102.

THE DEFINITION AND
DEFENSE OF FREEDOM*

The Mises Institute has worked for more than two decades to advance one purpose: the cause of economic freedom in academia and public life. The two comments on our work that I hear most often are: (1) you guys are doing a great job, and (2) it is not working.

On the first point, I can only thank our generous supporters and faculty who make it all happen. They have enabled us to create an intellectual infrastructure that combines the ideals of the sanctuary and the tactics of intellectual guerrilla warfare, at once reflective and separate as well as passionate and expansionist. For those who are not yet members, join us please.

On the second point, that our work has not yet yielded a free society, it is not difficult to observe that the government is growing and liberty is shrinking in many areas. But rather than fall into despair, consider that liberty is not easy to achieve or sustain absent a deep cultural commitment.

Mises taught that all societies in all times, and their governing structures, are the result of the ideas prevalent in the culture. He took it for granted that no government is liberal by nature. They all want maximum power and money for themselves, and can only obtain it at the expense of the people, since government itself produces nothing.

Consider the mentality of most presidents, justices, and senators, and the incentives they face. Expanding the reach of government power is just considered integral to the job description. They may choose to expand in one area as versus another based

---

*August 2005

on the *quid pro quos* they owe for the past election and the next one, but the idea of diminishing overall government makes no sense to them—any more than it makes sense for a cook to encourage dieting, or a housing contractor to encourage cave-dwelling. Once a politician or bureaucrat tastes power, he or she becomes a member of the governing caste, which means advancing the public sector first.

Totalitarianism, in this view, is not an aberration in history but the expected result of any state that is not restrained by the ideological convictions of the public. The state can use any ideological excuse—the need for community as in communism, the desire for national greatness as with fascism, the call for central economic planning as in the New Deal, or the urge to wage war for security—but the result is always the same.

It is the public belief in liberty—originating with the intellectual class—that ultimately restrains the state. If the population is passive and uninformed by any contrary voices, the state can succeed in its evil aims. Where cultural convictions are intense and intolerant of power, as well as embrace the inviolable right to person and property, liberty prevails. Either the government is afraid to act in a way contrary to popular sentiment or it is already so powerless that it is denied any ability to act despotically even if it wanted to.

What this suggests is that the most important work to do for liberty is intellectual work. An ideological force of resistance must thrive and have a voice. Intellectuals committed to liberty need support for their work. They need the freedom to write and speak and research. There must be a means to disseminate their ideas and attract young thinkers. There must be a means in place to propagate these ideas in forms that reach the largest number of social and business leaders, as well as professionals of all sorts. These ideas must further have a component that attracts the broadest possible support from the public.

The Mises Institute has worked to put all this in place, and in this way the efforts are succeeding most remarkably. Before 20 years ago, the Austrian School's prospects were sinking, libertarian theory had been marginalized in cultural affairs, there were very few consistent advocates of liberty speaking to public affairs (neither welfare nor warfare), and the number of sympathetic professors teaching was small and under fire.

Every one of these indicators has dramatically changed. This is progress. Incredible progress. No, the regime has not fallen but it has been restrained. After 9-11, when the regime saw its main chances to enact an all-powerful state that curbed liberties in every direction, the Mises Institute stood largely alone in saying no. I can tell you that we paid a high price. These are frightening times to be a libertarian, times when the head of the world empire declares that you are either for his policies or for the terrorists. This sends chills down the spine of every dissident.

And yet we look around today and we see two main trends. First, the state is advancing far less than it might have hoped three years ago. It faces opposition at every turn, and skepticism about its every action. We owe this to a level of public resistance. Every dissident voice assists in this regard. Second, we see private enterprise on the march as never before, transforming our lives, melting borders to capital, and gaining ever more opportunities for fighting against tyranny and advancing liberty.

No, our job is far from over. Indeed, it begins anew every day. But we only need to imagine a world in which there are no advocates of liberty, no support structures for dissident intellectuals, no conferences for students to learn an alternative, and no sanctuaries that keep the flame alive in dark times. Would we be better off? Far from it. The presence of the Mises Institute and its activities work to provide a brake on power and a guide for the future.

If you ever feel pessimistic about the prospects for freedom, I invite you to visit our offices. We have the archives and papers of Ludwig von Mises and Murray Rothbard, among other great champions of freedom. At a time when major libraries are throwing out books, we are accumulating the world's greatest library on liberty. We have about 30,000 volumes now.

All summer our offices were full of some of the smartest, most dedicated, most promising students I'd ever been around. They are as hard working as they are idealistic, and they come to us to read and study the forbidden books of our time, those works by Mises, Rothbard, Hayek, and others who are champions of freedom.

These students know that freedom is not popular among the intelligentsia. They experience it every day in class, where they face professors who disparage capitalism and offer a thousand plans for reconstructing the world in cockamamie ways.

The truth is that freedom hasn't been treated favorably in academia for the better part of a century. In the 1930s, for example, we were told that freedom was not an option. We could be fascists or communists (or perhaps democratic socialists) but freedom was outmoded and silly and unworkable.

But great minds like Mises could not be intimidated. They continued to speak. They paid a price, but they kept the philosophical flame burning. They were told that their ideas were outmoded and ineffective but they were not deterred.

Nor must we permit ourselves to be intimidated or deterred today. By publishing books and journals and offering materials that make the case for freedom, we are fighting the battle of ideas—and ideals, Mises tells us, are more powerful than armies.

Our ideal is freedom.

Now, the word freedom is bandied about a lot these days, so let me be clear that I don't mean freedom the way the proposed Iraqi Constitution means it. Here we have a document where every invocation of rights and liberties is qualified with the deadly phrase: except by law.

Most Americans who know about what real freedom means can only scoff at such nonsense. We know that if we put government in charge of regulating our freedoms, it is only a matter of time before we have no freedom left. Government wants us to do what it wants us to do, not what we want to do.

If there are no limits placed on government, if our freedom under law is not guaranteed as an absolute principle, the final result is that government will have all power and all property, and we will have none. That is the way the world works, from the ancient times until the end of time.

In all of human history, we can count the number of principled statesmen like Ron Paul on two hands. George Washington said that if men were angels we wouldn't need government. We might clarify that if all statesmen were like Ron Paul, we wouldn't need restraints on government. But we know that is not the case.

The definition of freedom is not complicated. Freedom means that which the government does not control. You are free when the government cannot steal your income, when it cannot tell you what to say or with whom you may or may not associate. You are free when the government cannot take your kids and send them to far-flung wars to kill and be killed. You are free when you control your life, your property, your church, your business, and your future. You are free when the government cannot inflate away your savings, tax away your profits, lay waste to your dividends by regimenting corporate life, or controlling how much of what you buy and sell and from where.

The Mises Institute has made a new backpack for students, and it sports the following quotation from Mises: "Government is the negation of liberty." I'm pleased to report that these are very popular on campus right now. They also explain where other students can go to find information.

The Mises Institute may not be able to persuade the faculty to read a big treatise on economics and society, or attend one of our conferences. We may never convert the literature and sociology departments in the Ivy League to the cause of the free market.

But still, it gives some satisfaction to know that we can drive them crazy by encouraging their students to declare where they stand. Until true freedom arrives—and some day it will—we must be pleased with all such seemingly small victories. Together with serious intellectual work, dedicated teaching efforts, the publishing of journals and books, and employing every effort to reach the broadest possible audience, we all do our part to prepare the way for a peaceful and prosperous world.

103.
We Need an Angel Like Clarence*

As the war drags on and the state expands its reach in nearly every area of life, I'm detecting another moment of despair sweeping through libertarian ranks. Why aren't all our efforts making a difference? What are we doing wrong? Are we just wasting our time with our publications, conferences, scholarships, editorials, vast web presence, recruitments of thousands of young people? Have our educational efforts ever made any difference?

There are a thousand reasons to object to this line of thought. Let us speak to the moral and strategic ones directly. Despair is a vice that squelches and defeats the human spirit. Hope, on the other hand, creates and builds. It is true in business, sports, and intellectual life. We must see success in the future in order to achieve it.

Murray Rothbard used to wonder why people who believe that liberty is unachievable or that activism of any sort is futile became libertarian in the first place. Would a team that is convinced that it will lose every game practice or come together at all? Would an entrepreneur who is convinced that he or she will go bankrupt ever invest a dime?

---

*December 2006

Perhaps you could say that a person has no choice but to follow the truth even when it is obvious that failure is inevitable. And truly there is some virtue in doing so. But as a practical matter, it makes no sense to waste one's time doing something that is futile when one could be doing something that is productive and at least potentially successful.

So should libertarian activists be doing something else with their time?

Here is the crucial matter to consider. What might have been the fate of liberty if no one had cared about it in the last 100 years? That is an important way to look at this issue, one that accords with Frédéric Bastiat's emphasis on looking not only at the seen but also at the unseen. He urged us to look at the unseen costs of state intervention. I ask that we look at the unseen benefits of activism on the part of liberty. We need to look at the statism that we do not experience, and what the world would be like if it weren't for the efforts of libertarians.

We need an angel like Clarence to show us that world that might have been.

Less than a century ago, in our own country, the state was in its heyday. Socialism was the intellectual fashion, even more so than today. The income tax was seen as the answer to fiscal woes. Inflation and central banking would solve our problems with money. Antitrust regulation and litigation would achieve perfect industrial organization. World war would end despotism, or so that generation believed.

Preposterously, a small faction that would later be dominant in public life believed that if we could just pass national legislation against drinking, sobriety would prevail. Fathers would become responsible, sons would become educated, churches would fill with pious worshippers, and even poverty—which people then as now associated with substance abuse—would be a thing of the past. Speech should be thoroughly controlled and dissidents suppressed. Healthcare should be cartelized. The environment should be protected. The state would uplift us in every way.

If that trend had continued, we would have had totalitarianism right here at home. If the state had had its way—and the state is always happy with more power and money—there would have been no zone of freedom left to us, and we would live as people have always lived when the state controlled every aspect of life: in the absence of civilization. It would have been a catastrophe.

But it didn't happen. Why? Because people objected, and they kept objecting for the remainder of the century. An antiwar movement put a major dent in the war and led to an unraveling of the state afterwards—and kept us out of more wars for many years. Public outrage at the income tax led to keeping a lid on it. Inflation was kept in check by intellectuals who warned of the effects of central banking. So too with antitrust action, which has been set back by libertarian ideology. Free speech has also been protected through activism.

The alcohol prohibitionists managed to pass a constitutional amendment banning all liquor—think of that!—but their victory was short lived. Public opinion rose up against them and the amendment was eventually repealed. It was a magnificent reversal, brought about mainly by the force of public ideology that said it was causing more harm than good and violating people's rights.

We can look forward in time and see another bout of statism during the New Deal and World War II. But the state faced resistance. FDR and Truman hated, spied on, and harassed their opponents, but their opponents prevailed. FDR was stymied in his attempts to further the state, which is why he turned to war. Wartime planning and price controls were beaten back against Truman's objections. The same was true with Vietnam and the draft. The war ended because public opinion turned against it. Reality conformed more closely to the critics' views than to the proponents' views. We won.

Nixon limited traffic speed to 55 mph by national decree. But another major rollback of the state happened and that was repealed. Then Carter did some good things, like deregulate trucking, and he did it because of public pressure and the triumph of free-market economics.

Again, what we need to take into account are the unseen benefits of activism. Had the advocates of liberty never spoken up, never written books, never taught in the classroom, never written editorials, and never advanced their views in any public or private forum, would the cause of liberty have been better off or even the same? No way.

You have to do the counterfactual in order to understand the impact of ideology. Libertarian ideology, in all its forms, has literally saved the world from the state, which always and everywhere wants to advance and never roll back. If it does not advance and if it does roll back (however rarely), it is to the credit of public ideology.

Don't think for a second that it doesn't matter. Most of the time the impact is hard to measure and even sometimes hard to detect. Libertarian ideas are like stones dropping into water, which make waves in so many directions that no one is sure where they come from.

But there are times when the Mises Institute has made a direct hit, and we know from personal testimony that we've caused bureaucrats and politicians to fly into a rage at what we are saying and what we are doing. If you think public opinion doesn't matter to these people, think again. They are terrified about the impressions the public has of their work. They can be completely demoralized by public opposition.

We live in times of incredible prosperity, unlike any we've ever known. This is due solely to the zones of freedom that remain in today's world, technology and communication among them. Why are these sectors freer and hence more productive than the rest? Because this is an area in which we've achieved success. The state is terrified to touch the Internet for fear of public hostility.

Again let me ask the question: does anyone really believe that these zones of freedom are best protected when there is no public advocacy of the libertarian cause? Would Bush feel more or less secure in the continued conduct of his egregious war if the antiwar movement shut up and dried up? Would entrepreneurs feel more or less at liberty to invest if there were no advocates for their cause working in public and intellectual life?

When measuring the success of the freedom movement, these are the sorts of questions we have to ask. It is not enough to observe that the world has yet to conform to our image. We need to take note of the ways in which the world has not conformed to the state's image. No state is liberal by nature, said Mises. Every state wants to control all. If it does not do so, the major reason is that freedom-minded intellectuals are making the difference.

If it were otherwise, why would the state care so intensely about suppressing ideas with which it disagrees? Why would there be political censorship? Why would the state bother with propaganda at all?

Ideas matter. More than we know. Why haven't we won? Because we are not doing enough and our ranks are not big enough. We need to do what we are doing on ever-grander scales. We need to make ever-better arguments on behalf of liberty. And we need to have patience, just like the prohibitionists and socialists had patience to see their agenda to the end. They've had their day. Our time will come, provided that we don't listen to the counsel of despair.

The angel Clarence says in *It's a Wonderful Life* that, "Each man's life touches so many other lives. When he isn't around he leaves an awful hole, doesn't he?"

It's something for anyone who advocates liberty to think about before he bails out.

INDEX

Printed in Great Britain
by Amazon